ERP SYSTEMS

ERP SYSTEMS

Dimpi Srivastava
M.C.A., M. Phil., M.Tech.
Sr. Lecturer, Department of Computer Application
M.I.E.T Group of Institutions, Meerut

Aarti Batra
M.C.A., M.Tech.
Lecturer, Department of Computer Application
M.I.E.T Group of Institutions, Meerut

TECHSAR™

NEW DELHI

Published and Printed by

Techsar Pvt. Ltd.
4435-36/7, Ansari Road, Daryaganj,
New Delhi–110 001 (India)
E-mail : tech_info@techsarworld.com
Website: www.techsarworld.com

ISBN 978-93-80578-15-6

Reprint 2025

Dedicated to
our parents and family

PREFACE

The entire concept of ERP systems is based on the premise that for successful management of enterprise, as a whole, an enterprise-wide information system is a requisite. ERP systems integrate accounting, distribution, manufacturing, human resources, payroll and other business processes into a single integrated application. Selection of right ERP package as well as right ERP vendor will mark the success of ERP implementation.

This book on ERP systems provides a glimpse on the evolution of ERP, its benefits, ERP market and the life cycle of ERP. It elaborates the ERP system concepts, implementation strategies and methodologies. The book has been written in a simple and easy to understand language. It covers the latest syllabi of ERP systems for B. Tech., M.C.A and M.B.A students of various universities. Learning points included in the chapters will serve as a useful learning tool for the students. Review exercise provided at the end of each chapter will also provide useful practice session to the students.

We take this opportunity to express our gratitude to col. Dr. D.K. Bhola, Dr. Pushpendra Singh Dhama, Dr. Swati Singh, Dr. Rupal Joshi, Dr. Anita Rawat, Mr. S.P. Singh, Ms. Savita Kumari Singh, Ms. Shilpi Khanna, Ms. Prerna Garg, Mrs. Abhilasha, Mr. Tanweer Alam, Mr. Dinesh Khushwaha, Mr V.P. Maurya, Mr. Jyotirmay Patel, Mr. Vinod Kumar, Mr. Nagresh Singh Mrs. Nitasha Varshney, Mr. Santosh Prasad Gupta, Mr. Gufran Ahmad Ansari, Mr. Yogesh, Mr. Shivpoojan Singh, Mr. Vivek Kumar Goel, Mr. Mohammad Vakil, Mrs. Kumud Arora, Dr. V.B. Dhawan, Mr. Sunil Kumar Pandey, Mr. P.K. Bharti, Sh. Bhagwan Dutt Batra, Mr. Deepak Bagchi, for their support and well wishes.

We specially want to thank Dr. Mayank Garg, Director, MIT, Meerut for his whole-hearted support to this endeavour.

Constructive suggestions and comments for the future improvement of this volume are invited.

Dimpi Srivastava
Aarti Batra

CONTENTS

1

Chapter

An Introduction to ERP

HIGHLIGHTS

- **ERP Systems**
  - Characteristics of ERP Systems
  - Evolution of ERP
  - Myths about ERP
  - ERP Benefits and
  - Custom built and Packaged approaches

Information technology and information systems enable the firms to gain a competitive advantage. Today, extensive information systems are required that can automate and integrate the business information and processes. An enterprise-wide information system integrates all aspects of a business to support business strategies for better decision making and faster response time. Enterprise Resource Planning (ERP) systems can, in essence, be thought of as enterprise-wide information system. Today, ERP systems are becoming more and more powerful as new frontiers for ERP are continuously being explored.

Enterprise Resource Planning is a complex information system that provides a seamless integration of information flow throughout the organization. ERP systems, today, serve as a significant strategic tool of competition. K. Kumar and J.V. Hillegersberg define ERP systems as "configurable information system packages that integrate information and information-based processes within and across functional areas in an organization."

J. Manetti defines ERP as "a method for effective planning and control of all resources needed to take, make, ship and account for customer order."

1.1 CHARACTERISTICS OF ERP SYSTEMS

ERP systems have the following characteristics:

1. ERP systems are large scale, end-to-end business processing systems.
2. ERP systems provide easy and secure access to information in a real-time environment.
3. ERP systems are function-rich and integrate majority of a business's processes and operations.
4. ERP systems affect major departments in a company and tend to create changes in many business processes of the organization.
5. ERP systems are commercial software packages that are either designed as mainframe applications or designed to work on a client server environment.
6. An ERP software package can be customized to suit the specific business's needs of any organization.
7. ERP systems provide support for multiple currencies and languages.
8. An ERP system makes use of an enterprise-wide database to provide timely, relevant and shared information in an easy-to-use format.

1.1.1 Why do Companies Need ERP?

In the 1980's, companies used big mainframe computers that performed calculations (e.g., MRP system) and managed the financial records. Personal computers (PC's) were provided to every manager in every department to help them become efficient and thus, work better. But both the mainframes and PC's had their own limitations. While mainframes didn't provide timely and relevant information, the PC's could not store huge corporate databases.

The need for systems that could integrate all information flow in the company and at the same time make an efficient use of desktop technology gave way to the current ERP systems. ERP systems brought together MRP-II systems and the client/server technologies to provide for the following:

1. Integrating all the business functions of the enterprise.
2. Integrating all the systems running in different locations.
3. Transparency of information across the whole organization.

Figure 1.1 shows the pre-ERP scenario, in which, most departments had their own database and information systems which were not integrated with each other. As a result, the performance of the organization was not very good. With the arrival of ERP systems, as shown in Figure 1.2, business functions throughout the organization were integrated with each other. A single enterprise wide database system shared throughout an enterprise resulted in far better performance and improved quality.

LEARNING POINTS

1. An enterprise-wide information system integrates all aspects of a business to support all business strategies for better decision making and faster response time.
2. Enterprise Resource Planning (ERP) systems can, in essence, be thought of as enterprise-wide information system.
3. J. Manetti defines ERP as "a method for effective planning and control of all resources needed to take, make, ship and account for customer order."

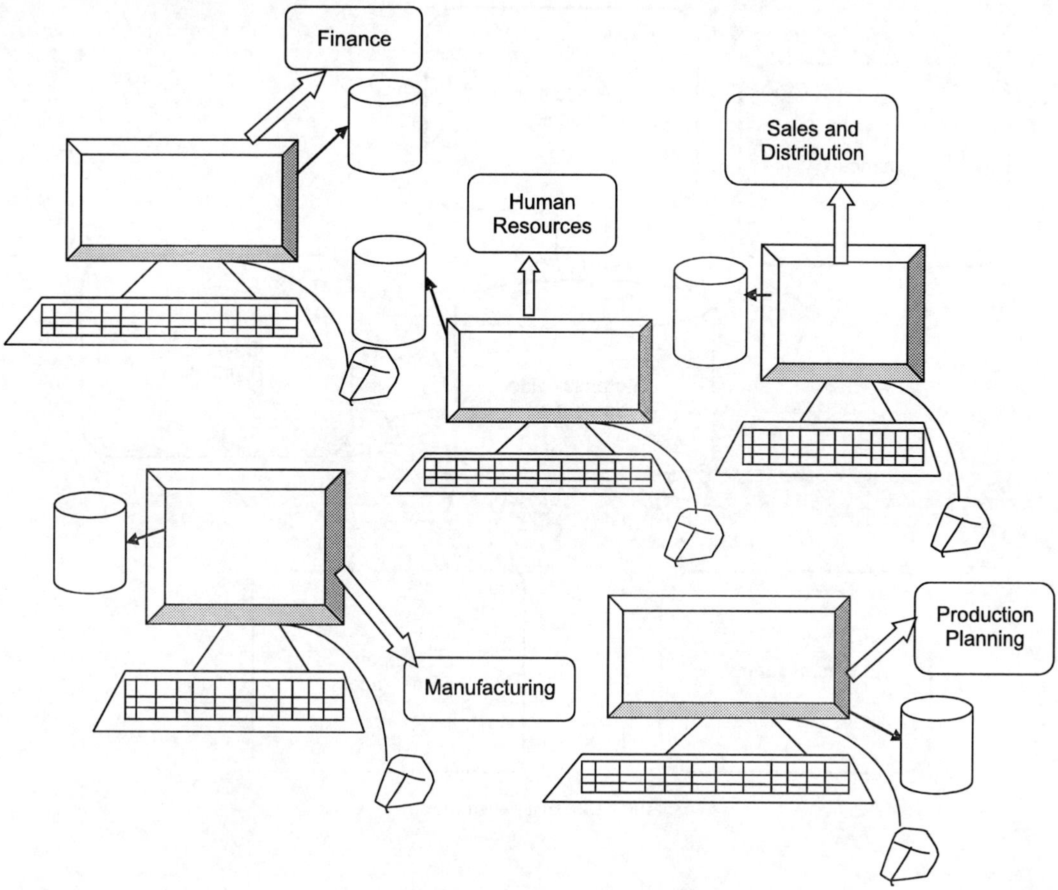

Fig. 1.1. Pre-ERP Information system

4. ERP systems are function-rich and integrate majority of a business's processes and operations.
5. ERP systems provide support for multiple currencies and languages.

1.2 EVOLUTION OF ERP

ERP plays a significant role within corporations today. ERP systems have gradually evolved from inventory management and control systems (1960's) to ERP-II (2000 onwards). In 1960's inventory management and control systems were used by the organizations to maintain an appropriate level of stock in the warehouse. Inventory management activities included identifying inventory shortage, providing replenishment techniques, monitoring inventory usage, reconciling the inventory balance and reporting stock status.

During 1970's many companies realized that by properly planning inventory requirements, unnecessary piling of large volumes of inventory could be avoided. This realization led to materials requirement planning (MRP) systems. Materials requirement planning utilizes computerized

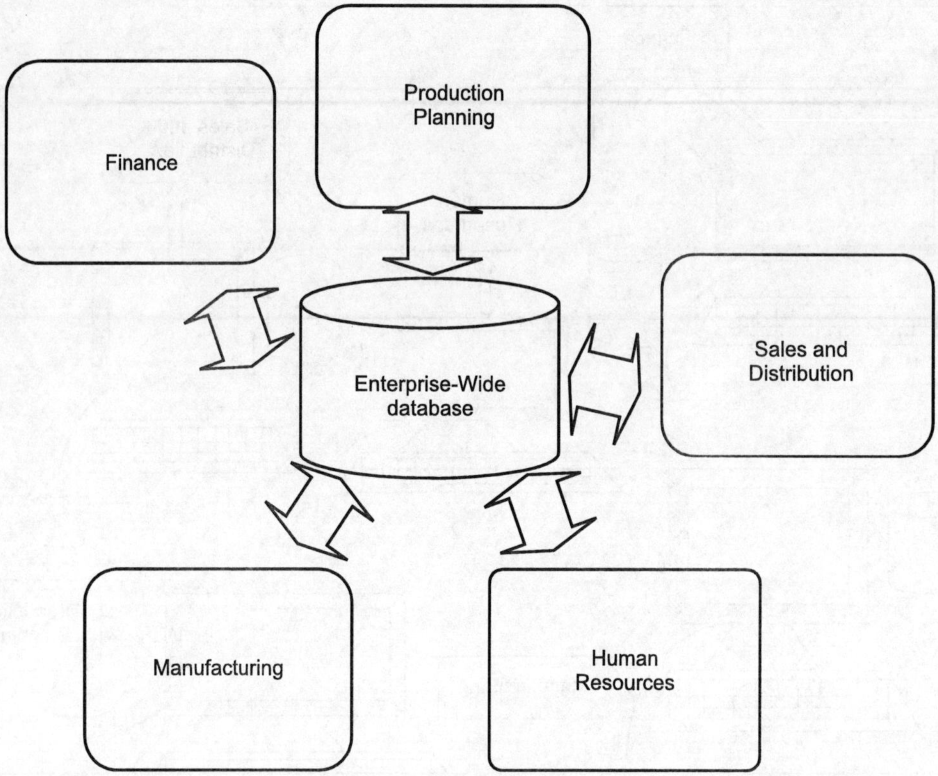

Fig. 1.2. ERP systems

methods to generate schedules for inventory purchase. MRP systems are used to plan and control effective and efficient resource utilization for better quality and increased productivity. With the passage of time, capacity planning and feedback was included in the MRP systems to improve the quality of the materials requirement schedules generated by the MRP systems. These systems were called closed-loop MRP systems.

In the 1980's MRP was expanded to MRP-II, to bring together all the major business processes under a standard computerized planning system. MRP-II extended MRP to shop floor activities and distribution management. MRP-II also provided support to financial planning by converting materials requirement schedules into capital requirements. Manufacturing requirements planning (MRP-II) helped coordinate manufacturing processes from product planning, parts purchasing, inventory control to product distribution. Figure 1.3 shows MRP-II systems.

In the early 1990's, more functional areas were included into manufacturing requirements planning. These functional areas mainly comprised product design, information warehousing, materials planning, communications, finance, human resource and project management. This led to the arrival of ERP systems—that covered all activities of an enterprise. ERP systems are therefore considered a natural extension of MRP-II. An ERP system integrates business activities across functional departments and may include application modules such as marketing, finance, manufacturing etc.

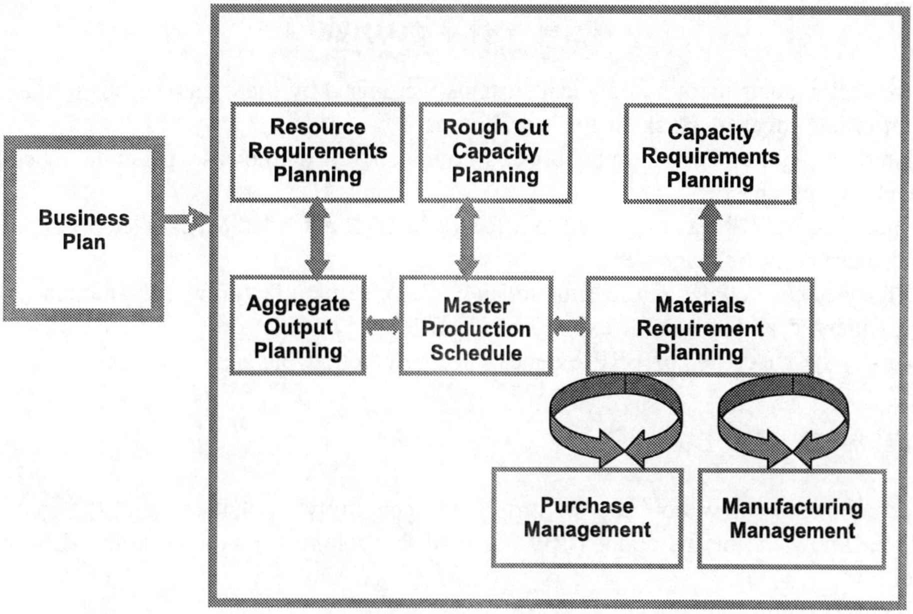

Fig. 1.3. MRP-II systems
(Adapted from Source: http://www.inter-log.net/modules/production_management/production_management_production_management__p080.htm)

The next evolution stage is of collaborative commerce (or ERP-II). ERP-II extends ERP to external business entities in order to, help companies compete better. With an ERP system working in the background, e-business can be easily accomplished.

Figure 1.4 illustrates the evolution of ERP system.

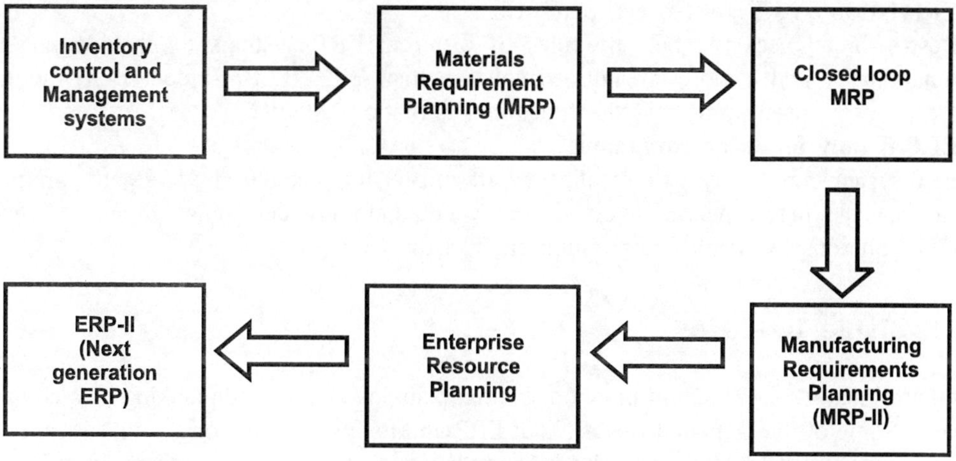

Fig. 1.4. Evolution of ERP systems

LEARNING POINTS

1. Inventory management and control systems were used by the organizations to maintain an appropriate level of stock in the warehouse.
2. Materials requirement planning utilizes computerized methods to generate schedules for inventory purchase.
3. In the 1980's MRP was expanded to MRP-II. MRP-II extended MRP to shop floor activities and distribution management.
4. ERP systems included more functional areas into manufacturing requirements planning and emerged as the natural extension of MRP-II.
5. ERP-II, the successor of ERP extends ERP to external business activities.

1.3 MYTHS ABOUT ERP

ERP is a completely new concept. In order to successfully implement an ERP system it is important to know the myths about ERP. Some of the common myths regarding ERP systems are as follows:

1. **ERP is a computer system**
   Though computers are an integral part of ERP systems, yet ERP is a broader concept that includes organization's goals and objectives, the working style and the people.
2. **ERP is only for manufacturing firms**
   ERP can be used in any company that wants to be competitive. ERP is gradually spreading to other sectors such as retail, insurance, banking and healthcare industries.
3. **ERP systems can generate all the reports**
   ERP systems provide a limited number of reports. For example, Oracle Advanced Collections provides only eight reports. Organizations will require to custom-build the reports by employing a third-party reporting tool. ERP software can be customized to generate large lists of reports needed by an organization.
4. **ERP is same as best-of-breed products**
   Best-of-breed uses the best modules of different ERP systems to provide increased functionality and a more streamlined solution than ERP. Best-of-breed (BOB) solutions are therefore used to address the functional limitations of ERP.
5. **ERP is only for large companies**
   ERP systems are costly, as a result, they are mostly implemented by large enterprises that can bear the huge expenses involved. ERP vendors are now designing simpler and cheaper ERP solutions for small and medium enterprises.

1.3.1 Evolving Realities

ERP systems intend to facilitate information sharing, planning and decision making on a company-wide basis. Some of the facts and issues about ERP and its implementation are discussed below:

1. Traditional ERP systems were large, complex and expensive. An enormous effort was required to implement them.

2. ERP systems often introduce large-scale change in the business processes of the organization.
3. ERP systems replace tangles of complicated computer applications with a single integrated information system.
4. Implementing an ERP system is a significant investment for an enterprise.
5. ERP systems often require adjustment and fine-tuning to meet the specific needs of the company.
6. Many of the underlying problems of the legacy systems are inherent in ERP systems.
7. ERP software can run on multiple platforms and follow client server architecture.
8. ERP is an investment in business, technology and people.

LEARNING POINTS

1. Some of the common myths regarding ERP systems are as follows: ERP is a computer system, ERP is only for manufacturing firms, ERP systems can generate all the reports and ERP is only for large companies.
2. ERP is, in fact, a broader concept that includes organization's goals and objectives, the working style and the people.
3. Best-of-breed (BOB) solutions are used to address the functional limitations of ERP.
4. ERP vendors are now designing simpler and cheaper ERP solutions for small and medium enterprises.
5. ERP systems often introduce large-scale change in the business processes of the organization.
6. Many of the underlying problems of the legacy systems are inherent in ERP systems.

1.4 ERP BENEFITS

ERP systems help companies compete better. ERP provides a large number of benefits to the company. ERP improves the enterprise IT architecture, improves the business processes and delivers enhanced revenues and profitability. According to Gary Forger, "ERP acts as a planning backbone for a company's business processes."

As shown in Figure 1.5, ERP systems provide the following benefits:

1. **Integrated Management**
   ERP systems manage all the business processes with a single, integrated and shared enterprise-wide information system. The same ERP system manages functions and activities as different as the bills of materials, efficient handling of order processing, production schedule, effective management of human resource, allocating costs and facilitating on-time delivery of products to the customers. ERP systems facilitate the synchronization of activities within the departments such as manufacturing, finance, human resource etc.
2. **Decision Making**
   ERP systems automate the data entry process and help in monitoring, sharing and tracking information throughout the organization. By providing accurate, timely and relevant information to the employees, the ERP systems aid in decision making capability of the employees.

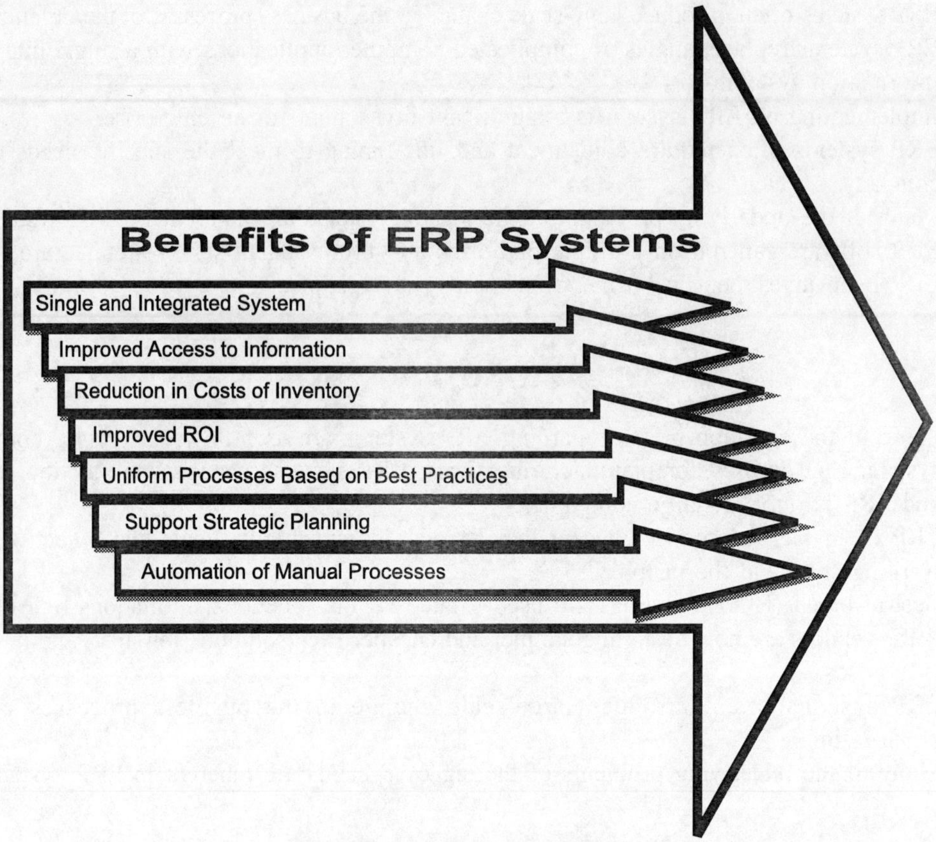

Fig. 1.5. Benefits of ERP systems

3. **Provides Proper Resource Utilization**
   ERP systems aim to obtain the most value from the resources and equipment of the company. ERP systems contribute to efficient resource utilization by minimizing the inventory, producing products only-on-demand and delivering products to the customers speedily.
4. **Reduces Lead-time**
   ERP systems reduce the lead-time by making the inventory management system more efficient and using latest technology such as EFT (electronic funds transfer) and EDI (electronic data interchange).
5. **Reduces cycle time**
   Time between the receipt of a customer order and the delivery of the required product is the cycle time. ERP systems help in reducing the cycle time for both make-to-order and make-to-stock items.
6. **Provides on-time delivery/shipment**
   ERP systems ensure on-time delivery of products to customers. With ERP companies are able to deliver highly customized products with the lead-time of standard off-the- shelf products.

7. **Increases customer satisfaction**
ERP systems increase customer satisfaction by providing on-time delivery of products customized to their needs. These systems also facilitate faster response time to customers.
8. **Provides better procurement process**
A procurement system helps the company to order right material at the right time and acquire the raw materials and components at comparatively low costs. ERP systems dynamically control the purchasing of raw materials.
9. **Provides vendor management**
ERP systems—integrated with SCM (supply chain management) and EDI (electronic data interchange)—monitor vendor activities and manage their suppliers efficiently.
10. **Reduces quality-related costs**
Some quality-related costs include costs of scraps, rework, repair and service costs, costs of inspecting by external inspectors, evaluation costs of new products and training. ERP systems have tools for implementing total quality management programs within an enterprise. Materials inspection systems support process supervision and control. The quality management systems in ERP packages facilitate improvement of manufacturing methods. Specification control system in ERP packages helps support documenting specifications. These systems help in reducing quality-related costs.
11. **Provides more flexibility**
ERP systems provide a seamless integrated flow of information across the enterprise, enabling the enterprise to respond quickly to the changing market conditions. This improves the flexibility of the enterprise as a whole.
12. **Improves corporate image**
With ERP systems the company restructures its processes to the so called "best practices: so that all activities across the enterprise are smoothly coordinated. This improves the corporate image.

The pros and cons of ERP systems and best-of-breed systems have been illustrated in Table 1.1 and Table 1.2 respectively.

Table 1.1 Pros and Cons of Integrated ERP Systems

S No.	Pros of ERP Systems	Cons of ERP Systems
1.	Large suppliers with significant resources and international support.	Perhaps not the best possible functionality in all areas.
2.	All data available in one system.	A release update affects the entire system, which can make it more complex to implement.
3.	Contact with one supplier.	Requires a relatively large project demanding significant internal resources from the entire organization for implementation.
4.	Support a business process methodology. Online data from all functional areas is always accessible for people with the right security level.	
5.	Continuous development with new releases.	
6.	Requires knowledge of only one system or platform. Also, it has one user interface and dialog.	

Table 1.2 Pros and Cons of Autonomous Best-of-Breed Systems

S No.	Pros	Cons
1.	Easy to replace in a system-by-system approach, which decreases risk.	Need many custom interfaces.
2.	Less sensitive. One system can freeze, but the others can continue. Also, maintenance on one system can be done without affecting the others.	Data warehouse needed to access all data at the same time.
3.	The best solution can be selected for the actual demand.	Require knowledge of many systems and possibly platforms.
4.		Require contact with many suppliers.
5.		Do not support a business process method.
6.		Complex maintenance, as when changes in one system mean changes in interfaces and other systems. Upgrades for parts of the system may require new interfaces, and may not be able to be upgraded.
7.		Local, small suppliers with limited international support.
8.		Different user interfaces for every system.

LEARNING POINTS

1. ERP systems manage all the business processes with a single, integrated and shared enterprise-wide information system.
2. ERP systems automate the data entry process and help in monitoring, sharing and tracking information throughout the organization.
3. ERP systems—integrated with SCM (supply chain management) and EDI (electronic data interchange)—monitor vendor activities and manage their suppliers efficiently.

1.5 CUSTOM-BUILT AND PACKAGED APPROACHES

ERP systems are commercial software packages that integrate transactions-oriented data and the business processes throughout the enterprise. The enterprise must make a careful choice while selecting an ERP package for use. If the misfit between the ERP package and the business processes of the enterprise is large then modifications will be required. These modifications are often time-consuming, costly and risky. It leads to a situation in which the enterprise must either customize its ERP software to suit the business's needs or change many of its business processes to adapt to the ERP software package.

Almost every analyst of the ERP implementation process strongly advises companies to avoid modifying the ERP software. The analyst in fact advises the enterprise to maintain the existing ERP software functionality and to change their business procedures to adapt to ERP software.

Table 1.3 shows the comparison of Customize and Configure Approaches.

Table 1.3: Comparison of Customize and Configure Approaches

S No.	Attribute	Customize	Configure
1.	Functionality	More control over functionality	Less control over functionality
2.	Cost	Higher	Lower
3.	Upgrades	More Difficult	Easier
4.	Support	Reduced vendor support	Full vendor support

Proposed by S. Rao, the decision tree model provides four options for the selection of an ERP package.

The options are as follows:

1. **Buying a ready-made package from the market.**
   Enterprises can go for tailor-made ERP packages available in the market like SAP, Baan, Oracle, PeopleSoft etc.
2. **Develop own ERP package**
   Enterprises can develop a custom-built ERP package, specific to the enterprise's requirements, with the help of an in-house IT department.
3. **Engaging the services of a software company to develop the ERP package specific to your requirements.**
   Enterprises can develop a custom-built ERP package, specific to the enterprise's requirements, with the help of a software solution provider.
4. **Enhancing the capabilities in the existing system.**

LEARNING POINTS

1. ERP systems are commercial software packages that integrate transactions-oriented data and the business processes throughout the enterprise.
2. Enterprises can either go for tailor-made ERP packages available in the market like SAP, Baan, Oracle, PeopleSoft etc. or develop a custom-built ERP package, specific to the enterprise's requirements, with the help of an in-house IT department or with the help of a software solution provider.

SUMMARY

An Enterprise Resource Planning (ERP) system is an integrated set of software programs that supports the core business activities such as manufacturing, logistics, sales and marketing, finance and human resources of an organization. As ERP systems integrate all the business activities in an organization the ERP systems provide a winning edge to the organization in the global competitive environment.

The advancement in manufacturing requirements planning (MRP-II) led to the evolution of ERP systems. ERP-II, the successor of ERP extends ERP to include suppliers as well as customers in its gamut of activities and draw maximum benefits from internet. After making their presence felt in large-scale enterprises for a long time, the ERP vendors are now shifting towards small and medium-sized enterprises (SME's). The ERP vendors have built a new generation of ERP software that is easy to install, easy to manage, function-specific and has low start-up-costs.

ERP implementation is often accompanied with large scale changes in the business processes of an organization. This often results in significant investment to be made by the management.

Some of the benefits provided by an ERP system implementation include proper resource utilization, reduced lead time, reduced cycle-time, increased customer satisfaction, on-time delivery of products and services, more flexibility and good corporate image.

The ERP packages available from ERP vendor may not address the specific business requirements of an organization. In such a situation either the business processes of the organization are changed to use the ready-made off-the-shelf ERP package or the ERP package is modified to address the business needs of the organization. The later is referred to as "customization". Customization is often time-consuming and expensive.

An organization can also develop its own ERP solution to meet its specific business needs. The ERP solution can be custom-built either by the in-house implementation team or by a software solution provider.

POINTS TO REMEMBER

1. An enterprise-wide information system integrates all aspects of a business to support strategies for better decision making and faster response time.
2. An Enterprise Resource Planning (ERP) system is a complex information system that provides seamless integration of information flow throughout the organization.
3. An ERP software package is often customized to suit the specific needs of a business firm.
4. Materials Requirement Planning (MRP) system is used to plan and control effective and efficient resource utilization for better quality and increased productivity.
5. Closed-loop MRP systems involves capacity planning and feedback mechanism to improve the quality of the materials requirement schedules generated by the MRP systems.
6. Manufacturing Requirements Planning (MRP-II) extended MRP to shop floor activities and distribution management.
7. ERP systems are considered a natural extension of MRP-II. They cover all major activities of an enterprise.
8. ERP-II extends ERP to external business entities.
9. Best-of-breed brings the best modules of different ERP systems to work together for better functionality.
10. ERP systems provide several benefits to an organization. They include integrated management, better decision making, proper resource utilization, reduction in lead-time, reduction in cycle-time and increased customer satisfaction.
11. The options available for the selection of an ERP package include-buying a ready made package from the market, develop own ERP package, engage the services of a software company to develop an ERP package to meet your specific requirements and the last option is to enhance the capabilities of an existing system.

REVIEW QUESTIONS

1. What is an enterprise-wide information system?
2. Give an example of an enterprise-wide information system.
3. Explain enterprise resource planning and list down the characteristics of ERP systems.
4. Why do companies need ERP systems?
5. Discuss the evolution of ERP systems.
6. What is collaborative commerce?
7. State and comment on some of the myths about ERP systems.
8. Discuss some of the evolving realities about ERP systems.
9. What are legacy systems? Discuss the problems associated with the legacy systems.
10. "Many of the underlying problems of the legacy system are inherent in ERP systems". Discuss.
11. What are the benefits of ERP systems?
12. What are the four options for selecting an ERP package?
13. What do you understand by custom-built and packaged approaches? Differentiate between the two.
14. What are the reasons for companies adopting ERP systems?
15. What are the advantages and disadvantages of in-house custom-built ERP with respect to the off-the-shelf ready-made available ERP package?
16. What are the drivers of ERP? Give suitable illustrations.

OBJECTIVE QUESTIONS

SECTION A

TICK THE CORRECT ANSWER

1. Some of the characteristics of the ERP systems include:
   (a) ERP systems are large-scale, end-to-end business processing systems.
   (b) ERP systems provide access to information in a real-time environment.
   (c) ERP systems are function-rich and integrate majority of a business's processes and operations.
   (d) ERP systems affect major departments in a company and tend to create changes in many business processes.
   (e) All of above.

2. The Inventory Management activities include:
   (a) Identifying inventory shortage.
   (b) Providing replenishment techniques.
   (c) Monitoring inventory usage.
   (d) Reconciling the inventory balance and reporting stock status.
   (e) All of above.

3. During 1970's many companies realized that by properly planning inventory requirements, unnecessary piling of large volumes of inventory could be avoided. This realization led to:
(a) Materials requirement planning (MRP) systems.
(b) Manufacturing Requirements Planning.
(c) ERP systems.
(d) DSS.
(e) EIS.

4. MRP-II extended ________to shop floor activities and distribution management.
(a) MRP.
(b) ERP.
(c) ERP-II.
(d) All of above.
(e) None of above.

5. Some of the common myths regarding ERP systems are as follows:
(a) ERP is a computer system.
(b) ERP is only for manufacturing firms.
(c) ERP systems can generate all the reports.
(d) ERP is same as best-of-breed products.
(e) All of above.

6. ERP systems are mostly implemented by large enterprises because:
(a) ERP systems are costly.
(b) ERP systems are large scale, end-to-end business processing systems.
(c) Traditional ERP systems were large and complex.
(d) ERP systems often introduce large-scale change in the business processes of the organization.

7. ERP System is intended to facilitate:
(a) Information sharing.
(b) Planning.
(c) Decision making on a company-wide basis.
(d) All of above.

8. Some of the facts about ERP and its implementation are:
(a) Traditional ERP systems were large, complex and expensive.
(b) ERP systems often introduce large-scale change in the business processes of the organization.
(c) ERP systems replace tangles of complicated computer applications with a single integrated information system.
(d) Implementing an ERP system is a significant investment for an enterprise.
(e) All of above.

9. Some of the facts about ERP and its implementation are:
(a) ERP systems often require adjustment and fine-tuning to meet the specific needs of the company.
(b) Many of the underlying problems of the legacy systems are inherent in ERP systems.
(c) ERP software can run on multiple platforms and follow client server architecture.
(d) ERP is an investment in business, technology and people.
(e) All of above.

10. ERP provides a large number of benefits to the company. The benefits include:
(a) ERP improves the enterprises IT architecture.
(b) Improves the business processes.
(c) Delivers enhanced revenues and profitability.
(d) All of above.

11. ERP systems contribute to efficient resource utilization by:
(a) Minimizing the inventory.
(b) Producing only-on-demand products.
(c) Delivering products to the customers speedily.
(d) All of above.

12. ERP systems reduce the lead-time by making the inventory management system more efficient and using latest technology such as ______________.
(a) Only EFT (electronic funds transfer).
(b) Only EDI (electronic data interchange).
(c) Both EFT (electronic funds transfer) and EDI (electronic data interchange).
(d) None of above.

13. ERP systems provide the following benefits:
(a) Decision making.
(b) Provides proper resource utilization.
(c) Reduces lead-time.
(d) Reduces cycle time.
(e) All of above.

14. ERP systems provide for the following:
(a) On-time delivery/shipment.
(b) Increased customer satisfaction.
(c) Better procurement process.
(d) Vendor management.
(e) All of above.

15. An ERP system provides the following:
(a) Improves corporate image.
(b) Reduces quality-related costs.
(c) More flexibility.
(d) All of above.

16. Proposed by S. Rao, the decision tree model provides options for the selection of an ERP package, which are as follows:
(a) Buying a ready-made package from the market.
(b) Engaging the services of a software company to develop the ERP package specific to your requirements.
(c) Develop own ERP package.
(d) Enhancing the capabilities in the existing system.
(e) All of above.

17. The ERP vendors have built a new generation of ERP software that has the following characteristics:
(a) Easy to install.

(b) Easy to manage.
(c) Function-specific.
(d) Has low start-up-costs.
(e) All of above.

18. The ERP packages available from ERP vendor may not address the specific business requirements of an organization. In such a situation:
(a) The business processes of the organization are changed to use the ready-made off-the-shelf ERP package.
(b) The ERP package is modified to address the business needs of the organization.
(c) Either (a) or (b).
(d) Neither (a) nor (b).

SECTION B

STATE TRUE OR FALSE

1. Mainframes didn't fair well at providing timely and relevant information and PC's could not store huge corporate databases.
2. The need for systems that could integrate all information flow in the company and at the same time make efficient use of desktop technology gave way to ERP systems.
3. ERP systems brought together MRP-II systems and the client/server technologies to integrate all the functions of the enterprise.
4. In the pre-ERP scenario, most departments had their own database and information systems which were fully integrated with each other.
5. In the pre-ERP scenario, the performance of the organization was very good.
6. With the arrival of ERP systems business functions were integrated with each other.
7. A single enterprise-wide database system shared throughout an enterprise results in better performance and improved quality.
8. In 1960's, Inventory Management and Control systems were used by the organizations to maintain an appropriate level of stock in the warehouse.
9. ERP is gradually spreading to other sectors such as retail, insurance, banking and health-care industries.
10. ERP systems provide a limited number of reports. Organizations will require to custom-build the reports by employing a third-party reporting tool.
11. One of the limitations of ERP software is that it cannot be customized to generate large lists of reports needed by an organization.
12. Best-of-breed uses the best modules of different ERP systems to provide increased functionality and a more streamlined solution than ERP.
13. Best-of-breed (BOB) solutions are used to address the functional limitations of ERP.
14. ERP is only for manufacturing firms.
15. ERP is same as best-of-breed products.
16. ERP systems are costly, as a result, they are mostly implemented by large enterprises that can bear the huge expenses involved.

17. ERP vendors are now designing simpler and cheaper ERP solutions for small and medium enterprises.

18. ERP Systems do not facilitate information sharing, planning and decision making on a company-wide basis.

19. Traditional ERP systems were large, complex and expensive. An enormous effort was required to implement them.

20. ERP systems often introduce large-scale change in the business processes of the organization.

21. ERP systems replace tangles of complicated computer applications with a single integrated information system.

22. Implementing an ERP system is a significant investment for an enterprise.

23. It is a myth that ERP systems often require adjustment and fine-tuning to meet the specific needs of the company.

24. The underlying problems of the legacy systems are not inherent in ERP systems.

25. ERP software cannot run on multiple platforms and do not follow client server architecture.

26. ERP is an investment in business, technology and people.

27. ERP improves; the enterprise IT architecture, business processes and delivers enhanced revenues and profitability.

28. The same ERP system manages functions and activities as different as the bills of materials, efficient handling of order processing, production schedule, effective management of human resource, allocating costs and facilitating on-time delivery of products to the customers.

29. ERP systems facilitate the synchronization of activities within the departments such as manufacturing, finance, human resource etc.

30. ERP systems aim to obtain the most value from the resources and equipment of the company.

31. ERP systems contribute to efficient resource utilization by minimizing the inventory, producing products only-on-demand and delivering products to the customers speedily.

32. An ERP system increases the lead-time by making the inventory management system more efficient and using latest technology such as EFT (electronic funds transfer) and EDI (electronic data interchange).

33. Time between the receipt of a customer order and the delivery of the required product is the cycle time.

34. ERP systems help in reducing the cycle time for both make-to-order and make-to-stock items.

35. With ERP companies are able to deliver highly customized products with the lead-time of standard off-the-shelf products.

36. Materials inspection systems support process supervision and control.

37. The Quality Management systems in ERP packages facilitate improvement of manufacturing methods.

38. ERP systems are commercial software packages that integrate transactions-oriented data and the business processes throughout the enterprise.

39. Proposed by S. Rao, the decision tree model provides four options for the selection of an ERP package. The options are as follows: buying a ready-made package from the market, develop own ERP package and engaging the services of a software company to develop the ERP package specific to your requirements, enhancing the capabilities in the existing system.

40. Enterprises can go for tailor-made ERP packages available in the market like SAP, Baan, Oracle, PeopleSoft etc.
41. Enterprises can develop a custom-built ERP package, specific to the enterprise's requirements, with the help of either an in-house IT department or a software solution provider.

SECTION C

FILL IN THE BLANKS

1. ERP systems have gradually evolved from ____________ to ________.
2. Materials Requirement Planning utilizes __________ methods to generate schedules for inventory purchase.
3. With the passage of time, _________ was included in the MRP systems to improve the quality of the materials requirement schedules generated by the MRP systems. These systems were called______________.
4. In the 1980's, MRP was expanded to__________, to bring together all the major business processes under a standard computerized planning system.
5. MRP-II also provided support to financial planning by converting materials requirement schedules into______.
6. ERP systems are considered a natural extension of_____.
7. _________ extends ERP to external business entities in order to help companies compete better.
8. Though computers are an integral part of ERP systems, yet ERP is a broader concept that includes______________, the working style and the people.
9. Best-of-breed uses the best ____________of different ERP systems to provide increased ___________ and a more streamlined solution than ERP.
10. Best of breed (BOB) solutions are used to address the _____________of ERP.
11. ERP systems are_________, as a result, they are mostly implemented by large enterprises that can bear the huge expenses involved.
12. ERP vendors are now designing simpler and cheaper ERP solutions for __________.
13. ERP system is intended to facilitate ________, planning and decision making on a company-wide basis.
14. Traditional ERP systems were large, _______ and expensive.
15. ERP systems often introduce large-scale change in the ___________of the organization.
16. ERP systems replace tangle of complicated computer applications with a single ___________system.
17. Implementing an ERP system is a significant ___________for an enterprise.
18. ERP systems often require______________to meet the specific needs of the company.
19. Many of the underlying problems of the __________ are inherent in ERP systems.
20. ERP software can run on multiple _________ and follow ___________architecture.
21. ERP is an investment in business, _____________ and people.
22. According to Gary Forger, "ERP acts as a ___________ for a company's business processes."

23. ERP systems ____________ the data entry process and help in monitoring, sharing and tracking ________________throughout the organization.

24. By providing accurate, timely and relevant information to the employees, ERP systems aid _____________of the employees.

25. ERP systems contribute to efficient __________ by minimizing the inventory, producing products only-on-demand and delivering products to the customers speedily.

26. ERP systems reduce the lead-time by making the inventory management system more efficient and using latest technology such as __________ and _____________.

27. Time between the receipt of a customer order and the delivery of the required product is the_________.

28. ERP systems help in ______________the cycle time for both make-to-order and make-to-stock items.

29. With ERP companies are able to deliver highly ____________ products with the lead-time of standard________________.

30. ERP systems increase customer satisfaction by providing on-time delivery of products _________ to their needs.

31. A _____________ helps the company to order right material at right time and acquire the raw materials and components at comparatively low costs.

32. ERP systems dynamically control the _________ of raw materials.

33. ERP systems integrated with ___________________ and EDI (electronic data interchange) monitor vendor activities and manage their suppliers efficiently.

34. _______ systems have tools for implementing total quality management programmes within an enterprise.

35. ______________in ERP packages helps support documenting specifications.

36. ERP systems provide a seamless integrated flow of information across the enterprise, enabling the enterprise to respond quickly to the changing_____________. This improves the flexibility of the enterprise as a whole.

37. With _________ the company restructures its processes to the so called "best practices: so that all activities across the enterprise are smoothly coordinated. This improves the________.

38. ERP systems are commercial software packages that integrate __________and the business processes throughout the enterprise.

39. The enterprise must make a careful choice while _________ an ERP package for use.

40. If the misfit between the ERP package and the business processes of the enterprise is large then _________ will be required.

41. The modifications are often________, costly and risky.

42. The enterprise must either __________ its ERP software to suit the business's needs or change many of its _____________ to adapt to the ERP software package.

43. Almost every analyst of the ERP implementation process strongly advises companies to __________the ERP software.

44. The analyst in fact advises the enterprise to maintain the existing ERP software functionality and to change their _____________ to adapt to ERP software.

45. Proposed by S. Rao, the decision tree model provides ________ options for the selection of an ERP package.

46. Enterprises can go for __________ available in the market like SAP, Baan, Oracle, PeopleSoft etc.

47. Enterprises can develop a ________ ERP package, specific to the enterprise's requirements, with the help of either _________ department or a software solution provider.

ANSWERS

SECTION A

(1) e (2) e (3) a (4) a (5) e (6) a (7) d (8) e (9) e (10) d
(11) d (12) c (13) e (14) e (15) d (16) e (17) e (18) c.

SECTION B

(1) True (2) True (3) True (4) False (5) False (6) True (7) True (8) True
(9) True (10) True (11) False (12) True (13) True (14) False (15) False (16) True
(17) True (18) False (19) True (20) True (21) True (22) True (23) False (24) False
(25) False (26) True (27) True (28) True (29) True (30) True (31) True (32) False
(33) True (34) True (35) True (36) True (37) True (38) True (39) True (40) True
(41) True.

SECTION C

(1) Inventory management and control systems, ERP-II **(2)** computerised **(3)** Capacity Planning and Feedback, closed-loop MRP systems **(4)** MRP-II **(5)** capital requirements **(6)** MRP-II **(7)** ERP-II **(8)** organization's goals and objectives **(9)** modules, functionality **(10)** functional limitations **(11)** costly **(12)** small and medium enterprises **(13)** information sharing **(14)** complex **(15)** business processes **(16)** integrated information **(17)** investment **(18)** adjustment and fine-tuning **(19)** legacy systems **(20)** platforms, client server **(21)** technology **(22)** planning backbone **(23)** automate, information **(24)** decision making capability **(25)** resource utilization **(26)** EFT (electronic funds transfer), EDI (electronic data interchange) **(27)** cycle time **(28)** reducing **(29)** customized, off-the- shelf products **(30)** customized **(31)** procurement system **(32)** purchasing **(33)** SCM (supply chain management) **(34)** ERP **(35)** Specification control system **(36)** market conditions **(37)** ERP systems, corporate image **(38)** transactions-oriented data **(39)** selecting **(40)** modifications **(41)** time-consuming **(42)** customize, business processes **(43)** avoid modifying **(44)** business procedures **(45)** four **(46)** tailor-made ERP packages **(47)** custom-built, in-house IT.

2

Chapter

ERP Life Cycle

HIGHLIGHTS

- **ERP Life cycle**
  - ERP Life cycle, as suggested by Markus & Tanis
  - ERP Life cycle Framework by Esteves and Pastor

ERP systems are complex systems and require proper planning and total support (support from management, employees and end-users) for its successful implementation. A successful ERP implementation raises the productivity of the enterprise and results in increased customer satisfaction. A company is likely to benefit more if it is able to fully integrate ERP into day-to-day business operations of the company. An effective ERP system will be able to accommodate rapidly changing business conditions.

2.1 ERP LIFE CYCLE

An ERP system goes through several phases during its whole life within the hosting enterprise. These phases constitute the life cycle of ERP.

2.1.1 ERP Life Cycle, as Suggested by Markus & Tanis

According to Markus & Tanis, an ERP life cycle has four phases.

1. **Chartering**

   This phase involves making decisions that will affect the business positively and analyze the impact of ERP on the business. The decision to adopt ERP is made only after a great deal of careful planning.

2. **Project**
   This phase involves changing management programmes and culture. Also, ERP software is customized to suit the requirements of the business. Other activities include software development, testing and troubleshooting.
3. **Shakedown**
   In this phase, the ERP system is monitored and evaluated for performance.
4. **Onward and Outward**
   This phase involves system maintenance, providing support to users, obtaining results and upgrading the systems.

Figure 2.1 shows ERP life cycle as suggested by Markus & Tanis.

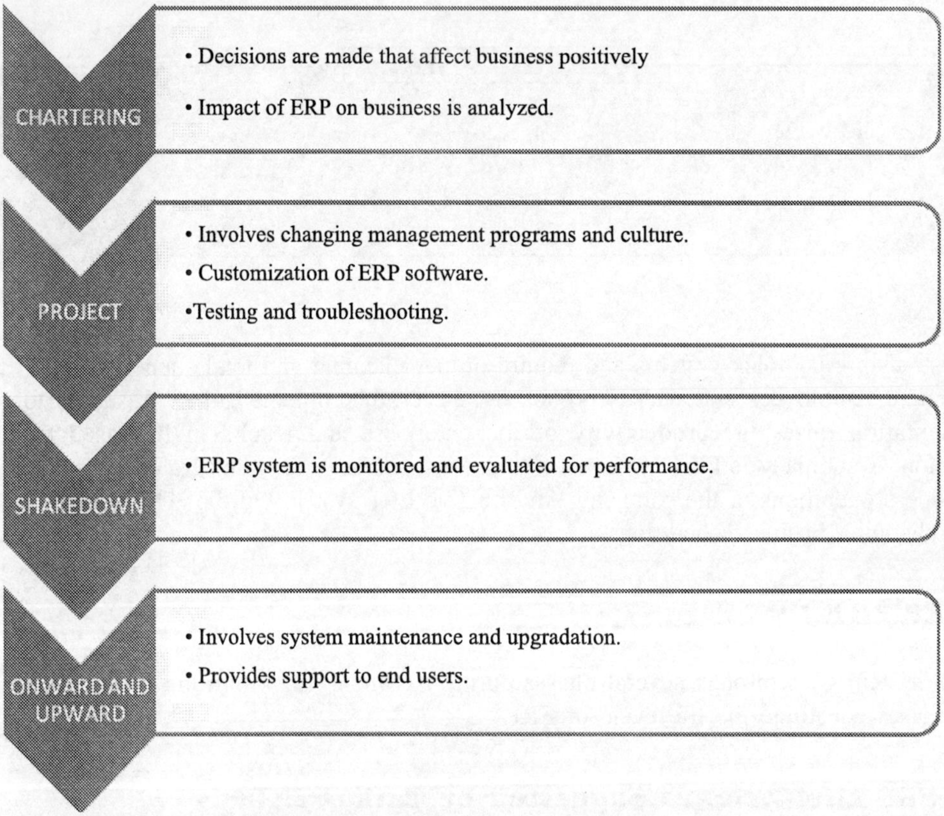

Fig. 2.1. ERP Lifecycle Framework as proposed by Markus and Tanis

LEARNING POINTS

1. An ERP system goes through several phases during its whole life within the hosting enterprise. These phases constitute the lifecycle of ERP.
2. ERP Lifecycle, as suggested by Markus & Tanis constitutes four phases- Chartering, Project, Shakedown, Onward and Outward.

3. In chartering phase, crucial decisions are taken in an attempt to have a positive impact of ERP system on the business.
4. Project phase involves customization of ERP software package, testing, troubleshooting as well as changing the management programs and culture.
5. In shakedown phase the system is monitored and evaluated for performance.
6. System maintenance and up-gradation of ERP is carried out in onward and upward phase of ERP Lifecycle.

2.1.2 ERP Lifecycle Framework by Esteves and Pastor

The ERP Lifecycle Framework given by Esteves and Pastor include the following phases as shown in Figure 2.2.

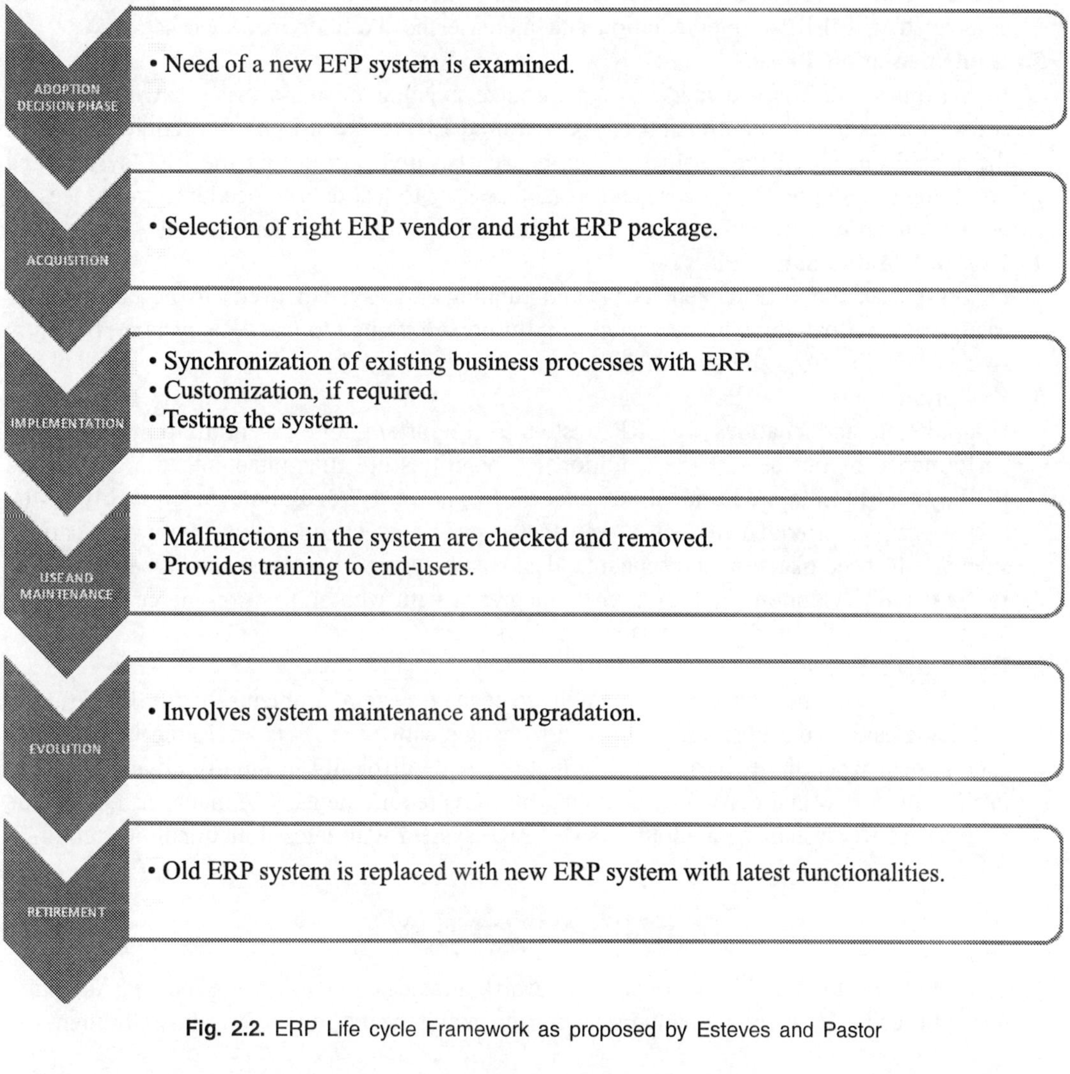

Fig. 2.2. ERP Life cycle Framework as proposed by Esteves and Pastor

1. **Adoption Decision Phase**
   In this phase, the need of a new ERP system is examined for the organization. The business requirements, the nature of the operations and the goals and objectives of the company are carefully studied. What impact the ERP system will have on the company is also determined before deciding to go for ERP adoption. It is necessary to assess the organization's readiness, management's support and IT skills required before the ERP adoption decision is taken.
2. **Acquisition Phase**
   This phase involves selecting the vendor and the ERP software that best addresses the needs of the business. The pricing models offered by different vendors, the functionality of different ERP products, training required are some of the factors that are considered for selecting an ERP package from a vendor.
   The selection of a right ERP package for the organization will minimize the risk often associated with ERP implementation and increase the likelihood of success.
3. **Implementation Phase**
   In this phase, efforts are made to synchronize existing business process with the ERP software package. Customization of the acquired ERP software may be required to meet the specific needs of the business. This phase also involves testing the ERP system and providing training on the new system. It is necessary to test data, procedures and processes before launch of ERP system in order to minimize errors after deployment.
4. **Use and Maintenance Phase**
   In this phase, the ERP system is up and running. The system needs to be corrected in case of any malfunctions in the system. End-users are trained to use ERP system efficiently so that benefits from the system are obtained.
5. **Evolution Phase**
   Upgradation and changes in ERP system is important and essential to improve the performance of business. Here, additional capabilities are integrated into the company's ERP system to obtain additional advantages. In "upwards" evolution, functionality in the ERP system is provided in such a way that it enables decision making with applications such as advanced planning and schedule, data warehouses and business intelligence systems. In "outward" evolution, ERP system is integrated with web and E-Commerce. It delivers added value to the traditional business ERP system.
6. **Retirement Phase**
   An ERP system may become vulnerable to legacy system problems in the long run as technologies and the business state of art change with time. It is advisable to retire the ERP system when the ERP system begins to provide difficulty in modifying and evolving itself to meet new and constantly changing business requirements. The manager may decide to replace ERP system with another newer ERP system with latest functionalities required.

LEARNING POINTS

1. Esteves & Pastor's ERP life cycle framework includes the following phases: adoption decision, acquisition, implementation, use and maintenance, evolution and retirement.

2. In adoption decision phase, the need of a new ERP system is examined for the organization.
3. Acquisition phase involves evaluation of ERP vendor and ERP software. Selection of right ERP package and right ERP vendor will reduce the risk associated with ERP implementation to a great extent.
4. In implementation phase, efforts are made to synchronize existing business processes with ERP software package. Customization is done, if required.
5. In use and maintenance phase, any malfunctions in the system are corrected. End-users are given training to work efficiently on the ERP systems.
6. In evolution phase, attempts are made to evolve ERP systems both "upwards" and "onwards". ERP system is integrated with web and e-commerce.
7. In retirement phase, old ERP system is replaced with the new ERP system with latest functionalities required.

SUMMARY

The different phases that an ERP system goes through within the organization constitute the life cycle of ERP. According to Markus and Tanis, an ERP life cycle consists of chartering, project, shakedown and onward & upward. In chartering phase, ERP adoption decision is taken. Project phase involves activities such as customization, testing etc. Monitoring and performance evaluation activities are carried out during the shakedown phase of ERP life cycle. The last phase-"onward and upward" involves maintenance and upgradation activities to be carried out.

According to Esteves and Pastor, ERP life cycle consists of the following phases: Adoption Decision, Acquisition, Implementation, Use & Maintenance, Evolution and Retirement phase. In adoption decision, the first phase of ERP life cycle, a careful examination of the business needs of organization is done before deciding to adopt ERP system. Acquisition phase involves the selection of the right ERP vendor and right ERP package to meet business requirements.

Implementation phase involves customization of ERP software and testing data as well as the processes and procedures to ensure correctness of ERP system. Use and maintenance phase deals with the corrections of any malfunctions that may occur in the working of the ERP system. It also involves training the end-users to ensure the effective use of ERP systems. Evolution phase is concerned with performing upgradations in ERP systems. The ERP system is integrated with web and e-commerce technologies to deliver more benefits to their customers.

POINTS TO REMEMBER

1. An ERP system life cycle consists of several phases through which the system goes during its whole life within an enterprise.
2. According to Markus and Tanis, an ERP life cycle has four phases: chartering, project, shakedown and onward & upward.
3. In chartering phase, decisions are made that affect business favourably.
4. Project phase involves changing culture of organization, customization and testing.
5. In shakedown phase, ERP system is monitored and evaluated for performance.
6. In "onwards and upwards", system is upgraded and end-user training is provided.

7. According to Esteves and Pastor, an ERP life cycle framework consists of the following phases: adoption decision, acquisition, implementation, use & maintenance, evolution and retirement.
8. In adoption decision phase, a careful examination of the business needs of the organization is done before taking the decision of ERP adoption.
9. Acquisition phase involves selection of best ERP package and vendor for the business needs of the organization.
10. Implementation phase involves customization, testing and troubleshooting.
11. Use and maintenance phase deals with correcting any malfunctions in the system.
12. In evolution phase, upgradations such as integrating the system with e-commerce and web are performed.
13. Retirement phase involves the replacement of the old system with new ERP system.

REVIEW QUESTIONS

1. Explain the various stages of ERP life cycle.
2. Explain ERP life cycle as suggested by Esteves and Pastor.
3. Explain ERP life cycle as suggested by Markus and Tanis.

OBJECTIVE QUESTIONS

SECTION A

TICK THE CORRECT ANSWER

1. According to Markus & Tanis, an ERP life cycle has the following phases:
   (a) Chartering.
   (b) Project.
   (c) Shakedown.
   (d) Onward and outward.
   (e) All of above.
2. ______________ phase involves making decisions that will affect the business positively and analyze the impact of ERP on the business.
   (a) Chartering.
   (b) Project.
   (c) Shakedown.
   (d) Onward and outward.
3. Project phase involves:
   (a) Making decisions that will affect the business positively.
   (b) Changing management programs and culture.
   (c) Monitoring ERP system.
   (d) Providing support to users.

4. Project phase involves:
   (a) Changing management programmes and culture.
   (b) Customization of ERP software to suit the requirements of the business.
   (c) Software development.
   (d) Testing and troubleshooting.
   (e) All of above.

5. The ERP system is monitored and evaluated for performance in the phase:
   (a) Chartering.
   (b) Project.
   (c) Shakedown.
   (d) Onward and outward.

6. Software development, testing and troubleshooting are activities included in:
   (a) Chartering.
   (b) Project.
   (c) Shakedown.
   (d) Onward and outward.

7. System maintenance, providing support to users, obtaining results and upgrading the systems are activities included in:
   (a) Chartering.
   (b) Project.
   (c) Shakedown.
   (d) Onward and outward.

8. The ERP life cycle framework, given by Esteves and Pastor, include the following phases:
   (a) Adoption Decision Phase.
   (b) Acquisition Phase.
   (c) Implementation Phase.
   (d) Use and Maintenance Phase.
   (e) All of above.

9. In Adoption Decision Phase, the following activities are performed:
   (a) The need of a new ERP system is examined for the organization.
   (b) Business requirements, the nature of the operations and the goals and objectives of the company are carefully studied.
   (c) Assessing the organization's readiness, management's support and IT skills required before the ERP adoption decision is taken.
   (d) All of above.

10. Acquisition Phase involves the following:
   (a) Selecting the vendor and the ERP software that best addresses the needs of the business.
   (b) Evaluating pricing models offered by different vendors, the functionality of different ERP products.
   (c) Examining the requirement for training for selecting an ERP package from a vendor.
   (d) All of above.

11. In Implementation Phase following activities are performed:
   (a) Efforts are done to synchronize existing business processes with the ERP software package.

(b) Customization of the acquired ERP software to meet the specific needs of the business.
(c) Testing the ERP system in order to minimize errors after deployment.
(d) Providing training on the new system.
(e) All of above.

12. In__________ the ERP system is up and running.
(a) Implementation Phase.
(b) Use and Maintenance Phase.
(c) Evolution Phase.
(d) Retirement Phase.
(e) None of above.

13. Additional capabilities are integrated into the company's ERP system to obtain additional advantages in _________ phase.
(a) Implementation Phase.
(b) Use and Maintenance Phase.
(c) Evolution Phase.
(d) Retirement Phase.
(e) None of above.

14. In _________ evolution functionality in the ERP system is provided in such a way that it enables decision making with applications such as advanced planning and schedule, data warehouses and business intelligence systems.
(a) Upwards
(b) Outwards
(c) Downwards
(d) None of above

15. In "outward" evolution:
(a) ERP system is integrated with web and e-Commerce.
(b) Any malfunctions in the ERP system are corrected.
(c) ERP system is replaced with another newer ERP system with latest functionalities required.
(d) None of above.

16. It is advisable to retire the ERP system when the ERP system begins to provide difficulty in modifying and evolving itself to meet new and constantly changing business requirements. The phase is called __________.
(a) Use and Maintenance Phase.
(b) Retirement Phase.
(c) Evolution Phase.
(d) Implementation Phase.

SECTION B

STATE TRUE OR FALSE

1. ERP systems are complex systems and require proper planning and total support (support from management, employees and end-users) for its successful implementation.

2. A company is likely to benefit more if it is able to fully integrate ERP into day-to-day business operations of the company.
3. An effective ERP system will be able to accommodate rapidly changing business conditions.
4. An ERP system goes through several phases during its whole life within the hosting enterprise. These phases constitute the life cycle of ERP.
5. According to Markus & Tanis, an ERP life cycle has four phases: Chartering, Project, Shakedown, Onward and Outward.
6. Project Phase involves making decisions that will affect the business positively and analyze the impact of ERP on the business.
7. Chartering Phase involves changing management programmes and culture.
8. ERP software is customized to suit the requirements of the business.
9. In Shakedown Phase, the ERP system is monitored and evaluated for performance.
10. Onward and Outward phase involves system maintenance, providing support to users, obtaining results and upgrading the systems.
11. The ERP Lifecycle Framework, given by Esteves and Pastor, consists of six phases.
12. The selection of a right ERP package for the organization will minimize the risk often associated with ERP implementation and increase the likelihood of success.
13. In Implementation Phase, efforts are made to synchronize existing business process with the ERP software package.
14. It is necessary to test data, procedures and processes before launch of ERP system in order to minimize errors after deployment.
15. Customization of the acquired ERP software may be required to meet the specific needs of the business.
16. Implementation phase does not involve testing the ERP system and providing training on the new system.
17. End-users are trained to use ERP system efficiently so that benefits from the system are obtained.
18. Upgradation and changes in ERP system is important and essential to improve the performance of business.
19. In "outward" evolution, functionality in the ERP system is provided in such a way that it enables decision making with applications such advanced planning and schedule, data warehouses and business intelligence systems.
20. In "upwards" evolution, ERP system is integrated with web and e-Commerce.
21. Integrating ERP system with web and e-Commerce delivers added value to the traditional business ERP system.
22. An ERP system may become vulnerable to legacy system problems in the long run as technologies and the business state of art change with time.
23. The manager may decide to replace ERP system with another newer ERP system with latest functionalities required.

SECTION C

FILL IN THE BLANKS

1. A successful ERP implementation raises the ____________ of the enterprise and results in increased customer satisfaction.

2. An ERP system goes through several phases during its whole life within the hosting enterprise. These phases constitute the__________.
3. According to Markus & Tanis, an ERP life cycle has _______ phases.
4. ________ Phase involves making decisions that will affect the business positively and analyze the impact of ERP on the business.
5. The decision to adopt ERP is made only after a great deal of ________ planning.
6. Project Phase involves changing ____________ and culture.
7. Activities included in _______ are software development, testing and troubleshooting.
8. ERP software is customized to suit the ________ of the business.
9. In Shakedown Phase, the ERP system is ______________ and ______________ for performance.
10. ______________ Phase involves system maintenance, providing support to users, obtaining results and upgrading the systems.
11. ______________ and upgradation of ERP is carried out in onward and upward phase of ERP life cycle.
12. The selection of a right ERP package for the organization will ________ the risk often associated with ERP implementation and ______ the likelihood of success.
13. In __________ phase, efforts are done to synchronize existing ____________ with the ERP software package.
14. It is necessary to test______, procedures and processes before launch of ERP system in order to minimize ________ after deployment.
15. ___________ Phase also involves testing the ERP system and providing training on the new system.
16. ____________ of the acquired ERP software may be required to meet the specific needs of the business.
17. __________ are trained to use ERP system efficiently so that benefits from the system are obtained.
18. Upgradation and changes in ______________ is important and essential to improve the performance of business.
19. In _________evolution functionality in the ERP system is provided in such a way that it enables decision making with applications such as advanced planning and schedule, data warehouses and business intelligence systems.
20. In _________ evolution, ERP system is integrated with web and e-commerce.
21. Integrating ERP system with web and _________ delivers added value to the traditional business ERP system.
22. An ERP system may become vulnerable to _____________ problems in the long run as technologies and the business state of art change with time.
23. The manager may decide to replace ERP system with another newer ___________ with latest functionalities required.

ANSWERS

SECTION A

(1) e **(2)** a **(3)** b **(4)** e **(5)** c **(6)** b **(7)** d **(8)** e **(9)** d **(10)** d
(11) e **(12)** b **(13)** c **(14)** a **(15)** a **(16)** b.

SECTION B

(1) True **(2)** True **(3)** True **(4)** True **(5)** True **(6)** False **(7)** False **(8)** True
(9) True **(10)** True **(11)** True **(12)** True **(13)** True **(14)** True **(15)** True **(16)** False
(17) True **(18)** True **(19)** False **(20)** False **(21)** True **(22)** True **(23)** True.

SECTION C

(1) productivity **(2)** ERP life cycle **(3)** four **(4)** chartering **(5)** Careful **(6)** management programmes **(7)** project phase **(8)** Requirements **(9)** monitored, evaluated **(10)** onward and outward **(11)** system maintenance **(12)** minimize, increase **(13)** implementation phase, business process **(14)** data, errors **(15)** Implementation **(16)** customization **(17)** end-users **(18)** ERP system **(19)** upwards **(20)** outward **(21)** e-commerce **(22)** legacy system **(23)** ERP system.

3
Chapter
ERP Market

HIGHLIGHTS

- **ERP Market**
  - Indian ERP Market
  - Global ERP Market
  - ERP in Large Enterprises
  - ERP for Small and Medium Enterprises
  - ERP Market Players

The ERP market for large enterprises as well as small and medium enterprises (referred to as SME or SMB) is undoubtedly promising as ERP is the latest high-end information technology solution that improves the business processes of the companies to gain competitive advantage. The ERP market is a segmented market. Though ERP originated in the manufacturing sector, today, the ERP systems have a much broader scope. As ERP systems spread to cover all basic functions of the enterprise, regardless of its nature of business, the ERP market scenario appears to be very active.

3.1 INDIAN ERP MARKET

India with its vast pool of talented professionals has become the most active market for the ERP vendors. The Indian ERP market is expected to reach Rs. 1550 crore ($341 million) according to IDC, over the next five years. Of this, the SME potential in India for enterprise class is projected to Rs. 728 crore (%160 million)—47 percent of the overall ERP market. SME's are becoming the popular choice of most ERP vendors in India.

According to ARC advisory, the ERP market in India was $83 million in the year 2004 and is forecast to be over $250 million in near future. Figure 3.1 shows the market share of the ERP vendors in India.

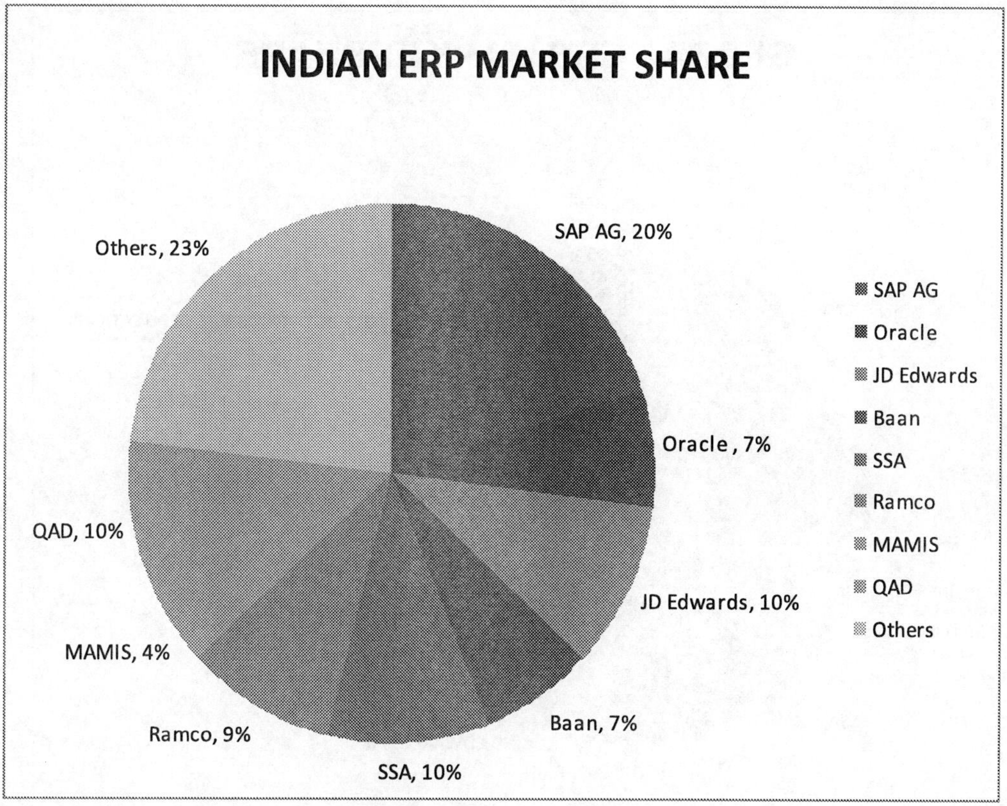

Fig. 3.1. Indian ERP Market Share

LEARNING POINTS

1. Though ERP originated in the manufacturing sector, today, the ERP systems have a much broader scope.
2. As ERP systems spread to cover all basic functions of the enterprise, regardless of its nature of business, the ERP market scenario appears to be very active.
3. According to ARC advisory, the ERP market in India was $83 million in the year 2004 and is forecast to be over $250 million in near future.

3.2 GLOBAL ERP MARKET

The world-wide market for the ERP products continues to grow across a diverse set of industries and continents. It is expected to grow at a compounded annual growth rate (CA GR) of 4.8 per cent over the next three years exceeding $21 billion in 2010. This forecast has been done by ARC advisory Group Study. Figure 3.2 shows the global ERP market share.

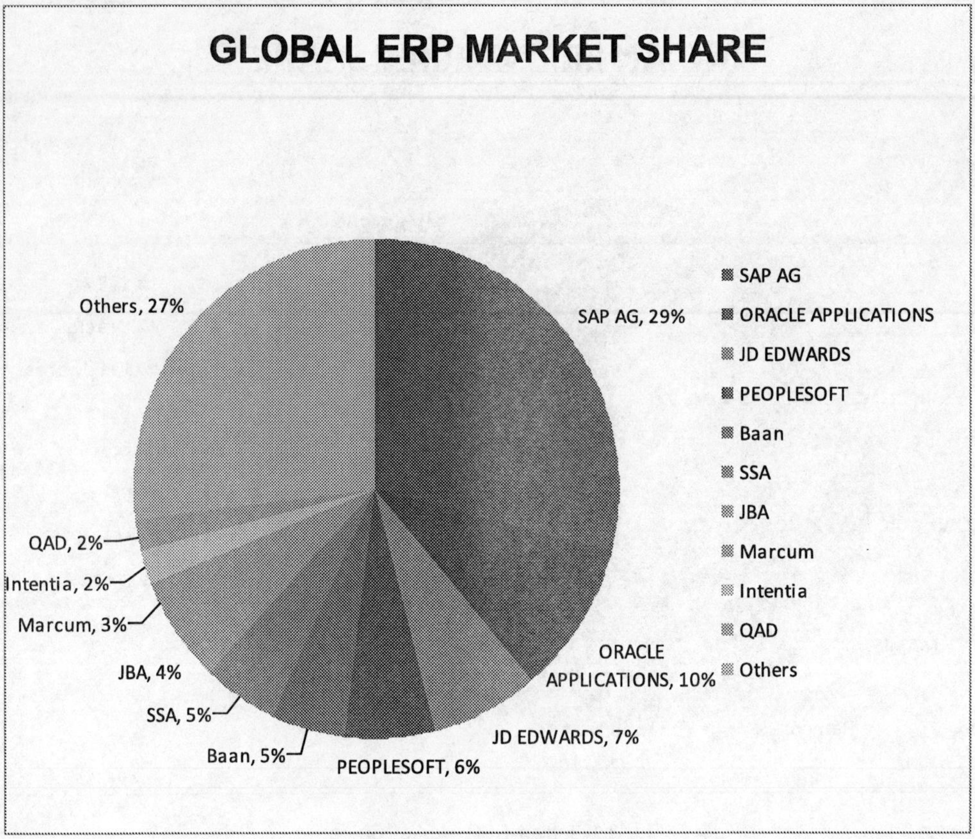

Fig. 3.2. Global ERP Market Share

The leading players such as SAP, Oracle, Baan, PeopleSoft, Ramco Systems are likely to continue to dominate the global ERP market in future. Globally, the mid-range and SME markets continue to be a major focus area for ERP vendors. SME market sector has fuelled the growth of the global ERP market in recent years.

LEARNING POINTS

1. The world-wide market for the ERP products continues to grow across a diverse set of industries and continents.
2. It is expected to grow at a compounded annual growth rate (CA GR) of 4.8 per cent over the next three years exceeding $21 billion in 2010. This forecast has been done by ARC advisory Group Study.

3.3 ERP IN LARGE ENTERPRISES

ERP is especially suitable for large enterprises that are capable of spending a large amount of money on their enterprise resource planning efforts. Over the years the number of large enterprises without ERP have turned out to be negligible, this has forced the ERP vendors to move their focus to small and medium enterprises. The reason why all the big corporations have successfully implemented ERP is quite simple. Today, a large enterprise cannot exist if it is without an ERP system. In order to improve the business performance and gain competitive advantage the company necessarily has to adapt to ERP. Moreover the awareness created by ERP vendors and IT researchers have also contributed a lot in bringing ERP to the large-scale enterprises.

LEARNING POINT

1. ERP is especially suitable for large enterprises that are capable of spending a large amount of money on their enterprise resource planning efforts.

3.4 ERP FOR SMALL AND MEDIUM ENTERPRISES

Recently ERP vendors have started addressing the business needs of the small and medium enterprises. As the number of large enterprises without ERP became negligible SME's turned to be the greener and fresher pastures for ERP vendors. The market prospects for ERP in SME's are high with SME's willing to refine their business operations and go ahead with ERP implementation and ERP vendors all set to provide special ERP business applications, priced lower compared to ERP packages for large firms, to tap this promising market sector. For example, J.D. Edwards offer customers a component based approach in which customers can select parts of the specific enterprise solution and purchase only what they require for the organization.

SME's often have to face many problems with regards to ERP. Some of these problems are as follows:

1. The requirement of the small and medium enterprises is limited while the ERP product exceeds their specifications in all ways (including the costs of the product). This problem can be solved by the vendor by providing a package designed to meet the specific requirements of the enterprise at an affordable cost. The component-based approach (devised by ERP vendor J.D. Edwards) will work well to address this problem.
2. SME's often fail to realize the importance of restructuring and redefining the business processes. Above all SME's often put the entire blame for the failure of the system on the ERP vendor.
3. The small and medium enterprises often demand a very low price from the vendor. In most cases either the ERP vendor fails to offer the product at such a low quotation or delivers a low quality product that will not provide many benefits to the organization. It may happen that all the efforts go in vain.
4. SME's often face the difficulty of selecting the right ERP vendor. Formerly SME's were catered to by smaller vendors only. But now big ERP players have intervened increasing

the number of ERP vendors from among the branded players and small vendors. The decision should be in favour of a vendor and product that meets the requirements of the SME.

5. As big ERP vendors don't offer source code to SME's, a lot of functional errors may occur thereby jeopardizing the very purpose of ERP.
6. If the SME's decide to go for big ERP vendor then the requirement for customization will be more. This may result in a bad experience for both the vendor and the organization.

Figure 3.3 illustrates an ERP implementation model in small and medium enterprises.

ERP IMPLEMENTATION MODEL

CASUAL CONDITIONS

- Need for system integration
- Changes in organizational structure
- Need for an excellent IT infrastructure
- Need for improving existing business processes

INTERVENING CONDITIONS

✓ ***Organizational***
- Need of good project team
- End-user involvement consultants

✓ ***Technological***
- Inadequate expertise to handle legacy systems
- Need for new hardware

✓ ***Project Management***
- Proper project plan
- Support from top management
- Need for troubleshooting

CONTEXT

✓ ***Organizational***
- Political factors
- Organizational culture

✓ ***Environment***
- Globalization

✓ ***IT***
- Adoption of SAP
- Adequate IT infrastructure

STRATEGIES

✓ ***Organizational***
- Training
- Overall Project Management

✓ ***Technological***
- Sound methodology
- Avoid customization
- Best implementation strategy

CONSEQUENCES

✓ ***Organizational***
- Business process reengineering
- Improved performance
- Better career prospects
- Change in attitude of employees

✓ ***Technological***
- Use of latest tools and technology
- Continuous improvement of systems
- Introduction of new SAP projects

Fig. 3.3. A Model for ERP Implementation in SME

3.4.1 Open Source ERP in SME's

An open source ERP application refers to the ERP software programs that can be copied and reproduced without even paying the ERP licence fees or at a reduced cost. Free licensing has helped the SME's to go ahead with ERP implementation with little investment. As SME's cannot afford to invest a high amount of money, open source ERP has come as a blessing. ERP outsourcing, Open source ERP and ERP applications designed specifically for SME's have contributed a lot in the growth of ERP market for small and medium enterprises.

3.4.2 Understanding the Tiers in SMB

The small and medium enterprises (SME's) are divided into four groups (called tiers) based on their finance and amount of resources as well as their attitude towards IT strategy and implementation of the strategy. Tier 1 SMB's are SMB's that view IT solutions as an integrated part of the company strategy and implement IT solutions to make their company grow faster. According to Sau Lam, New York based research analyst at AMI-Partners, Tier 1 SMB's account for the smallest percentage of the SMB universe. They are more likely to purchase ERP packages directly from the packaged software vendor. Tier 2 SMB's has comparatively less resources and finance than Tier 1 SMB's and tend to deal with value added resellers. The tier 2 market is the largest of all the four tiers in terms of the number of potential users. The Tier 3 SMB's include those companies that implement IT solutions keeping a sharp eye on the costs and constantly trying to control the unnecessary expenditures. The Tier 3 SMB's prefer to purchase from Internet/ mail order resellers. They prefer solutions that require smaller budgets. Tier 4 SMB's include the companies that are on the verge of losing a large number of their potential customers and suppliers and are therefore compelled to implement IT solutions in order to sustain their business. The Tier 4 SMB's prefer regional and national retail chains.

LEARNING POINTS

1. The market prospects for ERP in SME's are high with SME's willing to refine their business operations and go ahead with ERP implementation and ERP vendors all set to provide special ERP business applications, priced lower compared to ERP packages for large firms, to tap this promising market sector.
2. As SME's cannot afford to invest a high amount of money, open source ERP has come as a blessing.
3. The small and medium enterprises (SME's) are divided into four groups (called tiers) based on their finance and amount of resources as well as their attitude towards IT strategy and implementation of the strategy.

3.5 ERP MARKET PLAYERS

The ERP market has a large number of ERP vendors who are offering good ERP products to companies worldwide. The three primary ERP vendors include SAP, Baan and Oracle. Other ERP vendors include CODA, IBM, Ramco, Platinum to name a few.

Table 3.1 shows major ERP vendors and the products offered by them.

Table 3.1: Major ERP Vendors and their Products

S No.	Major ERP Vendors	Development Platforms	ERP Products
1.	Oracle	PL/SQL, XML	Oracle Applications
2.	PeopleSoft	SQL, XML	Peoplesoft select
3.	SAP	ABAP, Java, XML	SAPR/2, SAPR/3
4.	Baan		Baan ERP Baan Front Office Baan Corporate Office Baan Supply Chain

3.5.1 SAP's Profile and its Products

SAP (Systems, Applications and Products in Data Processing) company was founded in the year 1972 and is based in Germany. SAP is the top vendor of the ERP market and has installations in more than 107 countries. The ERP software packages from SAP come in two versions. One is the mainframe version (SAP R/2) and the other is the client/ server version of the ERP package (SAP R/3). The company has an extensive library of more than eight hundred business processes.

3.5.1.1 SAP R/3

R/3 system is suitable for companies of all sizes and nature. It comprises powerful programs for accounting, production and materials management, quality management, sales and distribution, plant maintenance and human resource management. R/3 ERP package gets installed quickly and can run on the hardware platforms of leading ERP vendors. It is also directly linked to the Internet. SAP's Business Engineer is a complete toolkit that facilitates easy implementation of R/3.

3.5.2 Baan's Profile and its Products

Baan Company was founded in the year 1978 by Jan and Paul baan. The company has dual headquarters in Netherlands and United States of America. The company provides component-based applications for front-office and back-office automation. It meets the needs of SMB's as well as large scale enterprises with its rich set of business modeling tools. Baan offers specific vertical industry solutions for automotive companies as well as aerospace and defense companies.

The Baan series-based product family consists of the following-BaanERP, BaanFrontOffice, BaanCorporate Office Solutions and BaanSupplyChain Solutions.

BaanERP consists of a number of interdependent modules such as manufacturing, finance, project and distribution to address the business needs of the enterprise. BaanERP tools facilitate creation of customer-specific ERP solution and easy integration of ERP products with third party products.

The company also provides run-time tools. Run-time tools provide independence to Baan ERP applications from computing environment specific issues. Baan IV makes use of both Java and Active X. Baan IV delivers web e-commerce capabilities through popular desktop browsers. Baan IV suite manages the sales order entry and tracking process via a web browser.

3.5.3 Oracle Corporation's Profile and its Products

The company was founded in 1977 and has its headquarters in Redwood Shores, California. It is the second largest software company in the world. Oracle Applications consists of over forty-five modules for manufacturing, financial, projects, front office, supply chain and human resources. Each of the modules is web-enabled. Oracle Applications support multiple currencies. It is available in twenty-nine languages.

3.5.4 QAD

Founded in the year 1979, QAD is now a leading provider of ERP applications to manufacturing industries. QAD's ERP addresses the needs of single-site and multinational companies. QAD's ERP includes the following solution suites-QAD's Financials, QAD customer management, QAD manufacturing, QAD supply chain, QAD services and support, QAD enterprise asset management, QAD analytics and QAD interoperability.

QAD enterprise applications support multiple currencies and allow multiple bank accounts in separate currencies. QAD's ERP solutions support multiple or proportional consolidation.

QAD's MFG/PRO software provides solution for manufacturing, distribution, financial, supply chain and service management. MFG/PRO is available in twenty-six languages. MFG/PRO synchronizes distributed operations within the enterprise and can be scaled to meet the growing needs of business. Qwizard is a value added tool for MFG/PRO software. It provides easy to use business modeling and learning tools.

3.5.5 System Software Associates, Inc. (SSA)

SSA was founded in 1981 and has its headquarters in Chicago, USA. SSA offers advanced ERP system software to address the needs of enterprises on a global scale. BPCS Client/ Sever products provide reconfigurability option to its customers. This allows companies to adjust their systems according to the changing market conditions easily and quickly. BPCS Client/ Server is based on Distributed Object Computing Architecture (DOCA).

3.5.6 Ramco

Ramco is a global ERP software provider with customers in thirty-five countries. Ramco Business Process Delivery System (BPDS) provides maximum flexibility to execute a business process strategy. Ramco ERP makes use of pure service oriented architecture (SOA). With Ramco's ERP OnDemand small and medium enterprises can get exactly the processes they need at a small price. ERP OnDemand modules include the following: Financials, Supply Chain Management (SCM), Customer Relationship Management (CRM), manufacturing, Business Analytics and Multi-Entity Management.

3.5.7 PeopleSoft Inc.

Established in 1987, PeopleSoft Inc. offers innovative industry specific ERP solutions. PeopleSoft ERP solutions run on a variety of hardware and database platforms. PeopleSoft Select is a complete ERP package provided by PeopleSoft to address the business needs of medium-sized firms. PeopleSoft also offers self-service applications enabling customers to perform some administrative tasks with the help of a Work list and Query interface on PeopleSoft Web Client.

PeopleSoft Implementation Toolkit helps in the identification of the implementation approach and strategy that will best suit your ERP project. PeopleSoft has also integrated popular OLAP tools such as Cognos PowerPlay and Arbor Essbase with its ERP solutions.

3.5.8 JD Edwards World Solutions Company

JD Edwards was formed in 1977 by three founders: Jack Thompsom, Dan Gregory and Ed McVaney. It is headquartered in Denver. The ERP solutions offer multi-currency, multi-language and multi-location capabilities. JD Edward's offers two application suites: OneWorld and WorldSoftware/WorldVision. OneWorld provides support to workflow, web based technology and integration of legacy, best-of-breed and third party products. OneWorld has been designed to provide a highly flexible solution to its customers. JDEdwards WorldSoftware allows customers to selectively integrate ERP software applications from among its diverse ERP product suites available for various industries. JD EdwardsWorldVision provides the customers with a graphical user interface.

LEARNING POINTS

1. The three primary ERP vendors include SAP, Baan and Oracle. Other ERP vendors include CODA, IBM, Ramco, Platinum to name a few.
2. The ERP software packages from SAP come in two versions. One is the mainframe version (SAP R/2) and the other is the client/ server version of the ERP package (SAP R/3).
3. The Baan series-based product family consists of the following-BaanERP, BaanFrontOffice, BaanCorporate Office Solutions and BaanSupplyChain Solutions.
4. BaanERP consists of a number of interdependent modules such as manufacturing, finance, project and distribution to address the business needs of the enterprise.
5. BaanERP tools facilitate creation of customer-specific ERP solution and easy integration of ERP products with third party products.
6. Oracle Applications consists of over forty-five modules for manufacturing, financial, projects, front office, supply chain and human resources. Each of the modules is web-enabled.

7. QAD"s ERP includes the following solution suites: QAD's Financials, QAD customer management, QAD manufacturing, QAD supply chain, QAD services and support, QAD enterprise asset management, QAD analytics and QAD interoperability.
8. SSA offers advanced ERP system software to address the needs of enterprises on a global scale. BPCS Client/Sever products provide reconfigurability option to its customers.
9. Ramco ERP makes use of pure service oriented architecture (SOA).
10. With Ramco's ERP OnDemand small and medium enterprises can get exactly the processes they need at a small price.
11. PeopleSoft Select is a complete ERP package provided by PeopleSoft to address the business needs of medium-sized firms.
12. JD Edward's offers two application suites: OneWorld and WorldSoftware/WorldVision. OneWorld provides support to workflow, web based technology and integration of legacy, best-of-breed and third party products.

SUMMARY

The ERP market has a bright future. The integration of ERP with latest technologies such as web and wireless along with its wider functional coverage has contributed to the high rise in the number of potential ERP customers. The ERP customers are both the large scale organizations as well as the small and medium sized business firms. According to IDC, the Indian ERP market is expected to reach Rs 1550 crore over the next five years.

According to ARC advisory group study, the global ERP market will exceed $21 billion in 2010. There has been a tremendous growth in the ERP market for small and medium-sized enterprises due to the availability of cheap ERP solutions designed to meet the specific business needs of SME's. ERP outsourcing and Open Source ERP has helped in reducing the costs of the ERP system further.

SME's are divided into four tiers on the basis of the amount of resource, finance, IT strategy. Tier 1 SME's view IT as an integral part of corporate strategy. As compared to tier1 SME's, Tier 2 SME's have less finance and resource. With even lesser resources and finance, tier 3 SME's strictly control their IT expenditure. Tier 4 SME's implement IT strategy in order to retain their customers that are almost on the verge of leaving them. IT strategy for Tier 4 SME's is a matter of necessity rather than a matter of choice.

Among the top ERP vendors are SAP, Oracle, Baan and Ramco. SAP R/3 consists of powerful programs for accounting, production and materials management, quality management, sales and distribution, plant maintenance and human resources. BaanERP from Baan consists of a number of interdependent modules such as manufacturing, finance, project and distribution. Baan IV delivers web e-commerce capabilities through web browsers to customers. Oracle Applications consists of over forty-five modules for manufacturing, finance, project, front office, supply chain and human resources.

QAD's MFG/PRO provides solution for manufacturing, distribution, finance, and supply chain and service management. BPCS Client/Server products from SSA Inc, provides reconfigurability option to its customers and is based on Distributed Object Computing architecture. Ramco ERP OnDemand modules include Financials, Supply Chain Management, Manufacturing, Business Analytics, multi-entity management and customer relationship management.

POINTS TO REMEMBER

1. Though ERP originated in the manufacturing sector, today, the ERP systems have a much broader scope.
2. As ERP systems spread to cover all basic functions of the enterprise regardless of its nature of business, the ERP market scenario appears to be very active.
3. According to ARC advisory, the ERP market in India was $83 million in the year 2004 and is forecast to be over $250 million by 2010.
4. The world-wide market for the ERP products continues to grow across a diverse set of industries and continents. It is expected to grow at a compounded annual growth rate (CAGR) of 4.8 percent over the next three years exceeding $21 billion in 2010. This forecast has been done by ARC advisory Group Study.
5. The market prospects for ERP in SME's are high with SME's willing to refine their business operations and go ahead with ERP implementation and ERP vendors all set to provide special ERP business applications, priced lower compared to ERP packages for large firms, to tap this promising market sector.
6. The small and medium enterprises (SME's) are divided into four groups (called tiers) based on their finance and amount of resources as well as their attitude towards IT strategy and implementation of the strategy.
7. The three primary ERP vendors include SAP, Baan and Oracle. Other ERP vendors include CODA, IBM, Ramco, Platinum to name a few.
8. The ERP software packages from SAP come in two versions. One is the mainframe version (SAP R/2) and the other is the client/ server version of the ERP package (SAP R/ 3).
9. The Baan series-based product family consists of the following: BaanERP, BaanFrontOffice, BaanCorporate Office Solutions and BaanSupplyChain Solutions.
10. Oracle Applications consists of over forty-five modules for manufacturing, financial, projects, front office, supply chain and human resources. Each of the modules is web-enabled.
11. QAD"s ERP includes the following solution suites-QAD's Financials, QAD customer management, QAD manufacturing, QAD supply chain, QAD services and support, QAD enterprise asset management, QAD analytics and QAD interoperability.
12. SSA offers advanced ERP system software to address the needs of enterprises on a global scale. BPCS Client/Sever products provide reconfigurability option to its customers.
13. With Ramco's ERP OnDemand small and medium enterprises can get exactly the processes they need at a small price.
14. PeopleSoft Select is a complete ERP package provided by PeopleSoft to address the business needs of medium-sized firms.
15. JD Edward's offers two application suites: OneWorld and WorldSoftware/WorldVision. OneWorld provides support to workflow, web based technology and integration of legacy, best-of-breed and third party products.

REVIEW QUESTIONS

1. Discuss the ERP market in India. What are the reasons for the growth of ERP market in India?
2. Discuss the global ERP market.
3. List down the major ERP players in global as well as in Indian ERP market.
4. Write a short note on QAD ERP system
5. Discuss the ERP products offered by Oracle Corporation
6. Discuss SAP's ERP package.
7. Are ERP products only for large business firms? Discuss.
8. Explain the need of ERP systems for large enterprises.
9. Discuss ERP's intervention in small and medium enterprises.
10. Discuss the problems faced by SME's with regards to ERP systems.
11. Write a short note on open source ERP in small and medium enterprises.
12. Explain the concept of tiers in SME's.
13. Write a short note on Baan ERP.
14. What are the reasons for the tremendous growth of ERP market?

OBJECTIVE QUESTIONS

SECTION A

TICK THE CORRECT ANSWER

1. ERP originated in the ________sector.
   (a) Manufacturing.
   (b) Production.
   (c) Retail.
   (d) None of above.
2. The Indian ERP market is expected to reach __________according to IDC, over the next five years.
   (a) Rs. 1550 crore.
   (b) Rs. 550 crore.
   (c) Rs. 100 crore.
   (d) Rs. 1075 crore.
3. The SME potential in India for enterprise class is projected to be _____ percent of the overall ERP market.
   (a) Forty-seven.
   (b) Sixty-two.
   (c) Thirty-eight.
   (d) Forty.
4. The world-wide market for the ERP products is expected to grow at a compounded annual growth rate (CAGR) of ________percent over the next three years exceeding $21 billion in 2010.

(a) 2.2
(b) 7.5
(c) 22.4
(d) 4.8

5. ___________ offer customers a component based approach in which customers can select parts of the specific enterprise solution and purchase only what they require for the organization.
(a) JD Edwards.
(b) Oracle.
(c) SAP.
(d) All of above.

6. SME's often have to face many problems with regards to ERP. Some of these problems are as follows:
(a) The requirement of the small and medium enterprises is limited while the ERP product exceeds their specifications in all ways (including the costs of the product).
(b) SME's often fail to realize the importance of restructuring and redefining the business processes.
(c) The small and medium enterprises often demand a very low price from the vendor.
(d) As big ERP vendors don't offer source code to SME's, a lot of functional errors may occur thereby jeopardizing the very purpose of ERP.
(e) All of above.

7. Select the most appropriate: SME's often fail to realize:
(a) The importance of restructuring and redefining the business processes.
(b) Importance of implementing ERP.
(c) Organizational politics.
(d) None of above.

8. An open source ERP application refers to:
(a) ERP software programs that can be copied and reproduced without even paying the ERP licence fees or at a reduced cost.
(b) ERP integrated with web.
(c) Traditional ERP.
(d) ERP package.

9. The small and medium enterprises (SME's) are divided into ________ groups (called tiers) based on their finance and amount of resources as well as their attitude towards IT strategy and implementation of the strategy.
(a) Three.
(b) Four.
(c) Five.
(d) Ten.

10. Which is true about Tier 1 SMB's?
(a) Tier 1 SMB's view IT solutions as an integrated part of the company strategy and implement IT solutions to make their company grow faster.
(b) Tier 1 SMB's account for the smallest percentage of the SMB.

(c) Tier 1 SMB's are more likely to purchase ERP packages directly from the packaged software vendor.
(d) All of above.

11. Which is true about Tier 2 SMB's?
(a) Tier 2 SMB's has comparatively less resources and finance than Tier 1 SMB's.
(b) Tier 2 SMB's tend to deal with value added resellers.
(c) The tier 2 market is the largest of all the four tiers in terms of the number of potential users.
(d) All of above.

12. Which is true about Tier 3 SMB's?
(a) Tier 3 SMB's implement IT solutions keeping a sharp eye on the costs and constantly trying to control the unnecessary expenditures.
(b) Tier 3 SMB does prefer to purchase from Internet/ mail order resellers.
(c) Tier 3 SMB does prefer solutions that require smaller budgets.
(d) All of above.

13. Which is true about Tier 4 SMB's?
(a) Tier 4 SMB's are companies on the verge of losing a large number of their potential customers and suppliers.
(b) Tier 4 SMB's are compelled to implement IT solutions in order to sustain their business.
(c) The Tier 4 SMB's prefer regional and national retail chains.
(d) All of above.

14. The _________ SMB's account for the smallest percentage of the SMB universe.
(a) Tier 1.
(b) Tier 2.
(c) Tier 3.
(d) Tier 4.

15. The _____ market is the largest of all the four tiers in terms of the number of potential users.
(a) Tier 1.
(b) Tier 2.
(c) Tier 3.
(d) Tier 4.

16. Tier 3 SMB's are those companies that:
(a) Implement IT solutions keeping a sharp eye on the costs and constantly try to control the unnecessary expenditures.
(b) Tend to deal with value added resellers.
(c) View IT solutions as an integrated part of the company strategy and implement IT solutions to make their company grow faster.
(d) None of above.

17. SAP (Systems, Applications and Products in Data Processing) company was founded in the year:
(a) 1972
(b) 1960
(c) 1980
(d) 2000

18. SAP R/3 system is suitable for companies of:
(a) Small size and simple in nature.
(b) Large size.
(c) Complex nature.
(d) All sizes and nature.

19. Which is true about SAP R/3 package?
(a) Gets installed quickly.
(b) Can run on the hardware platforms of leading ERP vendors.
(c) Both (a) and (b).
(d) None of above.

20. ______________ is a complete toolkit that facilitates easy implementation of R/3.
(a) SAP R/3.
(b) SAP R/2.
(c) SAP's Business Engineer.
(d) Qwizard.

21. Baan Company was founded in the year _________ by Jan and Paul Baan.
(a) 1978
(b) 1988
(c) 2001
(d) 1970

22. Baan Company has dual headquarters in _____________.
(a) Netherlands and United States of America.
(b) Germany and United States of America.
(c) Hong Kong and United States of America.
(d) Australia and Britain.

23. Baan Company provides component based applications for:
(a) Only back office automation.
(b) Only front office.
(c) Both front office and back office automation.
(d) Does not provide component based applications.

24. __________ offers specific vertical industry solutions for automotive companies as well as aerospace and defense companies.
(a) Baan.
(b) Oracle.
(c) SAP.
(d) JD Edwards.

25. The Baan series-based product family consists of the following:
(a) BaanERP.
(b) BaanFrontOffice.
(c) BaanCorporate Office Solutions.
(d) BaanSupplyChain Solutions.
(e) All of above.

26. Which is true about BaanERP?
(a) BaanERP consists of a number of interdependent modules to address the business needs of the enterprise.

(b) BaanERP tools facilitate creation of customer-specific ERP solution and easy integration of ERP products with third party products.
(c) Run-time tools provide independence to Baan ERP applications from computing environment specific issues.
(d) All of above.

27. Which is true about Baan IV?
(a) Baan IV makes use of both Java and Active X.
(b) Baan IV delivers web e-commerce capabilities through popular desktop browsers.
(c) Baan IV suite manages the sales order entry and tracking process via a web browser.
(d) All of above.

28. Oracle Company was founded in the year _______.
(a) 1977
(b) 1982
(c) 1972
(d) 2001

29. Oracle Applications consists of over _______ modules for manufacturing, financial, projects, front office, supply chain and human resources.
(a) Thirty-two.
(b) Forty-five.
(c) Twenty-six.
(d) Seventy.

30. In which year was QAD founded?
(a) 1975
(b) 1979
(c) 1990
(d) 1998

31. QAD's ERP addresses the needs of:
(a) Single-site companies.
(b) Multinational companies.
(c) Both single-site and multinational companies.
(d) Off-shore companies.

32. QAD enterprise applications support:
(a) Multiple currencies.
(b) Allow multiple bank accounts in separate currencies.
(c) Both (a) and (b).
(d) None of above.

33. QAD's MFG/PRO software that provides solution for manufacturing, distribution, financial, supply chain and service management is available in how many languages?
(a) Twenty-six.
(b) Thirty-three.
(c) Twenty-two.
(d) Fifteen.

34. Qwizard is a value added tool for:
(a) MFG/PRO software.

(b) SAP R/3.
(c) Baan IV.
(d) SAP R/2.

35. SSA was founded in _______ and has its headquarters in ________.
(a) 1981, Germany.
(b) 1981, Chicago (USA).
(c) 1979, Chicago (USA).
(d) 1988, Germany.

36. ________ Client/ Sever products provide reconfigurability option to its customers.
(a) BPCS.
(b) SAP R/2.
(c) Both (a) and (b).
(d) None of above.

37. ________ is based on Distributed Object Computing Architecture (DOCA).
(a) SAP R/2.
(b) BPCS Client/ Server.
(c) Qwizard.
(d) Baan IV.

38. Business Process Delivery System (BPDS), the product that provides maximum flexibility to execute a business process strategy is of:
(a) Oracle.
(b) SAP.
(c) Ramco.
(d) QAD.

39. PeopleSoft Inc. offers innovative industry specific ERP solutions to customers. In which year was it established?
(a) 1974
(b) 1979
(c) 1980
(d) 1987

40. _____________ is a complete ERP package provided by PeopleSoft to address the business needs of medium-sized firms.
(a) PeopleSoft Select.
(b) Qwizard.
(c) ERP OnDemand.
(d) BPCS.

41. PeopleSoft Implementation Toolkit helps in the identification of:
(a) Implementation approach that will best suit your ERP project.
(b) Implementation strategy that will best suit your ERP project.
(c) Implementation approach and strategy that will best suit your ERP project.
(d) None of above.

42. _____________has integrated popular OLAP tools such as Cognos PowerPlay and Arbor Essbase with its ERP solutions.
(a) PeopleSoft.

(b) Oracle.
(c) Both (a) and (b).
(d) SAP.

43. JD Edwards was formed in ________ by three founders-Jack Thompsom, Dan Gregory and Ed McVaney. It is headquartered in________.
(a) 1990, Britain.
(b) 1977, Denver.
(c) 1999, India.
(d) 1969, Russia.

44. The ERP solutions by JD Edwards offer the following capabilities:
(a) Multi-currency.
(b) Multi-language.
(c) Multi-location.
(d) All of above.

45. Which is true about JD Edwards OneWorld?
(a) Provides support to workflow, web based technology.
(b) Provides integration of legacy, best-of-breed and third party products.
(c) Has been designed to provide a highly flexible solution to its customers.
(d) All of above.

SECTION B

STATE TRUE OR FALSE

1. The ERP market for large enterprises as well as small and medium enterprises is undoubtedly promising as ERP is the latest high end information technology solution that improves the business processes of the companies to gain competitive advantage.
2. Though ERP originated in the manufacturing sector, today, the ERP systems have a much broader scope.
3. The Indian ERP market is expected to reach Rs. 1550 crore ($341 million) according to IDC, over the next five years.
4. Of this, the SME potential in India for enterprise class is projected to Rs. 728 crore (%160 million)—forty-seven percent of the overall ERP market.
5. SME's are becoming the popular choice of most ERP vendors in India.
6. According to ARC advisory, the ERP market in India was $200million in the year 2004 and is forecast to be over $1000 million by 2009.
7. The world-wide market for the ERP products is expected to grow at a compounded annual growth rate (CA GR) of **4.8** percent over the next three years exceeding $21 billion in 2010.
8. Globally, the mid range and SME markets continue to be a major focus area for ERP vendors.
9. ERP is especially suitable for large enterprises that are capable of spending a large amount of money on their enterprise resource planning efforts.

10. The awareness created by ERP vendors and IT researchers have also contributed a lot in bringing ERP to the large scale enterprises.
11. As the number of large enterprises without ERP became negligible SME's turned to be the greener and fresher pastures for ERP vendors.
12. ERP vendors all set to provide special ERP business applications, priced lower compared to ERP packages for large firms, to tap this promising market sector.
13. JD Edwards offers customers a component based approach in which customers can select parts of the specific enterprise solution and purchase only what they require for their organization.
14. The requirement of the small and medium enterprises is unlimited; this is a challenging task for ERP systems.
15. SME's often fail to realize the importance of restructuring and redefining the business processes.
16. SME's often face the difficulty of selecting the right ERP vendor.
17. Formerly SME's were catered to by smaller vendors only. But now big ERP players have intervened increasing the number of ERP vendors from among the branded players and small vendors.
18. As big ERP vendors don't offer source code to SME's, a lot of functional errors may occur thereby jeopardizing the very purpose of ERP.
19. If the SME's decide to go for big ERP vendor then the requirement for customization will be very less.
20. Customization is a bad experience for both the vendor and the organization.
21. An open source ERP application refers to the ERP software programs that can only be copied and reproduced after paying the ERP license fees.
22. Free licensing has helped the SME's to go ahead with ERP implementation with little investment.
23. As SME's cannot afford to invest a high amount of money, open source ERP has come as a blessing.
24. The small and medium enterprises (SME's) are divided into four tiers based on their finance and amount of resources as well as their attitude towards IT strategy and implementation of the strategy.
25. Tier 1 SMB's are SMB's that view IT solutions as an integrated part of the company strategy and implement IT solutions to make their company grow faster.
26. The Tier 2 SMB's account for the smallest percentage of the SMB universe.
27. Tier 1 SMB's are more likely to purchase ERP packages directly from the packaged software vendor.
28. Tier 2 SMB's has comparatively more resources and finance than Tier 1 SMB's.
29. The tier 2 market is the largest of all the four tiers in terms of the number of potential users.
30. The Tier 3 SMB's include those companies that implement IT solutions keeping a sharp eye on the costs and constantly try to control the unnecessary expenditures.
31. The Tier 3 SMB's prefer to purchase from Internet/ mail order resellers. They prefer solutions that require smaller budgets.
32. Tier 4 SMB's include the companies that are on the verge of losing a large number of their potential customers and suppliers and are therefore compelled to implement IT solutions in order to sustain their business.

33. The Tier 4 SMB's do not prefer regional and national retail chains.
34. The three primary ERP vendors include SAP, Baan and Oracle.
35. SAP (Systems, Applications and Products in Data Processing) company was founded in the year 1989 and is based in Australia.
36. The ERP software packages from SAP come in two versions. One is the mainframe version (SAP R/2) and the other is the client/ server version of the ERP package (SAP R/3).
37. R/3 system is suitable for companies of all sizes and nature.
38. A severe limitation of SAP R/3 ERP package is that it gets installed slowly and cannot run on the hardware platforms of leading ERP vendors.
39. SAP R/3 ERP package is directly linked to the Internet.
40. SAP's Business Engineer is a complete toolkit that facilitates easy implementation of R/3.
41. Baan Company was founded in the year 1978 by Jan and Paul Baan.
42. Baan offers specific vertical industry solutions for automotive companies as well as aerospace and defense companies.
43. The Baan series-based product family consists of the following-BaanERP, BaanFrontOffice, BaanCorporate Office Solutions and BaanSupplyChain Solutions.
44. BaanERP consists of a number of modules such as manufacturing, finance, project and distribution that are not dependent on each other.
45. The limitation of BaanERP tools is: BaanERP tools do not facilitate creation of customer-specific ERP solution and do not provide easy integration of ERP products with third party products.
46. Baan IV makes use of both Java and Active X.
47. Baan IV delivers web e-commerce capabilities through popular desktop browsers.
48. Oracle Corporation's was founded in 1960 and has its headquarters in Redwood Shores, California.
49. Oracle Applications consists of over forty five modules for manufacturing, financial, projects, front office, supply chain and human resources.
50. Oracle Applications do not support multiple currencies.
51. QAD was founded in the year 1979 and is now a leading provider of ERP applications to manufacturing industries.
52. QAD's ERP addresses the needs of single-site and multinational companies.
53. QAD"s ERP includes the following solution suites: QAD's Financials, QAD customer management, QAD manufacturing, QAD supply chain, QAD services and support, QAD enterprise asset management, QAD analytics and QAD interoperability.
54. QAD's MFG/PRO software provides solution for manufacturing, distribution, financial, supply chain and service management.
55. MFG/PRO is available in only English language.
56. MFG/PRO fails to synchronize distributed operations within the enterprise and cannot be scaled to meet the growing needs of business.
57. Qwizard is a value added tool for Baan IVsoftware that provides easy to use business modeling and learning tools.
58. System Software Associates, Inc. (SSA) was founded in 1981 and has its headquarters in Chicago, USA.

59. SSA offers advanced ERP system software to address the needs of enterprises on a global scale.
60. BPCS Client/ Sever products provide reconfigurability option to its customers.
61. BPCS Client/ Server is based on Distributed Object Computing Architecture (DOCA).
62. Ramco is a global ERP software provider with customers in thirty-five countries.
63. Ramco Business Process Delivery System (BPDS) provides maximum flexibility to execute a business process strategy.
64. Ramco ERP makes no use of pure service oriented architecture (SOA).
65. With Ramco's ERP OnDemand small and medium enterprises can get exactly the processes they need at a small price.
66. PeopleSoft Inc. established in 1987 offers innovative industry specific ERP solutions to customers.
67. People Soft ERP solutions cannot run on a variety of hardware and database platforms.
68. PeopleSoft Select is a complete ERP package provided by PeopleSoft to address the business needs of medium-sized firms.
69. PeopleSoft also offers self-service applications enabling customers to perform some administrative tasks with the help of a Work list and Query interface on PeopleSoft Web Client.
70. PeopleSoft Implementation Toolkit helps in the identification of the implementation approach and strategy that will best suit your ERP project.
71. PeopleSoft has also integrated popular OLAP tools such as Cognos PowerPlay and Arbor Essbase with its ERP solutions.
72. JD Edwards was formed in 1977 by three founders: Jack Thompsom, Dan Gregory and Ed McVaney.
73. JD Edwards offers two application suites: OneWorld and WorldSoftware/WorldVision.
74. OneWorld provides support to workflow, web based technology and integration of legacy, best-of-breed and third party products.
75. JDEdwards WorldSoftware allows customers to selectively integrate ERP software applications from among its diverse ERP product suites available for various industries.
76. JD EdwardsWorldVision does not provide the customers with a graphical user interface.

SECTION C

FILL IN THE BLANKS

1. The ________ for large enterprises as well as small and medium enterprises is undoubtedly promising as ERP is the latest high-end information technology solution that improves the business processes of the companies to gain competitive advantage.
2. Though ERP originated in the ________ sector, today, the ERP systems have a much broader scope.
3. The Indian ERP market is expected to reach Rs. ________ crore, according to IDC, over the next five years.
4. Of this, the SME potential in India for enterprise class is projected to _______ percent of the overall ERP market.

5. _______ are becoming the popular choice of most ERP vendors in India.
6. The world-wide market for the ERP products is expected to grow at a compounded annual growth rate (CAGR) of ______ percent over the next three years exceeding $21 billion in 2010.
7. Globally, the mid range and SME markets continue to be a major focus area for_______.
8. ERP is especially suitable for _______ enterprises that are capable of spending a large amount of money on their enterprise resource planning efforts.
9. The awareness created by ERP vendors and IT researches have also contributed a lot in bringing ________ to the large scale enterprises.
10. As the number of large enterprises without ERP became __________, SME's turned to be the greener and fresher pastures for ERP vendors.
11. ERP vendors all set to provide special ERP business applications, priced _________ compared to ERP packages for large firms, to tap SME market sector.
12. JD Edwards offer customers a _________ approach in which customers can select parts of the specific enterprise solution and purchase only what they require for the organization.
13. The requirement of the small and medium enterprises is _______.
14. SME's often fail to realize the importance of restructuring and redefining the__________.
15. The market prospects for ERP in SME's are _________.
16. SME's often face the difficulty of selecting the ________ vendor.
17. Formerly SME's were catered to by ________vendors only. But now _____ ERP players have intervened increasing the number of ERP vendors from among the branded players and small vendors.
18. As big ERP vendors don't offer _________ to SME's, a lot of __________ may occur thereby jeopardizing the very purpose of ERP.
19. If the SME's decide to go for big ERP vendor then the requirement for ___________ will be very high.
20. Customization is a bad experience for both the____________ and the_________.
21. An ____________ refers to the ERP software programs that can be copied and reproduced without even paying the ERP licence fees or at a reduced cost.
22. Free licensing has helped the ________ to go ahead with ERP implementation with little investment.
23. As SME's cannot afford to invest a high amount of money, _______ has come as a blessing.
24. The small and medium enterprises (SME's) are divided into ____ tiers based on their finance and amount of resources as well as their attitude towards IT strategy and implementation of the strategy.
25. _______ SMB's are SMB's that view IT solutions as an integrated part of the company strategy and implement IT solutions to make their company grow faster.
26. The Tier 1 SMB's, account for the __________ percentage of the SMB universe.
27. Tier 1 SMB's are more likely to purchase ERP packages directly from the________.
28. Tier 2 SMB's has comparatively ________ resources and finance than _________ SMB's and tend to deal with value added resellers.
29. The tier 2 market is the ______ of all the four tiers in terms of the number of potential users.
30. The _________ SMB's include those companies that implement IT solutions keeping a sharp eye on the costs and constantly try to control the unnecessary expenditures.

31. The Tier 3 SMB's prefer to purchase from __________ order resellers. They prefer solutions that require ________ budgets.

32. __________ SMB's include the companies that are on the verge of losing a large number of their potential customers and suppliers and are therefore compelled to implement IT solutions in order to sustain their business.

33. The Tier 4 SMB's prefer regional and national __________.

34. The three primary ERP vendors include ________, Baan and Oracle.

35. SAP (Systems, Applications and Products in Data Processing) company was founded in the year _______ and is based in __________.

36. The ERP software packages from SAP come in two versions. One is the ____________ and the other is the ________________.

37. SAP R/3 system is suitable for companies of all _______ and nature.

38. SAP R/3 ERP package gets installed __________ and can run on the _________ of leading ERP vendors.

39. SAP R/3 ERP package is directly linked to the __________.

40. SAP's ____________ is a complete toolkit that facilitates easy implementation of R/3.

41. Baan Company was founded in the year ________ by Jan and Paul Baan.

42. Baan offers specific vertical industry solutions for automotive companies as well as ___________ companies.

43. The _________ family consists of the following-BaanERP, BaanFrontOffice, BaanCorporate Office Solutions and BaanSupplyChain Solutions.

44. BaanERP consists of a number of ____________ modules such as manufacturing, finance, project and distribution to address the business needs of the enterprise.

45. BaanERP tools facilitate creation of customer-specific ERP solution and easy integration of ERP products with ________ products.

46. ________ makes use of both Java and Active X.

47. Baan IV delivers web and e-commerce capabilities through popular desktop ___________.

48. Oracle Corporation's was founded in _______ and has its headquarters in Redwood Shores, California.

49. Oracle Applications consists of over _______ modules for manufacturing, financial, projects, front office, supply chain and human resources.

50. Oracle Applications support _______ currencies.

51. QAD was founded in the year ______ and is now a leading provider of ___________ applications to manufacturing industries.

52. QAD's ERP addresses the needs of ________ and multinational companies.

53. QAD's ERP includes the following solution suites:_________, QAD customer management, ______________, QAD supply chain, QAD services and support, QAD enterprise asset management, QAD analytics and QAD interoperability.

54. QAD's _________ software provides solution for manufacturing, distribution, financial, supply chain and service management.

55. MFG/PRO is available in __________ languages.

56. MFG/PRO synchronizes __________ within the enterprise and can be scaled to meet the growing needs of business.

57. __________ is a value added tool for MFG/PRO software. It provides easy to use __________ and learning tools.
58. System Software Associates, Inc. (SSA) was founded in 1981 and has its headquarters in__________.
59. SSA offers advanced ERP system software to address the needs of enterprises on a __________scale.
60. BPCS Client/ Sever products provide _________ option to its customers.
61. BPCS Client/ Server, is based on_________________.
62. Ramco is a global ERP software provider with customers in ____________ countries.
63. Ramco Business Process Delivery System (BPDS) provides ___________ flexibility to execute a business process strategy.
64. Ramco ERP makes use of pure__________.
65. With Ramco's __________, small and medium enterprises can get exactly the processes they need at a small price.
66. ________ established in 1987 offers innovative industry specific ERP solutions to customers.
67. People Soft ERP solutions run on a variety of hardware and ____________ platforms.
68. ____________ is a complete ERP package provided by PeopleSoft to address the business needs of medium-sized firms.
69. PeopleSoft also offers ____________ enabling customers to perform some administrative tasks with the help of a Work list and ______ on PeopleSoft Web Client.
70. PeopleSoft ____________ helps in the identification of the implementation approach and strategy that will best suit your ERP project.
71. PeopleSoft has also integrated popular _________ such as Cognos PowerPlay and Arbor Essbase with its ERP solutions.
72. JD Edwards was formed in 1977 by three founders:__________, Dan Gregory and Ed McVaney.
73. JD Edward's offers two application suites: ________ and WorldSoftware/WorldVision.
74. OneWorld provides support to____________, web based technology and integration of legacy, best-of-breed and third party products.
75. JDEdwards ____________ allows customers to selectively integrate ERP software applications from among its diverse ERP product suites available for various industries.
76. JD Edwards WorldVision provides the customers with a ___________ interface.

ANSWERS

SECTION A

(1) a	**(2)** a	**(3)** a	**(4)** d	**(5)** a	**(6)** e	**(7)** a	**(8)** a	**(9)** b	**(10)** d
(11) d	**(12)** d	**(13)** d	**(14)** a	**(15)** b	**(16)** a	**(17)** a	**(18)** d	**(19)** c	**(20)** c
(21) a	**(22)** a	**(23)** c	**(24)** a	**(25)** e	**(26)** d	**(27)** d	**(28)** a	**(29)** b	**(30)** b
(31) c	**(32)** c	**(33)** a	**(34)** a	**(35)** b	**(36)** a	**(37)** b	**(38)** c	**(39)** d	**(40)** a
(41) c	**(42)** a	**(43)** b	**(44)** d	**(45)** d.					

SECTION B

(1) True **(2)** True **(3)** True **(4)** True **(5)** True **(6)** False **(7)** True **(8)** True **(9)** True **(10)** True **(11)** True **(12)** True **(13)** True **(14)** False **(15)** True **(16)** True **(17)** True **(18)** True **(19)** False **(20)** True **(21)** False **(22)** True **(23)** True **(24)** True **(25)** True **(26)** False **(27)** True **(28)** False **(29)** True **(30)** True **(31)** True **(32)** True **(33)** False **(34)** True **(35)** False **(36)** True **(37)** True **(38)** False **(39)** True **(40)** True **(41)** True **(42)** True **(43)** True **(44)** False **(45)** False **(46)** True **(47)** True **(48)** False **(49)** True **(50)** False **(51)** True **(52)** True **(53)** True **(54)** True **(55)** False **(56)** False **(57)** False **(58)** True **(59)** True **(60)** True **(61)** True **(62)** True **(63)** True **(64)** False **(65)** True **(66)** True **(67)** False **(68)** True **(69)** True **(70)** True **(71)** True **(72)** True **(73)** True **(74)** True **(75)** True **(76)** False.

SECTION C

(1) ERP market **(2)** manufacturing **(3)** 1550 **(4)** forty-seven **(5)** SME's **(6)** 4.8 **(7)** ERP vendors **(8)** large **(9)** ERP **(10)** negligible **(11)** lower **(12)** component based **(13)** limited **(14)** business processes **(15)** high **(16)** right ERP **(17)** smaller, big **(18)** source code, functional errors **(19)** customization **(20)** vendor, organization **(21)** open source ERP application **(22)** SME's **(23)** open source ERP **(24)** four **(25)** Tier 1 **(26)** Smallest **(27)** packaged software vendor **(28)** less, Tier 1 **(29)** largest **(30)** Tier 3 **(31)** Internet/ mail, smaller **(32)** Tier 4 **(33)** retail chains **(34)** SAP **(35)** 1972, Germany **(36)** mainframe version (SAP R/2), client/ server version of the ERP package (SAP R/3) **(37)** sizes **(38)** quickly, hardware platforms **(39)** Internet **(40)** Business Engineer **(41)** 1978 **(42)** aerospace and defense **(43)** Baan series-based product **(44)** Interdependent **(45)** third party **(46)** Baan IV **(47)** browsers **(48)** 1977 **(49)** forty-five **(50)** multiple **(51)** 1979, ERP **(52)** single-site **(53)** QAD's Financials, QAD manufacturing **(54)** MFG/PRO **(55)** twenty six **(56)** distributed operations **(57)** Qwizard, business modeling **(58)** Chicago, USA **(59)** global **(60)** reconfigurability **(61)** Distributed Object Computing Architecture (DOCA) **(62)** thirty five **(63)** maximum **(64)** service oriented architecture (SOA) **(65)** ERP OnDemand **(66)** PeopleSoft Inc **(67)** database **(68)** PeopleSoft Select **(69)** self-service applications, Query interface **(70)** Implementation Toolkit **(71)** OLAP tools **(72)** Jack Thompsom **(73)** OneWorld **(74)** Workflow **(75)** WorldSoftware **(76)** graphical user.

4

Chapter

ERP Modules

HIGHLIGHTS

- **ERP Modules**
  - Manufacturing
  - Finance
  - Sales and Distribution
  - Plant Maintenance
  - Materials Management
  - Human Resource
  - Quality Management

The purpose of ERP technology is to support all business processes of an organization, in order to support the company's strategic opportunities. A standard ERP package would deliver the company the benefits of "best practices" in the industry, eliminate maintenance costs (which were huge in the case of legacy systems) and provide better support and service.

The ERP software can either be custom-built software (developed in-house or by an external ERP solution provider) or package software. ERP packages are generalized off-the-shelf application software packages available with ERP vendor. Examples include SAP R/3 from SAP and Baan ERP from Baan Company. ERP packages are also referred to as tailor made ERP solutions.

All ERP packages contain many modules. The number and features of ERP modules may vary with ERP package. ERP modules can interface with an organization's own software with varying degrees of efforts. It is also possible to alter the ERP modules via the vendor's proprietary tools and proprietary or standard programming languages.

Some of the common ERP modules that are generally found in most of the ERP packages are finance, manufacturing, production planning, human resources, sales and distribution, quality management, plant maintenance and materials management.

4.1 MANUFACTURING

The manufacturing unit of the industry must respond to the demands of the customers quickly and effectively. The manufacturing planning and control is broadly categorized as either make-to-order manufacturing or make-to-stock. In make-to-stock production method, the manufacturer produces the end-item and places it in the inventory before he receives an order from a customer. Demand forecasting and market analysis are used in make-to-stock production method. In make-to-order production method, the manufacturer begins the production of the item only after he has received an order from the customer.

A robust ERP module for manufacturing must support a variety of business practices and production methods. It must also provide the flexibility for selecting either a combination of production methods or the best production method for each product at every stage of its manufacturing process. The manufacturing module may extend support to supply chain process.

Some of the major subsystems of the manufacturing module are as follows (shown in Figure 4.1):

1. **Materials and Capacity Planning**
   The subsystem helps in developing material plans from a variety of sources such as the master schedule, sales forecast and dependent and independent demand. Alternative plans can be simulated to decide which parts and assemblies to manufacture and which to purchase. A graphical production management tool helps in easy identification of changes in capacity utilization.
2. **Shop Floor Control**
   The shop floor control system provides flexible shop floor planning and control activities. The users are allowed to evaluate and adjust operation steps and components. The orders can be either rescheduled forward or rescheduled backward.
3. **Just-In-Time Manufacturing(JIT)**
   The just-in-time manufacturing seeks to reduce inventory levels of raw material, work-in-process and finished products. Based on actual performance the JIT subsystem tries to identify discrepancies. It monitors the production rates and daily output goals on a timely basis and adjusts them proactively.
4. **Quality Management**
   The quality management subsystem focuses on continuous improvement of manufacturing methods. The subsystem identifies and corrects the defects in product designs and production methods. An extensive history is maintained to improve the quality of product and find out the recurring problem.
5. **Cost Management**
   Detailed cost information is provided by the subsystem at various levels. It facilitates the manager to identify the cost drivers and reduce the product costs. The subsystem may have the feature to compare the estimates and production costs for different work centres, employees and machines.
6. **Engineering Data Management**
   The subsystem provides an automated link between engineering and production information. This facilitates reduction in data transfer time and increases design productivity.

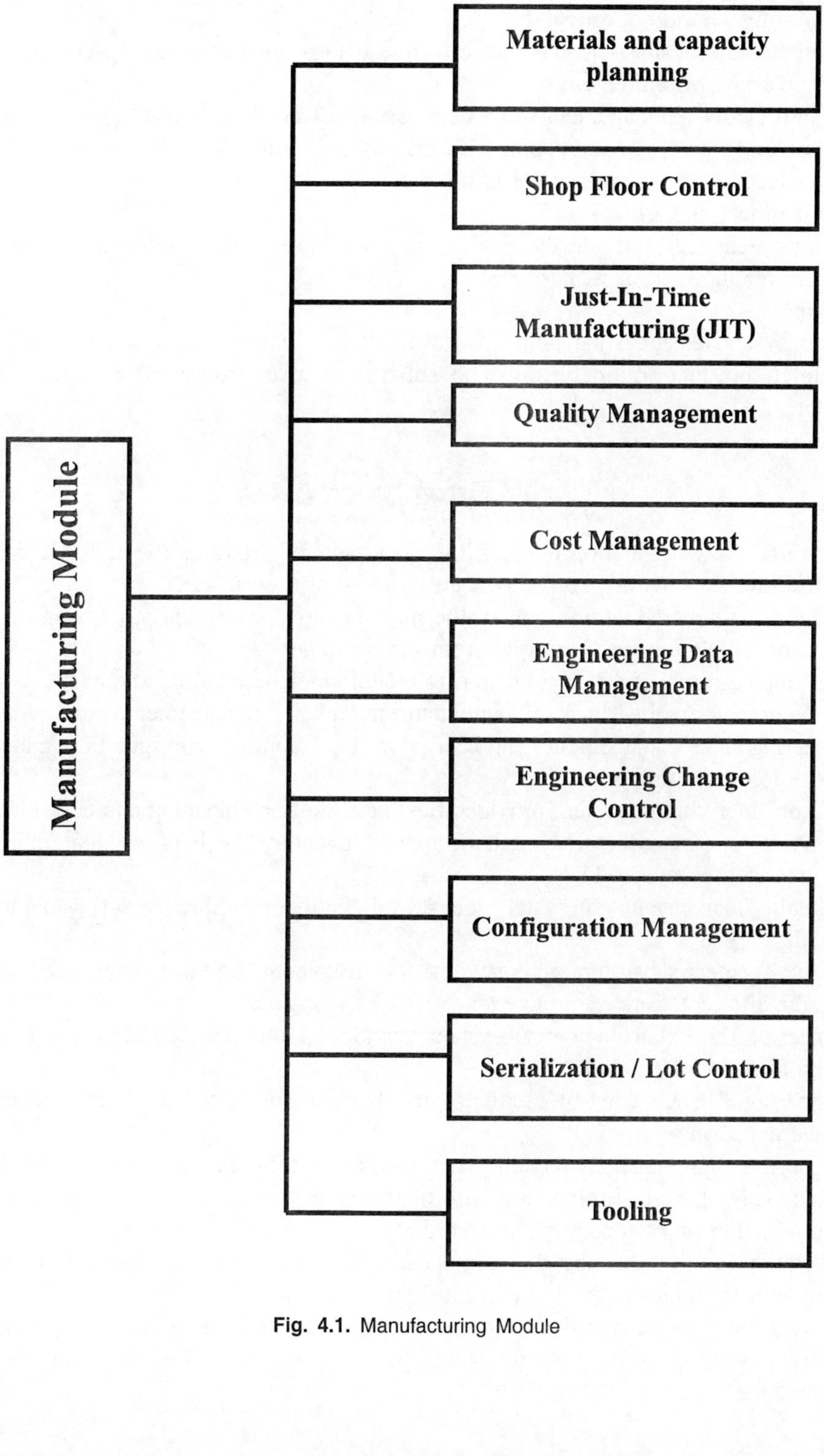

Fig. 4.1. Manufacturing Module

7. **Engineering Change Control**
   It facilitates the business to have an effective control over engineering change orders.
8. **Configuration Management**
   The configuration management subsystem uses a powerful analytical engine that interprets the knowledge base in conjunction with the customer selection. This results in the design and production of customer specific product.
9. **Serialization/Lot Control**
   The subsystem may provide the facility for pre-assigning the production orders with lot numbers for the present item.
10. **Tooling**
    The subsystem ensures that both the raw materials and the tools arrive together at the scheduled production operation. The subsystem also provides for tools repair and maintenance.

LEARNING POINTS

1. In make-to-stock production method, the manufacturer produces the end-item and places it in the inventory before he receives an order from a customer.
2. In make-to-order production method, the manufacturer begins the production of the item only after he has received an order from the customer.
3. Some major subsystems of manufacturing module include material and capacity planning, shop floor control, just-in-time manufacturing, quality management, cost management, engineering data management, engineering change control, configuration management, serialization and tooling.
4. The shop floor control system provides flexible shop floor planning and control activities.
5. The just-in-time manufacturing seeks to reduce inventory levels of raw material, work-in-process and finished products.
6. The quality management subsystem focuses on continuous improvement of manufacturing methods.
7. Cost management subsystem may have the feature to compare the estimates and production costs for different work centres, employees and machines.
8. Engineering Data Management subsystem provides an automated link between engineering and production information.
9. Engineering Change Control facilitates the business to have an effective control over engineering change orders.
10. The configuration management subsystem uses a powerful analytical engine that interprets the knowledge base in conjunction with the customer selection. This results in the design and production of customer specific product.
11. Serialization/Lot Control subsystem may provide the facility for pre-assigning the production orders with lot numbers for the present item.
12. Tooling subsystem ensures that both the raw materials and the tools arrive together at the scheduled production operation. The subsystem also provides for tools repair and maintenance.

4.2 FINANCE

ERP packages must meet the financial goals of your organization. Up-to-the minute financial information helps in making strategic decisions. Finance module integrates financial functionality across all business and geographical areas.

A Finance module generally has the following subsystems (shown in Figure 4.2):

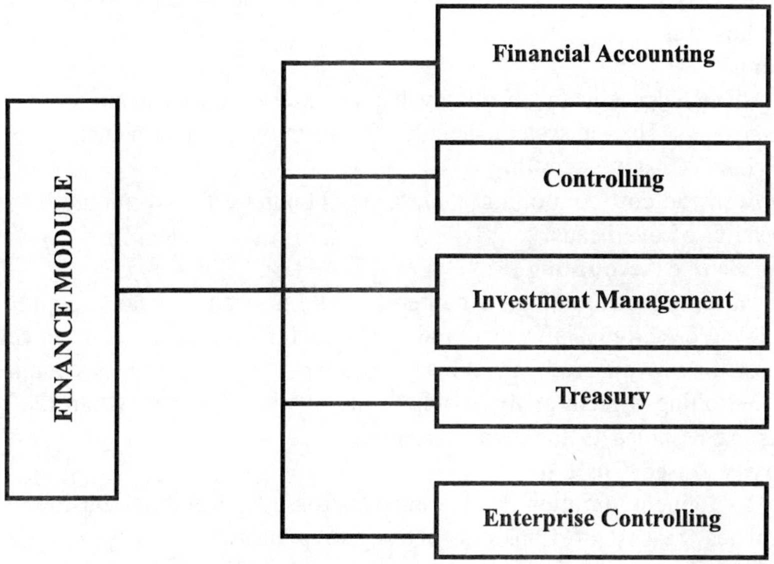

Fig. 4.2. Finance module

1. **Financial Accounting**

   The financial accounting system helps to keep track of financial data within an international framework of multiple languages, currencies and companies. Compliance with international accounting standards such as GAAP and IAS as well as local legal requirements are generally provided by the subsystem.

   The Financial accounting subsystem includes the following components:

   i. **General Ledger**

   General ledger provides support to all functions required in a financial accounting system such as real time simultaneous update of general ledger and sub-ledgers. It also facilitates parallel views of data in the general ledger and managerial accounting applications.

   ii. **Accounts Receivable and Payable**

   It facilitates payment automation with EFT (electronic funds transfer), document management, flexible reporting and an enterprise-wide credit management with workflow integration.

   iii. **Asset Accounting**

   The asset accounting component supports the management of machinery and equipment, leased assets, assets under construction and mass processing with work flow integration. It also provides detailed information on asset-related transactions to the general ledger. The asset accounting is integrated with plant maintenance module for better management of the company's asset.

iv. **Legal Consolidation**

Legal consolidation facilitates transfer of data from individual statements into consolidated report. Multiple views of the consolidated reports can be created. This enables easy and quick generation of reports about the legal entities or segments of your business.

2. **Controlling**

The subsystem helps you to effectively handle internal cost accounting. Custom reports can be generated. The subsystem includes the following components:

i. **Overhead Cost Controlling**

The overhead cost controlling component supports effective monitoring and efficient allocation of overheads.

ii. **Cost Centre Accounting**

In cost centre accounting, a center (area) for each logical grouping of product, employee or activity is formed and the costs for each such centre is calculated such as cost for raw materials, machinery or labor. The cost centre accounting subsystem of Controlling System analyzes where the overheads occur within the company and costs are assigned to the area of origin.

iii. **Activity Based Costing**

The component monitors and controls cross departmental business process and calculates the cost of a business activity or process.

iv. **Product Cost Controlling**

This subsystem is used to determine the costs of manufacturing a product or providing a service. It also enables us to find out the lowest price for which a product or service is profitable.

v. **Profitability Analysis**

Profitability analysis component of Finance module helps in examining the sources of returns, assigning revenues to costs according to market segment, making decisions regarding price determination, selection of customers and selection of distribution channels.

3. **Investment Management**

An investment programme hierarchy can be defined through the investment management component using any criteria, for e.g., product-wise. This enables efficient monitoring and distribution of budgets in order to avoid budget overrun.

4. **Treasury**

The component supports effective liquidity, portfolio and risk management. The treasury module includes the following components:

i. **Cash Management**

Cash management component provides information on sources and uses of funds to secure liquidity, so that, payment obligations are met when they become due. Incoming and outgoing payment flows are monitored and controlled. Analysis of financial transactions is also supported.

ii. **Treasury Management**
It is used to manage, analyze and support reporting for financial deals, positions and portfolios. Treasury is often fully integrated with all other modules of ERP.

iii. **Market Risk Management**
Market risk management provides various measures to analyze the risks involved. Risk measurement and control is an important function of this subsystem. All the current and the future cash flows as well as the financial deals that have been processed can be accessed by the component. By using simulation techniques upon the market data; the risk structure of "what-if' analysis is determined.

iv. **Funds Management**
This subsystem enables the company to manage its funds. It also determines how much of the budget has been utilized and monitors various expenditures of the company.

5. **Enterprise Controlling**
The module offers to optimize share holder value and meet the internal objectives for growth and investment.
The enterprise controlling subsystem includes the following:

i. **Executive Information System**
EIS provides information required to manage the organization. A drill down reporting facility is also provided to analyze the data interactively.

ii. **Profit Centre Accounting**
It is used to analyze the profitability of the internal responsibility centres of the organization. The profitability information is made available to the appropriate management and controlling departments.

iii. **Business Planning and Budgeting**
The component supports investment planning, budget release and tracking.

LEARNING POINTS

1. Finance module integrates financial functionality across all business and geographical areas.
2. A finance module generally includes the following subsystems-financial accounting, controlling, investment management, treasury and enterprise controlling.
3. The financial accounting system helps to keep track of financial data within an international framework of multiple languages, currencies and companies.
4. Activity Based costing component monitors and controls cross departmental business processes and calculates the cost of a business activity or process.
5. Profitability analysis helps in examining the sources of returns, assigning revenues to costs according to market segment, making decisions regarding price determination, selection of customers and selection of distribution channels.
6. Treasury component supports effective liquidity, portfolio and risk management.
7. Executive Information System (EIS) provides information required to manage the organization. A drill down reporting facility is also provided to analyze the data interactively.

4.3 SALES AND DISTRIBUTION

An efficient sales and distribution module helps the companies to improve sales as well as profit margins and customer satisfaction. The module must be integrated with the materials management and financial accounting module in order to achieve fast delivery and accurate billing support.

The module has the following subsystems (as shown in Figure 4.3)

1. **Master Data management**
   The master data management module keeps information about products, customers and suppliers. This information is used in decision making and automatic generation of various useful reports.

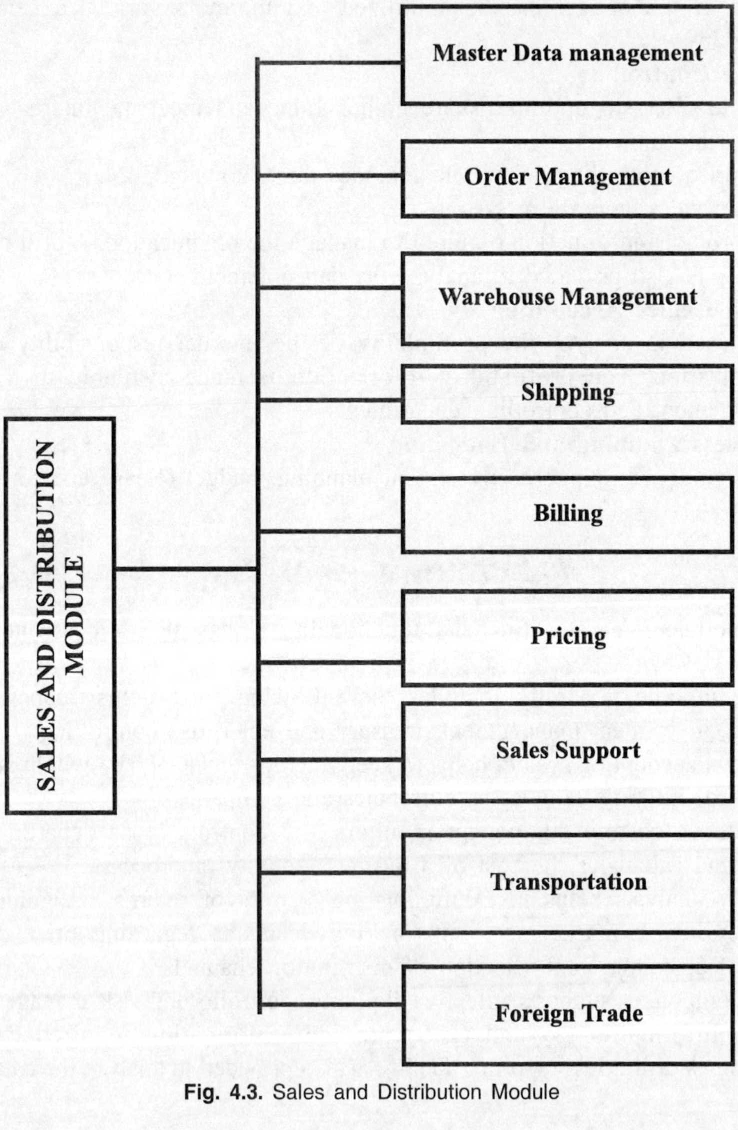

Fig. 4.3. Sales and Distribution Module

2. Order Management

The order data management module includes sales order management and purchase order management. The sales order management supports the sales operations of the company. The evaluation of sales performance can be done through the extensive report capabilities of the sales order management component. It also manages quotas, orders, customer discount and contract process. Tracking and tracing of schedules and follow-ups, multi-level customer credit reviews and blocking of orders are some other functionalities that are provided.

Purchase order management supports purchase decisions regarding price and quality of products. A purchase quotation can be sent to multiple suppliers through the system. Contract management, just-in-time schedules and vendor management are also provided. The vendor management tools help in checking the reliability of vendors.

3. Warehouse Management

It provides real-time information about the inventory levels and monitors all the inventory transactions. It includes the following components:

i. Inventory Planning

Inventory planning ensures that the customer receives the right order with respect to time, quantity and quality.

ii. Inventory handling

It monitors the warehouse inventory transaction that includes the receipt, issue and transfer of inventory.

iii. Inventory Location Assignment

It is used to detect the location of stored goods by criteria such as item, size, location availability etc.

iv. Inventory Reporting

It enables the company to offer customers' accurate delivery dates by knowing about its inventory status at single as well as multiple sites.

v. Inventory Analysis

It supports inventory forecasting and activity-based costing analysis to support warehousing activities.

vi. Lot Control

It provides lot tracking and tracing to trace the raw materials that the products require.

vii. Distribution Data Collection

It provides the communication link between inventory warehouse and the shipping system.

4. Shipping

The shipping module supports activities such as picking, packing, deliveries, printing and sending shipping output.

5. Billing

It supports various billing functions. Some of the billing functions include issue of invoices based on goods and services, canceling billing transactions and giving rebates.

6. Pricing

It keeps the information about prices and discounts of various items and provides this information to sales people.

7. **Sales Support**
   This subsystem helps the company to support its existing customers and add new customers to its existing customer base by providing up-to-date and useful information about inventory, sales and market trends to the sales people.
8. **Transportation**
   The transportation module provides effective transportation planning. This ensures that the shipment is dispatched without delay and it arrives on schedule. The module also performs functions such as freight calculation and settlement.
9. **Foreign Trade**
   The subsystem provides support to foreign trade processing activities.

LEARNING POINTS

1. An efficient sales and distribution module helps the companies to improve sales as well as profit margins and customer satisfaction.
2. The module must be integrated with the materials management and financial accounting module for fast delivery and accurate billing support.
3. The module has the following subsystems: Master Data management, Order Management, Warehouse Management, Inventory management, Shipping, Billing, Pricing, Sales Support, Transportation, and Foreign Trade.
4. The master data management module keeps information about products, customers and suppliers.
5. Order data management module includes sales order management and purchase order management.
6. Inventory management provides real-time information about inventory levels and monitors all the inventory transactions.

4.4 PLANT MAINTENANCE

The plant maintenance module handles the maintenance tasks for efficient working of equipment. It determines whether a repair or replacement of the machinery is needed. The module, thus, enables the company to achieve higher machine utilization.

It has the following components (as shown in Figure 4.4).

1. **Preventive maintenance Control**
   The subsystem is used to plan and control the machinery and equipment. Maintenance activities such as equipment lubrication, replacement of component and safety inspection of the equipment are closely monitored.
2. **Equipment Tracking**
   The subsystem provides equipment history to facilitate tracking of equipment. The information about acquisition, disposition and associations between different pieces of the equipment is included in the equipment history. A model and serial number is used to identify each piece of equipment.

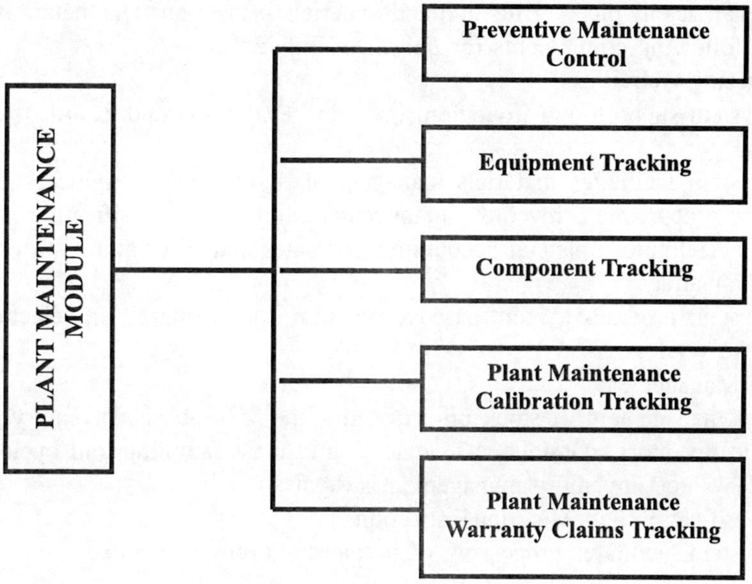

Fig. 4.4. Plant Maintenance

3. **Component Tracking**
   The subsystem is used to identify those components which have chronic repair problems.
4. **Plant Maintenance Calibration Tracking**
   It is used to track the calibration of the equipment in support of ISO9000 requirements.
5. **Plant Maintenance Warranty Claims Tracking**

The subsystem provides warranty related information for each item. This enables the company to recover the warranty.

LEARNING POINTS

1. Plant maintenance module handles the maintenance tasks for efficient working of equipments.
2. Preventive maintenance Control subsystem is used to plan and control the machinery and equipment.
3. Equipment tracking subsystem provides equipment history to facilitate tracking of equipment.
4. Plant Maintenance Calibration Tracking is used to track the calibration of the equipment in support of ISO9000 requirements.

4.5 MATERIALS MANAGEMENT

The module provides vendor evaluation, improves the procurement process by controlling the items costs and handles invoice verification and materials inspection. The materials management module has the following components (as shown in Figure 4.5)

1. Pre-Purchasing Activities
   The subsystem supports bid invitation, quotation evaluation and award of contract.
2. Purchasing
   The subsystem facilitates materials management. It performs activities such as material and service procurement, inventory management and invoice verification. It is integrated with cost accounting, financial accounting and sales and distribution system.
3. Vendor Evaluation
   The subsystem provides a point-based evaluation system, based on selection criteria, to evaluate the vendors.
4. Inventory Management
   It provides management of stock on a quantity and value basis. Inventory methods such as periodic inventory, continuous inventory, inventory sampling and cycle counting are supported by most inventory management systems.
5. Invoice Verification and Material Inspection
   The subsystem facilitates processing of invoices and credit memos.

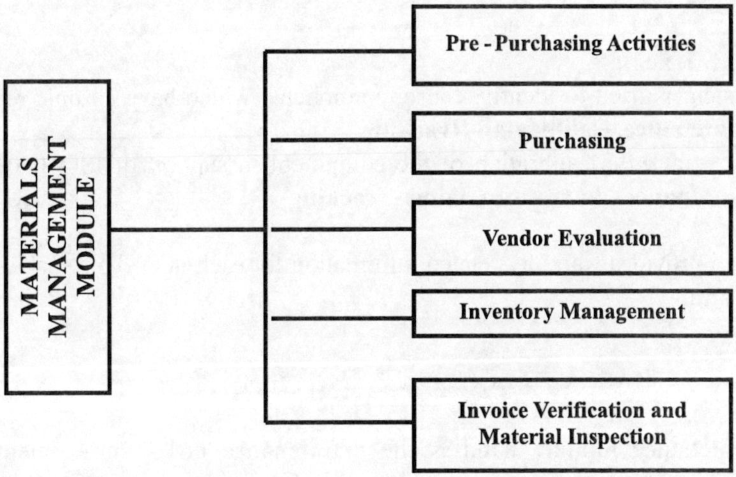

Fig. 4.5. Materials Management Module

LEARNING POINTS

1. Materials management module provides vendor evaluation, improves the procurement process by controlling the items costs and handles invoice verification and materials inspection.
2. Inventory Management provides management of stock on a quantity and value basis.

4.6 HUMAN RESOURCE

The human resource module offers easy access to employee data for personnel administration. The module also supports recruitment, travel management, payroll processing and personnel development.

Human resource module has the following components (as shown in the Figure 4.6):

1. **Payroll accounting**
   The component provides payroll functions. Payroll processing can be centralized or decentralized based on country or legal entities. The subsystem adapts itself to the policy changes, if any.
2. **Time Management**
   The subsystem facilitates daily processing of employee time data to determine the working hours of the employee. It also supports calculation of wages and incentives based on the employee time data. The shift planning component within time management assists in planning workforce requirements quickly. Employees can be assigned to the work area where they are required.
3. **Personnel Development**
   The component automates the process of matching the qualification of employees and external candidates with the job requirements. It also facilitates planning and management of training.
4. **Organizational Management**
   The module's graphical organizational charts enable the company to review its organizational structure easily.
5. **Personnel Management**
   The module provides a centralized employee database that facilitates personnel administration and recruitment processes to be carried out more efficiently.

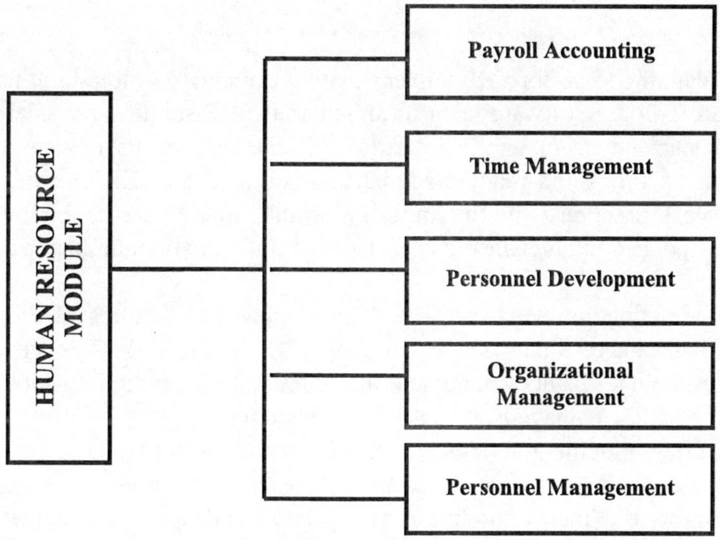

Fig. 4.6. Human Resource Module

LEARNING POINTS

1. The human resource module offers easy access to employee data for personnel administration.
2. Human resource module also supports recruitment, travel management, payroll processing and personnel development.
3. Human resource module generally has the following components: payroll accounting, time management, personnel development and organizational management.
4. Payroll accounting provides payroll functions.
5. Time Management subsystem facilitates daily processing of employee time data to determine the working hours of the employee.
6. Organizational management module's graphical organizational charts enable the company to review its organizational structure easily.

4.7 QUALITY MANAGEMENT

Quality management module of ERP system provides quality planning, quality inspection and quality control. The module is integrated with materials management, manufacturing and production planning, and sales and distribution module of the ERP system.

LEARNING POINT

1. Quality management module of ERP system provides quality planning, quality inspection and quality control.

SUMMARY

Any organization planning to go for ERP implementation can either custom-built the ERP software with the help of an in-house software team or an external ERP solution provider or purchase an off-the–shelf ERP package from an ERP vendor. All the options have their own merits and demerits. A standard off-the-shelf ready-made package by a reputed ERP vendor would provide the benefits of "best practices" in the industry. Some other benefits include reduction in development time, reduced maintenance costs, standard functionality and better customer service and support.

An ERP package contains many modules. The number and features of ERP modules may vary with the ERP package. Some of the common ERP modules that are generally found in most ERP packages include finance, manufacturing, sales and distribution, materials management, plant maintenance, quality management and human resources.

The manufacturing module provides the flexibility for selecting either a combination of production methods or the best production method for each of the product and at every stage of its manufacturing process. Finance module provides latest and updated financial information to support strategic decision making. A finance module may have the following subsystems: financial accounting, controlling, investment management, treasury and enterprise controlling.

An efficient sales and distribution module provides improved sales, higher profit margins and increased customer satisfaction to the company. It consists of the following subsystems: master data management, order management, warehouse management, shipping, billing, pricing, sales support, transportation and foreign trade. Plant maintenance module handles maintenance tasks for efficient working of equipment. It consists of the following components: preventive maintenance control, equipment tracking, component tracking, plant maintenance calibration tracking and plant maintenance warranty claims tracking.

Materials management module handles invoice verification and materials inspection. It has the following components: pre-purchasing activities, purchasing, vendor evaluation, inventory management, invoice verification and material inspection. Human resource module offers easy access to employee data for personnel administration. It comprises the following components: payroll accounting, time management, personnel development, organizational management and personnel management. Quality management module provides quality planning, quality inspection and quality control.

POINTS TO REMEMBER

1. A standard ERP package would deliver the company the benefits of "best practices" in the industry, eliminate maintenance costs (which were huge in the case of legacy systems) and provide better support and service.
2. All ERP packages contain many modules. The number and features of ERP modules may vary with ERP package.
3. ERP modules can interface with an organization's own software with varying degrees of efforts. It is also possible to alter the ERP modules via the vendor's proprietary tools and proprietary or standard programming languages.
4. Some of the common ERP modules that are generally found in most of the ERP packages are finance, manufacturing, production planning, human resources, sales and distribution, quality management, plant maintenance and materials management.
5. A robust ERP module for manufacturing must support a variety of business practices and production methods. It must also provide the flexibility for selecting either a combination of production methods or the best production method for each product at every stage of its manufacturing process.
6. The manufacturing module may extend support to supply chain process.
7. Some major subsystems of manufacturing module include material and capacity planning, shop floor control, just-in-time manufacturing, quality management, cost management, engineering data management, engineering change control, configuration management, serialization and tooling.
8. Finance module integrates financial functionality across all business and geographical areas. It generally includes the following subsystems: financial accounting, controlling, investment management, treasury and enterprise controlling.
9. The financial accounting system helps to keep track of financial data within an international framework of multiple languages, currencies and companies.
10. An efficient sales and distribution module helps the companies to improve sales as well as profit margins and customer satisfaction.

11. The sales and distribution module has the following subsystems: Master Data management, Order Management, Warehouse Management, Inventory management, Shipping, Billing, Pricing, Sales Support, Transportation, and Foreign Trade.
12. Plant maintenance module handles the maintenance tasks for efficient working of equipment. It determines whether a repair or replacement of the machinery is needed.
13. Materials management module provides vendor evaluation, improves the procurement process by controlling the items costs and handles invoice verification and materials inspection.
14. The human resource module offers easy access to employee data for personnel administration. The module also supports recruitment, travel management, payroll processing and personnel development.
15. Quality management module of ERP system provides quality planning, quality inspection and quality control. The module is integrated with materials management, manufacturing and production planning, and sales and distribution module of the ERP system.

REVIEW QUESTIONS

1. What are the advantages and disadvantages of in-house custom built ERP with respect to the off-the-shelf ready made available ERP package?
2. Discuss the common ERP modules that are generally found in most of the ERP packages.
3. What are the major subsystems of the manufacturing module?
4. What do you understand by just-in-time manufacturing? Give its advantages.
5. Discuss the various subsystems of the finance module.
6. Explain in brief the following modules:
   a) Sales and distribution
   b) Plant maintenance
   c) Materials Management
   d) Human Resource
   e) Quality management

OBJECTIVE QUESTIONS

SECTION A

TICK THE CORRECT ANSWER

1. A standard ERP package would deliver the company:
   (a) The benefits of "best practices" in the industry.
   (b) Eliminate maintenance costs (which were huge in the case of legacy systems).
   (c) Provide better support and service.
   (d) All of above.
2. The ERP software can be:
   (a) Custom-built software developed in-house.

(b) Custom-built software by an external ERP solution provider.
(c) Off-the-shelf application software packages available with ERP vendor.
(d) All of above.

3. Which is true about ERP packages?
(a) ERP packages are also referred to as tailor made ERP solutions.
(b) All ERP packages contain many modules.
(c) The number and features of ERP modules may vary with ERP package.
(d) ERP modules can interface with an organization's own software with varying degrees of efforts.
(e) All of above.

4. Demand forecasting and market analysis are used in __________ production method.
(a) Only make-to-stock.
(b) Both make-to-stock and make-to-order.
(c) Only make-to-order.
(d) None of above.

5. In make-to-order the manufacturer begins:
(a) The production of the item only after he has received an order from the customer.
(b) The manufacturer produces the end-item and places it in the inventory before he receives an order from a customer.
(c) The users are allowed to evaluate and adjust operation steps and components.
(d) None of above.

6. A robust ERP module for manufacturing must:
(a) Support a variety of business practices and production methods.
(b) Provide the flexibility for selecting either a combination of production methods or the best production method for each product at every stage of its manufacturing process.
(c) May extend support to supply chain process.
(d) All of above.

7. Some of the major subsystems of the manufacturing module are:
(a) Materials and Capacity Planning.
(b) Shop Floor Control.
(c) Engineering Data Management.
(d) Serialization/Lot Control.
(e) All of above.

8. The ______________ subsystem helps in developing material plans from a variety of sources such as the master schedule, sales forecast and dependent and independent demand.
(a) Materials and Capacity Planning.
(b) Just-In-Time Manufacturing.
(c) Cost Management.
(d) Engineering Data Management.

9. ________________ provides flexible shop floor planning and control activities.
(a) Shop Floor Control system.
(b) Materials and Capacity Planning.
(c) Serialization.
(d) Quality management.

10. Which is true about shop floor control system?
(a) Provides flexible shop floor planning and control activities.
(b) Users are allowed to evaluate and adjust operation steps and components.
(c) Orders can be either rescheduled forward or rescheduled backward.
(d) All of above.

11. Which is true about Just-In-Time Manufacturing (JIT)?
(a) Seeks to reduce inventory levels of raw material, work-in-process and finished products.
(b) Based on actual performance, the JIT subsystem tries to identify discrepancies.
(c) It monitors the production rates and daily output goals on a timely basis and adjusts them proactively.
(d) All of above.

12. The__________ subsystem of manufacturing module focuses on continuous improvement of manufacturing methods.
(a) Cost Management.
(b) Quality management.
(c) Just-In-Time Manufacturing.
(d) Engineering Data Management.

13. The Cost Management subsystem of manufacturing module provides:
(a) Detailed cost information at various levels.
(b) Facilitates the manager to identify the cost drivers.
(c) Reduce the product costs.
(d) All of above.

14. ____________ subsystem of manufacturing module provides an automated link between engineering and production information.
(a) Engineering Data Management.
(b) Engineering Change Control.
(c) Materials and Capacity Planning.
(d) None of above.

15. ___________ Subsystem of manufacturing module uses a powerful analytical engine that interprets the knowledge base in conjunction with the customer selection.
(a) Engineering Data Management.
(b) Engineering Change Control.
(c) Configuration Management.
(d) Just-In-Time Manufacturing.

16. ______________ Subsystem of manufacturing module facilitates the business to have an effective control over engineering change orders.
(a) Engineering Data Management.
(b) Configuration Management.
(c) Materials and Capacity Planning.
(d) None of above.

17. Which subsystem of manufacturing module may provide the facility for pre-assigning the production orders with lot numbers for the present item?
(a) Engineering Data Management.
(b) Engineering Change Control.

(c) Configuration Management.
(d) None of above.

18. Treasury subsystem is a part of:
(a) Manufacturing.
(b) Finance.
(c) Sales and distribution.
(d) Quality management.

19. Financial accounting subsystem of Finance module does not include which component?
(a) General Ledger.
(b) Inventory Planning.
(c) Asset Accounting.
(d) Legal Consolidation.

20. The asset accounting component provides for the following:
(a) Supports the management of machinery and equipment, leased assets, assets under construction and mass processing with work flow integration.
(b) Provides detailed information on asset-related transactions to the general ledger.
(c) Integrated with plant maintenance module for better management of the company's asset.
(d) All of above.

21. Legal Consolidation component of financial accounting provides:
(a) Transfer of data from individual statements into consolidated report.
(b) Multiple views of the consolidated reports can be created.
(c) Easy and quick generation of reports about the legal entities or segments of your business.
(d) All of above.

22. The Controlling subsystem of Finance module does not contain ___________.
(a) Overhead Cost Controlling.
(b) Cost Centre Accounting.
(c) Activity Based Costing.
(d) Product Cost Controlling.
(e) None of above.

23. Profitability analysis component of Finance module helps in:
(a) Examining the sources of returns.
(b) Assigning revenues to costs according to market segment.
(c) Making decisions regarding price determination.
(d) Selection of customers and distribution channels.
(e) All of above.

24. The ___________ subsystem of Finance module enables efficient monitoring and distribution of budgets in order to avoid budget overrun.
(a) Investment Management.
(b) Treasury.
(c) Controlling.
(d) Financial accounting.

25. Treasury component supports:
(a) Effective liquidity.
(b) Effective portfolio.
(c) Effective risk management.
(d) All of above.

26. The treasury module includes the following components:
(a) Cash Management.
(b) Treasury Management.
(c) Market Risk Management.
(d) Funds Management.
(e) All of above.

27. Which is true about market risk management component of treasury subsystem of Finance module?
(a) Market risk management provides various measures to analyze the risks involved.
(b) Risk measurement and control is an important function of this subsystem.
(c) By using simulation techniques upon the market data, the risk structure of "what-if' analysis is determined.
(d) All of above.

28. The enterprise controlling subsystem of Finance module has the components:
(a) Executive Information System.
(b) Profit Centre Accounting.
(c) Business Planning and Budgeting.
(d) All of above.

29. Which subsystem of Finance module supports effective liquidity, portfolio and risk management?
(a) Enterprise Controlling.
(b) Treasury.
(c) Financial Accounting.
(d) Investment Management.
(e) None of above.

30. Sales and distribution module includes the component:
(a) Master Data management.
(b) Order Management.
(c) Warehouse Management.
(d) Shipping.
(e) All of above.

31. Master Data management subsystem of Sales and Distribution module keeps information about:
(a) Products.
(b) Customers.
(c) Supplier.
(d) All of above.
(e) None of above.

32. Which is true about the order data management sub-module of Sales and Distribution module?
(a) Includes sales order management and purchase order management.
(b) It also manages quotas, orders, contracts process and customer discount.
(c) Tracking and tracing of schedules and follow-ups, multi-level customer credit reviews and blocking of orders are some other functionalities that are provided.
(d) All of above.

33. Which is not true about Warehouse Management?
(a) It provides real-time information about the inventory levels.
(b) It Includes sales order management and purchase order management.
(c) It monitors all the inventory transactions.
(d) It includes Inventory Planning and Inventory handling.

34. Which___________ subsystem of sales and distribution module provides real-time information about the inventory levels and monitors all the inventory transactions?
(a) Master Data management.
(b) Order Management.
(c) Warehouse Management.
(d) Shipping.

35. _________ Subsystem of sales and distribution module helps the company to support its existing customers and add new customers to its existing customer base by providing up-to-date and useful information about inventory, sales and market trends to the sales people.
(a) Sales Support.
(b) Shipping.
(c) Foreign Trade.
(d) Order Management.

36. Which is true about plant maintenance module?
(a) Handles the maintenance tasks for efficient working of equipment.
(b) It determines whether a repair or replacement of the machinery is needed.
(c) Enables the company to achieve higher machine utilization.
(d) All of above.

37. Plant maintenance module includes:
(a) Preventive Maintenance Control.
(b) Equipment Tracking.
(c) Component Tracking.
(d) Plant Maintenance Calibration Tracking.
(e) All of above.

38. _______________ subsystem of Plant maintenance module is used to plan and control the machinery and equipment
(a) Preventive Maintenance Control.
(b) Equipment Tracking.
(c) Component Tracking.
(d) Plant Maintenance Warranty Claims Tracking.
(e) None of above.

39. ______________ Subsystem of Plant maintenance module provides equipment history to facilitate tracking of equipment:

(a) Equipment Tracking.
(b) Component Tracking.
(c) Plant Maintenance Calibration Tracking.
(d) Plant Maintenance Warranty Claims Tracking.

40. Component tracking subsystem of Plant maintenance module is used to ______________.

(a) Plan and control the machinery and equipment.
(b) Identify those components which have chronic repair problems.
(c) Provides equipment history to facilitate tracking of equipment.
(d) Track the calibration of the equipment in support of ISO9000 requirements.

41. Materials Management module provides:

(a) Vendor evaluation.
(b) Improves the procurement process by controlling the items costs.
(c) Handles invoice verification and materials inspection.
(d) All of above.

42. Materials management module does not have____________ component:

(a) Pre-Purchasing Activities.
(b) Vendor Evaluation.
(c) Inventory Management.
(d) Invoice Verification and Material Inspection.
(e) None of above.

43. Which is true about purchasing subsystem of Materials management module?

(a) It facilitates materials management.
(b) Performs activities such as material and service procurement, inventory management and invoice verification.
(c) It is integrated with cost accounting, financial accounting and sales and distribution system.
(d) All of above.

44. Purchasing subsystem of Materials management module contains:

(a) Material and Service Procurement.
(b) Inventory management.
(c) Invoice verification.
(d) All of above.

45. Which is true about the human resource module?

(a) Offers easy access to employee data for personnel administration.
(b) Supports recruitment, payroll processing and personnel development.
(c) Supports travel management.
(d) All of above.

46. Human resource module contains:

(a) Payroll accounting.
(b) Time Management.
(c) Personnel Development.
(d) Organizational Management.
(e) All of above.

47. Payroll processing in Payroll accounting component of Human resource module can be
- **(a)** Centralized.
- **(b)** Decentralized based on country or legal entities.
- **(c)** Either (a) or (b).
- **(d)** None of above.

48. Time Management subsystem of Human resource module facilitates:
- **(a)** Daily processing of employee time data to determine the working hours of the employee.
- **(b)** Calculation of wages and incentives based on the employee time data.
- **(c)** Planning workforce requirements quickly.
- **(d)** All of above.

49. ________________module's graphical organizational charts enable the company to review its organizational structure easily.
- **(a)** Organizational Management.
- **(b)** Personnel Management.
- **(c)** Personnel Development.
- **(d)** Time Management.

50. Quality management module of ERP system provides:
- **(a)** Quality Planning.
- **(b)** Quality Inspection.
- **(c)** Quality Control.
- **(d)** All of above.

SECTION B

STATE TRUE OR FALSE

1. The purpose of ERP technology is to support all of the organizational business processes in order to support the company's strategic opportunities.
2. A standard ERP package would deliver the company the benefits of "best practices" in the industry, eliminate maintenance costs (which were huge in the case of legacy systems) and provide better support and service.
3. The ERP software can either be custom-built software (developed in-house or by an external ERP solution provider) or a package software.
4. ERP packages are also referred to as tailor made ERP solutions.
5. All ERP packages contain many modules.
6. The number and features of ERP modules cannot vary with ERP package.
7. ERP modules can interface with an organization's own software with varying degrees of efforts.
8. It is impossible to alter the ERP modules via the vendor's proprietary tools and proprietary or standard programming languages.
9. The manufacturing unit of the industry must respond to the demands of the customers quickly and effectively.
10. The manufacturing planning and control is broadly categorized as either make-to-order manufacturing or make-to-stock.

11. In make-to-order production method, the manufacturer produces the end-item and places it in the inventory before he receives an order from a customer.
12. Demand forecasting and market analysis are used in make-to-order production method.
13. In make-to-stock production method, the manufacturer begins the production of the item only after he has received an order from the customer.
14. A robust ERP module for manufacturing must support a variety of business practices and production methods.
15. A robust ERP module for manufacturing must also provide the flexibility for selecting either a combination of production methods or the best production method for each product at every stage of its manufacturing process.
16. The manufacturing module cannot extend support to supply chain process.
17. Materials and Capacity Planning subsystem helps in developing material plans from a variety of sources such as the master schedule, sales forecast and dependent and independent demand.
18. Alternative plans can be simulated to decide which parts and assemblies to manufacture and which to purchase.
19. A graphical production management tool fails to easily identify changes in capacity utilization.
20. The shop floor control system does not provide flexible shop floor planning and control activities.
21. In the shop floor control system, the users are not allowed to evaluate and adjust operation steps and components. The orders can be neither rescheduled forward nor rescheduled backward.
22. Just-In-Time Manufacturing (JIT) seeks to increase inventory levels of raw material, work-in-process and finished products.
23. Based on actual performance, the JIT subsystem tries to identify discrepancies.
24. JIT subsystem monitors the production rates and daily output goals on a timely basis and adjusts them proactively.
25. Quality Management subsystem focuses on continuous improvement of manufacturing methods.
26. Cost Management facilitates the manager to identify the cost drivers and reduce the product costs.
27. General Ledger does not facilitate parallel views of data in the general ledger and managerial accounting applications.
28. Asset Accounting facilitates payment automation with EFT (electronic funds transfer), document management, flexible reporting and an enterprise-wide credit management with workflow integration.
29. Accounts Receivable and Payable component supports the management of machinery and equipment, leased assets, assets under construction and mass processing with work flow integration.
30. Legal Consolidation facilitates transfer of data from individual statements into consolidated report.
31. Controlling subsystem helps you to effectively handle internal cost accounting.

32. Overhead Cost controlling component supports effective monitoring and efficient allocation of overheads.

33. The cost centre accounting subsystem of Controlling System analyzes where the overheads occur within the company and costs are assigned to the area of origin.

34. Product Cost Controlling component monitors and controls cross departmental business process and calculate the cost of a business activity or process.

35. Activity Based costing subsystem is used to determine the costs of manufacturing a product or providing a service.

36. Profitability analysis component of Finance module helps in examining the sources of returns, assigning revenues to costs according to market segment and making decisions regarding price determination and selection of customers, distribution channels.

37. An investment programme hierarchy can be defined through the investment management component using any criteria, for e.g., product-wise. This enables efficient monitoring and distribution of budgets in order to avoid budget overrun.

38. Treasury management component support effective liquidity, portfolio and risk management.

39. Treasury management component provides information on sources and uses of funds to secure liquidity, so that payment obligations are met when they become due. Incoming and outgoing payment flows are monitored and controlled.

40. Cash Management is used to manage, analyze and support reporting for financial deals, positions and portfolios.

41. Market Risk Management provides various measures to analyze the risks involved Risk measurement and control is an important function of this subsystem.

42. By using simulation techniques upon the market data the risk structure of "what-if' analysis is determined by the Market risk management component.

43. The funds Management subsystem enables the company to manage its funds. It also determines how much of the budget has been utilized and monitors various expenditures of the company.

44. Enterprise Controlling module offers to optimize share holder value and meet the internal objectives for growth and investment.

45. Executive Information System (EIS) provides information required to manage the organization. A drill down reporting facility is also provided to analyze the data interactively.

46. Business Planning and Budgeting is used to analyze the profitability of the internal responsibility centres of the organization. The profitability information is made available to the appropriate management and controlling departments.

47. Profit Centre Accounting component supports investment planning, budget release and tracking.

48. The master data management module only keeps information about products and not about customers and suppliers.

49. The order data management module includes sales order management and purchase order management.

50. The Purchase order management supports the sales operations of the company.

51. Purchase order management supports purchase decisions regarding price and quality of products.

52. Warehouse Management does not provide real-time information about the inventory levels.

53. Inventory handling ensures that the customer receives the right order with respect to time, quantity and quality.

54. Inventory Planning monitors the warehouse inventory transaction that includes the receipt, issue and transfer of inventory.

55. Inventory Reporting is used to detect the location of stored goods by criteria such as item, size, location availability etc.

56. Inventory Location Assignment enables the company to offer customers' accurate delivery dates by knowing about its inventory status at single as well as multiple sites.

57. Inventory Analysis supports inventory forecasting and activity-based costing analysis to support warehousing activities.

58. Lot Control provides lot tracking and tracing to trace the raw materials that the products require.

59. Distribution Data Collection provides the communication link between inventory warehouse and the shipping system.

60. Shipping module supports activities such as picking, packing, deliveries, printing and sending shipping output.

61. Billing supports various billing functions. Some of the billing functions include issue of invoices based on goods and services, canceling billing transactions and giving rebates.

62. Pricing keeps the information about prices and discounts of various items and provides this information to sales people.

63. Sales Support subsystem helps the company to support its existing customers and add new customers to its existing customer base by providing up-to-date and useful information about inventory, sales and market trends to the sales people.

64. The transportation module does not ensure that the shipment is dispatched without delay and it arrives on schedule.

65. The plant maintenance module handles the maintenance tasks for efficient working of equipment.

66. Equipment tracking subsystem is used to plan and control the machinery and equipment. Maintenance activities such as equipment lubrication, replacement of component and safety inspection of the equipment are closely monitored.

67. Preventive maintenance Control subsystem provides equipment history to facilitate tracking of equipment.

68. Component tracking subsystem is used to identify those components which have chronic repair problems.

69. Plant Maintenance Warranty Claims Tracking is used to track the calibration of the equipment in support of ISO9000 requirements.

70. Plant Maintenance Calibration tracking subsystem provides warranty related information for each item. This enables the company to recover the warranty.

71. Materials management module provides vendor evaluation, improves the procurement process by controlling the items costs and handles invoice verification and materials inspection.

72. Purchasing subsystem of materials management module supports bid invitation, quotation evaluation and award of contract.

73. Pre-Purchasing Activities subsystem of materials management module facilitates materials management.

74. Inventory Management subsystem of materials management module provides a point-based evaluation system based on a selection criteria to evaluate the vendors.
75. Inventory Management subsystem of materials management module provides management of stock on a quantity and value basis.
76. Inventory methods such as periodic inventory, continuous inventory, inventory sampling and cycle counting are not supported by most inventory management systems.
77. Invoice Verification and Material Inspection subsystem of materials management module facilitates processing of invoices and credit memos.
78. The human resource module offers easy access to employee data for personnel administration.
79. Payroll accounting component provides payroll functions.
80. Time Management subsystem only facilitates monthly processing of employee time data to determine the working hours of the employee.
81. Personnel Development component automates the process of matching the qualification of employees and external candidates with the job requirements. It also facilitates planning and management of training.
82. Organizational Management module's graphical organizational charts enable the company to review its organizational structure easily.
83. Personnel Development module provides a centralized employee database that facilitates personnel administration and recruitment processes to be carried out more efficiently.
84. Quality Management module of ERP system provides quality planning, quality inspection and quality control. The module is integrated with materials management, manufacturing and production planning, and sales and distribution module of the ERP system.

SECTION C

FILL IN THE BLANKS

1. The purpose of ERP technology is to support the business processes of an organization in order to support the organization's_________________.
2. A standard ERP package would deliver the company, the benefits of "best practices" in the industry, eliminate ___________costs (which were huge in the case of legacy systems) and provide better support and service.
3. The ERP software can either be _____________software (developed in-house or by an external ERP solution provider) or a ______________software.
4. ERP packages are also referred to as ___________ERP solutions.
5. All ERP packages contain many____________.
6. The number and features of ERP modules may _________with ERP package.
7. ERP modules can interface with an organization's own software with varying degrees of____________.
8. It is also possible to alter the ERP modules via the vendor's ___________tools and proprietary or __________programming languages.
9. The manufacturing unit of the industry must respond to the demands of the customers' __________and effectively.

10. The manufacturing planning and control is broadly categorized as either ____________ manufacturing or make-to-stock.

11. In ____________ production method, the manufacturer produces the end-item and places it in the inventory before he receives an order from a customer.

12. Demand forecasting and market analysis are used in ____________production method.

13. In ____________ production method, the manufacturer begins the production of the item only after he has received an order from the customer.

14. A robust ERP module for ____________ must support a variety of business practices and production methods.

15. A robust ERP module must also provide the flexibility for selecting either a combination of production methods or the ________ production method for each product at every ________of its manufacturing process.

16. The manufacturing module may extend support to ________ process.

17. ______________ Subsystem of manufacturing module helps in developing material plans from a variety of sources such as the master schedule, sales forecast and dependent and independent demand.

18. A graphical production management tool helps in easy identification of changes in___________.

19. The _________ control subsystem of manufacturing module provides flexible shop floor planning and control activities.

20. In the shop floor control subsystem of manufacturing module the users are allowed to evaluate and adjust _________and components. The orders can be either rescheduled ___________or _________.

21. Just-In-Time Manufacturing (JIT) subsystem of manufacturing module seeks to ________ inventory levels of raw material, work-in-process and finished products.

22. Based on actual performance the __________ subsystem of manufacturing module tries to identify discrepancies.

23. JIT subsystem of manufacturing module monitors the production rates and daily output goals on a _______ basis and adjusts them proactively.

24. _______ Subsystem of manufacturing module focuses on continuous improvement of manufacturing methods.

25. Cost Management subsystem of manufacturing module provides detailed cost information at various_____.

26. _____________ Subsystem of manufacturing module facilitates the manager to identify the cost drivers and reduce the product costs.

27. Engineering Data Management subsystem of manufacturing module provides an ________ between engineering and production information. This facilitates __________ in data transfer time and increases design productivity.

28. _______ Subsystem of manufacturing module facilitates the business to have an effective control over engineering change orders.

29. ______________ Subsystem of manufacturing module uses a powerful analytical engine that interprets the knowledge base in conjunction with the customer selection. This results in the design and production of ___________ product.

30. Serialization/Lot Control subsystem of manufacturing module may provide the facility for pre-assigning the production orders with __________ for the present item.

31. __________ Subsystem of manufacturing module ensures that both the __________ and the tools arrive together at the scheduled production operation.

32. Finance module integrates ___________ functionality across all business and geographical areas.

33. A ________ module generally has Financial Accounting subsystem.

34. The financial accounting system helps to keep track of financial data within an international framework of ___________ languages, currencies and companies.

35. Compliance with international accounting standards such as GAAP and IAS as well as local legal requirements are generally provided by the ___________ subsystem.

36. General Ledger component of Financial Accounting subsystem of Finance module provides support to all functions required in a financial accounting system such as real time simultaneous __________ of general ledger and sub-ledgers.

37. Accounts Receivable and Payable component of Financial Accounting subsystem of Finance module facilitates _____________ with EFT (electronic funds transfer), document management, flexible reporting and an enterprise-wide credit management with workflow integration.

38. _________ Component of Financial Accounting subsystem of Finance module supports the management of machinery and equipment, leased assets, assets under construction and mass processing with work flow integration.

39. Asset accounting component of Financial Accounting subsystem of Finance module provides detailed information on __________ transactions to the general ledger.

40. Legal Consolidation component of Financial Accounting subsystem of Finance module facilitates transfer of data from individual statements into___________. Multiple views of the consolidated reports can be created. This enables easy and quick generation of reports about the _________ entities or segments of your business.

41. _________ Subsystem of Finance module helps you to effectively handle internal cost accounting.

42. Overhead Cost controlling component of controlling subsystem of Finance module supports effective monitoring and efficient allocation of________________.

43. The cost centre accounting component of controlling subsystem of Finance module analyzes where the _______ occur within the company and costs are assigned to the________.

44. ___________ Component of controlling subsystem of Finance module monitors and controls cross departmental business process and calculate the cost of a business activity or process.

45. ________________ Component of controlling subsystem of Finance module is used to determine the costs of manufacturing a product or providing a service. It also enables us to find out the lowest price for which a product or service is profitable.

46. _____________ Component of controlling subsystem of Finance module helps in examining the sources of returns, assigning revenues to costs according to market segment, making decisions regarding price determination and selection of customers and distribution channels.

47. An investment programme hierarchy can be defined through the investment management subsystem of finance module using ______ criteria, for e.g., product-wise. This enables efficient monitoring and distribution of budgets in order to avoid________.
48. Treasury subsystem of finance module supports effective______, ____________ and risk management.
49. _____________ Component of treasury subsystem of finance module provides information on sources and uses of funds to secure liquidity so that payment obligations are met when they become due. Incoming and ________ payment flows are monitored and controlled.
50. __________ Component of treasury subsystem of finance module is used to manage, analyze and support reporting for financial deals, positions and portfolios.
51. By using ________ upon the market data; the risk structure of "what-if" analysis is determined by the Market risk management component of treasury subsystem of finance module.
52. Funds Management component of treasury subsystem of finance module, enables the company to manage its _________. It also determines how much of the budget has been _________ and monitors various expenditures of the company.
53. Enterprise Controlling subsystem of finance module offers to ________ share holder value and meet the internal objectives for growth and investment.
54. Executive Information System provides ________ required to manage the organization. A _________ reporting facility is also provided to analyze the data interactively.
55. ________________ Component of Enterprise Controlling subsystem of finance module is used to analyze the profitability of the internal responsibility centres of the organization.
56. The Business Planning and Budgeting component of Enterprise Controlling subsystem of finance module is used for _________, budget release and tracking.
57. An efficient ___________ module helps the companies to improve sales as well as profit margins and customer satisfaction.
58. ___________ Subsystem of sales and distribution module keeps information about products, customers and suppliers. This information is used in ____________and automatic generation of various useful reports.
59. Order Management Subsystem of sales and distribution module includes _________ management and ______ management.
60. The sales order management supports the _______ operations of the company.
61. __________ Management supports purchase decisions regarding price and quality of products. A purchase quotation can be send to __________suppliers through the system.__________, just-in-time schedules and vendor management are also provided.
62. __________ Subsystem of sales and distribution module provides real-time information about the inventory levels and monitors all the inventory transactions.
63. Inventory planning component of warehouse management subsystem of sales and distribution module ensures that the customer receives the _________ with respect to time, quantity and quality.
64. ________________ Component of warehouse management subsystem of sales and distribution module monitors the warehouse inventory transaction that includes the receipt, issue and transfer of inventory.

65. Inventory Location Assignment component of warehouse management subsystem of sales and distribution module is used to detect the ________ of stored goods by criteria such as item, size, location availability etc.

66. ________________ Component of warehouse management subsystem of sales and distribution module enables the company to offer customers' accurate delivery dates by knowing about its inventory status at single as well as multiple sites.

67. Inventory Analysis component of warehouse management subsystem of sales and distribution module supports inventory forecasting and activity-based costing analysis to support ___________ activities.

68. Lot Control component of _____________ Subsystem of sales and distribution module provides lot tracking and tracing to trace the raw materials that the products require.

69. Distribution Data Collection component of warehouse management subsystem of sales and distribution module provides the communication link between inventory warehouse and the ___________ system.

70. __________ Subsystem of sales and distribution module supports activities such as picking, packing, deliveries, printing and sending shipping output.

71. ________ Subsystem of sales and distribution module supports various billing functions.

72. _______ Subsystem of sales and distribution module keeps the information about prices and discounts of various items and provides this information to sales people.

73. Sales Support subsystem of sales and distribution module helps the company to support its existing customers and add new customers to its existing customer base by providing up-to-date and useful information about_______, sales and _________ to the sales people.

74. Transportation subsystem of sales and distribution module provides effective _______ planning.

75. Foreign Trade subsystem of sales and distribution module provides support to ________________ activities.

76. The ___________ module handles the maintenance tasks for efficient working of equipment. It determines whether a replacement or _________ of the machinery is needed.

77. ___________ Subsystem of Plant maintenance module is used to plan and control the machinery and equipment. __________ Activities such as equipment lubrication, replacement of component and safety inspection of the equipment are closely monitored.

78. Equipment tracking subsystem of Plant maintenance module provides _________ to facilitate tracking of equipment.

79. Component tracking subsystem of Plant maintenance module is used to identify those components which have ____________ repair problems.

80. Plant Maintenance Calibration Tracking subsystem of Plant maintenance module is used to track the calibration of the equipment in support of ___________ requirements.

81. Plant Maintenance Warranty Claims tracking subsystem of Plant maintenance module provides __________ information for each item. This enables the company to recover the warranty.

82. Materials Management module provides vendor evaluation, improves the procurement process by controlling the items costs and handles ___________ and materials inspection.

83. _____________ Subsystem of Materials Management module supports bid invitation, quotation evaluation and award of contract.

84. ________ Subsystem of Materials Management module facilitates materials management and performs activities such as material and service procurement, inventory management and invoice verification.

85. Vendor Evaluation subsystem of Materials Management module provides a ________ evaluation system based on a selection criteria to evaluate the________.

86. Inventory Management subsystem of Materials Management module provides management of stock on a ________ and value basis.

87. Inventory methods such as periodic inventory, continuous inventory, inventory sampling and cycle counting are supported by most ____________systems.

88. ____________ Subsystem of Materials Management module facilitates processing of invoices and credit memos.

89. The human resource module offers ________access to ______ data for personnel administration.

90. Payroll accounting subsystem of Human resource module provides ________ functions.

91. Payroll processing can be _______ or _________ based on country or legal entities. The subsystem adapts itself to the policy changes, if any.

92. Time Management subsystem of Human resource module facilitates daily processing of employee time data to determine the __________ of the employee.

93. Time Management subsystem of Human resource module also supports calculation of _________ and incentives based on the employee time data.

94. The ________ component within time management assists in planning workforce requirements quickly. Employees can be assigned to the work area where they are required.

95. ________ Subsystem of Human resource module automates the process of matching the qualification of employees and external candidates with the job requirements.

96. The __________ module's graphical organizational charts enable the company to review its organizational structure easily.

97. ____________ Subsystem of Human resource module provides a centralized employee database that facilitates personnel administration and recruitment processes to be carried out more efficiently.

98. ______________ Module of ERP system provides quality planning, quality inspection and quality control.

ANSWERS

SECTION A

(1) d	**(2)** d	**(3)** e	**(4)** a	**(5)** a	**(6)** d	**(7)** e	**(8)** a	**(9)** a	**(10)** d
(11) d	**(12)** b	**(13)** d	**(14)** a	**(15)** c	**(16)** d	**(17)** d	**(18)** b	**(19)** b	**(20)** d
(21) d	**(22)** e	**(23)** e	**(24)** a	**(25)** d	**(26)** e	**(27)** d	**(28)** d	**(29)** b	**(30)** e
(31) d	**(32)** d	**(33)** b	**(34)** c	**(35)** a	**(36)** d	**(37)** e	**(38)** a	**(39)** a	**(40)** b
(41) d	**(42)** e	**(43)** d	**(44)** d	**(45)** d	**(46)** e	**(47)** c	**(48)** d	**(49)** a	**(50)** d.

SECTION B

(1) True **(2)** True **(3)** True **(4)** True **(5)** True **(6)** False **(7)** True **(8)** False **(9)** True **(10)** True **(11)** False **(12)** False **(13)** False **(14)** True **(15)** True **(16)** False **(17)** True **(18)** True **(19)** False **(20)** False **(21)** False **(22)** False **(23)** True **(24)** True **(25)** True **(26)** True **(27)** False **(28)** False **(29)** False **(30)** True **(31)** True **(32)** True **(33)** True **(34)** False **(35)** False **(36)** True **(37)** True **(38)** True **(39)** False **(40)** False **(41)** True **(42)** True **(43)** True **(44)** True **(45)** True **(46)** False **(47)** False **(48)** False **(49)** True **(50)** False **(51)** True **(52)** False **(53)** False **(54)** False **(55)** False **(56)** False **(57)** True **(58)** True **(59)** True **(60)** True **(61)** True **(62)** True **(63)** True **(64)** False **(65)** True **(66)** False **(67)** False **(68)** True **(69)** False **(70)** False **(71)** True **(72)** False **(73)** False **(74)** False **(75)** True **(76)** False **(77)** True **(78)** True **(79)** True **(80)** False **(81)** True **(82)** True **(83)** False **(84)** True.

SECTION C

(1) strategic opportunities **(2)** maintenance **(3)** custom built, package **(4)** tailor made **(5)** modules **(6)** vary **(7)** efforts **(8)** proprietary, standard **(9)** quickly **(10)** make-to-order **(11)** make-to-stock **(12)** make-to-stock **(13)** make-to-order **(14)** manufacturing **(15)** best, stage **(16)** supply chain **(17)** Materials and capacity planning **(18)** capacity utilization **(19)** shop floor **(20)** operation steps, forward, backward **(21)** reduce **(22)** JIT **(23)** timely **(24)** Quality Management **(25)** levels **(26)** cost management **(27)** automated link, reduction **(28)** engineering change control **(29)** configuration management, customer specific **(30)** lot numbers **(31)** tooling, raw materials **(32)** financial **(33)** finance **(34)** multiple **(35)** Financial Accounting subsystem **(36)** update **(37)** payment automation **(38)** asset accounting **(39)** asset related **(40)** consolidated report, legal **(41)** controlling **(42)** overheads **(43)** overheads, area of origin **(44)** activity based costing **(45)** product cost controlling **(46)** Profitability analysis **(47)** any, budget overrun **(48)** liquidity, portfolio **(49)** cash management, outgoing **(50)** treasury management **(51)** simulation techniques **(52)** funds, utilized **(53)** optimize **(54)** information, drill down **(55)** profit centre accounting **(56)** investment planning **(57)** sales and distribution **(58)** master data management, decision making **(59)** sales order, purchase order **(60)** sales **(61)** purchase order, multiple, contract management **(62)** warehouse management **(63)** right order **(64)** inventory handling **(65)** location **(66)** inventory reporting **(67)** warehousing **(68)** warehouse management **(69)** shipping **(70)** shipping **(71)** billing **(72)** pricing **(73)** inventory, market trends **(74)** transportation **(75)** foreign trade processing **(76)** plant maintenance, repair **(77)** preventive maintenance control, maintenance **(78)** equipment history **(79)** chronic **(80)** ISO 9000 **(81)** warranty related **(82)** invoice verification **(83)** pre-purchasing activities **(84)** purchasing **(85)** point based, vendors **(86)** quantity **(87)** inventory management **(88)** invoice verification and materials inspection **(89)** easy, employee **(90)** payroll **(91)** centralized, decentralized **(92)** working hours **(93)** wages **(94)** shift planning **(95)** personal development **(96)** organizational management **(97)** personnel management **(98)** quality management.

5
Chapter
Framework for Evaluating ERP Acquisition

HIGHLIGHTS

- **ERP Modules**
  - Framework for Evaluating ERP Acquisition

It is expected that ERP vendors will go one step further in increasing their market share, by addressing the business's needs of small and medium enterprises (SME's). As the small and medium enterprises can't afford the expensive ERP systems designed for large enterprises, the ERP vendors need to come up with simpler and cheaper ERP solution suitable for SME's.

The adoption of an ERP system can have a profound impact on the overall organizational structure of an SME. In order to evaluate the acquisition of an ERP system within SME's, a framework is required that will verify the suitability of the ERP systems to the organizational complexity of the SME's. Business complexity and business transformation need to be carefully assessed by the framework being used for evaluating the ERP acquisition within the enterprise.

5.1 FRAMEWORK FOR EVALUATING ERP ACQUISITION

Ravarini et al., developed a simple framework for evaluating ERP acquisition within the small and medium enterprise. The framework is a bidirectional matrix structure. The two dimensions are as follows:

1. **Business Complexity**
   It indicates the complexity of the business processes and the information flows. A high value for the business complexity will imply that the enterprise will need to adapt complex

IT solutions. In other words the technological changes are intensely required by the company to reduce its business complexity and improve its efficiency. Some of the factors that affect business complexity are as follows:

i. **Growth and development objectives**

ii. **Internationalization level**
Business complexity is directly proportional to the degree of internationalization of the company. Managing different legal and cultural issues, handling the rich diversity of customers and competition and the extent of divisionalization all contribute their share to the business complexity.

iii. **Diversification of Product**
A company will have a high business complexity if the company markets a large number and variety of business products.

iv. **Number of employees**
Business complexity increases with the increase in number of employees in a company. It is often difficult to handle a large number of employees as large groups can become quiet unwieldy.

v. **Degree of vertical integration**
The degree of vertical integration required by the company results in different levels of business complexity. As the number of dependencies among the various activities increases the business complexity also increases.

vi. **Degree of functional extension**
It refers to the number of strategic functions directly managed within the enterprise. A high degree of functional extension implies high business complexity.

2. **Business transformation levels**
Business transformation is the change in the way business is conducted. An ERP acquisition is almost always accompanied with a certain level of business transformation. The various levels to which the business may transform itself are as follows:

i. **Local Automation**
It involves automation of local, independent procedures in order to improve the efficiency of the procedures. Local automation requires only little efforts and improves the performance of the business processes.

ii. **Internal Integration**
It deals with integrating the business processes and the information system of the company. As with local automation the internal integration improves the performance of the business. The business process structures remain unchanged in both local automation and internal integration transformation levels.

iii. **Business Process Reengineering**
This level involves a partial or complete redesign of the various business processes of the company. BPR brings out the deficiencies in the existing system and gives way to implementing new systems and improving the existing systems. BPR is time-consuming and also expensive.

iv. **Business network redesign**
In this level the changes overcome the boundaries of the company and extend further to the external relationships. Business partners can interact with each other through

EDI and continuous information exchange and competence sharing is facilitated by the business process integration.

v. **Redefinition of company boundaries**

This business transformation level is characterized by the formation and management of strong inter-organization relationships.

The framework suggests the most suitable approach for ERP acquisition within the SME by presenting a cross analysis between the two dimensions: business complexity and business transformation level.

Figure 5.1 suggests the approaches and their respective positions.

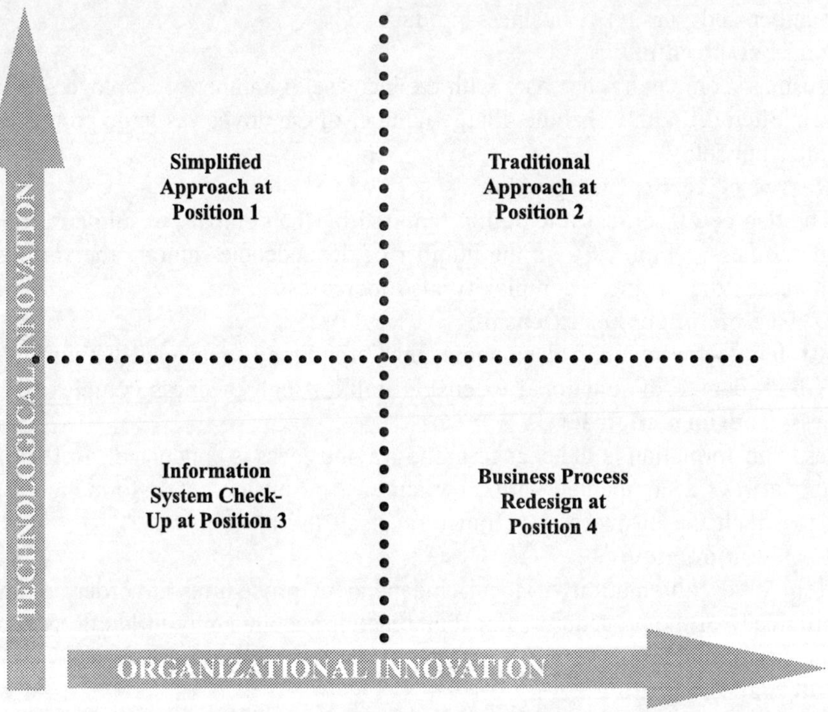

Fig. 5.1. Framework for evaluating ERP acquisition within SME's

1. **Simplified approach at position 1**

   It may happen that the enterprise is not ready for the organizational impacts it would be subjected to by business process reengineering. But the enterprise nevertheless feels the need to have an ERP system as the business complexity is quite high. In this case the simplified approach for ERP acquisition would be most appropriate.

   Simplified approach implies implementation of ERP without BPR. In this approach the company adapts its business processes in accordance with the requirements of the ERP system. The enterprise postpones the reengineering of critical business processes to a more appropriate time.

Some of the advantages of the simplified approach include the following:

i. The time required for implementation of the ERP system is less.
ii. Adoption process is easier and cheaper.
iii. It requires comparatively less or no structural changes.

The effectiveness of the simplified approach depends on the flexibility of the existing information system. From the organizational perspective the simplified approach has a lower impact on the SME structure-involving less structural changes, a short-term impact and low financial resources.

As the simplified approach just provides the automation and the integration of business processes it is unable to give a high performance enhancement in the business. As BPR can be considered following the implementation of the ERP system by the company, therefore, the ERP system implemented should be flexible enough to map its procedures on the reengineering business processes through the adjustment of the various parameter values of the ERP system.

2. **Traditional approach at position 2**
   Traditional approach is the most obvious choice for a company that is ready to redesign its organization structure and the business processes; and is also characterized by high business complexity. Traditional approach usually involves significant impacts from both cultural and organizational perspectives and higher investments.

   In traditional approach BPR is considered a prerequisite of ERP implementation. SME's are often characterized by the absence of long term planning, inadequate technological and organizational innovations, skill shortage, financial limitations, organizational resistance to changes and lack of training. Since business process reengineering will deal with all these SME's characteristics it is expected that the traditional approach will bring about a dramatical change in the company and facilitate a high performance improvement.
3. **Information system check-up at position 3**
   This position is marked with a low value for the business complexity as well as high resistance within the organization for any changes in the existing system. Such a situation does not justify the acquisition of an ERP system. In Information system check-up the existing IT applications and infrastructure of the company is analyzed and some modifications are made to make the existing information system more suitable. This approach is suitable when a company has a low business complexity and the employees are providing resistance to any changes in the organization structure.
4. **Business Process Redesign at position 4**
   It may happen that a company with a low complexity wants to redesign its organizational structure. This situation strongly advocates for exploiting the benefits of business process reengineering. The business processes should be redesigned to increase the performance. The company needs to verify the coverage level of the existing software applications. If the coverage level is found to be too low then the company must seriously consider the acquisition of an ERP system.

SUMMARY

The adoption of an ERP system can have a profound impact on the overall organization structure of an SME. Ravarini et al. developed a simple framework for evaluating the acquisition of ERP in an organization. The framework is a bi-dimensional matrix structure with the following dimensions: business complexity and business transformational levels. Business complexity indicates the complexity of the information flow as well as the business processes. Some of the factors that affect the business complexity include growth and development objectives, internationalization level, diversification of product, number of employees, degree of vertical integration and degree of functional extension.

Business transformation is the change in the way business is conducted. An ERP acquisition is almost always accompanied with a certain level of business transformation. Various business transformation levels include the following: local automation, internal integration, business process reengineering and business network redesign and redefinition of company boundaries. Local automation involves automation of local independent business procedures.

In internal integration, the information system is integrated with the business processes. Business process reengineering involves a partial or a complete redesign of the business processes of the organization. In business network redesign, the changes are extended to the external relationships. Technology such as EDI facilitates the transfer of information between companies. Business network redesign attempts to achieve competence and skill sharing between companies. The last transformation level, redefinition of company boundaries deals with the formation and management of strong inter-organizational relationships.

The framework suggests the most suitable approach that should be taken by the SME for ERP acquisition. Simplified approach at position 1 implies the implementation of ERP systems without a prior undertaking of business process reengineering. The simplified approach is advised when a company, characterized by high business complexity, strongly requires an ERP system to support its operations but the organization is not in a position to afford the changes that will accompany business process reengineering.

Traditional approach at position 2 is the most obvious choice for a company that is ready to redesign its organization structure and the business processes; and is also characterized by high business complexity.

Business process reengineering is considered a prerequisite of ERP implementation in the traditional approach. It is considered the most suitable approach for companies characterized by high business complexity that are ready to redesign its business processes and organization structure. Business process reengineering is the best approach to consider when the business complexity of the company is high and the company is ready for changes in the organizational structure.

In Information system check-up the existing IT applications and infrastructure of the company is analyzed and some modifications are made to make the existing information system more suitable. This approach is suitable when a company has a low business complexity and the employees are providing resistance to any changes in the organization structure.

POINTS TO REMEMBER

1. In order to evaluate the acquisition of an ERP system within SME's, a framework is required that will verify the suitability of the ERP systems to the organizational complexity of the SME's.
2. Business complexity and business transformation need to be carefully assessed by the framework being used for evaluating the ERP acquisition within the enterprise.
3. Ravarini et al., developed a simple framework for evaluating ERP acquisition within the small and medium enterprise. The framework is a bidirectional matrix structure having two dimensions: Business Complexity and Business Transformation levels.
4. Business complexity indicates the complexity of the information flow as well as the business processes.
5. Business transformation is the change in the way business is conducted. An ERP acquisition is almost always accompanied with a certain level of business transformation. Various business transformation levels include the following: local automation, internal integration, business process reengineering, business network redesign and redefinition of company boundaries.
6. The framework suggests the most suitable approach that should be taken by the SME for ERP acquisition. Simplified approach at position 1 implies the implementation of ERP systems without a prior undertaking of business process reengineering.
7. Traditional approach at position 2 is the most obvious choice for a company that is ready to redesign its organizational structure and the business processes; and is also characterized by high business complexity.
8. Information system check-up at position 3 is marked with a low value for the business complexity as well as high resistance within the organization for any changes in the existing system.
9. Business Process Redesign at position 4 strongly advocates for exploiting the benefits of business process reengineering. The business processes should be redesigned to increase the performance.

REVIEW QUESTIONS

1. Discuss the framework developed by Ravarini et al., for evaluating ERP acquisition within the small and medium enterprise.
2. Write short notes on the following:
   a. Business Complexity
   b. Business transformation levels
   c. Simplified approach
   d. Traditional approach
   e. Information system check-up
   f. Business Process Redesign
3. Explain business process reengineering.

OBJECTIVE QUESTIONS

SECTION A

TICK THE CORRECT ANSWER

1. It is expected that ERP vendors will go one step further in their share for increasing their market share, by addressing the business's needs of__________.
(a) Small and medium enterprises.
(b) Large enterprises.
(c) Only manufacturing sector.
(d) None of above.

2. As the small and medium enterprises can't afford the expensive ERP systems designed for large enterprises, the ERP vendors need to come up with __________ ERP solution suitable for SME's.
(a) Simpler.
(b) Cheaper.
(c) Both (a) and (b).
(d) None of above.

3. The adoption of an ERP system can have a profound impact on the ________ of an SME.
(a) Business expendture.
(b) Business transformation level.
(c) Organizational structure.
(d) None of above.

4. In order to evaluate the acquisition of an ERP system within SME's, a framework is required that will verify the suitability of the _____ systems to the organizational complexity of the SME's.
(a) SCM.
(b) ERP.
(c) Both (a) and (b)
(d) None of above.

5. __________ need to be carefully assessed by the framework being used for evaluating the ERP acquisition within the enterprise.
(a) Business complexity.
(b) Business transformation.
(c) Both (a) and (b).
(d) None of above.

6. Ravarini et al., developed a simple framework for evaluating ERP acquisition within the____________.
(a) Small and medium enterprise.
(b) Large enterprises.
(c) Both (a) and (b).
(d) None of above.

7. The framework is a bidirectional matrix structure. The dimensions are:
   (a) Business complexity.
   (b) Business transformation.
   (c) Management skills.
   (d) Both (a) and (b).
   (e) All of above.
8. Business Complexity indicates the complexity of the____________.
   (a) Only Business processes.
   (b) Only the information flows.
   (c) Both (a) and (b).
   (d) None of above.
9. A ________ value for the business complexity will imply that the enterprise will need to adapt to complex IT solutions.
   (a) Low.
   (b) High.
   (c) Very low.
   (d) None of above.
10. The technological changes are intensely required by the company to___________.
    (a) Reduce its business complexity.
    (b) Improve its efficiency.
    (c) Handle advanced needs of customers.
    (d) All of above.
11. Business complexity is ________ proportional to the degree of internationalization of the company.
    (a) Inversely.
    (b) Directly.
    (c) Either (a) or (b) depending upon company.
    (d) None of above.
12. __________ contribute their share to the business complexity.
    (a) Managing different legal and cultural issues.
    (b) Handling the rich diversity of customers and competitions.
    (c) The extent of divisionalization.
    (d) All of above.
13. A company will have a high business complexity if the company __________.
    (a) Markets a large number of business products.
    (b) Markets a large variety of business products.
    (c) Dependencies among activities in the company are large.
    (d) All of above.
14. It is often difficult to handle a large number of employees as large groups can become quiet unwieldy. This statement is:
    (a) True.
    (b) False.
    (c) Depends upon organization.
    (d) None of above.

15. The degree of ____________ required by the company, will result in different levels of business complexity.
(a) Customization.
(b) Vertical integration.
(c) Both (a) and (b).
(d) None of above.

16. As the number of dependencies, among the various activities decreases the business complexity ________.
(a) Increases.
(b) Decreases.
(c) Remains constant.
(d) Increases exponentially.

17. Degree of functional extension refers to the number of ________ directly managed within the enterprise.
(a) Strategic functions.
(b) Employees.
(c) Resources.
(d) Changes.

18. ________ is the change in the way business is conducted.
(a) Business transformation.
(b) Business complexity.
(c) Both (a) and (b).
(d) None of above.

19. The various levels to which the business may transform itself are:
(a) Local Automation.
(b) Internal Integration.
(c) Business Process Reengineering.
(d) Business network redesign.
(e) All of above.

20. __________ involves automation of local, independent procedures in order to improve the efficiency of the procedures.
(a) Internal Integration.
(b) Business Process Reengineering.
(c) Business network redesign.
(d) None of above.

21. ________ deals with integrating the business processes and the information system of the company.
(a) Internal Integration.
(b) Business network redesign.
(c) Local Automation.
(d) Both (a) and (c).

22. The business process structures change completely in ____________ levels.
(a) Local automation.
(b) Internal integration transformation.

(c) Both local automation and internal integration transformation.
(d) None of above.

23. _______ Level involves a partial or complete redesign of the various business processes of the company.
(a) Business Process Reengineering.
(b) Local automation.
(c) Both local automation and Business Process Reengineering.
(d) None of above.

24. What does BPR do?
(a) BPR helps in bringing out the deficiencies in the existing system.
(b) BPR gives way to implementing new systems.
(c) BPR helps in improving the existing systems.
(d) All of above.

25. BPR is considered:
(a) Time-consuming.
(b) Expensive.
(c) Both time-consuming and expensive.
(d) Neither time-consuming nor expensive.

26. In __________ level, the changes overcome the boundaries of the company and extend further to the external relationships.
(a) Local Automation.
(b) Internal Integration.
(c) Business Process Reengineering.
(d) Business Network Redesign.

27. The business transformation level __________ is characterized by the formation and management of strong inter-organization relationships.
(a) Internal Integration.
(b) Business Process Reengineering.
(c) Redefinition of company boundaries.
(d) None of above.

28. The framework developed by Ravarini et al. suggests the most suitable approach for ERP acquisition within the SME by presenting a cross analysis between the two dimensions- ______________ and ____________.
(a) Business complexity and business transformation level.
(b) Profit and expenditure.
(c) IT skills and management.
(d) None of above.

29. The Simplified approach, in the framework developed by Ravarini et al., is at__________.
(a) Position 1.
(b) Position 2.
(c) Position 3.
(d) Position 4.

30. It may happen that the enterprise is not ready for the organizational impacts it would be subjected to by business process reengineering. But the enterprise nevertheless feels the need to have an ERP system as the business complexity is quite high. Which approach for ERP acquisition would be most appropriate in this case?
(a) The simplified approach.
(b) The traditional approach.
(c) Information system check-up.
(d) Business process redesign.

31. Simplified approach implies:
(a) Implementation of ERP without BPR.
(b) Implementation of BPR without ERP.
(c) Implementation of ERP with BPR.
(d) Implementation of neither ERP nor BPR.

32. In ________ approach the company adapts its business processes in accordance with the requirements of the ERP system.
(a) Traditional.
(b) Simplified.
(c) Information system check-up.
(d) Business Process Redesign.

33. Some of the advantages of the simplified approach include:
(a) The time required for implementation of the ERP system is less.
(b) Adoption process is easier and cheaper.
(c) It requires comparatively less or no structural changes.
(d) All of above.

34. The effectiveness of the ______ approach depends on the flexibility of the existing information system.
(a) Simplified.
(b) Traditional
(c) Information system check-up.
(d) Business Process Redesign.

35. From the organizational perspective the simplified approach has:
(a) A lower impact on the SME structure-involving less structural changes
(b) A short-term impact.
(c) Low financial resources.
(d) All of above.

36. As the ________ just provides the automation and the integration of business processes it is unable to give a high performance enhancement in the business.
(a) Simplified approach.
(b) Traditional approach.
(c) Information system checkup.
(d) Business Process Redesign.

37. At which position is the Traditional approach, in the framework developed by Ravarini et al.
(a) Position 1.
(b) Position 2.

(c) Position 3.
(d) Position 4.

38. Which approach is the most obvious choice for a company that is ready to redesign its organization structure and the business processes; and is also characterized by high business complexity?
(a) Simplified.
(b) Traditional.
(c) Information system check-up.
(d) Business Process Redesign.

39. Traditional approach usually involves significant impacts from:
(a) Both cultural and organizational perspectives and higher investments.
(b) Cultural and organizational perspectives.
(c) Higher investments.
(d) None of above.

40. In which approach is BPR considered a prerequisite of ERP implementation?
(a) Traditional.
(b) Simplified.
(c) Information system check-up.
(d) Business Process Redesign.

41. SME's are often characterized by:
(a) The absence of long term planning.
(b) Inadequate technological and organizational innovations.
(c) Skill shortage and financial limitations.
(d) Organizational resistance to changes and lack of training.
(e) All of above.

42. The Information system check-up approach, in the framework developed by Ravarini et al., is at _______.
(a) Position 1.
(b) Position 2.
(c) Position 3.
(d) Position 4.

43. Information system check-up position is marked with:
(a) A high value for the business complexity.
(b) Low resistance within the organization for any changes in the existing system.
(c) Both (a) and (b).
(d) None of above.

44. Which is true for Information system check-up?
(a) The existing IT applications are analyzed.
(b) Infrastructure of the company is analyzed.
(c) Some modifications are made to make the existing information system more suitable.
(d) All of above.

45. The Information system check-up approach is suitable when a company has:
(a) A low business complexity.
(b) High resistance by the employees to any changes in the organization structure.

(c) Both (a) and (b).
(d) None of above.

46. At which position is Business Process Redesign approach, in the framework developed by Ravarini et al.?
(a) Position 1.
(b) Position 2.
(c) Position 3.
(d) Position 4.

47. It may happen that a company with a low ________ wants to redesign its organizational structure.
(a) Complexity.
(b) Number of employees.
(c) Financial resource.
(d) Customer base.

48. The situation in which a company with a low complexity wants to redesign its organizational structure strongly advocates for exploiting the benefits of ________.
(a) Business process reengineering.
(b) Information system.
(c) EDI.
(d) None of above.

49. The business processes should be redesigned to:
(a) Increase the performance.
(b) Bring dramatical change in organization.
(c) Reduce workforce.
(d) Reduce training needs.

50. The company needs to verify the coverage level of the existing software applications. If the coverage level is found to be ________ then the company must seriously consider the acquisition of an ERP system.
(a) Too low.
(b) High.
(c) Very high.
(d) Medium.

51. With the increase in number of employees in a company the business complexity of an organization ________.
(a) Increases.
(b) Decreases.
(c) Remains constant.
(d) Increases exponentially.

SECTION B

STATE TRUE OR FALSE

1. It is expected that ERP vendors will go one step further in increasing their market share, by addressing the business's needs of small and medium enterprises (SME's).
2. As the small and medium enterprises can't afford the expensive ERP systems designed for large enterprises, the ERP vendors need to come up with simpler and cheaper ERP solution suitable for SME's.
3. The adoption of an ERP system can have a profound impact on the overall organizational structure of an SME.
4. In order to evaluate the acquisition of an ERP system within SME's, a framework is required that will verify the suitability of the ERP systems to the organizational complexity of the SME's.
5. Business complexity and business transformation need to be carefully assessed by the framework being used for evaluating the ERP acquisition within the enterprise.
6. Ravarini et al., developed a simple framework for evaluating ERP acquisition within the small and medium enterprise.
7. The framework is a bidirectional matrix structure. The two dimensions are as follows: Business Complexity and Business transformation levels.
8. Business Complexity indicates the complexity of the business processes and the information flows.
9. A low value for the business complexity will imply that the enterprise will need to adapt complex IT solutions.
10. The technological changes are intensely required by the company to reduce its business complexity and improve its efficiency.
11. Business complexity is inversely proportional to the degree of internationalization of the company.
12. Managing different legal and cultural issues, handling the rich diversity of customers and competition and the extent of divisionalization all contribute their share to the business complexity.
13. A company will have a high business complexity if the company markets a small number and variety of business products.
14. It is often difficult to handle a large number of employees as large groups can become quiet unwieldy.
15. The degree of vertical integration, required by the company, will result in different levels of business complexity.
16. As the number of dependencies among the various activities decreases the business complexity increases.
17. Degree of vertical integration refers to the number of strategic functions directly managed within the enterprise.
18. A high degree of functional extension does not imply high business complexity.
19. Business transformation is the change in the way business is conducted.

20. An ERP acquisition is almost always accompanied with a certain level of business transformation.

21. The various levels to which the business may transform itself are as follows: Local Automation, Internal Integration, Business Process Reengineering and Business network redesign.

22. Local Automation involves automation of local, independent procedures in order to improve the efficiency of the procedures.

23. Local automation requires only little efforts and improves the performance of the business processes.

24. Internal Integration deals with integrating the business processes and the information system of the company.

25. As with local automation, the internal integration improves the performance of the business.

26. The business process structures change completely in both local automation and internal integration transformation levels.

27. Business Process Reengineering level involves a partial or complete redesign of the various business processes of the company.

28. BPR brings out the deficiencies in the existing system and gives way to implementing new systems and improving the existing systems.

29. BPR is neither time-consuming nor expensive.

30. In Business network redesign level, the changes overcome the boundaries of the company and extend further to the external relationships.

31. The business transformation level "Redefinition of company boundaries" is characterized by the formation and management of strong inter-organization relationships.

32. The framework developed by Ravarini et al., suggests the most suitable approach for ERP acquisition within the SME by presenting a cross analysis between the two dimensions: business complexity and business transformation level.

33. The Simplified approach, in the framework developed by Ravarini et al., is at position 1.

34. It may happen that the enterprise is not ready for the organizational impacts it would be subjected to by business process reengineering. But the enterprise nevertheless feels the need to have an ERP system as the business complexity is quite high. In this case the traditional approach for ERP acquisition would be most appropriate.

35. Simplified approach implies implementation of ERP without BPR.

36. In Simplified approach the company adapts its business processes in accordance with the requirements of the ERP system.

37. Some of the advantages of the simplified approach include the following: the time required for implementation of the ERP system is less, adoption process is easier and cheaper and it requires comparatively less or no structural changes.

38. The effectiveness of the simplified approach depends on the flexibility of the existing information system.

39. From the organizational perspective the simplified approach has a lower impact on the SME structure involving less structural changes, a short-term impact and low financial resources.

40. As the simplified approach just provides the automation and the integration of business processes it is unable to give a high performance enhancement in the business.

41. As BPR can be considered following the implementation of the ERP system by the company, therefore, the ERP system implemented should be flexible enough to map its procedures on the reengineering business processes through the adjustment of the various parameter values of the ERP system.

42. The Traditional approach, in the framework developed by Ravarini et al., is at position 3.

43. Simplified approach is the most obvious choice for a company that is ready to redesign its organization structure and the business processes; and is also characterized by high business complexity.

44. Traditional approach usually involves significant impacts from both cultural and organizational perspectives and higher investments.

45. In traditional approach BPR is not considered as a prerequisite of ERP implementation.

46. SME's are often characterized by the absence of long term planning, inadequate technological and organizational innovations, skill shortage, financial limitations, organizational resistance to changes and lack of training.

47. Since business process reengineering will deal with all these SME's characteristics it is expected that the traditional approach will bring about a dramatical change in the company and facilitate a high performance improvement.

48. The Information system check-up approach, in the framework developed by Ravarini et al., is at position 3.

49. Information system check-up position is marked with a high value for the business complexity as well as low resistance within the organization for any changes in the existing system.

50. In Information system check-up, the existing IT applications and infrastructure of the company is analyzed and some modifications are made to make the existing information system more suitable.

51. The Information system check-up approach is suitable when a company has a low business complexity and the employees are providing high resistance to any changes in the organization structure.

52. The Business Process Redesign approach, in the framework developed by Ravarini et al., is at position 4.

53. It may happen that a company with a low complexity wants to redesign its organizational structure.

54. The situation in which a company with a low complexity wants to redesign its organizational structure strongly advocates for exploiting the benefits of business process reengineering.

55. The business processes should be redesigned to increase the performance.

56. The company needs to verify the coverage level of the existing software applications. If the coverage level is found to be too low then the company must seriously consider the acquisition of an ERP system.

57. Business complexity increases with the increase in number of employees in a company.

SECTION C

FILL IN THE BLANKS

1. As the small and medium enterprises can't afford the expensive ERP systems designed for large enterprises, the ERP vendors need to come up with __________ and __________ ERP solution suitable for SME's.
2. The adoption of an ERP system can have a profound impact on the overall __________ of an SME.
3. In order to evaluate the acquisition of an ERP system within SME's, a framework is required that will verify the __________ of the ERP systems to the __________ of the SME's.
4. Business complexity and business transformation need to be carefully assessed by the __________ being used for evaluating the ERP acquisition within the enterprise.
5. __________ developed a simple framework for evaluating ERP acquisition within the small and medium enterprise.
6. The framework developed by Ravarini et al., is a __________ matrix structure. The two dimensions are: __________ and __________.
7. Business Complexity indicates the complexity of the __________ and the information flows.
8. A __________ value for the business complexity will imply that the enterprise will need to adapt complex IT solutions. In other words the technological changes are __________ required by the company to reduce its business complexity and improve its efficiency.
9. Business complexity is __________ proportional to the degree of internationalization of the company.
10. Managing different legal and cultural issues, handling the rich diversity of customers and competition and the extent of divisionalization all contribute their share to the__________.
11. A company will have a high business complexity if the company markets a large __________ and __________ of business products.
12. The business complexity of any company increases with the __________ in number of employees in a company.
13. It is often difficult to handle a large number of employees as large groups can become quiet__________.
14. The degree of __________required by the company results in different levels of business complexity.
15. As the number of dependencies among the various activities __________ the business complexity also increases.
16. Degree of__________ refers to the number of strategic functions directly managed within the enterprise.
17. A high degree of functional extension implies __________ business complexity.
18. __________ is the change in the way business is conducted.
19. An __________ is almost always accompanied with a certain level of business transformation.
20. The various levels to which the business may transform itself are as follows: __________, __________, __________and business network redesign.

21. ____________ involves automation of local, independent procedures in order to improve the efficiency of the procedures.

22. _________ deals with integrating the business processes and the information system of the company.

23. As with local automation, the internal integration serves to _________ the performance of the business.

24. The business process structures remain ________ in both local automation and internal integration transformation levels.

25. Business Process reengineering level involves a partial or complete redesign of the various ____________of the company.

26. BPR brings out deficiencies in the existing system and gives way to implementing new systems and improving the existing systems. BPR is ________ and also expensive.

27. In Business network redesign level the changes overcome the _________ of the company and extend further to the_________. Business partners can interact with each other through ________and continuous information exchange and competence sharing is facilitated by the business process integration.

28. Redefinition of company boundaries is characterized by the formation and management of ___________ inter-organization relationships.

29. The framework suggests the most _______ approach for ERP acquisition within the SME by presenting a cross analysis between the two dimensions: business complexity and business transformation level.

30. It may happen that the enterprise is not ready for the organizational impacts it would be subjected to by business process reengineering. But the enterprise nevertheless feels the need to have an ERP system as the business complexity is quite high. In this case the ___________ for ERP acquisition would be most appropriate.

31. Simplified approach implies implementation of ERP without__________.

32. In Simplified approach the company adapts its ___________ in accordance with the requirements of the ERP system.

33. The time required for implementation of the ERP system is _______ in the simplified approach.

34. Adoption process is ________and _________ in the simplified approach.

35. The effectiveness of the simplified approach depends on the flexibility of the existing_______.

36. From the organizational perspective the simplified approach has a _______ impact on the SME structure involving less structural changes, a short-term impact and low financial resources.

37. As the simplified approach just provides the automation and the integration of business processes it is unable to give a _______ performance enhancement in the business.

38. As BPR can be considered following the implementation of the ERP system by the company, therefore, the ERP system implemented should be _________ enough to map its procedures on the reengineering business processes through the adjustment of the various _________ of the ERP system.

39. _________________ Approach is the most obvious choice for a company that is ready to redesign its organization structure and the business processes; and is also characterized by high business complexity.

40. Traditional approach usually involves significant impacts from both ____________ perspectives and higher investments.
41. In traditional approach, ______ is considered a prerequisite of ERP implementation.
42. ________ are often characterized by the absence of long term planning, inadequate technological and organizational innovations, skill shortage, financial limitations, organizational resistance to changes and lack of training.
43. Since business process reengineering will deal with all these SME's characteristics it is expected that the ___________ will bring about a dramatical change in the company and facilitate a high performance improvement.
44. Information system check-up at position 3 is marked with a __________ for the business complexity as well as_______________ resistance within the organization for any changes in the existing system.
45. A situation characterized by low value for the business complexity as well as high resistance within the organization for any changes in the existing system does not justify the __________ of an ERP system.
46. In_____________, the existing IT applications and infrastructure of the company is analyzed and some modifications are made to make the existing information system more suitable.
47. It may happen that a company with a low complexity wants to redesign its____________. This situation strongly advocates for exploiting the benefits of___________.
48. In Business Process Redesign at position 4, the business processes should be __________ to increase the performance.
49. If the coverage level of the existing software applications is found to be too ______ then the company must seriously consider the acquisition of an________.

ANSWERS

SECTION A

(1) a (2) c (3) c (4) b (5) c (6) a (7) d (8) c (9) b (10) d
(11) b (12) d (13) d (14) a (15) b (16) b (17) a (18) a (19) e (20) d
(21) a (22) d (23) a (24) d (25) c (26) d (27) c (28) a (29) a (30) a
(31) a (32) b (33) d (34) a (35) d (36) a (37) b (38) b (39) a (40) a
(41) e (42) c (43) d (44) d (45) c (46) d (47) a (48) a (49) a (50) a
(51) a

SECTION B

(1) True (2) True (3) True (4) True (5) True (6) True (7) True (8) True
(9) False (10) True (11) False (12) True (13) False (14) True (15) True (16) False
(17) False (18) False (19) True (20) True (21) True (22) True (23) True (24) True
(25) True (26) False (27) True (28) True (29) False (30) True (31) True (32) True
(33) True (34) False (35) True (36) True (37) True (38) True (39) True (40) True

(41) True **(42)** False **(43)** False **(44)** True **(45)** False **(46)** True **(47)** True **(48)** True **(49)** False **(50)** True **(51)** True **(52)** True **(53)** True **(54)** True **(55)** True **(56)** True **(57)** True.

SECTION C

(1) simpler, cheaper **(2)** organizational structure **(3)** suitability, organizational complexity **(4)** framework **(5)** Ravarini et al **(6)** bidirectional, business Complexity, business transformation levels **(7)** business processes **(8)** high, intensely **(9)** directly **(10)** business complexity **(11)** number, variety **(12)** increase **(13)** unwieldy **(14)** vertical integration **(15)** increases **(16)** functional extension **(17)** high **(18)** business transformation **(19)** ERP acquisition **(20)** local automation, internal integration, business process reengineering **(21)** local automation **(22)** internal integration **(23)** improve **(24)** unchanged **(25)** business processes **(26)** time-consuming **(27)** boundaries, external relationships, EDI **(28)** strong **(29)** suitable **(30)** simplified approach **(31)** BPR **(32)** business processes **(33)** less **(34)** easier, cheaper **(35)** information system **(36)** lower **(37)** high **(38)** flexible, parameter values **(39)** traditional **(40)** cultural and organizational **(41)** BPR **(42)** SME's **(43)** traditional approach **(44)** low value, high **(45)** acquisition **(46)** Information system check-up **(47)** organizational structure, business process reengineering **(48)** redesigned **(49)** low, ERP system.

6

Chapter

Analytical Hierarchy Process

HIGHLIGHTS

- **Analytical Hierarchy Process Method**

Analytical Hierarchy Process is a method used for formalizing decision making when the number of choices are limited, each choice has a number of attributes and it is difficult to formalize some of those attributes. In this method we first decide the relative importance of the attributes by comparing each pair of attributes and ranking them on a certain scale. The next step comprises evaluating all the choices on each attribute.

Analytical hierarchy process makes use of phrases like "of equal importance", "strongly more important than", etc. to extract the preferences of the decision makers. In other words, the decision making depends on the use of these phrases in analytical hierarchy process.

6.1 ANALYTICAL HIERARCHY PROCESS METHOD

The method can be best illustrated with the help of an example.

Ram Mohan has job offers from four companies: BigWing, DeltaCare, Joyce Constructions and CrativeMinds Ltd. He is finding it difficult to decide which company to join. A number of factors such as location, salary, job profile and long term projects need to be considered carefully before he makes his final decision.

RamMohan wants a method that will assist him in making the correct decision by taking into consideration the factors and their relative importance. Analytical hierarchy process does just the same; it would serve as the best way for him to use analytical hierarchy process to solve his problem. Analytical hierarchy process would first formalize the relative importance and then evaluate each choice.

The following steps should be followed carefully in this technique.

Step 1. Decide the relative importance of the objectives (attributes/factors)

The scale used for ranking is as follows:

Table 6.1: Objectives Ranking Table

S No.	Objective statement	Score
1	Objective 'i' and 'j' are of equal importance	1
2	Objective 'i' is weakly more important than 'j'	3
3	Objective 'i' is strongly more important than 'j'	5
4	Objective 'i' is very strongly more important than 'j'	7
5	Objective 'i' is absolutely more important than 'j'	9
6	Intermediate values may be assigned	Any one of the intermediate values-2,4,6 ,8

i. Set a_{ii}=1 in the objective preference table
ii. If a_{ij}=k then we set a_{ji}=1/k in the objectives preference table.

Ram Mohan makes the following entries in his objective preference table based on his own preference s of location, salary, job profile and long-term prospects.

Table 6.2: Objectives Preferences

	Location	Salary	Job profile	Long term prospects
Location	1	1/5	1/3	1/2
Salary	5	1	2	4
Job profile	3	1/2	1	3
Long term prospects	2	1/4	1/3	1

Step 2. Determine the overall weight to be assigned to each objective. The weight assigned will lay between values 0 and 1.

The weights are determined as follows:

i. Take each entry and divide that entry in the table by the sum of the entries of the column it appears in.

For example, the location, location entry will work as follows: 1/ (1+5+3+2) =.091

ii. Average across each row to get the average values for each objective. This average value is the overall weight to be assigned to the objective in each row.

After completing these two steps, Ram Mohan gets the following table:

Table 6.3: Weights of Objectives

	Location	Salary	Job profile	Long term prospects	Average
Location	.091	.102	.091	.059	.086
Salary	.455	.513	.545	.471	.496
Job profile	.273	.256	.273	.353	.289
Long term prospects	.182	.128	.091	.118	.130

Step 3. The next step is to evaluate all the choices (in this case job) on each objective. The relative weight of each choice with regard to each objective is then obtained by average across the rows.

For example, suppose Ram Mohan gives the following preference values to the four jobs when taking location into consideration alone.

Table 6.4: Table of Preference Values

	BigWing	DeltaCare	JoyceConstructions	CreativeMinds ltd.
BigWing	1	1/2	1/3	5
DeltaCare	2	1	1/2	7
Joyce Constructions	3	2	1	9
CreativeMinds ltd.	1/5	1/7	1/9	1

He then begins to calculate the relative scores for 'location' objective by first normalizing (dividing the entry by the sum of entries in the column) and then averaging across the rows to get the relative weights of each job with regards to 'location'.

Table 6.5: Relative Location Scores

	BigWing	DeltaCare	Joyce Constructions	CreativeMinds	Average
BigWing	.161	.137	.171	.227	.174
DeltaCare	.322	.275	.257	.312	.293
Joyce Constructions	.484	.549	.514	.409	.489
CreativeMind	.032	.040	.057	.045	.044

The entries in the last column (average column) represent the relative location scores for the jobs.

That is, .174 is the relative location score for BigWing Company, .293 for DeltaCare, .489 for Joyce Constructions and .044 for CreativeMinds ltd.

Note: Ram Mohan performs step 3 for the remaining objectives salary, job profile and long term prospects

Step 4. Construct the table that shows the relative scores for each job, objective pair.

Note: He then constructs the main table with the various jobs marked as columns and the various objectives as rows of the table.

The relative scores for each objective (obtained from tables in step 3) appear as rows in the main table.

Suppose Ram Mohan gives the relative values for the objectives as follows:

Table 6.6: Relative Scores Table for each objective job pair

	BigWing	DeltaCare	Joyce Constructions	CreativeMinds
Location	.174	.293	.489	.044
Salary	.050	.444	.312	.194
Job profile	.210	.038	.354	.398
Long term prospects	.510	.012	.290	.188

Step 5. The job value is now calculated with the help of relative scores table values and the weights of objectives (in table 3).

RamMohan calculates the value for each job as follows:

The value for BigWing can be calculated as follows:
(.174)(.086)+(.050)(.496)+(.210)(.289)+(.510)(.130)=.164.
Similarly, the value for DeltaCare can be calculated as follows:
(.293)(.086)+(.444)(.496)+(.038)(.289)+(.012)(.130)=.256
The values for Joyce Construction and CreativeMinds ltd. are .335 and .238 respectively.
Ram Mohan, therefore, decides to join Joyce Constructions as the job value for Joyce Constructions is the highest.

Analytical Hierarchy process is being used in a large number of applications as it provides some structure on a decision making process.

LEARNING POINTS

1. Analytical Hierarchy Process is a method used for formalizing decision making when the number of choices are limited, each choice has a number of attributes and it is difficult to formalize some of those attributes.
2. In this method, we first decide the relative importance of the attributes and then rank them on a certain scale. The next step comprises evaluating all the choices on each attribute.
3. Analytical Hierarchy process is being used in a large number of applications as it provides some structure on a decision making process.

SUMMARY

Analytical Hierarchy Process (AHP) method is used for formalizing decision making when the number of choices is limited. Also, each choice has a number of attributes (also referred to as objectives or factors) where some of these attributes may be difficult to formalize. AHP assists in decision making by taking into consideration the factors for each choice and evaluating them to make the correct decision.

Analytical hierarchy process includes the following steps: the first step decides the relative importance of the objectives. In the second step the overall weight to be assigned to each objective is determined. In the third step all the choices on each objective are calculated and then the relative weights of each choice with regard to each objective are obtained by averaging across the rows.

In the fourth step, a table that shows the relative scores for each choice, objective pair is constructed. In the last step, the choice value is calculated for each choice. This calculation is done with the help of relative score values (table constructed in fourth step) and weight values of the objective (values determined in second step). The highest choice value becomes the selected choice.

POINTS TO REMEMBER

1. Analytical Hierarchy Process is a method used for formalizing decision making when the number of choices are limited, each choice has a number of attributes and it is difficult to formalize some of those attributes.

2. Analytical hierarchy process makes use of phrases like "of equal importance", "strongly more important than", etc. to extract the preferences of the decision makers.
3. In this method, we first decide the relative importance of the attributes and then rank them on a certain scale. The next step comprises evaluating all the choices on each attribute.
4. Analytical Hierarchy process is being used in a large number of applications as it provides some structure on a decision making process.
5. Steps performed in AHP are as follows:
   (a) Decide relative importance of the objectives.
   (b) Determine overall weight to be assigned to each objective.
   (c) Evaluate all the choices on each objective.
   (d) Construct the table that shows the relative scores for each choice objective pair.
   (e) Calculate the choice value with the help of relative scores table values and weights of objectives.
   (f) The choice with the highest value is selected.

REVIEW QUESTIONS

1. What is analytical hierarchy process? Why is it used?
2. Explain how AHP can be used to evaluate and select the ERP solution. Explain using any assumption if required.
3. Write a short note on fuzzy hierarchical analysis (FHA)
4. Give some of the limitations of AHP.

OBJECTIVE QUESTIONS

SECTION A

TICK THE CORRECT ANSWER

1. Analytical Hierarchy Process is a method used for formalizing decision making
   (a) When the number of choices is limited.
   (b) Each choice has a number of attributes.
   (c) It is difficult to formalize some of those attributes.
   (d) All of above.
2. In Analytical Hierarchy Process method we first:
   (a) Decide relative importance of the objectives.
   (b) Determine overall weight to be assigned to each objective.
   (c) Evaluate all the choices on each objective.
   (d) Construct the table that shows the relative scores for each choice objective pair.
3. Which is true about Analytical Hierarchy Process?
   (a) It is a method used for formalizing decision making when the number of choices are limited, each choice has a number of attributes and it is difficult to formalize some of those attributes.

(b) It makes use of phrases like "of equal importance", "strongly more important than", etc. to extract the preferences of the decision makers.
(c) Analytical Hierarchy process is being used in a large number of applications as it provides some structure on a decision making process.
(d) Both (a) and (b).
(e) All of above.

4. The second step in Analytical Hierarchy Process method is:
(a) The overall weight to be assigned to each objective is determined.
(b) All the choices on each objective are calculated and then the relative weights of each choice with regard to each objective are obtained by averaging across the rows.
(c) A table that shows the relative scores for each choice, objective pair is constructed.
(d) The choice value is calculated for each choice.

5. The third step in Analytical Hierarchy Process method is:
(a) The overall weight to be assigned to each objective is determined.
(b) All the choices on each objective are calculated and then the relative weights of each choice with regard to each objective are obtained by averaging across the rows.
(c) A table that shows the relative scores for each choice, objective pair is constructed.
(d) The choice value is calculated for each choice.

6. The fourth step in Analytical Hierarchy Process method is:
(a) The overall weight to be assigned to each objective is determined.
(b) All the choices on each objective are calculated and then the relative weights of each choice with regard to each objective are obtained by averaging across the rows.
(c) A table that shows the relative scores for each choice, objective pair is constructed.
(d) The choice value is calculated for each choice.

7. The last step in Analytical Hierarchy Process method is:
(a) The overall weight to be assigned to each objective is determined.
(b) All the choices on each objective are calculated and then the relative weights of each choice with regard to each objective are obtained by averaging across the rows.
(c) A table that shows the relative scores for each choice, objective pair is constructed.
(d) The choice value is calculated for each choice with the help of relative scores table values and weights of objectives and the choice with the highest value is selected.

SECTION B

STATE TRUE OR FALSE

1. Analytical Hierarchy Process is a method used for formalizing decision making when the number of choices are limited, each choice has a number of attributes and it is difficult to formalize some of those attributes.
2. In this method we first decide the relative importance of the attributes by comparing each pair of attributes and ranking them on a certain scale. The next step comprises evaluating all the choices on each attribute.
3. Analytical hierarchy process does not make use of phrases like "of equal importance", "strongly more important than", etc. to extract the preferences of the decision makers.

4. Analytical Hierarchy process is being used only in a small number of applications as it does not provide any structure on a decision making process.
5. Each choice in Analytical Hierarchy Process (AHP) method has a number of attributes (also referred to as objectives or factors) where some of these attributes may be difficult to formalize.
6. AHP assists in decision making by taking into consideration the factors for each choice and evaluating them to make the correct decision.
7. In the first step of Analytical hierarchy process, the relative importance of the objectives is decided.
8. In the second step of Analytical hierarchy process, the overall weight to be assigned to each objective is determined.
9. In the third step of Analytical hierarchy process, a table that shows the relative scores for each choice, objective pair is constructed.
10. In the fourth step of Analytical hierarchy process, all the choices on each objective are calculated and then the relative weights of each choice with regard to each objective are obtained by averaging across the rows.
11. In the last step of Analytical hierarchy process, the choice value is calculated for each choice. This calculation is done with the help of relative score values (table constructed in fourth step) and weight values of the objective (values determined in second step).
12. The lowest choice value becomes the selected choice.

SECTION C

FILL IN THE BLANKS

1. Analytical Hierarchy Process is a method used for formalizing decision making when the number of choices are__________, each choice has a number of attributes and it is __________ to formalize some of those attributes.
2. In Analytical Hierarchy Process method, we first decide the relative importance of the __________by comparing each pair of attributes and ranking them on a certain scale.
3. The second step in Analytical Hierarchy Process method comprises of evaluating all the __________ on each attribute.
4. Analytical hierarchy process makes use of phrases like “of equal importance”, “strongly more important than”, etc. to extract the __________ of the__________.
5. Analytical Hierarchy process is being used in a large number of applications as it provides some structure on __________.
6. Each choice in Analytical Hierarchy Process method has a number of __________ (also referred to as objectives or factors) where some of these attributes may be __________ to formalize.
7. AHP assists in __________ by taking into consideration the factors for each choice and evaluating them to make the correct decision.
8. The __________ step of Analytical hierarchy process method decides the relative importance of the objectives.

9. In the second step of Analytical hierarchy process method, the __________ to be assigned to each objective is determined.
10. In the third step of Analytical hierarchy process method, all the choices on each objective are calculated and then the _____________ of each choice with regard to each objective are obtained by averaging across the____________.
11. In the _________ step of Analytical hierarchy process method, a table that shows the relative scores for each choice, objective pair is constructed.
12. In the last step, the _________ is calculated for each choice. This calculation is done with the help of relative score values (table constructed in fourth step) and ________ values of the objective (values determined in second step).
13. The ___________ choice value becomes the selected choice.

ANSWERS

SECTION A

(1) **d** (2) **a** (3) **e** (4) **a** (5) **b** (6) **c** (7) **d.**

SECTION B

(1) True **(2)** True **(3)** False **(4)** False **(5)** True **(6)** True **(7)** True **(8)** True **(9)** False **(10)** False **(11)** True **(12)** False.

SECTION C

(1) limited, difficult **(2)** attributes **(3)** choices **(4)** preferences, decision makers **(5)** decision making process **(6)** attributes, difficult **(7)** decision making **(8)** first **(9)** overall weight **(10)** relative weights, rows **(11)** fourth **(12)** choice value, weight **(13)** highest.

7
Chapter
ERP Implementation

HIGHLIGHTS

- **ERP IMPLEMENTATION**
  - ERP Implementation Phases
  - Implementation Strategies, Approaches and Methodology
  - Role of Consultants, Vendors and End-users in ERP Implementation
  - Critical Success Factors
  - ERP Effectiveness Model
  - ERP Success Inhibitors and Accelerators
  - Hidden Cost in ERP Implementation
  - Return of Investment in ERP Implementation

Implementing an ERP System is a large undertaking. It usually becomes a mind-altering experience for the people involved in its implementation. As ERP implementation is a complex, resource-consuming and risky activity, the company must follow a sound methodology. A sound implementation methodology will effectively increase the chances of success of the ERP implementation. A successful ERP implementation also depends upon the implementation approach and the implementation strategies chosen by the organization.

7.1 ERP IMPLEMENTATION PHASES

The different phases involved in implementation of an ERP system shown in Figure 7.1 are as follows:

1. **Pre-Evaluation Screening of ERP packages**
   It is a short phase that deals with eliminating those ERP packages that are not at all suitable for the business processes of the company. It supports the package evaluation phase by limiting the number of packages to be evaluated to just a few.

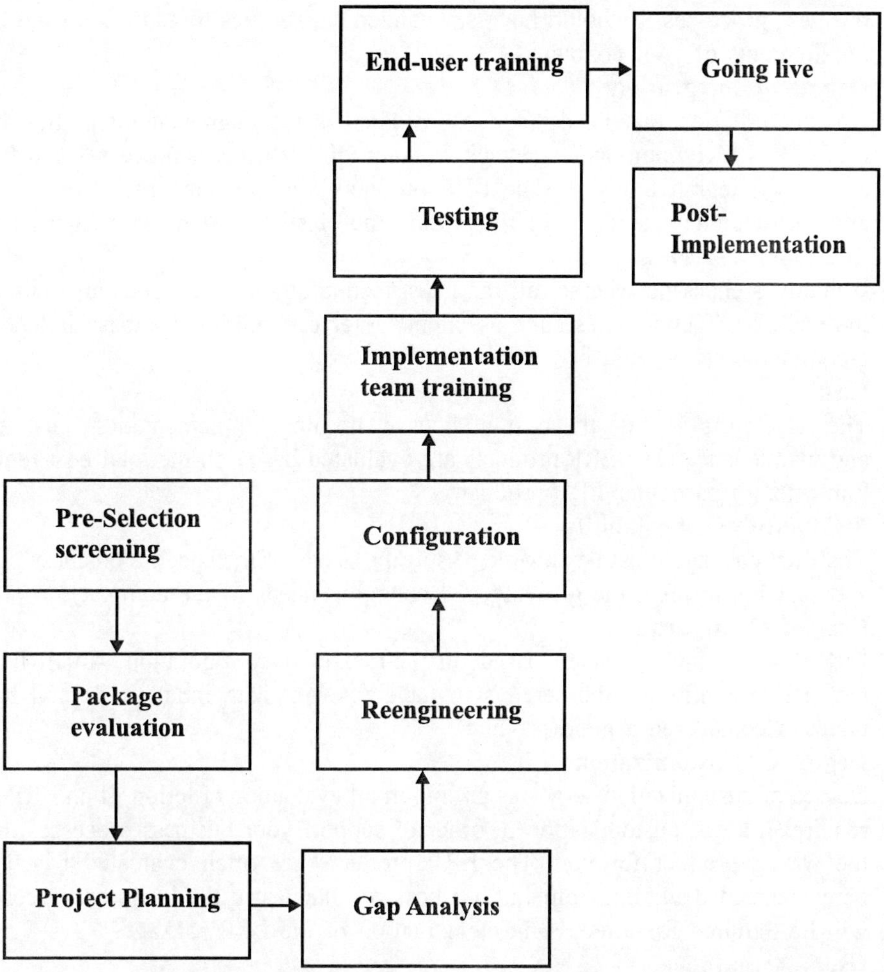

Fig. 7.1. Different Phases of ERP Implementation Life cycle

2. **Package Evaluation**

   This phase has a lot of significance in the ERP implementation life cycle. The success of an ERP implementation depends largely on the ERP package selected for implementation. A right ERP package selected will almost decide the success of the implementation. The evaluation and selection of ERP software is a complex task. This task must be accomplished as a fact-based process that minimizes the risks associated and helps to make a well-informed decision. The evaluation and selection of an ERP package involves considering the following criteria:

   i. **Functional Fit**

   It involves checking whether all functional aspects of the business are duly covered in the ERP package. The ERP package should be functionally-fit with the company's business processes. It should have specialized capabilities to address all the business requirements of your company.

ii. **Degree of Integration**
Another criterion that needs to be considered is the degree of integration between the various ERP components. Check whether all the business processes and functions are fully integrated or not. The ERP products are evaluated based on efforts and amount of money required for integrating the existing system with ERP package.

iii. **Technology /Trends**
It involves checking whether all the latest technology and IT trends are supported by the package. Technologies such as client/server capabilities, database independence, e-commerce etc. should be included.

iv. **Cost**
The total costs include the cost of license, training, implementation, customization and maintenance. The ERP products are evaluated based on the total cost required to implement a particular ERP product.

v. **Flexibility and Scalability**
The ERP package must be flexible to suit the needs of the specific business processes and scalable to meet the growing and changing needs of the company.

vi. **Ease of Configuration**
ERP products are evaluated based on their ease of configuration. An ERP product that easily configures the screens to have relevant data input fields and back-end tables is considered a good product.

vii. **Degree of Customization**
Degree of customization serves as an important evaluation criterion. If an ERP product requires a lot of customization in order to support your business processes then it is the wrong product for you. The ERP products are often evaluated based on the percentage of deviation from the business or changes in the business processes that will be required for effective implementation of the ERP package.

viii. **Users Acceptance**
It is defined as the percentage of acceptance of the user friendliness of the screens/ interfaces as well as the process flows by the users. The higher the rate of acceptance, the more user-friendly the product is considered to be.

ix. **Quick Implementation**
An ERP package is considered to be good if it requires less time to get implemented. Implementation time thus becomes a good evaluation criterion for ERP products.

x. **Complexity**
ERP packages are often big, complex and require maintenance. A complex ERP package will make the ERP implementation a difficult exercise.

Some other evaluation criteria for ERP products include ability to support multi-site planning and control, local support infrastructure, availability of the reference sites, performance level, easy information retrieval, standardized practices, security, internationalization and availability of regular updates. The evaluation of the ERP packages based on the above-mentioned criteria enables the company to select the best ERP package that best meets the needs and practices of the company.

The key to successful ERP implementation is selecting the right ERP software and the right ERP vendor who will provide you with a fast and effective implementation. The ERP vendors should be evaluated based on the functionality of their applications and their ability to support business transformation in order to achieve the objectives of the company. The ability of the vendor to transform the business processes can be determined as follows:

i. **Evaluate his interest in helping the company to achieve the defined objectives.** A good ERP vendor will provide the company with a preliminary implementation. He would plan even before the contract is signed. He would assist the team to identify and learn the complex business processes of the company. He would explain the business value to be derived from ERP system, the support of the system to the day-to-day operations of the company and the installation details to the implementation team.
ii. **Check the customer references of the ERP vendor.** The references should be checked carefully in order to understand the implementation success rate of the vendor. Checking the customer references ensures that the claims of the vendor are substantiated and not just brochure-ware. Effectively rating the vendor's track record and true capabilities is an important factor to consider when selecting an ERP vendor.
iii. **Completely understand the implementation methodology of the vendor.** The implementation methodology of the ERP vendor should be highly tailor-able to the specific needs and expertise of the company. An implementation methodology that is well-tailored to the known requirements of the company will help the company to achieve the desired results and ensure that maximum return on investment (ROI) is received. While selecting the ERP vendor, some traits need to be considered. They include technical expertise, domain knowledge, adequate manpower, project management skills and good involvement.

Some evaluation criteria for vendors are as follows:

i. **Operational coverage**
It deals with finding out whether the vendor is a local developer or a truly international organization.
ii. **Range of business applications**
It is important to find out the number of departmental functions and the business applications that the ERP vendor supports.
iii. **Company character and direction**
The ERP vendor company's objectives, policies and working style are considered to decide whether to select the vendor or not.
iv. **Training offered by the ERP vendor**
The vendor selected should provide training to users at various levels and in various details. A good ERP vendor will provide familiarization programmes for all the employees of the company, executive programmes for the top management and functional training for the members of the implementation team as well as end-user training.
v. **Vendor's experience**
The vendor's experience is an important criterion to evaluate the vendors. A vendor who has a long existence in the field will certainly provide better support and service.

vi. **Vendor's financial position**
The vendors may be evaluated based on their financial track record.

vii. **Pricing models offered by vendors**
The pricing models being offered by different vendors must be examined carefully. If a vendor's quote is far below that of other vendors then the deal is "too good to be true". In case you select such a vendor then chances are either vendor is not providing you with all the features or benefits or the ERP vendor is going to leave you, plagued later, with hidden costs.

3. **Project Planning**
This phase designs the implementation process. Project planning builds a road map that is used throughout the implementation. The implementation team develops the project plan using the project planning tools (gnatt charts etc.). Bernard Golden, CEO, Navica Inc., a consulting firm in San Carlos, California highlighted the significance of a project plan when he said "don't do any project without a plan, particularly an ERP project which touches almost every part of your organization." An ERP project implementation will be successful only if it has been approached with a great deal of careful planning.

A committee is constituted to develop the project plan. It meets periodically to review the progress and frame the future course of actions. It is also called implementation team. Project planning involves preparing time schedules, fixing deadlines, identifying the roles and assigning responsibilities. Various organizational resources that will be utilized for the implementation effort are determined. Crucial decisions such as when to start the ERP implementation, how to do it and when it should be completed are taken in this phase. Deciding what to do in case of contingencies, the corrective actions that should be taken when the situation is out of control and how to monitor the progress constitutes the important points that are well planned by the implementation team in this phase.

A good project plan will describe all the activities in an implementation. It will include the entire technical area to support technical project management. It will address interfaces, data conversion and authorizations to avoid mistakes at a later stage.

It would prove beneficial to involve users in your ERP project planning phase. Andy Klee, president of Klee Associates Inc., a consulting firm in Cedaredge, Colombia said "Involve users in your ERP Project planning phase". He further added "the software is not going to do you much good if you don't have employee buy-in."

4. **Gap Analysis**
Gap analysis is the process that identifies the gaps by mapping the expectations of the company with the capabilities of the ERP product.

5. **Business Process Reengineering**
Business Process Reengineering is a more efficient way to do business. It analyses the various business processes of the organization in order to identify and practice the best way of doing work. Hammer and Champy defined BPR as "the fundamental rethinking and radical redesign of business processes to achieve dramatic improvements in critical, contemporary measures of performance such as cost, quality, service and speed."

Business Process Reengineering reduces the workforce size. But the involvement of ERP in BPR tries to do away with this ill effect of BPR. It works together with BPR to bring a change in the business and still keep the jobs of thousand of employees save. BPR and ERP together give way to implement new systems and the long pending improvements in the existing systems.

Business Process Reengineering is seen as a prerequisite for going ahead with ERP implementation by most of the ERP experts. The ERP experts often suggest doing an in-depth BPR study before taking up ERP implementation.

BPR attempts to maximize the business productivity through restructuring and reorganizing the business processes, information workflows, human resources as well as the divisions and departments in the organization. BPR involves the following activities:

i. **Understand**
   In this step attempts are made to understand the existing system.

ii. **Simplify**
   It deals with drafting and framing the possibilities and ways to simplify or improve or eliminate the processes in the existing system.

iii. **Automate**
   It deals with implementing the new system with the help of ERP.

6. **Installation and Configuration**
   Installation and configuration phase is considered to be the main functional area in the ERP implementation life cycle. In this phase attempts are made to synchronize the existing practices of the company with the ERP package. Modification of the ERP software results in problems such as code errors and difficulty when upgrading to new versions. Therefore the ERP experts strongly advise the company going for ERP implementation to avoid modifying their ERP software. The ERP software configuration is complex, time consuming and costly.

7. **Training of Implementation Team**
   It is imperative that the implementation team is given a rigorous training by the ERP vendor and the hired consultants on how to implement the ERP system.

8. **Testing**
   The testing phase enables the implementation team to discover problems that may require some minor modifications before the ERP system goes live. Testing your ERP system with real case and extreme case scenarios will allow the implementation team to identify any errors in the process and information flows before live deployment. It is crucial to test all of the company data, procedures and processes in order to find the weak links in the ERP system. These bugs should then be fixed before the launch of the system.

   The testing phase helps the implementation team to minimize the errors after deployment as well as maximize the potential of the new system.

9. **Going live**
   In this phase the old system is removed and the new system is officially proclaimed operational. The company will use the new ERP system for doing business.

10. **End User Training**
    The end users need to be trained in order to ensure the acceptance and readiness of the new system. Some organizations use an in-house training approach while other organizations prefer using training consultants.

11. Post-Implementation

In this phase the system is upgraded as and when new versions or technologies are introduced. The post-implementation phase includes regular monitoring of the system, tuning the hardware or software and performing audit of the ERP system.

LEARNING POINTS

1. As ERP implementation is a complex, resource-consuming and risky activity, the company must follow a sound methodology.
2. The different phases involved in implementation of an ERP system include: Pre-Evaluation Screening of ERP packages, project planning, package evaluation, gap analysis, business process reengineering, installation and configuration, training of implementation team, testing, going live, end user training, post-implementation.
3. Pre-Evaluation Screening of ERP packages is a short phase that deals with eliminating those ERP packages that are not at all suitable for the business processes of the company
4. Evaluation and selection of ERP software must be accomplished as a fact-based process that minimizes the risks associated and helps to make a well-informed decision.
5. The evaluation and selection of an ERP package involves considering the following criteria: functional fit, degree of Integration, technology /trends, cost, flexibility and scalability, ease of Configuration, degree of Customization, users Acceptance, quick implementation and complexity.
6. The ERP vendors should be evaluated based on the functionality of their applications and their ability to support business transformation in order to achieve the objectives of the company.
7. Project planning phase designs the implementation process. It builds a road map that is used throughout the implementation. The implementation team develops the project plan using the project planning tools (gnatt charts etc.)
8. Gap analysis is the process that identifies the gaps by mapping the expectations of the company with the capabilities of the ERP product.
9. Business Process Reengineering is a more efficient way to do business. It analyses the various business processes of the organization in order to identify and practice the best way of doing work.
10. Installation and configuration phase is considered to be the main functional area in the ERP implementation life cycle. In this phase attempts are made to synchronize the existing practices of the company with the ERP package.
11. The testing phase enables the implementation team to discover problems that may require some minor modifications before the ERP system goes life.
12. In going live phase the old system is removed and the new system is officially proclaimed operational. The company will use the new ERP system for doing business.

7.2 IMPLEMENTATION STRATEGIES

The different strategies for implementing ERP can be classified into organizational, technical and people strategies. The implementation strategies help to overcome the resistance of the workers to the ERP system and thereby the success of the ERP implementation.

1. **Organizational Strategies**
   The organizational strategies include change strategy development, change management techniques, project management, communication and coordination, organizational structure and resources, IS function characteristics, managerial style and ideology.
2. **People strategies**
   The people strategies include management and staff attitudes, user involvement and training.
3. **Technical strategies**
   They include adequacy of in-house technical expertise, time and cost of ERP implementation, ERP complexity and various technical aspects of the ERP installation.

   The top management must analyze the two fundamental sources of employee's resistance to ERP implementation-perceived risk and employee habit. Habit simply refers to the current practices that a person routinely performs. Perceived risks refer to an employee's perception of the risk associated with the decision to accept the new system.

Some of the change management strategies for ERP implementation are as follows:

1. **Effective Communication system**
   A major strategy for changing the attitudes of the potential users of the new ERP system is to establish an effective communication system. An effective communication strategy is to inform the potential users about the various benefits of the ERP system. Another communication strategy is to provide users a general description of how the implemented ERP system will work. This strategy will ensure a receptive attitude for the new ERP system from the users.
2. **Cost Minimization Strategy**
   The top management can use the cost Minimization Strategy to influence the effective components of users' attitudes. In this strategy the user's adoption costs are kept to a minimum and the users are convinced by the change agents that their net outcome of the ERP adoption process will be positive. The cost Minimization Strategy should operate at both the individual worker and the influential groups' level. An employee will develop an interest in the new ERP system if he is made to understand that the ERP system will enhance his job. Similarly, if the influential groups are convinced that change in the balance of power in the organization will be in their favour then they will develop a positive adoption attitude for the new system.
3. **Differentiation Strategy**
   A user's perceived high quality of the ERP system has a positive impact on his attitude towards the system. An ERP system that is user friendly will have good chances of success where as an ERP system with an unwieldy user interface will not be accepted by the users.
4. **Providing Hands-on Training**
   ERP users will be reluctant to use the new system if they do not know how it works. Training provides hands-on experience to the users. Trained users are able to appreciate the quality attributes as well as the potential benefits of the ERP system. Training also

helps in developing positive attitudes of the users towards the system as the users are now not only aware of how the system works but also know the benefits the new system has to offer.

5. **Carefully timing the introduction of the new system**
   The management should delay the introduction of the ERP system until a positive attitude is developed and sustained among the potential users. It will be a bad experience if the ERP system is introduced at a time when a critical mass of employees is not ready for the change.
6. **Ensuring the support of opinion leaders**
   A very effective implementation strategy is to ensure the support of well known individuals and opinion leaders. If the group leaders are convinced to participate effectively in the ERP implementation process then the other employees also show their readiness.
7. **Management's commitment and support**
   The management has to play the main role in successful ERP implementation. The management must be sure that the employee's anxiety and resistance to the ERP system is well under control. The management must participate in creating effective awareness among the employees for the new system. The complete support and commitment of the management is the ultimate strategy that will help set the stage for ERP implementation success.

LEARNING POINTS

1. The implementation strategies help to overcome the resistance of the workers to the ERP system and thereby the success of the ERP implementation.
2. The different strategies for implementing ERP can be classified into organizational, technical and people strategies.
3. Organizational strategies include change strategy development, change management techniques, project management, communication and coordination, organizational structure and resources, IS function characteristics, managerial style and ideology.
4. People strategies include management and staff attitudes, user involvement and training.
5. Technical strategies include adequacy of in-house technical expertise, time and cost of ERP implementation, ERP complexity and various technical aspects of the ERP installation.
6. Some of the change management strategies for ERP implementation are as follows: effective communication system, cost minimization strategy, differentiation strategy, providing hands-on training, carefully timing the introduction of the new system, ensuring the support of opinion leaders.
7. The top management can use the Cost Minimization Strategy to influence the affective components of users' attitudes.

7.3 IMPLEMENTATION APPROACHES

ERP implementation is complex, costly, resource-consuming and risky activity. The implementation approach chosen by the organization decides the costs and risks of the ERP implementation project. Three different approaches to ERP implementation include big-bang, phased or skeleton and parallel approach. Each implementation approach has its own pros and cons. After carefully evaluating the pros and cons of all the three implementation approaches, an organization should select the implementation approach that works best for that organization.

7.3.1 Big-Bang Approach

In big-bang approach the switch between using the old systems and using the new ERP system happens at once. Every person starts using the new system at the same date and from that day onwards the old system is not used. For example, Quantum Corp. closed its operation world-wide for eight days to switch the systems. In big-bang implementation fewer interfaces are required between the different modules, the costs are generally reduced compared to the phased approach and the implementation time is shorter.

Big-bang approach focuses the organization for intense but relatively shorter time duration than phased approach. Big-bang approach not only addresses the long-term resource shortages but also condenses the pain of an ERP implementation project into short duration. A big-bang implementation approach is considered to be more risky than phased approach. Due to the short time duration; the ERP project is often rushed, the details are overlooked and fewer learning opportunities are incorporated in this approach.

The advantages of big-bang approach are as follows:

1. Shorter implementation time.
2. Low implementation cost.
3. No need for temporary interfaces.
4. The need to maintain and change legacy system is limited.

Some of the disadvantages of this approach are as follows:

1. Huge peak resources may be required.
2. The new system once implemented cannot readily go back to the legacy system.
3. The working of the system cannot be demonstrated until the system gets fully installed.
4. The implementation team gets fewer hands-on opportunities to gain knowledge.

7.3.2 Skeleton or Phased Approach

The Skeleton implementation is a phased approach. It provides usable functionality incrementally whether by functional business area or geography. In the Phased Approach the system component is brought online serially. The system component is then operated and its performance is observed. If the performance of the component is found to be satisfactory then the implementation team moves on to the implementation of the next phase. With the successful completion of each phase the system is a little nearer to be fully adopted.

The biggest advantage of Skeleton approach is that the project implementation team gets enough time to plan, customize and test the system. Lessons learnt from the previous phases are utilized in the next phase to avoid making costly mistakes.

But Skeleton or Phased Approach lacks the urgency and focus of a big-bang approach. This often leads to "change fatigue" which is often harmful for the project implementation. The employees lose focus and feel exhausted.

Some of the advantages of the Skeleton approach are as follows:

1. The peak resource requirements are less as compared to big-bang approach.
2. Risks in the phased approach are low.
3. Legacy system can be returned.
4. Implementation team gains knowledge in each phase.
5. The time between development of the system and its use is reduced.
6. The project manager can demonstrate the working system.

Its disadvantages are as follows:

1. The need to maintain and revise legacy systems is more.
2. There is a higher risk of losing personnel to turnover.
3. Implementation time is more.
4. There is a heavy use of temporary interfaces.
5. Involves higher cost.

7.3.3 Parallel Approach

In this approach the old system and the new system run parallel in the organization. The advantage of the parallel approach is that the users can get used to the new system and meanwhile do their work using the old system.

LEARNING POINTS

1. The implementation approach chosen by the organization decides the costs and risks of the ERP implementation project.
2. Each implementation approach has its own pros and cons. After carefully evaluating the pros and cons of all the three implementation approaches, an organization should select the implementation approach that works best for that organization.
3. Three different approaches to ERP implementation include big-bang, phased or skeleton and parallel approach.
4. In big-bang approach the switch between using the old systems and using the new ERP system happens at once. Every person starts using the new system at the same date and from that day onwards the old system is not used.
5. The Skeleton implementation is a phased approach. It provides usable functionality incrementally whether by functional business area or geography. In the Phased Approach the system component is brought online serially.
6. In the Parallel approach the old system and the new system are running parallel in the organization. The advantage of the parallel approach is that the users can get used to the new system and meanwhile do their work using the old system.

7.4 IMPLEMENTATION METHODOLOGY

An ERP implementation methodology is a roadmap to an ERP implementation. The purpose of the implementation methodology is to deliver the implementation according to the specifications, within budget and on time. A structured and well-constructed implementation methodology focuses on defined processes, users and strategies to provide a clear understanding of the business environment and goals. A good implementation methodology leads to the shortest path to pay-off and fewest risks. The implementation team should strictly adhere to the methodology for success. The implementation methodology provided by the vendor or in-house consultants must be highly tailor-able to the needs of the company. Both the ERP vendors as well as the consultants have developed their own implementation methodologies.

An ERP implementation methodology serves as a model to deliver measurable return on investment quickly and effectively. The ERP vendors and consulting firms develop the implementation methodology through refinements and application of best practices based on their expertise and industry experiences gained over several years in business.

Some ERP methodologies are "Accelerated SAP" from SAP, "The Total Solution" from Ernst and Young LLP, "Fast Track Work plan" from Deloitte and Touche.

7.4.1 Accelerated SAP (ASAP)

SAP has introduced an effective implementation methodology called "Accelerated SAP". It is also referred to as ASAP. ASAP is a detailed project plan by SAP that describes all the activities in an ERP implementation. SAP makes use of its extensive knowledge gained from implementing thousands of R/3 SAP modules to date in designing this implementation methodology. ASAP helps to reduce the SAP implementation time to less than six months.

ASAP implementation methodology consists of five phases. These are as follows:

1. **Project Preparation**
   In project preparation phase proper planning and an assessment of the organization's readiness to change is done. It deals with determining the following:
   - **i.** All the decision makers of the company are in support of the implementation project.
   - **ii.** The objectives of the project are clear.
   - **iii.** An efficient decision making process exists and the company is ready for change.
2. **Business Blueprint**
   It is Accelerated SAP visual model of the future state of the business. During this phase the broad scope of the SAP's R/3 module is narrowed down to fit the industry-specific processes. The business blueprint model supports the implementation team to clearly define the scope and focus on the specific R/3 processes that are required to conduct the business smoothly and efficiently.
3. **Realization**
   In this phase the R/3 system is configured. It is Accelerated SAP two-step process. In the first step the baseline system is configured. In the second step the ERP system is fine-tuned to meet the necessary requirements of the business.

4. **Final Preparation**
   This phase involves making necessary adjustments to the system, conducting final system tests and completing the training of the end users.
5. **Go Live and Support**
   This phase involves developing procedures and measures to review the benefits of the R/3 investment on an ongoing basis.

7.4.2 The Total Solution

"The Total Solution" methodology has been developed by Ernst and Young LLP, Accelerated SAP consulting firm. This system reengineering approach has five components. These are as follows:

1. **Value proposition**
   In this phase the implementation team finds out the value of the implementation project by considering the following points:
   - **i.** Is the technology investment justified?
   - **ii.** Does the technology match with the objectives and goals of the company?
   - **iii.** Is the management ready to support the change?
   - **iv.** Is the organization ready for change?
   - **v.** What are the milestones that will measure the progress of the implementation project?
   - **vi.** Who are the decision makers?
   - **vii.** Is value being delivered throughout the process?

After carefully considering these points, the business case is built for the company. If the business case makes sound business sense then the implementation team moves to the second phase.

2. **Reality Check**
   In this phase the readiness of the organization for change is assessed. Hidden agendas, if any, are discovered as well as the expectations of the management are figured out. Doing this reality check is important as it helps the implementation team to prepare its implementation strategy accordingly and come up with a system that will fully meet the expectations of the company.
3. **Aligned Approach**
   The short term and the long term expectations from the system are set. The implementation is preceded in well defined modules by adhering to Accelerated SAP "best-fit approach. The results of each module completed are communicated to the management. An effective communication keeps the management well-informed and alert.
4. **Success Dimension**
   In this phase teamwork is emphasized. People with good skills in process management, change management, knowledge management and industry skills are absorbed into the project implementation team to ensure the project's success.
5. **Delivering Value**
   This phase deals with measuring results of the system.

7.4.3 The Fast Track Work Plan

The Fast Track methodology developed by Deloitte and Touche consulting firm enhances and accelerates the ERP implementation project. The five implementation phases of the Fast Track Work plan methodology include scoping and planning, visioning and targeting, redesign, configuration, testing and delivery. The implementation methodology helps the company to achieve a high quality business transformation speedily.

Table 7.1 gives some ERP implementation methodologies developed by different ERP vendors and consultancy firms.

Table 7.1: ERP Implementation Methodologies

S. No	ERP Implementation Methodologies	ERP Provider
1.	Oracle Application Implementation Methodology (AIM)	Oracle
2.	Accelerated SAP	SAP
3.	The Total Solution	Ernst & Young LLP
4.	The Fast Track Work Plan	Deloitte & Touche Consulting Group/ ICS

LEARNING POINTS

1. An ERP implementation methodology is a roadmap to an ERP implementation. The purpose of the implementation methodology is to deliver the implementation according to the specifications, within budget and on time.
2. Some ERP methodologies are "Accelerated SAP" from SAP, "The Total Solution" from Ernst and Young LLP, "Fast Track Work plan" from Deloitte and Touche.
3. SAP has introduced an effective implementation methodology called "Accelerated SAP". It is also referred to as ASAP.
4. ASAP implementation methodology consists of five phases. These are as follows: project preparation, business blueprint, realization, final preparation, go live and support
5. "The Total Solution" methodology has been developed by Ernst and Young LLP. This system reengineering approach has five components. These are as follows: value proposition, reality check, aligned approach, success dimension, delivering value.
6. The Fast Track methodology developed by Deloitte and Touche consulting firm enhances and accelerates the ERP implementation project. The five implementation phases of the Fast Track Work plan methodology include scoping and planning, visioning and targeting, redesign, configuration, testing and delivery. The implementation methodology helps the company to achieve a high quality business transformation speedily.

7.5 ROLE OF CONSULTANTS, VENDORS AND USERS IN ERP IMPLEMENTATION

The ERP vendors, consultants and the end users all have a significant role to play in a successful ERP implementation. An ERP vendor is a software firm that design, develop and implement ERP packages. Consultants are the people who specialize in developing effective techniques and methodologies for ensuring a successful ERP implementation. End users are the people who will use the ERP system to do their work in the company. The ERP vendors, consultants and end-users are considered to be the three major players in an ERP implementation.

7.5.1 Role of ERP Vendors

An ERP vendor has many responsibilities to fulfill. An ERP vendor needs to have qualified, in-house and client-centric consultants that are capable of advising, instructing, applying best solutions and resolving issues. A vendor who has implementation consultants on staff has a higher rate of ERP implementation success than an ERP vendor who uses third party consultants. An ERP vendor needs to perform absolutely well as most of the time it is the ERP vendor who is blamed when the anticipated results from the new system do not materialize.

Some of the responsibilities of an ERP vendor are as follows:

1. An ERP vendor should deliver the product along with its documentation to the company after the contract has been signed.
2. The vendor should provide a preliminary implementation plan even before the contract is signed.
3. The software provider must identify and learn about the various business processes of the company. A qualified vendor will show the company how the ERP software will support the day-to-day operations of the company and meet the needs of the business.
4. The vendor should suggest best ways to implement the system. Most ERP vendors have by now developed effective implementation methodologies that are industry-specific.
5. The ERP vendor should fix any problem in the software that the implementation team encounters. The vendor must carry out the customization process if the company has taken decision to customize the ERP system to suit the business processes of the organization.
6. The vendor should carefully review the software competencies in the organization and take all necessary steps to remove the software deficiencies before going ahead with running the ERP system.
7. The vendor should conduct a formal survey to understand and document the current business processes and give appropriate suggestions for improvement.
8. The vendor must support company's project manager in developing, documenting, monitoring and managing the scope of project plan.

The different roles that an ERP vendor has to play are as follows:

1. **Innovator**
   ERP vendors are frequently coming out with inventions and modular improvements.
2. **Advisor**
   ERP vendor plays the role of an advisor in all the implementation phases.
3. **Change Agent**
   The vendor will lead the company successfully through change process. As a change agent, the vendor will reduce the complexity of business transformation and will prepare organization ready for change.

4. Trainer
The vendor will provide initial training for key users of the company. The key users are people who will play lead roles in the implementation of the ERP system. The objective of the vendor training is to show the key users how the system works.

7.5.2 ERP Consultants

ERP consultants are firms who specialize in developing implementation strategies and time-related methodologies. The experts in the consulting firms have an in-depth understanding of the strengths and weaknesses of the various ERP products offered by different vendors. They have an extensive knowledge of the ERP market and are well-conversant with the tricks and techniques of the trade. The ERP consultants have several years of hands-on ERP implementation experience with several industries. The cost of consultants is very high. Though hiring the consultants will be expensive for the company, yet it promises to pay high dividends. It is, therefore, in the best interest of the company that the consultants are hired as they are people with necessary know-how, right methodology and good analytical skills.

Some of the responsibilities of the consultants are as follows:

1. The consultants are responsible for effectively administrating each implementation phase.
2. The consultants analyze the ERP package and the business processes and accordingly address the customization issue.
3. The consultants are required to defend the ERP vendor when such defense is technically correct.
4. The consultants need to safeguard the interest of the company.
5. The consultants need to ask questions from the vendor so that vendor claims are verified before the product is purchased from a particular vendor.
6. The consultants should develop a knowledge base and train the employees so that they are able to work effectively on the ERP system when the ERP implementation project is complete and the consultants have all left. The ERP consultant therefore has several roles to play: as an administrator, as an analyst, as a trainer and as a mediator between the company and the ERP vendor.
7. The ERP consultants often charge a high fee. Some of the reasons for the high consultancy fees are as follows:

ERP consultants usually operate in the "high risk-high reward" area.

i. The consultants are people who have invested significant amount of their time, money and effort in understanding the ERP software and market, gaining extensive knowledge of various industries and developing time tested implementation techniques and methodologies.
ii. ERP consultancy is given to the highest levels of management. As a result it is more expensive.
iii. As ERP consultants save a considerable amount of money for an organization they tend to charge a high fee.
iv. The high cost of the ERP consultants is justified by the fact that they have excellent communication skills, domain knowledge and software expertise.

v. The huge gap in the supply-demand for ERP consultants also contribute in raising the cost of the ERP consultants.

7.5.3 End-Users

End-users are the people who use the ERP system once it is in place. The success of an ERP system lies in the hands of the end users. A high ROI from the ERP system can only be achieved if the end-users accept the change readily and undergo training to develop new skill sets. This will enable them to work effectively with the new ERP system and deliver the benefits of automation to the company. End-user's involvement and participation is considered an important factor for the success of ERP implementation.

According to Hartwick and Barki user involvement refers to a psychological state of the individual and is defined as "the importance and personal relevance of a system to a user." The end-users should gain the knowledge and necessary skills to effectively use the system. This will improve their job performance and productivity. The effective use of the ERP system by the end-users results in improved cash flows, short response cycles and increased profits. End-users should effectively use the system to focus on solving important business problems. The most important contribution of end-users is providing feedback to the implementation team about the ERP system.

Some of the responsibilities of the end-users are as follows:

1. The involvement of the users in the early implementation stages makes it easier to understand the system's requirements, select the right ERP package and plan the customization issue.
2. The user's timely involvement during ERP implementation helps in early detection and correction of mistakes.
3. After implementation the users should help the company in modifying and upgrading the ERP system.
4. End-users who are frequently participating in the ERP implementation process and training programmes become experienced. These experienced users are easier to train as in-house experts.

LEARNING POINTS

1. The ERP vendors, consultants and end-users are considered to be the three major players in an ERP implementation.
2. An ERP vendor is a software firms that design, develops and implements ERP packages.
3. Consultants are the people who specialize in developing effective techniques and methodologies for ensuring a successful ERP implementation.
4. End-users are the people who will use the ERP system to do their work in the company. The involvement of the users in the early implementation stages makes it easier to understand the system's requirements, select the right ERP package and plan the customization issue.

5. Though hiring the consultants will be expensive for the company, yet it promises to pay high dividends. It is, therefore, in the best interest of the company that the consultants are hired as they are people with necessary know-how, right methodology and good analytical skills.

7.6 CRITICAL SUCCESS FACTORS

Critical success factors can be understood as essentially a small number of easily identifiable operational goals that are framed by the management and experts based on research done on the system and the broader environment. The critical success factors are believed to ensure ERP's success to an organization. The critical success factor approach is therefore used to define and measure the success of an ERP implementation in an organization.

Some critical success factors for ERP include the following:

1. A clear vision and support of top management.
2. Capabilities and expertise of the ERP software vendor. Selecting the most qualified ERP vendor can make the difference between a successful ERP implementation and a poor ERP implementation.
3. Suitability of the software and hardware.
4. Involvement of the end-users.
5. Education and training.
6. Effective project management.
7. Business process reengineering.
8. Teamwork and communication.

7.6.1 Holland and Light's Critical Success Factor Model

The critical success factor model designed by Holland and Light groups the critical success factors into strategic and tactical factors.

Figure 7.2 shows the critical success factors model by Holland and Light.

Strategic issues are factors that define the planning phase of a project. The strategic issues specify the need for a project mission, top management's approval and support as well as a well planned project schedule outlining individual action steps for implementation of project. The strategic factors appear most important at the outset of a project.

The strategic factors include business vision, support of the owner and top management, project schedule, ERP strategy and legacy systems. The legacy systems are systems that are no longer efficient and need to be improved so that they are able to perform well.

The tactical issues define the rollout or action phase of the project. They appear more important as the implementation phase moves close. Tactical factors include communication with all the affected parties or users, recruiting the necessary technical as well as business specialist, obtaining the underlying technology, acceptance from the end-users, troubleshooting throughout the project, monitoring and providing feedback at every stage of the ERP implementation project. Both strategic and tactical factors go hand-in-hand to provide success to the ERP implementation.

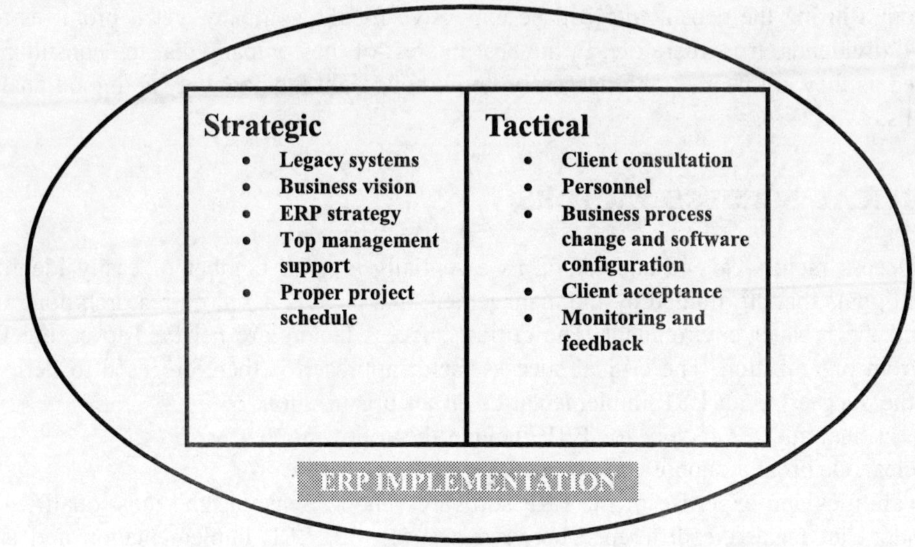

Fig. 7.2. Critical Success Factors Model by Holland and Light

7.6.1 Unified Critical Success Factor Model

The Unified critical success factor model for ERP implementation was developed through the application of grounded theory. In this model the critical success factors are divided in four perspectives.

The four perspectives are strategic, tactical, technological and organizational.

Figure 7.3 show the unified critical success factor model. The critical success factors included in this model are described below:

1. **Organizational Perspective-Strategic Factors**
   The organizational perspective is related with concerns like organizational structure and culture as well as the business processes of the organization. The factors included in this category are as follows:
   i. **Top management support**
   The support of top management is considered crucial for achieving the goals and objectives of the project and aligning these goals with the strategic business goals.
   ii. **Effective organizational change management**
   The organization will accept the new system easily if an effective change management approach has been used.
   iii. **Good project scope management**
   This factor includes both the scope-definition as well as the subsequent scope control. It is considered to be a key factor for ensuring the success of a project.
   iv. **Adequate project team competition**
   The project team should be a rich mix of IT specialists, vendor, consultants and business experts.

Fig. 7.3. Unified Critical Success Factor Model

v. **Comprehensive BPR**

Business process reengineering helps in modifying the business processes to fit the ERP technology.

vi. **Adequate project champion role**

A project champion is a person who possesses the position as well as the skills required to handle organizational change.

vii. **User involvement and participation**

If the involvement and participation of the end-users is high then there are good chances that ERP implementation will be successful.

viii. **Trust between partners**

The ERP implementation will have high chances of success if all the parties have trust between each other throughout the project.

2. **Organizational Perspective: Tactical Factors**

The critical success factors included are as follows:

i. **Dedicated Staff and consultants**

The dedication and commitment of the staff and consultants sets the path for the success of the ERP project.

ii. **Strong communication inwards and outwards**

In order to establish effective communication system within the organization an efficient sharing of information should take place between all the members of the implementation team. The results and objectives should also be communicated to the whole organization through proper channels in each stage of the ERP implementation.

iii. **Formalized project plan/ schedule**
A well-defined project schedule covering the details of all implementation activities along with an appropriate budget and resources for these activities will ensure the completion of the project on time and within budget.

iv. **Adequate training programme**
The training should be prepared to both the technical staff and the end-users. Training helps to reduce end-users resistance as well as increases the efficiency of the technical staff.

v. **Troubleshooting**
The implementation plan should include mechanisms for troubleshooting.

vi. **Appropriate usage of consultants**
Consultants support the vendor and the implementation team in all the phases of the ERP project. The consultants are people who have good experience and insight. They will solve the implementation problems and provide guidance to the management.

vii. **Empowered decision makers**
The members of the implementation team should have the authority to make quick decisions. This will help to reduce delays in implementation that are related with slow decision making.

3. **Technical Perspective: Strategic Factors**
The technological perspective focuses on aspects related to the particular ERP product, software as well as hardware requirements. They include the following:

i. **Adequate ERP implementation strategy**
Deciding which implementation strategy to follow is difficult as it often marks the success of the ERP project. It is important to carefully evaluate the pros and cons of "big-bang" and "phased" approach before going on ERP implementation.

ii. **Avoid customization**
Customization should be avoided as much as possible as the complexity and expense of customization is quite high. The organization should modify the business processes to fit into the ERP system.

iii. **Adequate ERP version**
The ERP version should include most of the functionality required by the organization. The latest version of ERP should be implemented.

4. **Technical Perspective- Tactical Factors**
The tactical factors include the following:

i. **Adequate software configuration**
Software configuration involves adopting the generic functionality of the ERP software package to the requirements of the organization. The system interfaces need to be configured according to the end-users requirement.

ii. **Legacy systems**
The legacy systems are traditional business and IT systems prior to ERP systems. These systems are considered good source of information for implementing ERP systems successfully.

7.6.2 Factors for ERP Implementation Failure

Implementing ERP is a difficult task. Various factors that cause ERP implementation to fail are as follows:

1. An overoptimistic management with unrealistic expectations.
2. A slow and poor feedback mechanism.
3. Inadequate organizational learning and training programmes.
4. Selecting the wrong vendor and the wrong ERP product.
5. Poor documentation.
6. Excessive customization of the ERP package.
7. Too much user resistance.
8. Lack of management support.
9. A poor implementation team with unclear vision.

LEARNING POINTS

1. Critical success factors can be understood as essentially a small number of easily identifiable operational goals that are framed by the management and experts based on research done on the system and the broader environment.
2. The critical success factor model designed by Holland and Light groups the critical success factors into strategic and tactical factors. Strategic issues are factors that define the planning phase of a project. The tactical issues define the rollout or action phase of the project. They appear more important as the implementation phase moves close.
3. The unified critical success factor model for ERP implementation was developed through the application of grounded theory. In this model the critical success factors are divided in four perspectives. The four perspectives are strategic, tactical, technological and organizational.
4. Various factors that cause ERP implementation to fail are as follows: an overoptimistic management with unrealistic expectations, a slow and poor feedback mechanism., inadequate organizational learning and training programmes, selecting the wrong vendor and the wrong ERP product, poor documentation, excessive customization of the ERP package, too much user resistance, lack of management support and a poor implementation team with unclear vision.

7.7 ERP EFFECTIVENESS MODEL

The ERP effectiveness model by Vinod Kumar et al., provides a structured road map for understanding the complex process as well as the critical issues in institutionalizing ERP systems in organizations. According to Markus and Tanis, the ERP adoption is an organizational innovation process. The institutionalization of an innovation is defined as an important post-implementation process in which the organization learns to deal with changes, stabilize technology and builds up new competencies by redefining the processes. Using best practices complimentary structure and norms evolve. During the institutionalization process the organization uses the innovation, learns to accept the introduced changes as well as begins to realize the benefits of the ERP system.

Though ERP systems provide benefits to the company by integrating enterprise-wide resources, revamping the business processes and using best practices; yet it limits the ability of the organization to embed the organization-specific knowledge in its systems. Also, according to Clemens and Rao, IT systems and technologies are not an innovation in themselves and organizations cannot depend on them to produce sustainable advantages because of their ready availability to all competitors at a price.

The differences in the ERP adoption process occur due to the differences in the organizational characteristics. Some characteristics of the organization that should be taken into consideration *a-priori* include centralization, complexity, and formalization, interconnectedness and organizational slack. These characteristics are described below:

1. Centralization
2. Complexity
3. Formalization
4. Interconnectedness
5. Organization slack

There are three stages in the ERP institutionalization model: technical, semantic and effective.

Figure 7.4 shows the ERP effectiveness model given by Kumar et al. The three levels-technical, semantic and effectiveness are discussed below:

1. **Technical Level**
   This stage is characterized by a high level of technical disorder. The main activities that are performed in this stage consist of resolving bugs, fine-tuning the systems and facing the technical challenges in order to provide a running system. Vendor support is gradually withdrawn and in-house team members are expected to control the situation. Communication, both inwards (to the team members) and outwards (to all people in the organization) plays an important role at this stage. In this stage the system gradually begins to lose what it imported from outside character.
2. **Semantic Level**
   In the semantic level, the ERP system has lost it has imported from outside character to a large extent. The technical issues have been resolved and semantic problems become the main point of concern in this stage. Though the people in the organization have started working on the new system, the roles and responsibilities need to be identified. The organization has to deal with problems related to inappropriate resource distribution and identification of roles. Efforts to reduce organizational disorder are the main focus of organization in semantic level.
3. **Effectiveness Level**
   In this stage, the organization focuses on effectiveness of ERP systems in improving the efficiency of organization's value creation process. This level deals with problems related to optimizing the outputs. In this stage, the technical and organizational disorders are quite low. The characteristics that are evident in this stage are as follows: organization has been restructured, new roles have emerged and the capabilities of ERP system are extended.

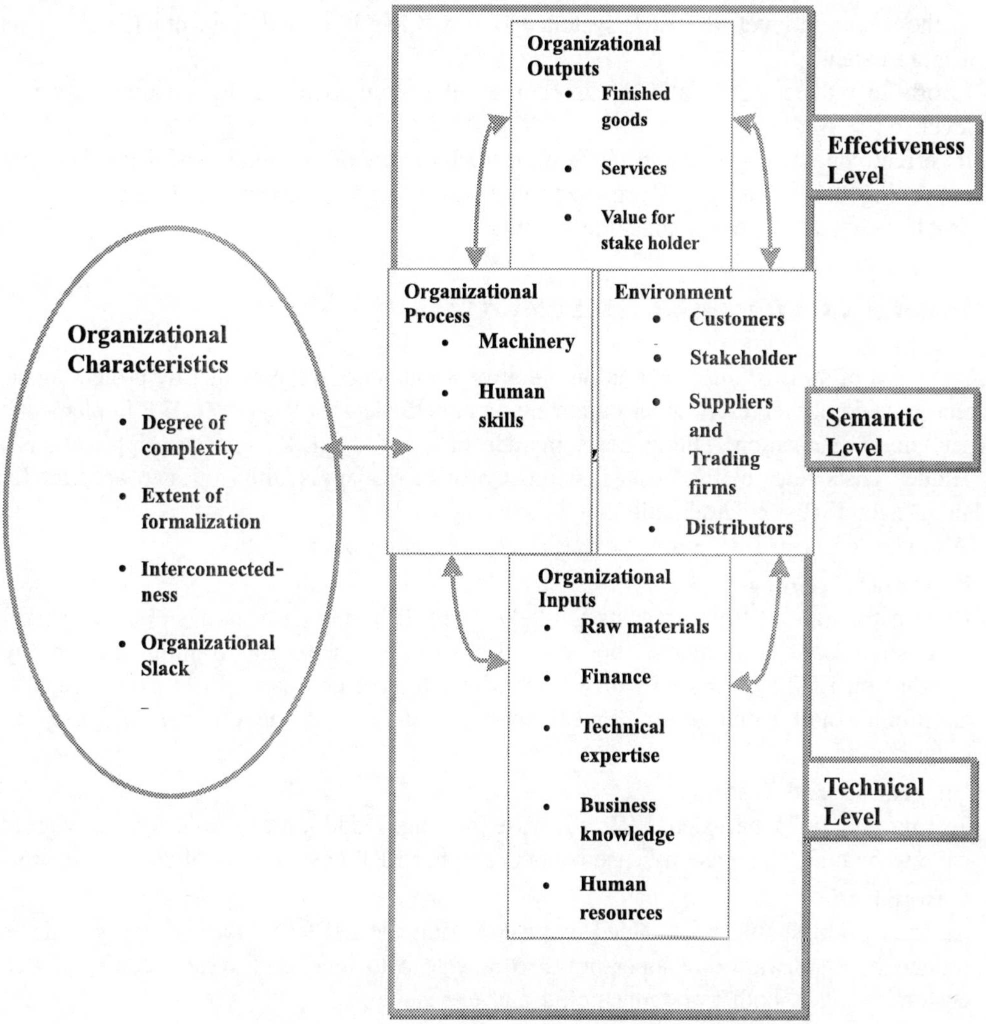

Fig. 7.4. ERP Effectiveness Model by Kumar et al.

LEARNING POINTS

1. The ERP effectiveness model by Vinod Kumar et al., provides a structured road map for understanding the complex process as well as the critical issues in institutionalizing ERP systems in organizations.
2. There are three stages in the ERP institutionalization model: technical, semantic and effective.
3. Technical Level stage is characterized by a high level of technical disorder. The main activities that are performed in this stage consist of resolving bugs, fine-tuning the systems and facing the technical challenges in order to provide a running system.

4. In the semantic level, the ERP system has lost it has imported from outside character to a large extent.
5. Efforts to reduce organizational disorder are the main focus of organization in semantic level.
6. In effectiveness stage, the organization focuses on effectiveness of ERP systems in improving the efficiency of organization's value creation process. This level deals with problems related to optimizing the outputs.

7.6 HIDDEN COST IN ERP IMPLEMENTATION

The direct costs of an ERP implementation are always included in the budget by project manager. But direct costs do not represent the accurate and complete picture of what an ERP implementation will cost your organization. Direct costs include costs of the ERP software applications and tools. Hidden costs refer to the costs that most project managers often miss to account for in their budgets for ERP implementation.

The hidden costs in ERP implementation are discussed below:

1. **Personnel Training**
   Underestimation of training costs is likely to result in budget overruns later. The training costs should not be reduced when budget has to be squeezed as training the employees to work on ERP systems will prove beneficial for the company. It will be wise to train an initial small batch of employees who can then train the other employees of the organization.
2. **Integration and Testing**
   Testing the links between ERP software packages and other corporate software that have to be built on a case by case basis is another ERP costs that is often underestimated.
3. **Customization**
   Customization should be avoided as customizing the ERP software not only calls for a trained ERP software developer but also may lead to increased system complexity. ERP customization is both time consuming and expensive.
4. **Data conversion**
   Data conversion is an important activity that determines the success of an ERP implementation. Migrating data from the legacy systems to the new ERP system is a costly affair. Companies often tend to underestimate the cost of data migration.
5. **ERP consultants**
   ERP consultants are required to guide the implementation team during ERP implementation.
   Other hidden costs include estimation of ERP implementation due to user resistance, additional applications and system downtime.

Table 7.2 lists the direct and indirect costs of ERP implementation.

Table 7.2: Direct and Indirect costs of ERP

S No.	Direct costs	Indirect costs
1.	Purchase of Primary Software	Equipment storage as well as office and clerical supplies
2.	Purchase of Third Party Software: ERP and Non-ERP	ERP consultants
3.		Integration and Testing
4.		Customization
5.		Personnel Training
6.		ERP conference attendance
7.		Audit costs
8.		Data conversion
9.		Estimation of ERP implementation costs due to user resistance, additional applications and system downtime

LEARNING POINTS

1. The direct costs of an ERP implementation are always included in the budget by project manager. Direct costs include costs of the ERP software applications and tools.
2. But direct costs do not represent the accurate and complete picture of what an ERP implementation will cost your organization. Hidden costs refer to the costs that most project managers often miss to account for in their budgets for ERP implementation.
3. The hidden costs in ERP implementation are discussed below: personnel training, integration and testing, customization, data conversion and ERP consultants.

7.9 ERP SUCCESS INHIBITORS AND ACCELERATORS

ERP implementation is a big venture. The factors that act as success accelerators for ERP implementation include the following:

1. High IT experience of the firm.
2. Increased user involvement and participation.
3. Having cross functional teams for managing software customization, if the customization necessary.
4. Effective monitoring and controlling system.
5. Clear vision and support of top management.
6. Expertise of ERP software vendor.
7. Effective project management.
8. Good communication and excellent team work.
9. Proper training.
10. Adequate project champion role.
11. Trust between partners.
12. Comprehensive Business Process Reengineering.
13. Adequate usage of consultants.
14. Empowered decision makers.
15. Document all functional areas that will be on the ERP system of the organization.

The success inhibitors for ERP implementation include the following:

1. Underestimating the implementation cost of ERP.
2. Cutting the ERP budget too soon.
3. Branding the ERP implementation as an IT project.
4. Failing to calculate ROI of ERP. In other words not having proper metrics.
5. Fear and mistrust among end-users.
6. Low or no IT experience of firm.
7. Customization of ERP system to a large extent.
8. Poor feedback mechanism.
9. Poor project management.
10. Lack of communication and team work.
11. Lack of trust between partners.
12. Lack of user involvement and participation.
13. Ignoring employees training needs.
14. Lack of commitment and support from top management.
15. Not selecting the most qualified ERP software vendor.
16. Inappropriate or no usage of consultants.
17. Lack of proper documentation.
18. Selecting the wrong ERP package.
19. Failing to realize the uniqueness of your business.

LEARNING POINTS

1. The factors that act as success accelerators for ERP implementation include the following: high IT experience of the firm, increased user involvement and participation, having cross functional teams for managing software customization, effective monitoring and controlling system, clear vision and support of top management, expertise of ERP software vendor, effective project management, good communication and excellent team work, proper training, adequate project champion role, trust between partners, comprehensive Business Process Reengineering, adequate usage of consultants, empowered decision makers, document all functional areas that will be on the ERP system of the organization.
2. The success inhibitors for ERP implementation include the following: underestimating the implementation cost of ERP, cutting the ERP budget too soon, branding the ERP implementation as an IT project, failing to calculate ROI of ERP, fear and mistrust among end-users, low or no IT experience of firm, customization of ERP system to a large extent, poor feedback mechanism, poor project management, lack of communication and team work, lack of trust between partners, lack of user involvement and participation, ignoring employees training needs, lack of commitment and support from top management, not selecting the most qualified ERP software vendor, inappropriate or no usage of consultants, lack of proper documentation, selecting the wrong ERP package, failing to realize the uniqueness of your business.

7.8 USEFUL GUIDELINES FOR ERP IMPLEMENTATION

ERP systems provide information support to manage all the functions of the business smoothly. Implementing ERP systems is a difficult task and needs to be handled carefully.

Following are some guidelines for implementing ERP successfully:

1. Understand your goals well before going for ERP implementation. The ERP package that meets most of your goals should be selected for implementation.
2. Plan the ERP project well in advance with the help of ERP experts. Select an ERP package that is compliant with industry standards.
3. Select the project manager who has good knowledge of the functional area and is experienced. If project manager with adequate experience is not available then the person who has been selected should be provided training on project management.
4. Be realistic in the cost projections. It is very important to get an accurate picture of the projected costs of an ERP. The cost for training and mentoring should be included. The ERP costs must also include cost of ongoing maintenance and future upgrades.
5. Limit the customization of ERP system as well as the scope of the project. Customizing ERP system to fit the existing business practice should be avoided as far as possible. Effectively limiting the scope of your project will help you to avoid "scope creep" in your project.
6. Develop a contract with legal and ERP expert review. The language of the contract should be unambiguous.
7. Single team atmosphere should be created. ERP implementation involves personnel from various departments. They should be brought together to work in a focused team oriented manner. A joint commitment from all the people involved in the implementation will eventually mark the success of the ERP project.
8. Involve ERP users in the project planning phase.
9. Ensure that the claims of the vendor are true by checking on the vendor's customer references.
10. Employ ERP consultants to provide support and guidance to the implementation team.

LEARNING POINTS

1. Some guidelines for implementing ERP successfully: understand your goals well before going for ERP implementation, plan the ERP project well in advance according to industry standards, select the project manager who has good knowledge of the functional area and is experienced, be realistic in the cost projections.
2. Other guidelines include the following: limit the customization of ERP system as well as the scope of the project, develop a contract with legal and ERP expert review, single team atmosphere should be created, involve ERP users in the project planning phase, ensure that the claims of the vendor are true by checking on the vendor's customer references, employ ERP consultants to provide support and guidance to the implementation team.

7.10 RETURN ON INVESTMENT OF ERP IMPLEMENTATION

The term return on investment (ROI) means that the decision makers evaluate the investment potential by comparing the magnitude as well as the timing of expected gains from a system to the investment costs on the system.

LEARNING POINT

1. The term return on investment (ROI) means that the decision makers evaluate the investment potential by comparing the magnitude as well as the timing of expected gains from a system to the investment costs on the system.

SUMMARY

ERP implementation is a complex, resource-consuming and risky activity. Following a sound implementation methodology effectively increases the chances of success of ERP implementation. The various phases of ERP implementation include pre-evaluation, screening of ERP packages, package evaluation, project planning, gap analysis, business process reengineering, installation and configuration, training of implementation team, testing, going live, end-user training and post-implementation.

The evaluation and selection of an ERP package involves considering the following criteria-functional fit, degree of integration, technology, cost, flexibility and scalability, ease of configuration, degree of customization, users acceptance criteria, quick implementation, level of complexity and security. The evaluation criteria for vendors include operational coverage, range of business applications, company's character and direction, training offered by vendor and vendor's experience.

ERP implementation strategies can be classified into organization, technical and people strategies. Organization strategies include change management techniques as well as managerial style and ideology. People strategies include user involvement and end-user training. Technical strategies include adequacy of technical expertise and deals with various technical aspects of ERP installation. In cost minimization strategy, the change agents try to convince users that the net outcome of ERP adoption process will be favourable to them.

The different approaches that are used to implement ERP include the following: big-bang, phased or skeleton and parallel approach. In big-bang approach, the shift from old system to new system happens at once as a whole. Big-bang approach therefore has a shorter implementation time. Skeleton approach is a phased approach. It provides usable functionality incrementally either by functional area or based on geography. An important advantage of phased approach is that the lessons learnt from previous phases are utilized in next phase to avoid making costly mistakes. But phased approach lacks the urgency and focus of a big-bang approach. In parallel approach, the old and new system runs parallel in the organization for some time.

The purpose of an implementation methodology is to deliver ERP implementation according to specifications, within budget and on-time. Some ERP implementation methodologies are "Accelerated SAP", from SAP, "The Total Solution" from Ernst and Young LLP, "Fast Track Work Plan" from Deloitte and Touche.

ERP vendors, consultants and end-users have a significant role to play in a successful ERP implementation. An ERP vendor plays the role of an innovator, an advisor, a change agent and a trainer. ERP consultants are people with necessary know-how, right methodology and good analytical skills. The cost of consultants is generally very high. End-users are the people who use the ERP system. User involvement and participation is considered an important factor for success of ERP implementation.

The critical success factors for ERP include a clear vision and support of top management, expertise of ERP vendor, suitability of software and hardware, user involvement and participation, education and training, effective project management, business process reengineering and team work.

Holland and Light's critical success factors (CSF) model groups CSF's into strategic and tactical factors. Strategic factors define the planning phase of a project and include business vision, strategy and top management support. Tactical issues, on the other hand, define the action phase of the project. Tactical factors include communication, technical expertise, user acceptance, troubleshooting and feedback.

Unified Critical Success Factor model divides CSF's into four perspectives: strategic, tactical, technological and organizational. Various factors that cause an ERP implementation to fail are: an overoptimistic management with unrealistic expectations, poor management support, slow and poor feedback mechanism, inadequate training programmes, selection of wrong ERP product or vendor, poor documentation, excessive customization, excessive user resistance, lack of management support and a poor implementation team with unclear vision.

ERP effectiveness model proposed by Vinod Kumar et al., provides a structured roadmap for understanding the complex process, as well as, the critical issues involved in institutionalizing ERP systems in organizations. ERP institutionalization model has three stages: technical, semantic and effective. Technical level is characterized by a high level of technical disorder. The main activities performed in this stage include resolving bugs, fine-tuning the system and facing technical challenges in order to provide a running system. In the semantic level, the semantic problems become the main point of concern. In the effectiveness level, the organization focuses on effectiveness of ERP system in improving the efficiency of an organization's value creation process.

Hidden costs refer to the costs that most project managers forget to include in their budget for ERP implementation. These include personnel training, integration and testing, customization, data conversion, consultancy charges and estimation costs of ERP implementation due to user resistance, additional applications and system downtime.

ERP success accelerators are as follows: high IT experience of firm, increased user involvement and participation, having cross functional team for managing software customization, presence of effective monitoring and controlling system, vendor expertise, clear vision and support of top management etc.

Some success inhibitors include: underestimating the implementation cost of ERP, cutting ERP budget to soon, involving only IT department, fear and mistrust among end-users, excessive customization, poor feedback mechanism, lack of communication and team work, lack of trust between vendor and firm, lack of proper documentation, lack of commitment and support from top management, ignoring the training needs of employees and failing to calculate ROI of ERP.

Some useful guidelines for ERP implementation include the following: understand the goals of an organization before going for ERP implementation, plan ERP project well in advance with the help of ERP experts, select a good project manager, be realistic in cost projections, limit customization of ERP system, involve end-users, ensure that the vendor claims are true and employ consultants.

Return on Investment (ROI) means that the decision makers evaluate the investment potential by comparing the magnitude, as well as, timing of expected gains from a system to the investment costs on the system.

POINTS TO REMEMBER

1. The different phases involved in implementation of an ERP system include: Pre-evaluation Screening of ERP packages, project planning, package evaluation, gap analysis, business process reengineering, installation and configuration, training of implementation team, testing, going live, end-user training, post-implementation.
2. The evaluation and selection of an ERP package involves considering the following criteria: functional fit, degree of integration, technology/trends, cost, flexibility and scalability, ease of configuration, degree of customization, users acceptance, quick implementation and complexity.
3. Project planning phase designs the implementation process. It builds a roadmap that is used throughout the implementation. The implementation team develops the project plan using the project planning tools (gnatt charts etc.).
4. Gap analysis is the process that identifies the gaps by mapping the expectations of the company with the capabilities of the ERP product.
5. Business process reengineering is a more efficient way to do business. It analyses the various business processes of the organization in order to identify and practice the best way of doing work.
6. Installation and configuration phase is considered to be the main functional area in the ERP implementation life cycle. In this phase attempts are made to synchronize the existing practices of the company with the ERP package.
7. The implementation strategies help to overcome the resistance of the workers to the ERP system and thereby the success of the ERP implementation. The different strategies for implementing ERP can be classified into organizational, technical and people strategies.
8. Some of the change management strategies for ERP implementation are as follows: effective communication system, cost minimization strategy, differentiation strategy, providing hands-on training, carefully timing the introduction of the new system, ensuring the support of opinion leaders.
9. The implementation approach chosen by the organization decides the costs and risks of the ERP implementation project. Three different approaches to ERP implementation include big-bang, phased or skeleton and parallel approach.
10. In big-bang approach the switch between using the old systems and using the new ERP system happens at once. Every person starts using the new system at the same date and from that day onwards the old system is not used.

11. The Skeleton implementation is a phased approach. It provides usable functionality incrementally whether by functional business area or geography.
12. In the Phased Approach the system component is brought online serially.
13. Some ERP methodologies are "Accelerated SAP" from SAP, "The Total Solution" from Ernst and Young LLP, "Fast Track Work plan" from Deloitte and Touche.
14. SAP has introduced an effective implementation methodology called "Accelerated SAP" (ASAP). ASAP implementation methodology consists of five phases. These are as follows: project preparation, business blueprint, realization, final preparation, go live and support.
15. An ERP vendor is a software firm that design, develop and implement ERP packages. Consultants are the people who specialize in developing effective techniques and methodologies for ensuring a successful ERP implementation.
16. End-users are the people who will use the ERP system to do their work in the company. The involvement of the users in the early implementation stages makes it easier to understand the system's requirements, select the right ERP package and plan the customization issue.
17. Critical success factors can be understood as essentially a small number of easily identifiable operational goals that are framed by the management and experts based on research done on the system and the broader environment.
18. The critical success factor model designed by Holland and Light groups the critical success factors into strategic and tactical factors. Strategic issues are factors that define the planning phase of a project. The tactical issues define the rollout or action phase of the project. They appear more important as the implementation phase moves close.
19. The ERP effectiveness model by Vinod Kumar et al., provides a structured roadmap for understanding the complex process as well as the critical issues in institutionalizing ERP systems in organizations. There are three stages in the ERP institutionalization model-technical, semantic and effective.
20. The direct costs of an ERP implementation are always included in the budget by project manager. Direct costs include costs of the ERP software applications and tools.
21. Hidden costs refer to the costs that most project managers often miss to account for in their budgets for ERP implementation.
22. Some of the factors that act as success accelerators for ERP implementation include the following: high IT experience of the firm, increased user involvement and participation, having cross functional teams for managing software customization, effective monitoring and controlling system, clear vision and support of top management, expertise of ERP software vendor, effective project management, good communication and excellent team work, proper training etc.
23. Some guidelines for implementing ERP successfully: understand your goals well before going for ERP implementation, plan the ERP project well in advance according to industry standards, select the project manager who has good knowledge of the functional area and is experienced, be realistic in the cost projections.

REVIEW QUESTIONS

1. "Implementing an ERP system is a significant investment". Discuss this statement.
2. Discuss the various phases in an ERP implementation life cycle.
3. Why is the pre-selection screening of ERP packages considered important?
4. What are the criteria on which ERP is selected?
5. "A right ERP package selected will almost decide the success of the implementation". Comment.
6. How will you select the right ERP vendor for implementing ERP system in your organization?
7. What is customization? Why is customization needed?
8. What is the drawback of over-customization?
9. What do you understand by "Project Planning"? What activities are performed in this phase of ERP lifecycle?
10. Explain gap analysis. What are the steps to carry out gap analysis?
11. ERP and BPR go hand-in hand. Comment. Is it possible to implement ERP without BPR? Explain.
12. Which phase is considered to be the main functional area in ERP implementation life cycle and why?
13. What is an ERP project team?
14. Why is it considered a good idea to train the implementation team?
15. How is the ERP system tested?
16. What do you mean by the term "going live". Is there a good time to "go live"? Discuss.
17. Discuss the importance of end user training.
18. What activities are performed in the post-implementation phase of an ERP system?
19. Explain some of the strategies that are used for implementing ERP.
20. Discuss the change management strategies for ERP implementation.
21. What do you understand by differentiation strategy?
22. What are the different approaches to ERP implementation? Discuss the circumstances in which a particular approach is suitable.
23. Explain the "big bang" approach to ERP implementation.
24. What are the advantages of big-bang approach?
25. What are the disadvantages of big-bang approach?
26. Explain the skeleton or phase approach.
27. Discuss the advantages and disadvantages of skeleton approach.
28. Explain the parallel approach to ERP implementation.
29. What do you understand by an implementation methodology? Explain the different implementation methodologies being used.
30. Explain the role of consultants in ERP implementation.
31. Explain the role of vendors in ERP implementation.
32. Discuss the different roles that an ERP vendor has to play.
33. What are the responsibilities of an ERP vendor?
34. What are the responsibilities of an ERP consultant?
35. Why do consultants charge a high fee?

36. Who are the end-users? What are the responsibilities of the end-users?
37. Explain the benefits of end-user training.
38. What are the reasons behind ERP implementation failure? What are the critical success factors for ERP implementation?
39. Explain the critical success factor model designed by Holland and Light.
40. Explain the unified critical success factor model.
41. Explain the ERP effectiveness model.
42. Discuss the three stages in the ERP institutionalization model.
43. Write a short note on the hidden costs in ERP implementation.
44. Discuss ERP success inhibitors and accelerators.
45. Give some useful guidelines for implementing ERP system successfully.
46. What do you understand by return on investment?
47. How can the benefits of ERP be measured and quantified? Further discuss how ROI of ERP is relevant.

OBJECTIVE QUESTIONS

SECTION A

TICK THE CORRECT ANSWER

1. Which is true about ERP implementation?
 (a) For most organizations, whether large scale or small and medium enterprises, ERP implementation opens the door for new opportunities.
 (b) Implementing an ERP system is a large undertaking.
 (c) It usually becomes a mind-altering experience for the people involved in its implementation.
 (d) As ERP implementation is a complex, resource-consuming and risky activity, the company must follow a sound methodology.
 (e) All of above.

2. A sound implementation methodology will:
 (a) Effectively increase the chances of success in implementing ERP.
 (b) Help to deliver the ERP implementation according to the specifications, within budget and on time.
 (c) Both (a) and (b).
 (d) None of above.

3. A successful ERP implementation depends upon:
 (a) Implementation approach.
 (b) Implementation methodology.
 (c) Implementation strategies chosen by the organization.
 (d) All of above.

4. ________________ is a short phase that deals with eliminating the ERP packages that are not at all suitable for the business processes of the company.

(a) Pre-evaluation Screening.
(b) Package Evaluation.
(c) Project Planning
(d) None of above.

5. Which is a true statement?
(a) The evaluation and selection of the right ERP software for the company is a complex task.
(b) The evaluation and selection of the right ERP software for the company must be accomplished as a fact-based process that minimizes the risks associated and helps to make a well-informed decision.
(c) The evaluation and selection of an ERP package involves considering the criteria: Functional Fit, Degree of Integration, Technology /Trends etc.
(d) All of above.

6. The ___________ criterion involves checking whether all functional aspects of the business are duly covered in the ERP package.
(a) Functional Fit
(b) Degree of Integration
(c) Degree of Customization
(d) None of above.

7. Degree of Integration involves:
(a) Checking whether all the business processes and functions are fully integrated or not.
(b) Checking whether all the latest technology and IT trends are supported by the package.
(c) Both (a) and (b).
(d) None of above.

8. The ERP package must be:
(a) Flexible.
(b) Scalable.
(c) Easily configurable.
(d) Both (a) and (b).
(e) All of above.

9. _____________ is defined as the percentage of acceptance of the user friendliness of the screens/interfaces as well as the process flows by the users.
(a) Degree of customization.
(b) Users acceptance.
(c) Degree of integration.
(d) None of above.

10. Other evaluation criteria for ERP products include:
(a) Ability to support multi-site planning and control.
(b) Local support infrastructure.
(c) Easy information retrieval.
(d) All of above.

11. The key to successful ERP implementation is:
(a) Selecting the right ERP software.
(b) Selecting the right ERP vendor.

(c) Both (a) and (b).
(d) All of above.

12. A good ERP vendor will:
(a) Assist the team to identify and learn complex business processes of the company.
(b) Explain the business value to be derived from ERP system.
(c) Provide familiarization programmes for all the employees of the company, executive programmes for the top management and functional training for the members of the implementation team as well as end-user training.
(d) All of above.

13. Which is a false statement?
(a) Effectively rating the vendor's track record and true capabilities is an important factor to consider when selecting an ERP vendor.
(b) The implementation methodology of the ERP vendor should be highly tailor-able to the specific needs and expertise of the company.
(c) While selecting the ERP vendor, some traits need to be considered. They include technical expertise, domain knowledge, adequate manpower, project management skills and good involvement.
(d) The ERP vendor company's objectives, policies and working style are not considered to decide whether to select the vendor or not.
(e) None of above.

14. An implementation methodology that is well-tailored to the known requirements of the company will:
(a) Help the company to achieve the desired results.
(b) Ensure that maximum return on investment (ROI) is received.
(c) Both (a) and (b).
(d) None of above.

15. The evaluation criteria for vendors include:
(a) Operational coverage.
(b) Range of business applications.
(c) Company character and direction
(d) Training offered by the ERP vendor
(e) All of above.

16. Operational coverage deals with finding out:
(a) Whether the vendor is a local developer or a truly international organization.
(b) The number of departmental functions and the business applications that the ERP vendor supports.
(c) Both (a) and (b).
(d) None of above.

17. The vendor selected should provide training to users:
(a) At various levels.
(b) In various details.
(c) Both (a) and (b).
(d) None of above.

18. A good ERP vendor will provide:
  (a) Familiarization programmes for all the employees of the company.
  (b) Executive programmes for the top management.
  (c) Functional training for the members of the implementation team.
  (d) End-user training.
  (e) All of above.

19. Vendors may be evaluated based on:
  (a) Experience.
  (b) Financial position.
  (c) Pricing models offered by vendors.
  (d) All of above.
  (e) None of above.

20. Which phase designs the implementation process?
  (a) Project Planning.
  (b) Gap Analysis.
  (c) Implementation phase.
  (d) None of above.

21. ____________ is the process that identifies the gaps by mapping the expectations of the company with the capabilities of the ERP product.
  (a) Project Planning.
  (b) Gap Analysis.
  (c) Implementation phase.
  (d) None of above.

22. Which is true about Business Process Reengineering?
  (a) Business Process Reengineering is a more efficient way to do business.
  (b) BPR analyses the various business processes of the organization in order to identify and practice the best way of doing work.
  (c) Business Process Reengineering reduces the workforce size.
  (d) All of above.

23. ___________ attempts to maximize the business productivity through restructuring and reorganizing the business processes, information workflows, human resources as well as the divisions and departments in the organization.
  (a) BPR.
  (b) ERP.
  (c) Extended ERP.
  (d) SCM.

24. _________________ Phase is considered to be the main functional area in the ERP implementation life cycle.
  (a) Package evaluation.
  (b) Project Planning.
  (c) Gap Analysis.
  (d) Installation and configuration.

25. Modification of the ERP software results in problems such as:
  (a) Code errors.

(b) Difficulty when upgrading to new versions.
(c) Both (a) and (b).
(d) None of above.

26. The ERP software configuration is often:
(a) Complex.
(b) Time consuming.
(c) Costly.
(d) All of above.

27. The __________ phase enables the implementation team to discover problems that may require some minor modifications before the ERP system goes life.
(a) Implementation.
(b) Testing.
(c) Going live.
(d) None of above.

28. Which is true about testing phase?
(a) Testing ERP system with real case and extreme case scenarios will allow the implementation team to identify any errors in the process and information flows before live deployment.
(b) The testing phase helps the implementation team to minimize the errors after deployment as well as maximize the potential of the new system.
(c) In this phase the old system is removed and the new system is officially proclaimed operational.
(d) Both (a) and (b).

29. In which phase is the old system removed and the new system is officially proclaimed operational?
(a) Implementation.
(b) End-User Training.
(c) Going live.
(d) None of above.

30. In __________ phase the system is upgraded as and when new versions or technologies are introduced.
(a) Implementation.
(b) Going live.
(c) Post-Implementation.
(d) None of above.

31. The ______________ phase includes regular monitoring of the system, tuning the hardware or software and performing audit of the ERP system.
(a) Implementation.
(b) Going live.
(c) Post-Implementation.
(d) None of above.

32. Which statement is true?
(a) The different strategies for implementing ERP can be classified into organizational, technical and people strategies.

(b) The implementation strategies help to overcome the resistance of the workers to the ERP system and thereby the success of the ERP implementation.

(c) The organizational strategies include change strategy development, change management techniques, project management, communication and coordination, organizational structure and resources, IS function characteristics, managerial style and ideology.

(d) All of above.

(e) None of above.

33. The people strategies include:

(a) Management and staff attitudes.

(b) User involvement.

(c) Training.

(d) All of above.

34. Technical strategies include:

(a) Adequacy of in-house technical expertise.

(b) Time and cost of ERP implementation.

(c) ERP complexity and various technical aspects of the ERP installation.

(d) All of above.

35. The fundamental sources of employee's resistance to ERP implementation that the top management must analyze include:

(a) Perceived risk.

(b) Employee habit.

(c) Both (a) and (b).

(d) None of above.

36. Habit simply refers to:

(a) The current practices that a person routinely performs.

(b) An employee's perception of the risk associated with the decision to accept the new system.

(c) Both (a) and (b).

(d) None of above.

37. Which strategy is not a change management strategy for ERP implementation?

(a) Effective Communication system.

(b) Cost Minimization Strategy.

(c) Differentiation Strategy.

(d) None of above.

38. Which strategy can the top management use to influence the affective components of users' attitudes?

(a) Effective Communication System.

(b) Cost Minimization Strategy.

(c) Differentiation Strategy.

(d) None of above.

(e) All of above.

39. Which is not true about Cost Minimization Strategy?

(a) In this strategy, the user's adoption costs are kept to a minimum and the users are convinced by the change agents that their net outcome of the ERP adoption process will be positive.

(b) The Cost Minimization Strategy should operate at both the individual worker and the influential groups' level.
(c) According to this strategy, a user's perceived high quality of the ERP system has a positive impact on his attitude towards the system.
(d) None of above.

40. Which statement is not true?
(a) A user's perceived high quality of the ERP system has a positive impact on his attitude towards the system.
(b) AN ERP system that is user friendly will have good chances of success whereas an ERP system with an unwieldy user interface will not be accepted by the users.
(c) Both (a) and (b).
(d) None of above.

41. What does training do?
(a) Training provides hands-on experience to the users.
(b) Trained users are able to appreciate the quality attributes as well as the potential benefits of the ERP system.
(c) Training also helps in developing positive attitudes of the users towards the system as the users are now not only aware of how the system works but also know the benefits the new system has to offer.
(d) All of above.

42. A very effective implementation strategy is to ensure the support of:
(a) Well known individuals.
(b) Opinion leaders.
(c) Both (a) and (b).
(d) None of above.

43. In __________approach, the switch between using the old systems and using the new ERP system happens at once.
(a) Big-bang.
(b) Skeleton.
(c) Parallel.
(d) None of above.

44. In big-bang implementation:
(a) Fewer interfaces are required between the different modules.
(b) The costs are generally reduced compared to the phased approach.
(c) The implementation time is shorter.
(d) All of above.

45. Which approach is considered to be more risky?
(a) Big-bang.
(b) Phased.
(c) Parallel.
(d) Both (b) and (c).

46. The advantages of big-bang approach are:
(a) Shorter implementation time
(b) Low implementation cost
(c) No need for temporary interfaces

(d) The need to maintain and change legacy system is limited
(e) All of above.

47. The disadvantages of big-bang approach are:
(a) Huge peak resources may be required.
(b) The new system once implemented cannot readily go back to the legacy system.
(c) The working of the system cannot be demonstrated until the system gets fully installed.
(d) The implementation team gets fewer hands-on opportunities to gain knowledge.
(e) All of above.

48. Which is not true about the Skeleton implementation?
(a) It is a phased approach.
(b) It provides usable functionality incrementally whether by functional business area or geography.
(c) The biggest advantage of Skeleton approach is that the project implementation team gets enough time to plan, customize and test the system.
(d) Skeleton or Phased Approach lacks the urgency and focus of a big-bang approach.
(e) None of above.

49. Some of the advantages of the skeleton approach are:
(a) The peak resource requirements are less as compared to big-bang approach.
(b) Risks in the phased approach are low. Also, legacy system can be returned.
(c) Implementation team gains knowledge in each phase.
(d) The time between development of the system and its use is reduced.
(e) All of above.

50. The disadvantages of the Skeleton approach are:
(a) The need to maintain and revise legacy systems is more.
(b) There is a higher risk of losing personnel to turnover.
(c) Implementation time is more. Also, involves higher cost.
(d) There is a heavy use of temporary interfaces.
(e) All of above.

51. Which is not true about parallel approach?
(a) In this approach, the old system and the new system are running parallel in the organization.
(b) The advantage of the parallel approach is that the users can get used to the new system and meanwhile do their work using the old system.
(c) The implementation team gets fewer hands-on opportunities to gain knowledge.
(d) None of above.

52. ________________ is a roadmap to an ERP implementation.
(a) ERP implementation strategy.
(b) ERP implementation approach.
(c) ERP implementation methodology.
(d) None of above.

53. The purpose of the implementation methodology is to:
(a) Deliver the implementation according to the specifications,.
(b) Deliver the implementation within budget.
(c) Deliver the implementation on time.
(d) All of above.

54. Which statement is true?

(a) A structured and well-constructed implementation methodology focuses on defined processes, users and strategies to provide a clear understanding of the business environment and goals.

(b) A good implementation methodology leads to the shortest path to pay-off and fewest risks.

(c) The implementation team should strictly adhere to the methodology for success.

(d) The implementation methodology provided by the vendor or in-house consultants must be highly tailor-able to the needs of the company.

(e) All of above.

55. ________________ develop the implementation methodology through refinements and application of best practices based on their expertise and industry experiences gained over several years in business.

(a) ERP vendors.

(b) Consulting firms.

(c) Both (a) and (b).

(d) None of above.

56. Who has developed the ERP methodology "Accelerated SAP"?

(a) SAP.

(b) Ernst and Young LLP.

(c) Deloitte and Touche.

(d) None of above.

57. Which is true about ASAP?

(a) ASAP helps to reduce the SAP implementation time to less than six months.

(b) ASAP implementation methodology consists of five phases.

(c) Both (a) and (b).

(d) None of above.

58. ____________ is Accelerated SAP visual model of the future state of the business.

(a) Business Blueprint.

(b) Realization

(c) Final Preparation.

(d) Go Live and Support.

59. During ____________ phase the broad scope of the SAP's R/3 module is narrowed down to fit the industry-specific processes.

(a) Business Blueprint.

(b) Realization

(c) Final Preparation.

(d) Go Live and Support.

(e) None of above.

60. Which is true about the business blueprint model?

(a) It supports the implementation team to clearly define the scope and focus on the specific R/3 processes that are required to conduct the business smoothly and efficiently.

(b) During the business blueprint phase the broad scope of the SAP's R/3 module is narrowed down to fit the industry-specific processes.

(c) Both (a) and (b).
(d) None of above.

61. In which phase is the R/3 system configured?
(a) Business Blueprint.
(b) Realization.
(c) Final Preparation.
(d) Go Live and Support.
(e) None of above.

62. "The Total Solution" methodology has been developed by ______________.
(a) SAP.
(b) Deloitte and Touche.
(c) Ernst and Young LLP.
(d) None of above.

63. In ____________ phase of "The Total Solution" methodology, the implementation team finds out the value of the implementation project.
(a) Reality Check.
(b) Value proposition.
(c) Aligned Approach.
(d) Success Dimension.

64. In _________phase of "The Total Solution" methodology, teamwork is emphasized.
(a) Reality Check.
(b) Value Proposition.
(c) Aligned Approach.
(d) Success Dimension.
(e) None of above.

65. Which phase of "The Total Solution" methodology, deals with measuring results of the system?
(a) Delivering Value.
(b) Value proposition.
(c) Aligned Approach.
(d) Success Dimension.
(e) None of above.

66. The ___________ methodology has been developed by Deloitte and Touche
(a) Fast Track.
(b) SAP.
(c) Total Solution.
(d) None of above.

67. An ERP vendor is:
(a) A software firm that designs, develops and implements ERP packages.
(b) The people who specialize in developing effective techniques and methodologies for ensuring a successful ERP implementation.
(c) The people who will use the ERP system to do their work in the company.
(d) All of above.

68. Which is not true about an ERP vendor?
- **(a)** An ERP vendor has no responsibilities to fulfill.
- **(b)** An ERP vendor needs to have qualified, in-house and client-centric consultants that are capable of advising, instrtucting, applying best solutions and resolving issues.
- **(c)** An ERP vendor is a software firm that design, develop and implement ERP packages.
- **(d)** None of above.

69. Which of the following is not a responsibility of an ERP vendor?
- **(a)** An ERP vendor should deliver the product along with its documentation to the company after the contract has been signed.
- **(b)** Vendor should provide a preliminary implementation plan even before the contract is signed.
- **(c)** The software provider must identify and learn about the various business processes of the company.
- **(d)** The vendor should suggest best ways to implement the system. Most ERP vendors have by now developed effective implementation methodologies that are industry-specific.
- **(e)** None of above.

70. The different roles that an ERP vendor has to play are:
- **(a)** Innovator and Advisor.
- **(b)** Trainer.
- **(c)** Change Agent
- **(d)** All of above.

71. Which is true about ERP consultants?
- **(a)** ERP consultants are firms who specialize in developing implementation strategies and time-related methodologies.
- **(b)** ERP consultants have an extensive knowledge of the ERP market and are well-conversant with the tricks and techniques of the trade.
- **(c)** The ERP consultants have several years of hands-on ERP implementation experience with several industries.
- **(d)** The cost of consultants is very high.
- **(e)** All of above.

72. The responsibilities of the consultants are:
- **(a)** The consultants are responsible for effectively administrating each implementation phase.
- **(b)** The consultants analyze the ERP package and the business processes and accordingly address the customization issue.
- **(c)** The consultants are required to defend the ERP vendor when such defense is technically correct.
- **(d)** The consultants need to safeguard the interest of the company.
- **(e)** All of above.

73. Which is not true?
- **(a)** The consultants need to ask questions from the vendor so that vendor claims are verified before the product is purchased from a particular vendor.

(b) The consultants should develop a knowledge base and train the employees so that they are able to work effectively on the ERP system when the ERP implementation project has completed and the consultants have all left.
(c) Both (a) and (b).
(d) None of above.

74. The ERP consultant play role as an:
(a) Administrator.
(b) Analyst.
(c) Trainer.
(d) Mediator between the company and the ERP vendor.
(e) All of above.

75. The ERP consultants often charge a high fee. The reasons for the high consultancy fees are:
(a) ERP consultants usually operate in the "high risk-high reward" area.
(b) The consultants are people who have invested significant amount of their time, money and effort in understanding the ERP software and market, gaining extensive knowledge of various industries and developing time tested implementation techniques and methodologies.
(c) ERP consultancy is given to the highest levels of management. As a result it is more expensive.
(d) As ERP consultants save a considerable amount of money for an organization they tend to charge a high fee.
(e) All of above.

76. Which is true about end-users?
(a) End-users are the people who use the ERP system once it is in place.
(b) The success of an ERP system lies in the hands of the end-users.
(c) A high ROI from the ERP system can only be achieved if the end-users accept the change readily and undergo training to develop new skill sets.
(d) End users involvement and participation is considered an important factor for the success of ERP implementation.
(e) All of above.

77. The effective use of the ERP system by the end users results in:
(a) Improved cash flows.
(b) Short response cycles.
(c) Increased profits.
(d) All of above.

78. Which is the most important contribution of end users to ERP implementation?
(a) Providing feedback to the implementation team about the ERP system.
(b) Working on the system.
(c) Improving cash flows.
(d) Putting up no resistance.
(e) None of above.

79. The responsibilities of the end users are:

(a) The involvement of the users in the early implementation stages makes it easier to understand the system's requirements, select the right ERP package and plan the customization issue.

(b) The user's timely involvement during ERP implementation helps in early detection and correction of mistakes.

(c) After implementation the users should help the company in modifying and upgrading the ERP system.

(d) All of above.

(e) None of above.

80. Which is not true about critical success factors?

(a) Critical success factors can be understood as essentially a small number of easily identifiable operational goals that are framed by the management and experts based on research done on the system and the broader environment.

(b) The critical success factors are believed to ensure ERP's success to an organization.

(c) The critical success factor approach is used to define and measure the success of an ERP implementation in an organization.

(d) All of above.

(e) None of above.

81. The critical success factors for ERP include:

(a) A clear vision and support of top management.

(b) Capabilities and expertise of the ERP software vendor.

(c) Suitability of the software and hardware.

(d) Effective project management.

(e) All of above.

82. Which is true about the strategic factors in the critical success factor model designed by Holland and Light?

(a) The strategic factors appear most important at the outset of a project.

(b) The strategic factors include business vision, support of the owner and top management, project schedule, ERP strategy and legacy systems.

(c) Both (a) and (b).

(d) None of above.

83. Which is true about the tactical factors in the critical success factor model designed by Holland and Light?

(a) Tactical factors appear more important as the implementation phase moves close.

(b) Tactical factors include communication with all the affected parties or users, recruiting the necessary technical as well as business specialist, obtaining the underlying technology, acceptance from the end-users, troubleshooting throughout the project, monitoring and providing feedback at every stage of the ERP implementation project.

(c) Both (a) and (b).

(d) None of above.

84. The ______________ model for ERP implementation was developed through the application of grounded theory.

(a) Unified critical success factor.

(b) Critical success factor model by Holland and Light.
(c) ERP effectiveness model by Vinod Kumar et al.
(d) None of above.

85. In unified critical success factor model, the critical success factors are divided in _______ perspectives.
(a) Two.
(b) Four.
(c) Five.
(d) None of above.

86. During the institutionalization process the organization:
(a) Uses the innovation.
(b) Learns to accept the introduced changes.
(c) Begins to realize the benefits of the ERP system.
(d) All of above.

87. There are ______________ stages in the ERP institutionalization model.
(a) Two
(b) Three.
(c) Four.
(d) None of above.

88. Which stage in the ERP institutionalization model by Vinod Kumar et al., is characterized by a high level of technical disorder?
(a) Technical.
(b) Semantic.
(c) Effectiveness.
(d) All of above.

89. Which is true about Semantic Level?
(a) In the semantic level, the ERP system has lost it has imported from outside character to a large extent.
(b) The technical issues have been resolved and semantic problems become the main point of concern in this stage.
(c) Efforts to reduce organizational disorder are the main focus of organization in semantic level.
(d) All of above.

90. In which stage, the organization focuses on effectiveness of ERP systems in improving the efficiency of organization's value creation process.
(a) Technical.
(b) Semantic.
(c) Effectiveness.
(d) None of above.

91. In which stage, the technical and organizational disorders are quite low?
(a) Technical.
(b) Semantic.
(c) Effectiveness.
(d) None of above.

92. Which is true about direct costs?

(a) The direct costs of an ERP implementation are always included in the budget by project manager

(b) Direct costs do not represent the accurate and complete picture of what an ERP implementation will cost your organization.

(c) Direct costs include costs of the ERP software applications and tools.

(d) All of above.

93. Hidden costs refer to:

(a) The costs that most project managers often miss to account for in their budgets for ERP implementation.

(b) Costs of the ERP software applications and tools.

(c) Costs of an ERP implementation that is always included in the budget by project manager.

(d) Management expenses.

94. The hidden cost does not include:

(a) Customization.

(b) Data conversion.

(c) ERP consultants.

(d) Costs of the ERP software applications and tools.

95. The factors that act as success accelerators for ERP implementation include:

(a) Increased user involvement and participation.

(b) Having cross functional teams for managing software customizations, if the customizations are necessary.

(c) Clear vision and support of top management.

(d) Expertise of ERP software vendor.

(e) All of above.

96. Some guidelines for implementing ERP successfully are:

(a) Plan the ERP project well in advance with the help of ERP experts.

(b) Select an ERP package that is compliant with industry standards.

(c) Select the project manager who has good knowledge of the functional area and is experienced.

(d) Be realistic in the cost projections.

(e) All of above.

97. Which is a false statement?

(a) It is very important to get an accurate picture of the projected costs of an ERP.

(b) The cost for training and mentoring should be included.

(c) The ERP costs must also include cost of ongoing maintenance and future upgrades.

(d) All of above.

(e) None of above.

SECTION B

STATE TRUE OR FALSE

1. Implementing an ERP system is a large undertaking.
2. As ERP implementation is a complex, resource-consuming and risky activity, the company must follow a sound methodology.
3. A sound implementation methodology will effectively increase the chances of success of the ERP implementation.
4. A successful ERP implementation depends upon the implementation approach and the implementation strategies chosen by the organization.
5. The pre-evaluation screening of ERP package is a short phase that deals with eliminating those ERP packages that are not at all suitable for the business processes of the company.
6. Package evaluation phase has a lot of significance in the ERP implementation life cycle.
7. A right ERP package selected will almost decide the success of the implementation.
8. The evaluation and selection of ERP software is a complex task. This task must be accomplished as a fact-based process that minimizes the risks associated and helps to make a well-informed decision.
9. Degree of integration involves checking whether all functional aspects of the business are duly covered in the ERP package.
10. The ERP package should be functionally-fit to the company's business processes.
11. The ERP products are not evaluated based on efforts and amount of money required for integrating the existing system with ERP package.
12. The ERP products are evaluated based on the total cost required to implementation a particular ERP product.
13. The ERP package must be flexible to suit the needs of the specific business processes and scalable to meet the growing and changing needs of the company.
13. ERP products are evaluated based on their ease of configuration.
14. An ERP product that easily configures the screens to have relevant data input fields and back-end tables is not considered as a good product.
15. Degree of customization does not serve as an important evaluation criterion. If an ERP product requires a lot of customization in order to support your business processes then it is the right product for you.
16. The ERP products are often evaluated based on the percentage of deviation from the business or changes in the business processes that will be required for effective implementation of the ERP package.
17. Users acceptance is defined as the percentage of acceptance of the user friendliness of the screens/interfaces as well as the process flows by the users.
18. The higher the rate of acceptance, the more user-friendly the product is considered to be.
19. Implementation time is a good evaluation criterion for ERP products.
20. ERP packages are often big, complex and require maintenance. A complex ERP package will make the ERP implementation a difficult exercise.
21. The key to successful ERP implementation is selecting the right ERP software and the right ERP vendor who will provide you with a fast and effective implementation.

22. The ERP vendors should be evaluated based on the functionality of their applications and their ability to support business transformation in order to achieve the objectives of the company.

23. A good ERP vendor will provide the company with a preliminary implementation plan even before the contract is signed.

24. The customer references of the ERP vendor should be checked carefully in order to understand the implementation success rate of the vendor. This is a false statement.

25. It is not necessary to completely understand the implementation methodology of the vendor.

26. The implementation methodology of the ERP vendor should be highly tailor-able to the specific needs and expertise of the company.

27. An implementation methodology that is well-tailored to the known requirements of the company will help the company to achieve the desired results and ensure that maximum return on investment (ROI) is received.

28. It is important to find out the number of departmental functions and the business applications that the ERP vendor supports.

29. The ERP vendor company's objectives, policies and working style are not considered to decide whether to select the vendor or not.

30. The vendor selected should provide training to users at various levels and in various details.

31. A good ERP vendor will provide familiarization programmes for all the employees of the company, executive programmes for the top management and functional training for the members of the implementation team as well as end-user training.

32. The vendor's experience is not an important criterion to evaluate the vendors.

33. The vendors may be evaluated based on their financial track record.

34. Package evaluation phase designs the implementation process.

35. Project planning builds a road map that is used throughout the implementation.

36. The implementation team develops the project plan using the project planning tools (gnatt charts etc.).

37. The committee constituted to develop the project plan is called implementation team.

38. Project planning involves preparing time schedules, fixing deadlines, identifying the roles and assigning responsibilities.

39. A good project plan will describe all the activities in an implementation. It will include the entire technical area to support technical project management and address interfaces, data conversion and authorizations to avoid mistakes at a later stage.

40. It would prove detrimental to involve users in your ERP project planning phase.

41. Gap analysis is the process that identifies the gaps by mapping the expectations of the company with the capabilities of the ERP product.

42. Business Process Reengineering analyses the various business processes of the organization in order to identify and practice the best way of doing work.

43. Business Process Reengineering reduces the workforce size.

44. Business Process Reengineering is seen as a prerequisite for going ahead with ERP implementation by most of the ERP experts.

45. The ERP experts never suggest doing an in-depth BPR study before taking up ERP implementation as it leads to more costs.

46. Planning phase is considered to be the main functional area in the ERP implementation life cycle.
47. Modification of the ERP software results in problems such as code errors and difficulty when upgrading to new versions.
48. It is imperative that the implementation team is given a rigorous training by the ERP vendor and the hired consultants on how to implement the ERP system.
49. The testing phase enables the implementation team to discover problems that may require some minor modifications before the ERP system goes live.
50. In going live phase, the old system is removed and the new system is officially proclaimed operational.
51. The end-users need to be trained in order to ensure the acceptance and readiness of the new system.
52. In testing phase, the system is upgraded as and when new versions or technologies are introduced.
53. The different strategies for implementing ERP can be classified into organizational, technical and people strategies.
54. The implementation strategies help to overcome the resistance of the workers to the ERP system and thereby the success of the ERP implementation.
55. Organizational strategies include change strategy development, change management techniques, project management, communication and coordination, organizational structure and resources, IS function characteristics, managerial style and ideology.
56. People strategies include management and staff attitudes, user involvement and training.
57. Technical strategies include adequacy of in-house technical expertise, time and cost of ERP implementation, ERP complexity and various technical aspects of the ERP installation.
58. The top management must analyze the two fundamental sources of employee's resistance to ERP implementation—perceived risk and employee habit.
59. A perceived risk simply refers to the current practices that a person routinely performs.
60. Habit refers to an employee's perception of the risk associated with the decision to accept the new system.
61. A major strategy for changing the attitudes of the potential users of the new ERP system is to establish an effective communication system.
62. The top management can use the Cost Minimization Strategy to influence the effective components of users' attitudes. In this strategy the user's adoption costs are kept to a minimum and the users are convinced by the change agents that their net outcome of the ERP adoption process will be positive.
63. The Cost Minimization Strategy should operate at both the individual worker and the influential groups' level.
64. If the influential groups are convinced that a change in the balance of power in the organization will be in their favour then they will develop a positive attitude for the new system.
65. A user's perceived high quality of the ERP system has a positive impact on his attitude towards the system.
66. Trained users are able to appreciate the quality attributes as well as the potential benefits of the ERP system.

67. The management should not delay the introduction of the ERP system until a positive attitude is developed and sustained among the potential users.
68. A very effective implementation strategy is to ensure the support of well known individuals and opinion leaders.
69. The complete support and commitment of the management is the ultimate strategy that will help set the stage for ERP implementation success.
70. The implementation approach chosen by the organization does not decide the costs and risks of the ERP implementation project.
71. Three different approaches to ERP implementation include big-bang, phased or skeleton and parallel approach.
72. In parallel approach, the switch between using the old systems and using the new ERP system happens at once.
73. In big-bang implementation, fewer interfaces are required between the different modules, the costs are generally reduced compared to the phased approach and the implementation time is shorter.
74. Big-bang approach focuses on the organization for intense but relatively shorter time duration than phased approach.
75. A big-bang implementation approach is considered to be less risky than phased approach.
76. The advantages of big-bang approach are: shorter implementation time, low implementation cost, no need for temporary interfaces, the need to maintain and change legacy system is limited.
77. The disadvantages of big-bang approach are: huge peak resources may be required; the working of the system cannot be demonstrated until the system gets fully installed and the implementation team gets fewer hands-on opportunities to gain knowledge.
78. The Skeleton implementation is a phased approach.
79. The Skeleton approach provides usable functionality incrementally whether by functional business area or geography
80. The biggest disadvantage of Skeleton approach is that the project implementation team gets less time to plan, customize and test the system.
81. Skeleton or Phased Approach lacks the urgency and focus of a big-bang approach.
82. The advantage of the skeleton approach is that the peak resource requirements are less as compared to big-bang approach.
83. Risks in the phased approach are low.
84. In parallel approach, the old system and the new system are running parallel in the organization.
85. The advantage of the parallel approach is that the users can get used to the new system and meanwhile do their work using the old system.
86. An ERP implementation methodology is a roadmap to an ERP implementation.
87. The purpose of the implementation methodology is to deliver the implementation according to the specifications, within budget and on time.
88. A good implementation methodology leads to the shortest path to pay-off and fewest risks.
89. The ERP vendors and consulting firms develop the implementation methodology through refinements and application of best practices based on their expertise and industry experiences gained over several

90. Accelerated SAP is a detailed project plan by SAP that describes all the activities in an ERP implementation.
91. ASAP helps to reduce the SAP implementation time to less than six months.
92. ASAP implementation methodology consists of seven phases.
93. "The Total Solution" methodology has been developed by Deloitte and Touche consulting firm.
94. The Fast Track methodology has been developed by Ernst and Young LLP consulting firm.
95. An ERP vendor is a software firm that design, develop and implement ERP packages.
96. Consultants are the people who specialize in developing effective techniques and methodologies for ensuring a successful ERP implementation.
97. End-users are the people who will use the ERP system to do their work in the company.
98. A vendor who has implementation consultants on staff has a higher rate of ERP implementation success than an ERP vendor who uses third party consultants.
99. An ERP vendor should deliver the product along with its documentation to the company after the contract has been signed.
100. The vendor should suggest best ways to implement the system. The vendor must carry out the customization process if the company has taken decision to customize the ERP system to suit the business processes of the organization.
101. The vendor should carefully review the software competencies in the organization and take all necessary steps to remove the software deficiencies before going ahead with running the ERP system.
102. ERP vendor plays the role of an advisor in all the implementation phases.
103. As a change agent, the vendor will reduce the complexity of business transformation and will prepare organization ready for change.
104. The ERP consultants have several years of hands-on ERP implementation experience with several industries.
105. The cost of consultants is very high.
106. The end users analyze the ERP package and the business processes and accordingly address the customization issue.
107. ERP consultancy is given to the highest levels of management. As a result it is more expensive.
108. A high ROI from the ERP system can only be achieved if the end users accept the change readily and undergo training to develop new skill sets.
109. End-users involvement and participation is not an important factor for the success of ERP implementation.
110. The effective use of the ERP system by the end-users results in improved cash flows, short response cycles and increased profits.
111. The most important contribution of end-users is providing feedback to the implementation team about the ERP system.
112. The involvement of the users in the early implementation stages makes it easier to understand the system's requirements, select the right ERP package and plan the customization issue.
113. The user's timely involvement during ERP implementation helps in early detection and correction of mistakes.

114. Critical success factors can be understood as essentially a small number of easily identifiable operational goals that are framed by the management and experts based on research done on the system and the broader environment.

115. The critical success factor model designed by Holland and Light groups the critical success factors into strategic and tactical factors.

116. The tactical issues are factors that define the planning phase of a project.

117. The strategic factors include business vision, support of the owner and top management, project schedule, ERP strategy and legacy systems.

118. The legacy systems are systems that are no longer efficient and need to be improved so that they are able to perform well.

119. The strategic issues define the rollout or action phase of the project. They appear more important as the implementation phase moves close.

120. Tactical factors include communication with all the affected parties or users, recruiting the necessary technical as well as business specialist, obtaining the underlying technology, acceptance from the end-users, troubleshooting throughout the project, monitoring and providing feedback at every stage of the ERP implementation project.

121. The unified critical success factor model for ERP implementation was developed through the application of grounded theory.

122. In unified critical success factor model the critical success factors are divided in four perspectives. The four perspectives are strategic, tactical, technological and organizational.

123. The ERP effectiveness model by Vinod Kumar et al., provides a structured road map for understanding the complex process as well as the critical issues in institutionalizing ERP systems in organizations.

124. The institutionalization of an innovation is defined as an important post-implementation process in which the organization learns to deal with changes, stabilize technology and builds up new competencies by redefining the processes.

125. There are three stages in the ERP institutionalization model-technical, semantic and effective.

126. Technical Level stage is characterized by a high level of technical disorder.

127. In the semantic level, the ERP system has lost it has imported from outside character to a large extent.

128. In effectiveness stage, the organization focuses on effectiveness of ERP systems in improving the efficiency of organization's value creation process.

129. The direct costs of an ERP implementation are always included in the budget by project manager.

130. Direct costs represent the accurate and complete picture of what an ERP implementation will cost your organization.

131. Direct costs include costs of the ERP software applications and tools.

132. Hidden costs refer to the costs that most project managers often miss to account for in their budgets for ERP implementation.

133. Underestimation of training costs is likely to result in budget overruns later.

134. The training costs should not be reduced when budget has to be squeezed as training the employees to work on ERP systems will prove beneficial for the company.

135. Customization should be avoided as customizing the ERP software not only calls for a trained ERP software developer but also may lead to increased system complexity.

136. Migrating data from the legacy systems to the new ERP system is a costly affair.

SECTION C

FILL IN THE BLANKS

1. Implementing an ERP System is a ____________ undertaking.
2. As ERP implementation is a complex, resource-consuming and risky activity, the company must follow a ____________ methodology.
3. A successful ERP implementation also depends upon the ____________ and the implementation strategies chosen by the organization.
4. ____________ is a short phase that deals with eliminating those ERP packages that are not at all suitable for the business processes of the company.
5. The success of an ERP implementation depends largely on the ____________ selected for implementation.
6. A ________ ERP package selected will almost decide the success of the implementation.
7. The evaluation and selection of ERP software is a complex task. This task must be accomplished as a ____________ process that minimizes the risks associated and helps to make a well-informed decision.
8. Functional Fit involves checking whether all ________ aspects of the business are duly covered in the ERP package.
9. The ERP package should be functionally-fit with the company's business____________.
10. The ERP package must be __________ to suit the needs of the specific business processes and ____________ to meet the growing and changing needs of the company.
11. An ERP product that easily configures the screens to have relevant ____________ fields and back-end tables is considered a good product.
12. If an ERP product requires a lot of ____________ in order to support your business processes then it is the wrong product for you.
13. The ERP products are often evaluated based on the percentage of ____________ from the business or changes in the business processes that will be required for effective implementation of the ERP package.
14. Users Acceptance is defined as the percentage of acceptance of the user friendliness of the screens/interfaces as well as the process flows by the users. The ____________ the rate of acceptance, the more user-friendly the product is considered to be.
15. An ERP package is considered to be good if it requires __________ time to get implemented.
16. The key to successful ERP implementation is selecting the right ERP software and the right ________ who will provide you with a fast and effective implementation.
17. The ERP vendors should be evaluated based on the functionality of their ____________ and their ability to support business transformation in order to achieve the objectives of the company.
18. Checking the customer references ensures that the claims of the vendor are substantiated and not just ____________.
19. The implementation methodology of the ERP vendor should be highly ____________ to the specific needs and expertise of the company.

20. An implementation methodology that is well-tailored to the known requirements of the company will help the company to achieve the desired results and ensure that __________ return on investment (ROI) is received.

21. The evaluation criteria for vendors are: Operational coverage, Range of business applications, Company character and direction, Training offered by the ERP vendor, Vendor's experience and financial position and _____________.

22. _____________ builds a roadmap that is used throughout the implementation.

23. The implementation team develops the project ________ using the project planning tools (gnatt charts etc.).

24. ________ involves preparing time schedules, fixing deadlines, identifying the roles and assigning responsibilities.

25. A good Project plan will describe all the ____________ in an implementation it will address interfaces, ____________ and authorization to avoid mistakes at a later stage.

26. ____________ is the process that identifies the gaps by mapping the expectations of the company with the capabilities of the ERP product.

27. Business Process Reengineering analyses the various business processes of the organization in order to identify and practice the __________ way of doing work.

28. ______________ is seen as a prerequisite for going ahead with ERP implementation by most of the ERP experts.

29. The ERP experts often suggest doing an in-depth __________ study before taking up ERP implementation.

30. BPR attempts to maximize the business productivity through restructuring and reorganizing the business__________, information workflows, human resources as well as the divisions and departments in the organization.

31. __________ of the ERP software results in problems such as code errors and difficulty when upgrading to new versions.

32. The ERP software configuration is complex, ____________ and costly.

33. It is crucial to test all of the company data, procedures and processes in order to find the ________in the ERP system. These bugs should then be ____________ before the launch of the system.

34. In _____________ phase the old system is removed and the new system is officially proclaimed operational. The company will use the new ERP system for doing business.

35. The end users need to be trained in order to ensure the __________ and readiness of the new system.

36. Some organizations use an in-house training approach while other organizations prefer using training____________.

37. In ________________ phase the system is upgraded as and when new versions or technologies are introduced.

38. The post-implementation phase includes regular monitoring of the system, tuning the hardware or software and performing __________of the ERP system.

39. The different strategies for implementing ERP can be classified into organizational, __________ and people strategies.

40. The implementation strategies help to overcome the ______________ of the workers to the ERP system and thereby the success of the ERP implementation.

41. The organizational strategies include change strategy development, change management techniques, ________________, communication and coordination, organizational structure and resources, _________________, managerial style and ideology.
42. The ______________ strategies include management and staff attitudes, user involvement and training.
43. ______________ strategies include adequacy of in-house technical expertise, time and cost of ERP implementation, ERP complexity and various technical aspects of the ERP installation.
44. The top management must analyze the two fundamental sources of employee's resistance to ERP implementation: _____________ and_____________.
45. Habit simply refers to the current ____________that a person routinely performs.
46. ________________refer to an employee's perception of the risk associated with the decision to accept the new system.
47. Some of the change management strategies for ERP implementation are: ______________, Cost Minimization Strategy and Differentiation Strategy
48. An effective communication strategy is to inform the potential users about the various ___________ of the ERP system.
49. The top management can use the ______________ Strategy to influence the effective components of users' attitudes. In this strategy the user's adoption costs are kept to a minimum and the users are convinced by the change agents that their net outcome of the ERP adoption process will be positive.
50. The Cost Minimization Strategy should operate at both the individual worker and the ________________ level.
51. If the influential groups are convinced that change in the ______________in the organization will be in their favour then they will develop a positive attitude for the new system.
52. A user's perceived ___________ of the ERP system has a positive impact on his attitude towards the system.
53. Training provides hands-on experience to the users. Trained users are able to appreciate the ______________ as well as the potential ___________ of the ERP system.
54. The management should _____________the introduction of the ERP system until a positive attitude is developed and sustained among the potential users.
55. It will be a bad experience if the ERP system is introduced at a time when a critical mass of ___________ is not ready for the change.
56. A very effective implementation strategy is to ensure the support of well known individuals and_____________.
57. The complete support and commitment of the ______________ is the ultimate strategy that will help set the stage for ERP implementation success.
58. The implementation ______________ chosen by the organization decides the costs and risks of the ERP implementation project.
59. The three different approaches to ERP implementation include: __________________, _______________and phased or skeleton approach.
60. In big-bang approach the switch between using the old systems and using the new ERP system happens__________.

61. In big-bang implementation fewer interfaces are required between the different modules; the costs are generally ___________ compared to the phased approach and the implementation time is_________.

62. _________ Approach focuses the organization for intense but relatively shorter time duration than phased approach.

63. Big-bang approach not only addresses the long-term __________shortages but also condenses the pain of an ERP implementation project into short duration.

64. A big-bang implementation approach is considered to be more _____________ than phased approach.

65. The Skeleton implementation is a __________ approach.

66. The biggest advantage of ___________ approach is that the project implementation team gets enough time to plan, customize and test the system.

67. Skeleton or Phased Approach lacks the urgency and __________ of a big-bang approach.

68. In _______________ approach, the old system and the new system are running parallel in the organization.

69. The purpose of the implementation methodology is to deliver the implementation according to the_____________, within ___________and on time.

70. The implementation methodology provided by the vendor or in-house consultants must be _____________to the needs of the company.

71. An ERP implementation methodology serves as a model to deliver measurable ______________ quickly and effectively.

72. The ERP vendors and consulting firms develop the implementation methodology through refinements and application of best practices based on their __________and ____________ gained over several years in business.

73. SAP has introduced an effective implementation methodology called______________.

74. ASAP helps to reduce the SAP implementation time to less than _______ months.

75. Business Blueprint is Accelerated SAP visual model of the _________ of the business.

76. "The Total Solution" methodology has been developed by _______________ consulting firm.

77. The _____________ methodology developed by Deloitte and Touche consulting firm enhances and accelerates the ERP implementation project.

78. The five implementation phases of the Fast Track Work plan methodology include scoping and planning, visioning and targeting, _______________, __________, testing and delivery.

79. An ERP _______________ is a software firm that designs, develops and implement ERP packages.

80. _____________ are the people who specialize in developing effective techniques and methodologies for ensuring a successful ERP implementation.

81. ___________ are the people who will use the ERP system to do their work in the company.

82. A vendor who has implementation consultants on staff has a _____________ rate of ERP implementation success than an ERP vendor who uses third party consultants.

83. An ERP vendor needs to perform absolutely well as most of the time it is the ERP vendor who is __________ when the anticipated results from the new system do not materialize.

84. An ERP vendor should deliver the product along with its ______________to the company after the contract has been signed.

85. Most ERP vendors have by now developed effective implementation methodologies that are_______________.

86. The vendor should carefully review the ________________ in the organization and take all necessary steps to remove the software deficiencies before going ahead with running the ERP system.

87. The different roles that an ERP vendor has to play are as follows: Innovator, Advisor, ____________ and Trainer.

88. ERP consultants have an in-depth understanding of the strengths and weaknesses of the various ERP products offered by___________.

89. The consultants need to ask questions from the vendor so that vendor claims are __________ before the product is purchased from a particular vendor.

90. The ERP consultant has several roles to play as an administrator, as an __________, as a trainer and as a mediator between the company and the ERP vendor.

91. ERP consultants usually operate in the _____________ area.

92. ERP consultancy is given to the __________ levels of management. As a result it is more__________.

93. The huge gap in the __________ for ERP consultants also contribute in raising the cost of the ERP consultants.

94. End-users _________ is considered an important factor for the success of ERP implementation.

95. The effective use of the ERP system by the end-users results in improved cash flows, ______________and increased profits.

96. The most important contribution of end-users is providing _________ to the implementation team about the ERP system.

97. The involvement of the users in the _____________ implementation stages makes it ______________to understand the system's requirements, select the right ERP package and plan the customization issue.

98. Critical success factors can be understood as essentially a small number of easily identifiable ____________ that are framed by the management and experts based on research done on the system and the broader environment.

99. The critical success factor model designed by ____________________groups the critical success factors into strategic and tactical factors.

100. Strategic issues are factors that define the __________ phase of a project.

101. The _________ issues specify the need for a project mission, top management's approval and support as well as a well planned project schedule outlining individual action steps for implementation of project.

102. The strategic factors appear most important at the ________ of a project.

103. The __________ systems are systems that are no longer efficient and need to be improved so that they are able to perform well.

104. The __________ issues define the rollout or action phase of the project.

105. The tactical issues appear more important as the ____________ phase moves close.

106. ________ Factors include communication with all the affected parties or users, recruiting the necessary technical as well as business specialist, obtaining the underlying technology, acceptance from the end users, troubleshooting throughout the project, monitoring and providing feedback at every stage of the ERP implementation project.

107. The unified critical success factor model for ERP implementation was developed through the application of __________ theory.

108. In unified critical success factor model, the critical success factors are divided in ________ perspectives. The four perspectives are ________, tactical, technological and ___________.

109. The _________________ model by Vinod Kumar et al., provides a structured roadmap, for understanding the complex process as well as the critical issues in ___________ ERP systems in organizations.

110. The institutionalization of an innovation is defined as an important _____________ process in which the organization learns to deal with changes, stabilize technology and builds up new competencies by redefining the____________.

111. During the institutionalization process the organization uses the innovation, learns to accept the introduced changes as well as begins to realize the ______ of the ERP system.

112. There are three stages in the ERP institutionalization model-technical, _________ and effective.

113. Technical Level stage is characterized by a high level of technical___________.

114. The main activities that are performed in technical level stage consist of__________ , fine-tuning the systems and facing the technical challenges in order to provide a running system.

115. In Technical Level stage, the system gradually begins to ______ it imported from outside character.

116. In the __________ level, the ERP system has lost it has imported from outside character to a large extent.

117. The technical issues have been resolved and semantic problems become the main point of concern in ___________ level stage.

118. Efforts to reduce ____________ are the main focus of organization in semantic level.

119. In ___________ stage, the organization focuses on effectiveness of ERP systems in improving the efficiency of organization's value creation process.

120. In Effectiveness Level stage, the technical and organizational disorders are quite_________.

121. The _______ costs of an ERP implementation are always included in the budget by project manager.

122. _________costs do not represent the accurate and complete picture of what an ERP implementation will cost your organization.

123. Direct costs include costs of the ERP ______________and tools.

124. ______ Costs refer to the costs that most project managers often miss to account for in their budgets for ERP implementation.

125. Underestimation of _________ costs is likely to result in budget overruns later.

126. Testing the links between ERP software packages and other corporate software that have to be built on a case by case basis is another ERP costs that is often___________.

127. Customization should be _________ as customizing the ERP software not only calls for a trained ERP software developer but it also may lead to increased system__________.

128. ERP customization is both _____________ and expensive.

129. Data conversion is an important activity that determines the success of an____________.

130. Migrating data from the legacy systems to the new ERP system is a _________affair. Companies often tend to underestimate the _______of data migration.

ANSWERS

SECTION A

(1) e **(2)** c **(3)** d **(4)** a **(5)** d **(6)** a **(7)** a **(8)** e **(9)** b **(10)** d
(11) c **(12)** d **(13)** d **(14)** c **(15)** e **(16)** a **(17)** c **(18)** e **(19)** d **(20)** a
(21) b **(22)** d **(23)** a **(24)** d **(25)** c **(26)** d **(27)** b **(28)** d **(29)** c **(30)** c
(31) c **(32)** d **(33)** d **(34)** d **(35)** c **(36)** a **(37)** d **(38)** b **(39)** c **(40)** d
(41) d **(42)** c **(43)** a **(44)** d **(45)** a **(46)** e **(47)** e **(48)** e **(49)** e **(50)** e
(51) c **(52)** c **(53)** d **(54)** e **(55)** c **(56)** a **(57)** c **(58)** a **(59)** a **(60)** c
(61) b **(62)** c **(63)** b **(64)** d **(65)** a **(66)** a **(67)** a **(68)** a **(69)** e **(70)** d
(71) e **(72)** e **(73)** d **(74)** e **(75)** e **(76)** e **(77)** d **(78)** a **(79)** d **(80)** e
(81) e **(82)** c **(83)** c **(84)** a **(85)** b **(86)** d **(87)** b **(88)** a **(89)** d **(90)** c
(91) c **(92)** d **(93)** a **(94)** d **(95)** e **(96)** e **(97)** e.

SECTION B

(1) True **(2)** True **(3)** True **(4)** True **(5)** True **(6)** True **(7)** True **(8)** True
(9) False **(10)** True **(11)** False **(12)** True **(13)** True **(14)** False **(15)** False **(16)** True
(17) True **(18)** True **(19)** True **(20)** True **(21)** True **(22)** True **(23)** True **(24)** False
(25) False **(26)** True **(27)** True **(28)** True **(29)** False **(30)** True **(31)** True **(32)** False
(33) True **(34)** False **(35)** True **(36)** True **(37)** True **(38)** True **(39)** True **(40)** False
(41) True **(42)** True **(43)** True **(44)** True **(45)** False **(46)** False **(47)** True **(48)** True
(49) True **(50)** True **(51)** True **(52)** False **(53)** True **(54)** True **(55)** True **(56)** True
(57) True **(58)** True **(59)** False **(60)** False **(61)** True **(62)** True **(63)** True **(64)** True
(65) True **(66)** True **(67)** False **(68)** True **(69)** True **(70)** False **(71)** True **(72)** False
(73) True **(74)** True **(75)** False **(76)** True **(77)** True **(78)** True **(79)** True **(80)** False
(81) True **(82)** True **(83)** True **(84)** True **(85)** True **(86)** True **(87)** True **(88)** True
(89) True **(90)** True **(91)** True **(92)** False **(93)** False **(94)** False **(95)** True **(96)** True
(97) True **(98)** True **(99)** True **(100)** True **(101)** True **(102)** True **(103)** True **(104)** True
(105) True **(106)** False **(107)** True **(108)** True **(109)** False **(110)** True **(111)** True **(112)** True
(113) True **(114)** True **(115)** True **(116)** False **(117)** True **(118)** True **(119)** False **(120)** True
(121) True **(122)** True **(123)** True **(124)** True **(125)** True **(126)** True **(127)** True **(128)** True
(129) True **(130)** False **(131)** True **(132)** True **(133)** True **(134)** True **(135)** True **(136)** True.

SECTION C

(1) large **(2)** sound **(3)** implementation approach **(4)** Pre Evaluation Screening of ERP packages **(5)** ERP package **(6)** right **(7)** fact-based **(8)** functional **(9)** processes **(10)** flexible, scalable **(11)** data input **(12)** customization **(13)** deviation **(14)** higher **(15)** less **(16)** ERP vendor **(17)** applications **(18)** brochure-ware **(19)** tailor-able **(20)** maximum **(21)** pricing models being offered by different vendors **(22)** Project Planning **(23)** plan **(24)** Project planning **(25)** activities, data conversion **(26)** Gap analysis **(27)** best **(28)** BPR **(29)** BPR **(30)** processes **(31)** Modification

(32) time consuming **(33)** weak links, fixed **(34)** Going live **(35)** acceptance **(36)** consultants **(37)** Post Implementation **(38)** audit **(39)** technical **(40)** resistance **(41)** project management, IS function characteristics **(42)** people **(43)** Technical **(44)** perceived risk, employee habit **(45)** practices **(46)** Perceived risks **(47)** effective communication system **(48)** benefits **(49)** cost Minimization **(50)** influential groups' **(51)** balance of power **(52)** high quality **(53)** quality attributes, benefits **(54)** delay **(55)** employees **(56)** opinion leaders **(57)** management **(58)** approach **(59)** big-bang, parallel approach **(60)** at once **(61)** reduced, shorter **(62)** Big-bang **(63)** resource **(64)** risky **(65)** phased **(66)** Skeleton **(67)** focus **(68)** Parallel Approach **(69)** specifications, budget **(70)** highly tailor-able **(71)** return on investment **(72)** expertise, industry experiences **(73)** "Accelerated SAP" **(74)** six **(75)** future state **(76)** Ernst and Young LLP **(77)** Fast Track **(78)** redesign, configuration **(79)** vendor **(80)** Consultants **(81)** End-users **(82)** higher **(83)** blamed **(84)** documentation **(85)** industry-specific **(86)** software competencies **(87)** Change Agent **(88)** different vendors **(89)** verified **(90)** analyst **(91)** "high risk-high reward" **(92)** highest, expensive **(93)** supply-demand **(94)** involvement and participation **(95)** short response cycles **(96)** feedback **(97)** early, easier **(98)** operational goals **(99)** Holland and Light **(100)** planning **(101)** strategic **(102)** outset **(103)** legacy **(104)** tactical **(105)** implementation **(106)** Tactical **(107)** grounded **(108)** four, strategic, organizational **(109)** ERP effectiveness, institutionalizing **(110)** post-implementation, processes **(111)** benefits **(112)** semantic **(113)** disorder **(114)** resolving bugs **(115)** lose **(116)** semantic **(117)** semantic **(118)** organizational disorder **(119)** Effectiveness Level **(120)** low **(121)** direct **(122)** Direct **(123)** software applications **(124)** Hidden **(125)** training **(126)** underestimated **(127)** avoided, complexity **(128)** time consuming **(129)** ERP implementation **(130)** costly, cost.

8
Chapter
Soft System Approach

HIGHLIGHTS

- SOFT SYSTEM METHODOLOGY
  - SSM as a Tool for Analyzing ERP

Soft Systems Methodology (SSM) is a methodology specifically designed for analyzing and modeling large and complex systems including human (soft) systems. SSM is used to evaluate the impacts of the ERP systems. It, therefore, serves as a valuable framework for the evaluation of ERP. The methodology also helps in identifying the value of ERP system to the organization, the level of impact of ERP implementation on the organization and the barriers to the ERP implementation.

8.1 SOFT SYSTEMS METHODOLOGY

The Soft Systems Methodology (SSM) was first introduced by Peter Chuckland in his book: *Systems Thinking, Systems Practice* in 1981. SSM is regarded as a "soft" operations research tool. Traditionally the research tools that existed in the field of operations research comprised "hard" mathematical and decision models. SSM methodology is used to analyze and model hard to define complex systems that integrate technology (hard) and human (soft) systems.

A human (soft) system is defined as the collection of activities and the relationship between these activities with people purposefully engaged in the activities. SSM methodology attempts to successfully deal with the more unpredictable and complex human side of the system. It recognizes that different individuals may have different outlook on the same situation and may suggest different preferable outcomes. SSM recognizes these differences and take these differences into consideration in order to ensure that the results of the analysis are acceptable to all the concerned parties.

Soft Systems Methodology addresses "fuzzy" problems. These problems arise when the objectives are not clear, multiple objectives exist and several perceptions for the problem exist. The SSM approach defines an acceptable improved path of action through an iterative process. Figure 8.1 shows the seven stages that form the complete process of Soft Systems Methodology. In this process the users, analysts and designers all work together to define the problem situation, generate and evaluate the alternatives and finally select the most acceptable solution.

The seven stages in SSM process tailored to the framework for ERP are discussed below:

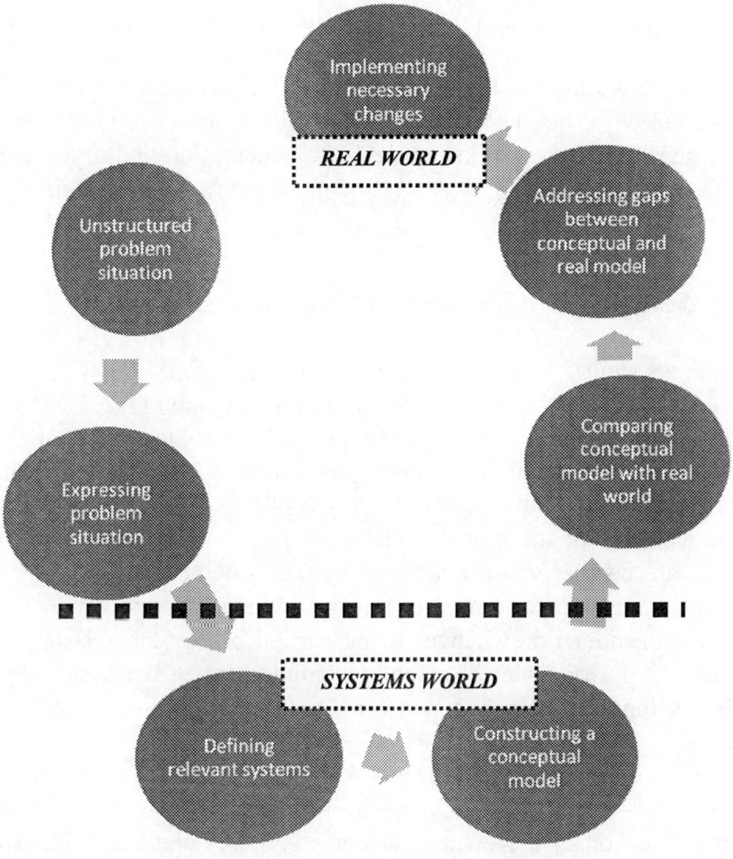

Fig. 8.1. Process of Soft Systems Methodology

Stage1. Unstructured Problem Situation

The problem situation is identified with the help of managers, employees or users and is represented in terms of a "rich picture" (an abstract drawing that describes all aspects of the system that are considered relevant to the problem definition).

It involves defining at a high level the organization, the system and the processes. The weaknesses are identified by checking the current performance of the system and conducting a thorough analysis of how the various business processes are currently being carried out in the organization. The analysts, managers and users all have a crucial role to play in this stage. They serve as active participants and exert certain level of control over the situation. By bringing their viewpoints and opinions into the analysis a true and correct problem situation will be identified.

Stage 2. Problem Situation Expressed

In this stage, the information about the problem situation is collected. The information generally includes structure of the organization, processes currently being carried out and the problems being faced by the people working in the organization as well as the viewpoint of the managers. This information is collected using the managers. This information is collected using techniques such as interviews, questionnaires, workshops, on-site observation and group decision making sessions. The tools such as QFD and Analytical Hierarchy Process can also aid in this elicitation.

Stage 3. Root Definition of Relevant Systems

The root definition is a succinct statement of the system that defines the system as "a system to do X, by Y, in order to achieve Z". It is expressed as a transformation process. The transformation process takes some input, transforms that input and produces a new form of the entity as an output of the system. The root definition of the system involves a certain view of the world. In the Soft Systems Methodology, the mnemonic 'CATWOE' guides the identification and development of the elements of the root definition:

Customer: these are people who are affected by the system.

Actor: Actors are the people who are perform activities in the system.

Transformation: constitutes the changes being carried out by the system.

Weltanschauung: the "world-view" or the viewpoints held of the system by the people.

Owners: system belong (s) to Person(s). He holds the authority to decide how (and if) the system will work.

Environment: constitutes the larger system within which the system under consideration exists.

The explicit identification of the owners, customers, actors and their viewpoints contribute to the successful implementation of the complex ERP systems. SSM considers the identification of the roles and needs of the customers, actors and owners as well as the top management support as critical for successful implementation.

Stage 4. Conceptual Models

In this stage, the conceptual model is constructed for the root definitions of stage 3. The conceptual model is mostly expressed in pictorial/flowchart form and essentially incorporates all the elements of the 'CATWOE' mnemonic. The conceptual model identifies the activities and their interactions that are necessary for the system to accomplish the goals and aims defined in the root definition of the stage 3.The models for the ERP systems are determined largely by the systems themselves and may include data flow diagrams, entity relationship diagrams, state transition diagrams, information systems planning matrices, etc.

Stage 5. Perform Comparison of the Conceptual Model to the Real World

The conceptual model is compared with the "real world" system. This comparison is done to identify the possible areas where improvements are necessary. A good comparison of the conceptual and the real world system will discover the problems or deficiencies that exist between what is happening ("rich picture") and what is desirable ("root definition") as defined by the conceptual model.

Stage 6. Feasible, Desirable Changes

In this stage, changes or improvements in the system are studied to address disconnects or gaps between the "real world" system and the "conceptual model" as identified in the stage 5. These changes will be carried out after a careful evaluation for feasibility determination has been performed. Deciding whether to customize the ERP software or to change the business processes to suit the ERP system is crucial to the success of the ERP system. The final agreement on what changes will be made forms an output of this stage.

Stage 7. Actions Needed for Improvement

Actions to improve constitute the last stage of the soft system methodology. Here the recommendations for the changes are implemented to ensure success of the ERP system.

LEARNING POINTS

1. Soft Systems Methodology (SSM) is a methodology specifically designed for analyzing and modeling large and complex systems including human (soft) systems.
2. SSM methodology is used to analyze and model hard to define complex systems that integrate technology (hard) and human (soft) systems.
3. A human (soft) system is defined as the collection of activities and the relationship between these activities with people purposefully engaged in the activities.
4. Soft Systems Methodology addresses "fuzzy" problems. These problems arise when the objectives are not clear, multiple objectives exist and several perceptions for the problem exist.
5. The SSM approach defines an acceptable improved path of action through an iterative process.
6. The first stage of SSM, problem situation unstructured, involves defining at a high level the organization, the system and the processes.

7. The conceptual model is expressed in pictorial/ flow chart form and identifies the activities as well as their interactions that are necessary for the system to accomplish the goals and aims defined in the root definition.
8. A good comparison of the conceptual model with the real-world system will discover the problems or deficiencies that exist between what is happening ("rich picture") and what is desired ("root definition") as defined by the conceptual model.
9. In the last stage, "actions to improve", recommendations for changes are implemented to ensure success of ERP system.

8.2 SSM AS A TOOL FOR ANALYZING ERP

Soft systems methodology has been applied in many settings. SSM has been used in the development of information system. For instance the Information System Devlopment model by Winter, et al., extends upon the concept of the information system as given by Peter Chuckland. Chuckland's view of an information system consists of two systems: a serving system and a served system. The actual organization consisting of purposeful organizational activity forms the served system. In another application, SSM is used as a framework for business process reengineering.

SSM is also used as a tool for analyzing the impact of ERP implementation. In addition to economic factors, SSM also tries to identify organizational, social and cultural aspects of the organization in order to rightly assess and evaluate the impact that ERP will have on the organization. Though the soft system methodology does not claim to identify and mitigate all the impacts of ERP on the organization by taking into account various aspects of the organization and the system.

LEARNING POINTS

1. SSM is used as a framework for business process reengineering.
2. It is also used as a tool for analyzing the impact of ERP implementation.

SUMMARY

Soft systems methodology (SSM) is specifically designed for analyzing and modeling large and complex systems including human (soft) systems. It is used to evaluate the impacts of the ERP system. It serves as the framework for evaluation of ERP systems.

A soft system is defined as the collection of activities and the relationship between these activities with people purposefully engaged in the activities. The SSM approach defines an acceptable improved path of action through an iterative process. The seven stages in SSM are: problem situation unstructured, problem situation expressed, root definition of relevant systems, conceptual model, comparison of the conceptual models with the real world, flexible and desirable changes and actions to improve.

In the first stage the problem situation is identified and represented in terms of a "rich picture". The second stage comprises information collection using various tools and techniques such as QFD, AHP, interviews, questionnaires, workshops, on-site observation etc. The third stage deals with the identification of the owners, customers, actors and their viewpoint. In the fourth stage, a conceptual model is constructed for the root definitions developed at stage 3. A root definition involves a certain view of the world. In the fifth stage, the conceptual model is compared with the 'real world' system. It helps in discovering the problems or deficiencies that exist between what is happening and what is desirable (the conceptual model).

In the sixth stage, the final agreement is drawn that decides what further changes and improvements will be made in the system. In the last stage of SSM the recommendations for changes (made in the previous stages) are implemented. SSM has been used in the development of the information system. In another application SSM is used as a framework for business process reengineering. SSM is also used as a tool for analyzing the impact of the ERP implementation.

POINTS TO REMEMBER

1. Soft systems methodology is a methodology specifically designed for analyzing and modeling large and complex systems including human (soft systems).
2. SSM serves as a valuable framework for the evaluation of ERP.
3. It is regarded as a tool for "soft" operations.
4. It deals with the complex and unpredictable human side of the system.
5. SSM process comprises seven steps (or stages). The stages are as follows:
   - **(a)** Identification of unstructured problem situation.
   - **(b)** Expressing the problem situation. In this stage, information about problem situation is collected.
   - **(c)** Root definition of relevant systems is formulated.
   - **(d)** Construction of conceptual models.
   - **(e)** Comparison of the conceptual models with the real world is done.
   - **(f)** Final agreement on feasible and desirable changes required is made.
   - **(g)** In this stage, recommendations for the changes (in step (f)) are implemented.
6. SSM is also used as a framework for business process reengineering.
7. In addition to economic factors, SSM also tries to identify organizational, social and cultural aspects of the organization in order to rightly assess and evaluate the impact that ERP will have on the organization.

REVIEW QUESTIONS

1. What is soft systems methodology?
2. Explain the different stages that constitute the soft systems methodology.
3. Discuss SSM as a tool for analyzing ERP.

OBJECTIVE QUESTIONS

SECTION A

TICK THE CORRECT ANSWER

1. The Soft Systems Methodology (SSM) was first introduced by whom and when?
   (a) Peter Chuckland in his book named "Systems Thinking, Systems Practice" in 1981.
   (b) Peter Chuckland in 1990.
   (c) S. Rao in 1978.
   (d) Kala Kota in 2000.
2. Which of the following is regarded as a "soft" operations research tool?
   (a) SSM.
   (b) ERP implementation.
   (c) Supply chain management.
   (d) CRM
3. Traditionally the research tools that existed in the field of operations research comprised of __________.
   (a) "Hard" mathematical.
   (b) Decision models.
   (c) Both (a) and (b).
   (d) None of above.
4. Which methodology is used to analyze and model hard to define complex systems that integrate technology (hard) and human (soft) systems?
   (a) Analytical Hierarchy Process.
   (b) SSM.
   (c) Accelerated SAP.
   (d) Total Solution.
5. A human (soft) system is defined as:
   (a) The collection of activities.
   (b) The relationship between the activities with people purposefully engaged in the activities.
   (c) The collection of activities and the relationship between these activities with people purposefully engaged in the activities.
   (d) None of above.
6. What does SSM methodology do?
   (a) SSM attempts to successfully deal with the more unpredictable and complex human side of the system.
   (b) SSM recognizes that different individuals may have different outlook on the same situation and may suggest different preferable outcomes.
   (c) SSM recognizes these differences and takes these differences into consideration in order to ensure that the results of the analysis are acceptable to all the concerned parties.
   (d) All of above.

7. Soft Systems Methodology addresses ________problems.
   (a) Fuzzy.
   (b) Maintenance.
   (c) Customization.
   (d) None of above.
8. When does a Fuzzy problem commonly arise?
   (a) The objectives are not clear.
   (b) Multiple objectives exist.
   (c) Several perceptions for the problem exist.
   (d) All of above.
9. The SSM approach defines an _________ path of action through an iterative process.
   (a) Acceptable.
   (b) Improved.
   (c) Both (a) and (b).
   (d) None of above.
10. Give the number of stages that form the complete process of Soft Systems Methodology.
    (a) Seven.
    (b) Five.
    (c) Ten.
    (d) Eight.
11. In SSM process the users, analysts and designers all work together to:
    (a) Define the problem situation.
    (b) Generate and evaluate the alternatives.
    (c) Finally select the most acceptable solution.
    (d) All of above.
    (e) None of above.
12. In ________________, the problem situation is identified with the help of managers, employees or users and is represented in terms of a "rich picture" (an abstract drawing that describes all aspects of the system that are considered relevant to the problem definition).
    (a) Stage 1: Unstructured Problem Situation.
    (b) Stage 2: Problem Situation Expressed.
    (c) Stage 3: Root Definition of Relevant Systems.
    (d) Stage 4: Conceptual Models.
13. Stage 1 "Unstructured problem situation" involves:
    (a) Defining at a high level the organization, the system and the processes.
    (b) Identifying the weaknesses by checking the current performance of the system and conducting a thorough analysis of how the various business processes are currently being carried out in the organization.
    (c) Both (a) and (b).
    (d) None of above.
14. In _________stage, the information about the problem situation is collected.
    (a) Stage 1: Unstructured Problem Situation.
    (b) Stage 2: Problem Situation Expressed.

(c) Stage 3: Root Definition of Relevant Systems.
(d) Stage 4: Conceptual Models.

15. The information about the problem situation generally includes:
(a) Structure of the organization.
(b) Processes currently being carried out.
(c) The problems being faced by the people working in the organization.
(d) The viewpoint of the managers.
(e) All of above.

16. Which technique is used to collect the information about the problem situation?
(a) Interviews.
(b) Questionnaires.
(c) Workshops.
(d) On-site observation and group decision making sessions.
(e) All of above.

17. The tool that can aid in eliciting the information about the problem situation is:
(a) QFD.
(b) Analytical Hierarchy Process.
(c) Both (a) and (b).
(d) None of above.

18. The root definition is a succinct statement of the system that defines the system as:
(a) System to do X.
(b) System to do X, by Y, in order to achieve Z.
(c) System to do X, by Y.
(d) None of above.

19. Which is true about stage 3: Root Definition of Relevant Systems?
(a) The root definition is a succinct statement of the system that defines the system as "system to do X, by Y, in order to achieve Z".
(b) The root definition of the system involves a certain view of the world.
(c) In the Soft Systems Methodology, the mnemonic CATWOE guides the identification and development of the elements of the root definition.
(d) All of above.

20. What does Weltanschauung mean?
(a) People who are performing activities in the system.
(b) The changes being carried out by the system.
(c) The "world-view" or the viewpoints held of the system by the people.
(d) None of above.

21. __________ are the people who are performing activities in the system.
(a) Owners.
(b) Actors.
(c) Employees.
(d) None of above.

22. In which stage is the conceptual model constructed for the root definitions of stage 3?
(a) Stage 1: Unstructured Problem Situation.
(b) Stage 2: Problem Situation Expressed.

(c) Stage 3: Root Definition of Relevant Systems.
(d) Stage 4: Conceptual Models.

23. Which is true about conceptual models?
(a) The conceptual model is mostly expressed in pictorial/flow chart form.
(b) The conceptual model essentially incorporates all the elements of the CATWOE mnemonic.
(c) The conceptual model identifies the activities and their interactions that are necessary for the system to accomplish the goals and aims defined in the root definition of the stage 3.
(d) All of above.

24. The models for the ERP systems are determined largely by the systems themselves and may include:
(a) Data flow diagrams.
(b) Entity relationship diagrams.
(c) State transition diagrams.
(d) Information systems planning matrices.
(e) All of above.

25. In__________ stage, the conceptual model is compared with the "real world" system.
(a) Stage 5: Perform comparison of the conceptual model to the Real World.
(b) Stage 6: Feasible, desirable changes.
(c) Stage 7: Actions needed for Improvement.
(d) None of above.

26. Which is true about stage 5?
(a) The comparison between conceptual models with the "real world" system is done to identify the possible areas where improvements are necessary.
(b) A good comparison of the conceptual and the real world system will discover the problems or deficiencies that exist between what is happening ("rich picture") and what is desirable ("root definition") as defined by the conceptual model.
(c) Both (a) and (b).
(d) None of above.

27. In stage 6: Feasible, desirable changes:
(a) Changes or improvements in the system are studied to address disconnects or gaps between the "real world system and the "conceptual model" as identified in the stage 5.
(b) These changes will be carried out after a careful evaluation for feasibility determination has been performed.
(c) Deciding whether to customize the ERP software or to change the business processes to suit the ERP system is crucial to the success of the ERP system.
(d) The final agreement on what changes will be made forms an output of this stage.
(e) All of above.

28. Which is the last stage of SSM methodology?
(a) Actions needed for improvement.
(b) Feasible, desirable changes.
(c) Perform comparison of the conceptual model to the real world.
(d) None of above.

29. Which is true about stage: Actions to improve of SSM?
 (a) It constitutes the last stage of the soft system methodology.
 (b) Here the recommendations for the changes are implemented to ensure success of the ERP system.
 (c) Both (a) and (b).
 (d) None of above.

30. ____________ is a tool for analyzing ERP.
 (a) SSM.
 (b) Accelerated SAP.
 (c) MFG/PRO.
 (d) None of above.

31. Which is true about SSM?
 (a) SSM has been used in the development of information system.
 (b) SSM is also used as a tool for analyzing the impact of ERP implementation.
 (c) In addition to economic factors, SSM also tries to identify organizational, social and cultural aspects of the organization in order to rightly assess and evaluate the impact that ERP will have on the organization.
 (d) The soft system methodology does not claim to identify and mitigate all the impacts of ERP on the organization by taking into account various aspects of the organization and the system.
 (e) All of above.

32. Which is true about SSM?
 (a) SSM is used as a framework for business process reengineering.
 (b) SSM is also used as a tool for analyzing the impact of ERP implementation.
 (c) Both (a) and (b).
 (d) None of above.

SECTION B

STATE TRUE OR FALSE

1. The Soft Systems Methodology (SSM) was first introduced by Peter Chuckland in his book named “Systems Thinking, Systems Practice” in 1961.
2. SSM is regarded as a “soft” operations research tool.
3. Traditionally the research tools that existed in the field of operations research comprised “hard” mathematical and decision models.
4. SSM methodology is used to analyze and model hard to define complex systems that integrate technology (hard) and human (soft) systems.
5. A human (soft) system is defined as the collection of activities.
6. SSM methodology attempts to successfully deal with the more unpredictable and complex human side of the system.
7. SSM fails to recognize that different individuals may have different outlook on the same situation and may suggest different preferable outcomes.

8. SSM recognizes these differences and take these differences into consideration in order to ensure that the results of the analysis are acceptable to all the concerned parties.
9. Soft Systems Methodology fails to address "fuzzy" problems.
10. Fuzzy problems arise when the objectives are clear, multiple objectives do not exist and only a single perception for the problem exists.
11. The SSM approach defines an acceptable improved path of action through an iterative process.
12. The complete process of Soft Systems Methodology consists of five stages.
13. In SSM process the users, analysts and designers all work together to define the problem situation, generate and evaluate the alternatives and finally select the most acceptable solution.
14. In stage 1: Unstructured Problem Situation, the problem situation is identified with the help of managers, employees or users and is represented in terms of a "rich picture" (an abstract drawing that describes all aspects of the system that are considered relevant to the problem definition).
15. The stage 1: Unstructured Problem Situation involves defining at a high level the organization, the system and the processes.
16. The analysts, managers and users do not have a crucial role to play in first stage.
17. In stage 2: Problem Situation Expressed, the information about the problem situation is collected.
18. The information in stage 2: Problem Situation Expressed generally includes structure of the organization, processes currently being carried out and the problems being faced by the people working in the organization as well as the viewpoint of the managers.
19. The information in stage 2: Problem Situation Expressed is collected using techniques such as interviews, questionnaires, workshops, on-site observation and group decision making sessions.
20. The tools such as QFD and Analytical Hierarchy Process can also aid in the elicitation of information in stage 2: Problem Situation Expressed.
21. The root definition is a succinct statement of the system that defines the system as "a system to do X, by Y, in order to achieve Z".
22. The root definition of the system involves a certain view of the world.
23. In the Soft Systems Methodology, the mnemonic CAWOE guides the identification and development of the elements of the root definition:
24. Actors are people who are affected by the system.
25. Customers are the people who are performing activities in the system.
26. Transformation constitutes the changes being carried out by the system.
27. Weltanschauung is the "world-view" or the viewpoints held of the system by the people.
28. Owner holds the authority to decide how (and if) the system will work.
29. Environment constitutes the larger system within which the system under consideration exists.
30. The explicit identification of the owners, customers, actors and their viewpoints contribute to the successful implementation of the complex ERP systems.
31. SSM does not consider the identification of the roles and needs of the customers, actors and owners as well as the top management support as critical for successful implementation.

32. In Stage 4: Conceptual Models, the conceptual model is constructed for the root definitions of stage 3.

33. The conceptual model is mostly expressed in pictorial/flow chart form and essentially incorporates all the elements of the CATWOE mnemonic.

34. The conceptual model identifies the activities and their interactions that are necessary for the system to accomplish the goals and aims defined in the root definition of the stage 3.

35. The models for the ERP systems are determined largely by the systems themselves and may include data flow diagrams, entity relationship diagrams, state transition diagrams, information systems planning matrices, etc.

36. In stage 5: Perform comparison of the conceptual model to the Real World; the conceptual model is compared with the "real world" system.

37. The comparison of the conceptual model to the Real World is done to identify the possible areas where improvements are necessary.

38. A good comparison of the conceptual and the real world system will discover the problems or deficiencies that exist between what is happening ("rich picture") and what is desirable ("root definition") as defined by the conceptual model.

39. In stage 6: Feasible, desirable changes, the recommendations for the changes are implemented to ensure success of the ERP system.

40. In stage 7: Actions needed for improvement, changes or improvements in the system are studied to address disconnects or gaps between the "real world system and the "conceptual model" as identified in the stage 5.

41. Deciding whether to customize the ERP software or to change the business processes to suit the ERP system is not crucial to the success of the ERP system.

42. Soft systems methodology has been applied in many settings.

43. SSM has been used in the development of information system.

44. SSM cannot be used as a framework for business process reengineering.

45. SSM is used as a tool for analyzing the impact of ERP implementation.

46. In addition to economic factors, SSM also tries to identify organizational, social and cultural aspects of the organization in order to rightly assess and evaluate the impact that ERP will have on the organization.

47. The soft system methodology does not claim to identify and mitigate all the impacts of ERP on the organization by taking into account various aspects of the organization and the system.

SECTION C

FILL IN THE BLANKS

1. The Soft Systems Methodology (SSM) was first introduced by __________ in his book named "Systems Thinking, Systems Practice" in 1981.
2. __________ is regarded as a "soft" operations research tool.
3. Traditionally the research tools that existed in the field of operations research comprised ____________ and___________.

4. SSM methodology is used to analyze and model hard to define complex systems that integrate technology (hard) and __________ systems.

5. A ____________ is defined as the collection of activities and the relationship between these activities with people purposefully engaged in the activities.

6. __________ Methodology attempts to successfully deal with the more unpredictable and complex human side of the system.

7. SSM recognizes that different __________ may have different outlook on the same situation and may suggest different preferable_________.

8. SSM recognizes these differences and take these differences into consideration in order to ensure that the results of the analysis are acceptable to_________.

9. Soft Systems Methodology addresses ________problems.

10. Fuzzy problems arise when the objectives are not________, ________objectives exist and several perceptions for the problem exist.

11. The SSM approach defines an acceptable improved path of action through an _________ process.

12. The complete process of Soft Systems Methodology has _________ stages.

13. In this process the users, analysts and designers all work together to _________the problem situation, generate and evaluate the ________ and finally select the ________ solution.

14. The SSM process has ________ stages in tailored to the framework for ERP.

15. In Stage 1: _________, the problem situation is identified with the help of_________, employees or users.

16. The problem situation in stage 1: Unstructured Problem Situation is represented in terms of a _______________.

17. A "rich picture" is an abstract drawing that describes all aspects of the system that are considered relevant to the_________.

18. In stage 2: Problem Situation Expressed, the information about the _________ is collected.

19. The information generally includes structure of the organization, _________ currently being carried out and the problems being faced by the people working in the organization as well as the viewpoint of the managers. This information is collected using the_________.

20. The information is collected using techniques such as interviews, __________, workshops, ____________, and group decision making sessions. The tools such as QFD and _______________can also aid in this elicitation.

21. The _____________ is a succinct statement of the system that defines the system as "as system to do X, by Y, in order to achieve Z".

22. The root definition of the system involves a certain view of the________.

23. In Soft Systems Methodology the mnemonic ____________, guides the identification and development of, the elements of the_____________.

24. ____________ are people who are affected by the system.

25. ________ are the people who are performing activities in the system.

26. Transformation constitutes the ________ being carried out by the system.

27. The term _____________ mean the "world-view" or the viewpoints held of the system by the people.

28. Owners hold the _______ to decide how (and if) the system will work.

29. ____________ constitutes the larger system within which the system under consideration exists.
30. The explicit identification of the owners, customers, __________and their viewpoints contribute to the successful implementation of the complex __________systems.
31. SSM considers the ___________of the roles and needs of the customers, actors and owners as well as the __________support as critical for successful implementation.
32. In ___________, the conceptual model is constructed for the _________ of stage 3.
33. The conceptual model is mostly expressed in ____________ form and essentially incorporates all the elements of the __________mnemonic.
34. The ________________identifies the activities and their interactions that are necessary for the system to accomplish the goals and aims defined in the root definition of the stage 3.
35. The models for the ERP systems are determined largely by the systems themselves and may include________________, entity relationship diagrams, state transition diagrams, information systems planning matrices, etc.
36. In________________, the conceptual model is compared with the ____________ system.
37. The conceptual model is compared with the real world system in order to identify the possible areas where ________ are necessary.
38. A ________ comparison of the conceptual and the real world system will discover the problems or deficiencies that exist between what is happening ("rich picture") and what is desirable ("root definition") as defined by the______________.
39. In______________, changes or improvements in the system are studied to address disconnects or gaps between the "real world system and the "conceptual model" as identified in the stage 5.
40. The changes will be carried out after a careful evaluation for ____________________has been performed.
41. Deciding whether to __________the ERP software or to change the business processes to suit the ERP system; is __________ to the success of the ERP system. The final agreement on what changes will be made forms an ________of this stage.
42. ________________ constitutes the last stage of the soft system methodology.
43. In Stage 7: Actions needed for improvement, the recommendations for the changes are _______________ to ensure success of the ERP system.
44. SSM is a tool for analyzing__________.
45. Soft systems methodology has been applied in many________.
46. SSM has been used in the development of ____________________. SSM is used as a framework for_________.
47. SSM is also used as a tool for analyzing the impact of_____________.
48. In addition to economic factors, SSM also tries to identify_______________, social and ________ aspects of the organization in order to rightly assess and evaluate the impact, that ERP will have on the organization.

ANSWERS

SECTION A

(1) a **(2)** a **(3)** c **(4)** b **(5)** c **(6)** d **(7)** a **(8)** d **(9)** c **(10)** a
(11) d **(12)** a **(13)** c **(14)** b **(15)** e **(16)** e **(17)** c **(18)** b **(19)** d **(20)** c
(21) b **(22)** d **(23)** d **(24)** e **(25)** a **(26)** c **(27)** e **(28)** a **(29)** c **(30)** a
(31) e **(32)** c.

SECTION B

(1) False **(2)** True **(3)** True **(4)** True **(5)** False **(6)** True **(7)** False **(8)** True
(9) False **(10)** False **(11)** True **(12)** False **(13)** True **(14)** True **(15)** True **(16)** False
(17) True **(18)** True **(19)** True **(20)** True **(21)** True **(22)** True **(23)** True **(24)** False
(25) False **(26)** True **(27)** True **(28)** True **(29)** True **(30)** True **(31)** False **(32)** True
(33) True **(34)** True **(35)** True **(36)** True **(37)** True **(38)** True **(39)** False **(40)** False
(41) False **(42)** True **(43)** True **(44)** False **(45)** True **(46)** True **(47)** True.

SECTION C

(1) Peter Chuckland **(2)** SSM **(3)** "hard" mathematical, decision models **(4)** human (soft) **(5)** human (soft) system **(6)** SSM **(7)** individuals, outcomes, **(8)** all the concerned parties **(9)** "fuzzy" **(10)** clear, multiple **(11)** iterative **(12)** seven **(13)** define, alternatives, most acceptable **(14)** seven **(15)** Unstructured Problem Situation, managers **(16)** "rich picture" **(17)** problem definition **(18)** problem situation **(19)** processes, managers **(20)** questionnaires, on-site observation, Analytical Hierarchy Process **(21)** root definition **(22)** world **(23)** CATWOE, root definition **(24)** Customers **(25)** Actors **(26)** changes **(27)** Weltanschauung **(28)** authority **(29)** environment **(30)** actors, ERP **(31)** identification, top management **(32)** Stage4: Conceptual Models, root definitions **(33)** pictorial/flow chart, CATWOE **(34)** conceptual model **(35)** data flow diagrams **(36)** Stage 5: Perform comparison of the conceptual model to the Real World, "real world" **(37)** improvements **(38)** good, conceptual model **(39)** Stage 6: Feasible, Desirable Changes **(40)** feasibility determination **(41)** customize, crucial, output **(42)** Stage 7: Actions needed for improvement **(43)** implemented **(44)** ERP **(45)** settings **(46)** information system, business process reengineering **(47)** ERP implementation **(48)** organizational, cultural.

9
Chapter
ERP and Related Technologies

HIGHLIGHTS

- **ERP AND RELATED TECHNOLOGIES**
  - Management Information System
  - Decision Support System
  - Executive Information System
  - Business Process Reengineering
  - Supply Chain Management
  - Customer Relationship Management
  - ERP and E-Commerce
  - OLAP, Data Warehouse and data Mining

The emergence of new technologies provides the business firms with many active tools to better conduct their business. For instance, the growth of Internet and Web has resulted in the globalization of customer and supplier networks. This has eventually created a number of new opportunities and methods to do business. Similarly, the ERP systems can be used to integrate the firms across geographic boundaries. The use of ERP systems in an organization allows the automatic introduction of the latest technologies such as Electronic Data Interchange (EDI), E-Commerce, etc.

Some of the technologies that are being used along with ERP, in order to overcome the limitations of a standalone ERP system and facilitate better decision making include management information system, decision support system, executive information system, data warehousing, data mining, on-line analytical processing, supply chain management and e-commerce. With the convergence of ERP, Data warehousing and Internet, the forerunners of the ERP system: MIS and DSS will be phased out.

9.1 MANAGEMENT INFORMATION SYSTEM

Management Information System (MIS) processes data into information which is sent to departments for appropriate decision making. MIS is essential to manage an organization effectively. MIS is mostly used at all levels of an organization. It is used to support the day-to-day activities (such as financial accounting systems), as well as, the long-term strategic goals and objectives of the organization.

MIS emerged in 1960s with the development of database management system (DBMS) to store and retrieve organized data. MIS extract useful management information from massive amounts of aggregated and summarized transaction data. MIS allows user-interactive queries to make routine (structured) decisions by implementing simple modeling and statistical techniques in the system.

An effective MIS system helps in the following activities: enhancing communication among the employees, recording and aggregating information, generation of reports, delivering reports throughout the organization, reducing manual activities with use of automated procedures and supporting the goals of the organization.

MIS system must meet the five elements of usability in order to function accurately and efficiently. These five elements are described below:

1. Timeliness: provide current information to users.
2. Accuracy: MIS system must correct errors promptly. Information should be free of errors
3. Consistence: information must be reliable. Data must be proceeds and compiled consistently.
4. Completeness: provide complete useful information in summarized form.
5. Relevance-provide relevant information for effective decision making.

A flawed MIS will cause operational risks and adversely affect the business activities of the organization. This is due to the fact that decisions taken by the management are wrong as they are based on ineffective, inaccurate and incomplete information obtained from the flawed MIS.

LEARNING POINTS

1. The use of ERP systems in an organization allows the automatic introduction of latest technologies such as Electronic Data Interchange (EDI), E-Commerce etc.
2. Management Information System (MIS) processes data into information which is sent to departments for appropriate decision making.
3. A flawed MIS will cause operational risks. This will have an adverse effect on the business activities of the organization.

9.2 DECISION SUPPORT SYSTEM

A decision support system is a computer based information system (CBIS) that supports the decision makers to take effective decisions quickly. DSS solves managerial problems by generating and evaluating decision alternatives. According to Sprague and Carlson, a decision support system must be able to perform the following activities: projection, deduction analysis, creation and comparison of decision alternatives, optimization and simulation.

A decision support system is no longer a voluntary system for an organization but, in fact, has become a strategic tool in the hands of the management for the survival of an organization. Some DSS applications include international business, accounting, auditing, marketing, finance etc.

Geographic information system (GIS) is a special category of DSS. GIS uses data visualization technology to support decision making with digitized maps. While MIS provides managers with routine reports, DSS facilitates ad-hoc queries. MIS is primarily used to support structured problems but DSS is used to solve unstructured and semi-structured problems.

Types of Decision Support Systems include the following:

1. **Knowledge based decision support systems**
   Knowledge based decision support systems are hybrid of DSS and expert systems (ES). KBDSS are used to solve a wide range of organizational problems. Knowledge acquisition serves as the major challenge in knowledge based systems.
2. **Group decision support systems**
   According to DeSanctis and Gallupe, a group DSS is "an interactive computer based system which facilitates solution of unstructured problems by a set of decision makers working together as a group. Group DSS has special technological requirements of software, hardware, operational procedures and people. Special functional capabilities such as anonymous input of the user's ideas, listing ideas of the group members are included in Group DSS software.
3. **Organizational decision support systems**
   Organizational DSS (ODSS) are DSS that provide various mechanisms to ensure that the decisions made throughout the organization are consistent with each other as well as are consistent with the overall organizational goals.
4. **Distributed decision making systems (DDM)**
   Distributed decision making systems (DDM) consists of several single user DSS, that, work together in a distributed environment.
5. **Active DSS**
   Active Decision Support Systems make use of new tools and technologies to develop a new generation of active and intelligent DSS. Active DSS will be equipped with intelligent interfaces and data mining tools.

LEARNING POINTS

1. A decision support system is a computer based information system (CBIS) that supports the decision makers to take effective decisions quickly.
2. Geographic information system (GIS) is a special category of DSS. GIS uses data visualization technology to support decision making with digitized maps.
3. There are different types of Decision Support Systems. They include: knowledge based DSS, Group DSS, Organizational DSS, Distributed decision making systems (DDM) and active DSS.

9.3 EXECUTIVE INFORMATION SYSTEM

Executive information system (EIS) is used to support the growing information needs of the executives. EIS provides timely and critical information to the top executives for identifying malfunctioning of organizational activities, monitoring the situation and controlling it. EIS is used to provide strategic planning, crisis management and strategic control and monitoring of all the business operations. An EIS has menu-driven, user-friendly interfaces to provide easy and flexible access to corporate information.

LEARNING POINTS

1. EIS is used to support the growing information needs of executives.
2. It is used to provide strategic planning, crisis management and strategic control and monitoring of all the business operations.

9.4 BUSINESS PROCESS REENGINEERING

Business process reengineering (BPR) is defined as "the functional rethinking and radical redesign of business processes to achieve dramatic improvements in critical, contemporary measures of performance such as cost, quality, service and speed." This definition of BPR was given by Michael Hammer and Champy. BPR provides a disciplined structured approach to organization that need to undergo a massive change for accomplishing the organization's goals and remain competitive.

BPR uses Information Technology. In fact, IT is a key factor that makes BPR work. In business process reengineering, the business processes are analyzed properly in order to identify the best way of performing jobs, the processes (jobs) are then changed accordingly. Depending upon the complexity of the business processes; some organizations may require only a partial, while others, a complete redesign of the business processes. The changes will not only affect the company's business procedures but also its organizational structure.

BPR came earlier than the popularization of ERP happened. The success of business process reengineering in the organization will determine ERP's potential effect. Similarly a failure of BPR in the organization will definitely lead to ERP implementation failure. BPR and ERP go hand-in-hand. BPR improves the business processes and ERP automates those improved business processes to deliver better accuracy and higher efficiency. Implementing BPR in an organization will ensure success to an ERP system implementation. As ERP systems facilitate seamless information flow across departmental boundaries and automates the business processes of the organization, ERP therefore, serves as an ideal solution for reengineering the business processes.

BPR provides the following benefits to the organization:

1. Improves the quality of products, services and operations.
2. Increases the efficiency of the organization.

BPR has continuously reduced the size of the workforce. As a consequence, the adoption of BPR approach has a challenging impact upon the organization.

LEARNING POINTS

1. Business process reengineering (BPR) is defined as "the functional rethinking and radical redesign of business processes to achieve dramatic improvements in critical, contemporary measures of performance such as cost, quality, service and speed." This definition of BPR was given by Michael Hammer and Champy.
2. Depending upon the complexity of the business processes; some organizations may require only a partial, while others, a complete redesign of the business processes.
3. BPR and ERP go hand-in-hand. BPR improves the business processes and ERP automates those improved business processes to deliver better accuracy and higher efficiency.

9.5 SUPPLY CHAIN MANAGEMENT

Supply Chain Management (SCM) refers to a wide variety of activities that firms and industries use to coordinate the key players in their procurement process. The concept of supply chain is usually supported by IT today. A supply chain that is being managed electronically with web-based software is referred to as an e-supply chain. A supply chain typically involves materials flows, information flows and financial flows. Supply chain management coordinates these flows among all the involved parties in the supply chain.

The supply chain involves three segments. These are as follows:

1. Upstream: The sourcing or procurement occur from external suppliers.
2. Downstream: The distribution or dispersal takes place.
3. Internal: The packaging, assembly or manufacturing occurs.

Some of the benefits that a supply chain management provides are as follows:

1. SCM reduces the uncertainty and risks along the supply chain.
2. SCM improves business processes by an effective coordination of information, material and financial flows among all parties involved in the supply chain.
3. SCM helps provide better service to the customers.
4. SCM decreases the inventory level and the cycle time.

A good supply chain management solution will improve critical business processes such as procurement-to-pay cycles, order-to-cash cycles and demand forecasting. Advanced planning and scheduling (APS) tools monitor and optimizes the entire supply chain to meet the specific needs of a company.

9.5.1 Push and Pull Approaches

In pull based approach to SCM the processes are initiated in response to an order from a customer.

The pull based approach is shown in Figure 9.1. Processes in pull based approach are also referred to as reactive processes because these processes react to the demands of the customers.

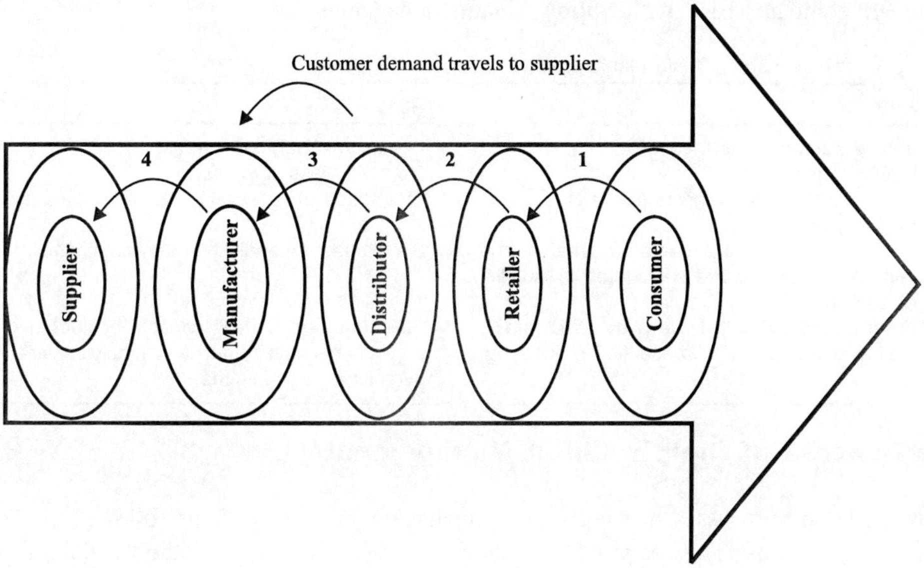

Fig. 9.1. Pull Based Approach

Figure 9.2 shows the push based approach to SCM. In push based model products are pushed to the customers in expectation of a customer order. The push based processes are referred to as speculative processes since they respond to demand forecast rather than actual customer demand.

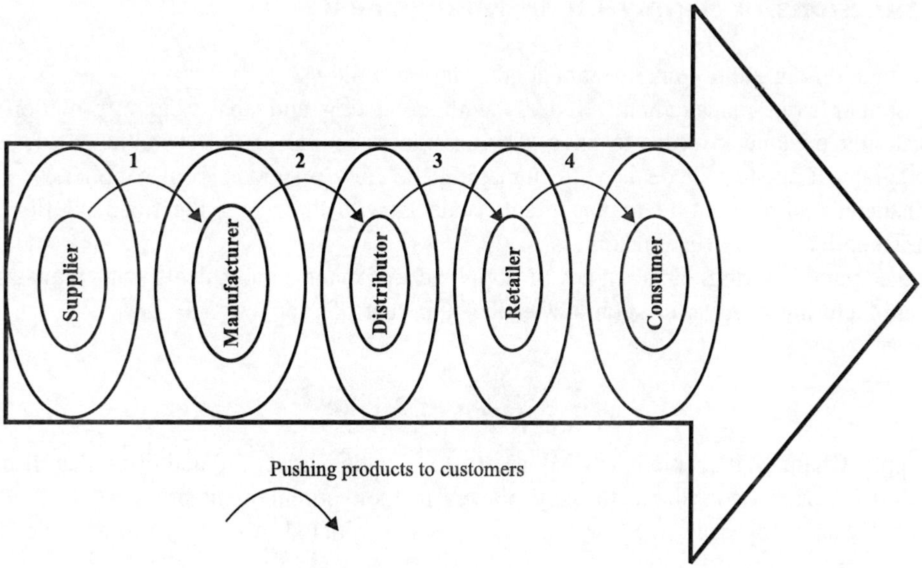

Fig. 9.2. Push Based Approach

Table 9.1 compares ERP with Supply Chain Management.

Table 9.1: ERP versus Supply Chain Management

S No.	ERP	SCM
1.	It covers more areas than SCM.	Covers relatively less areas.
2.	Highly complex.	Relatively less complex.
3.	The speed of processing requests is relatively slower.	The speed of processing requests is relatively fast.
3.	In ERP system, all the demand, capacity and material constraints are considered in isolation of each other.	Simultaneous handling of the constraints.
4.	**Functionality**: Relatively less dynamic: are mainly concerned with transaction processing.	**Functionality**: Usually capable of performing adjustments with regard to various constraints dynamically in real-time.

9.5.2 Elements of Supply Chain Management

There are three key processes in supply chain management. These are as follows:

1. Planning systems: The focus of the planning system is to ensure the availability of the right product at the right time and at right place.
2. Execution systems: The system enables the efficient movements of products and services through the supply chain. Providing operational efficiency is the main focus of execution systems.
3. Performance Measurement System: The system monitors and ensures the effectiveness of the supply chain. Use of web-based software agents and data warehousing allow the business operations to respond immediately to key business events.

9.5.3 Functions in Supply Chain Management

The key functions in supply chain management are as follows:

1. Customer asset management: It deals with collecting and analyzing information about customer demand in order to have a better understanding of the customer needs.
2. Integrated Logistics: It deals with managing the flow of goods from suppliers.
3. Financial and accounting management: It deals with managing the financial flows with the suppliers as well as customers.
4. Agile manufacturing: This aspect of supply chain management deals with managing the manufacturing process in such a way that the cost of production is low.

LEARNING POINTS

1. Supply Chain Management (SCM) refers to a wide variety of activities that firms and industries use to coordinate the key players in their procurement process.
2. In pull based approach to SCM the processes are initiated in response to an order from a customer.
3. In push based model products are pushed to the customers in expectation of a customer order.

4. The key functions in supply chain management include the following: Customer asset management, Integrated Logistics, Financial and accounting management, Agile manufacturing.

9.6 CUSTOMER RELATIONSHIP MANAGEMENT

According to Kala Kota and Robin, customer relationship management (CRM) is "an integrated sales, marketing and service strategy". Customer relationship management (CRM) systems focus on the key elements of the organization, that is, customers. A CRM system uses the CRM strategy that attempts to learn about the needs and preferences of customers in order to build healthier relations with the customers.

CRM systems support tracking past purchases and payments made by customers, updating the electronic customer profile, analyzing the behaviour of customers and providing updated online-answers to the frequently asked questions (FAQS) about various products and services. Today, most of the companies are realizing the need to integrate CRM systems with the other enterprise systems (ERP and SCM) in order to achieve business improvements and better financial performance. CRM systems include all the tools, technologies and procedures related with sales, marketing and post-sales customer service.

CRM systems can be implemented by introducing CRM software within the company either in strategically selected areas or getting it fully installed. A CRM system implemented partially has limited functionality. The lack of standards in CRM activities often makes the implementation of a CRM system difficult. CRM systems should be designed in such a way that they address cross-functional business processes. CRM vendors are now focusing on producing and delivering business process-based software solutions. These solutions are more flexible and highly configurable. Business process Management (BPM) is a new concept that attempts to overcome the limitations of the CRM systems.

Figure 9.3 illustrates the relation between ERP, SCM and CRM.

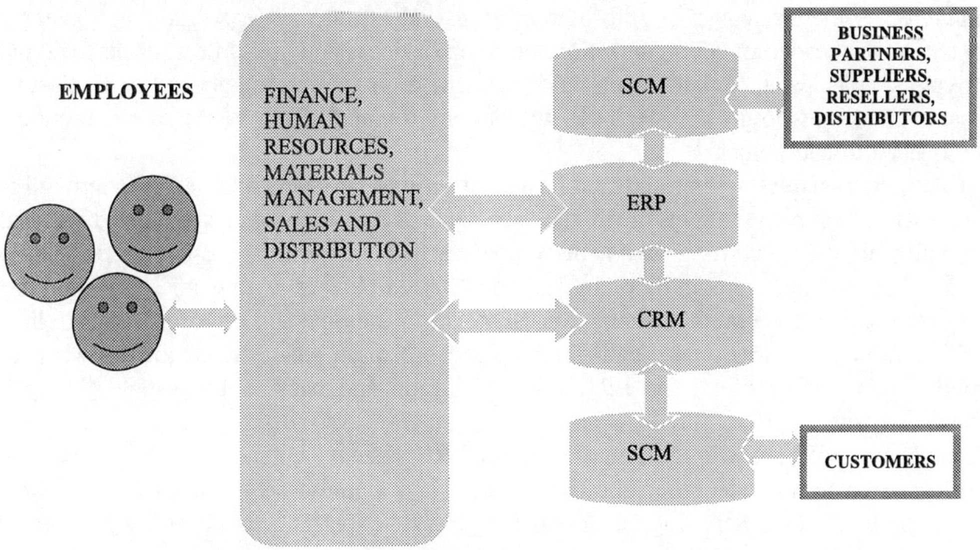

Fig. 9.3. Relationships between ERP, SCM and CRM

9.6.1 Elements of a CRM System

The main elements of a CRM system are:

1. Operational CRM
   Operational CRM centres on all the activities of the business that are related to sales, marketing and customer service.
2. Analytical CRM
   Analytical CRM deals with the collection and analysis of the data collected by the CRM system. Based on the results of the analysis different segments of customers and the relationship between them are identified. Analytical CRM provides support to decision making.
3. Collaborative CRM

Collaborative CRM facilitates the interaction with the customers by phone, fax or email.

LEARNING POINTS

1. According to Kala Kota and Robin, customer relationship management (CRM) is "an integrated sales, marketing and service strategy".
2. A CRM system uses the CRM strategy that attempts to learn about the needs and preferences of customers in order to build healthier relations with the customers.
3. The main elements of a CRM system are: Operational CRM, Analytical CRM and Collaborative CRM.

9.7 ERP AND E-COMMERCE

"E-commerce is the exchange of information across electronic networks at any stage in the supply chain whether within an organization, between business and consumers, or between public and private sectors whether paid or un-paid". Use of e-commerce together with ERP systems will enable companies to grow faster in the global environment. Both ERP and e-commerce are complimentary to each other.

E-Commerce enables selling and purchasing of various products and services through web. Without ERP a company cannot fulfill the web orders accurately and speedily. The need of implementing ERP systems is growing in companies that desire to use E-commerce for doing business. ERP systems were initially meant only for employees within an organization. But today's, tech-savvy customers demand access to information such as order status, invoice reconciliation etc., that was only meant for employees in past. Also, the customers want to get information that is free of all the ERP software jargon and easy to understand through the company's website.

Though a lot of hard work is required to fit ERP systems with e-commerce, the benefits obtained are significant. Integrating the ERP system and e-commerce requires careful planning to be done by the vendor. Selecting vendors having a good experience in developing e-commerce wares is a good choice to make.

ERP systems are complex and require a good deal of maintenance. The website will not be available to the public when the company shuts down the ERP system for maintenance work. This can be a costly affair. In order to prevent huge losses, most e-commerce veterans build flexibility into the connecting links between e-commerce and ERP systems. This means that the e-commerce applications can keep running on the web during the ERP system shut down for upgrades and fixes.

In order to make the ERP systems available over the web, the company's IT department will have to build two new channels of access into the company's ERP systems. One access channel will be used to provide access to the customers for information such as order status and billing from the company's ERP system. The other channel will provide access to the suppliers and business partners so that useful and relevant information is made available more easily and efficiently from the ERP system of the company. Middleware and EAI software take information from the ERP system.

Figure 9.4 illustrates EAI architecture. The information captured is then converted into a format that the e-commerce applications can understand.

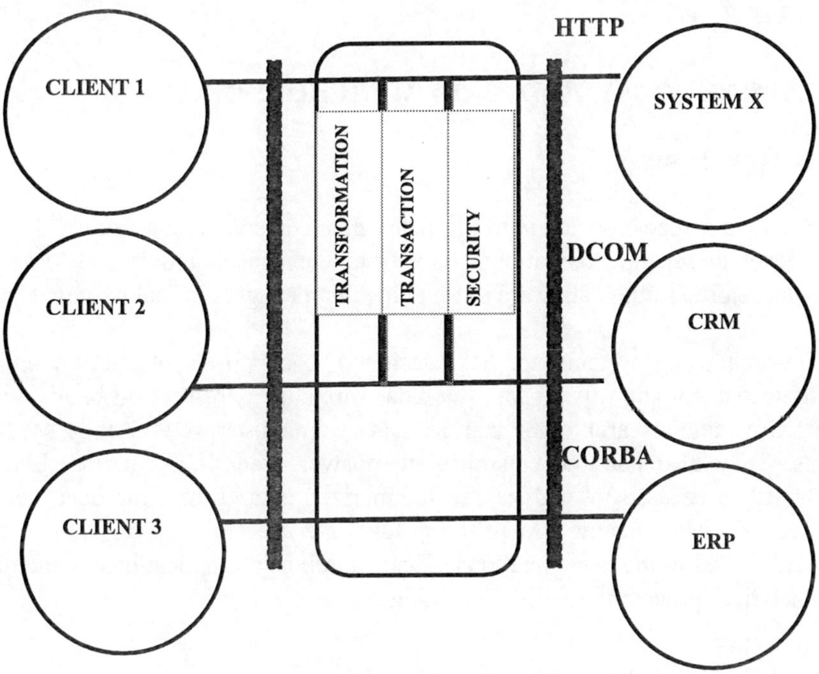

Fig. 9.4(a) EAI Architecture

LEARNING POINTS

1. E-commerce is the exchange of information across electronic networks at any stage in the supply chain whether within an organization, between business and consumers, or between public and private sectors whether paid or unpaid.

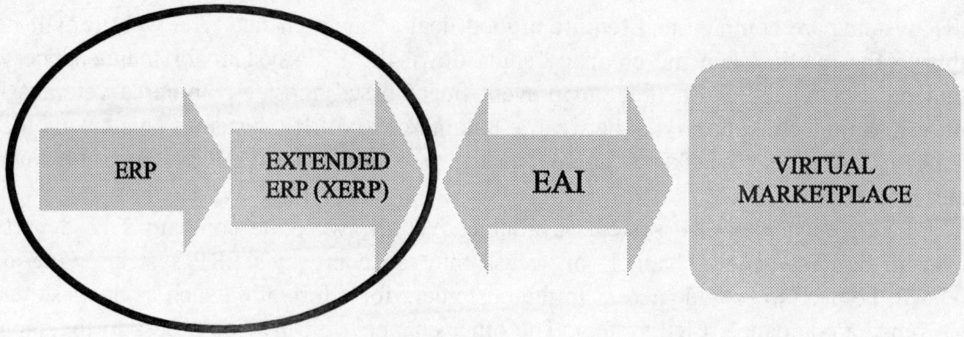

Fig. 9.4(b) ERP, EAI and virtual Marketplace

2. Integrating the ERP system and e-commerce requires careful planning to be done by the vendor. Selecting vendors having a good experience in developing e-commerce wares is a good choice to make.

9.8 DATA MINING, OLAP AND DATA WAREHOUSING

9.8.1 Data Warehouse

A data warehouse is a repository of multiple heterogeneous sources of data. A data warehouse is primarily meant to separate operational data from the data stored for performing business analysis. The data stored in the data warehouse helps the managers in making quick and effective decisions.

The data warehousing systems are now designed to support sophisticated online-analysis such as multidimensional analysis. Today, the data warehouses are used in banks, retail sectors, manufacturing firms and research organizations. Data warehouses were initially used to generate useful reports. They also had the capability to answer predefined queries. Later, the data warehouses began to be used to analyze the summarized data. Today, the data warehouses are used for strategic decision making. Data mining tools are used to discover knowledge from the vast pool of data stored in the data warehouse. Data warehouses applications include information processing, analytical processing and data mining.

9.8.1.1 Three-tier data warehouse architecture

The data warehouse normally has three tiers. The tiers are as follow:

1. Warehouse database server
2. OLAP server
3. Client tier

Warehouse database server is the bottom tier. It almost consists of a relational database system. OLAP server forms the middle tier of the data warehouse architecture. The topmost tier is the client tier. The client tier contains query tools, analysis, reporting tools and may also contain data mining tools.

9.8.1.2 Data warehouse models

Defining the architecture for a data warehouse is a challenging task. A data warehouse architecture must meet challenges such as data integration, information reuse and business intelligence. The data warehouse model should achieve data integration, promote information reuse and provide rich business intelligence.

A data model defines objects that are of interest to the organization and the rules that describe those objects and govern them. The three methodologies that are usually applied to the design and implementation of a data warehouse are as follows:

1. **Enterprise Data Modeling**
   Enterprise data model starts by using the conventional relational data modeling techniques. The data model describes the business in a conventional normalized database. A series of de-normalizations may then occur to improve performance. Enterprise data model is typically used by the corporations that possess a corporate-wide data model. In other words, an enterprise warehouse collects all details about subjects spanning the whole organization.
2. **Data Bus**
   This model is made up of a series of star schemas. The star schemas have gradually evolved over time.

   Data models are just views either directly on the star schemas or onto the aggregates of these star schemas. A data mart contains a subset of corporate-wide data that holds value only for a specific group of users.
3. **Process Neutral Model**
   In this data model all the embedded business rules have been removed. The advantage of this data model approach is that as the business processes change there is little or no change required to the data model. The approach is generally used by organizations that are characterized by a rapidly changing corporate environment.

Figure 9.5 illustrates the data warehouse architecture.

9.8.2 OLAP

OLAP stands for "Online Analytical Processing". An OLAP product is necessarily multi-dimensional. OLAP can be defined by five keywords: Fast Analysis of Shared Multi-dimensional Information (FASMI).

Fast: System will deliver responses to users in very less time.

Analysis: System will cope with any business logic and keep it simple for the users to understand.

Shared: System will implement all the security requirements for providing confidentiality. In case of multiple write concurrent update locking would be provided.

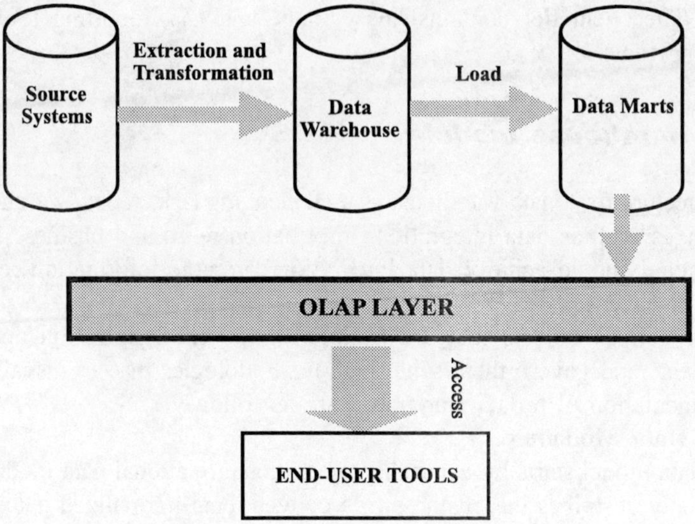

Fig. 9.5. Data Warehouse Architecture

Multi-dimensional: System will provide a multi-dimensional view of data to the users. Both simple and multiple hierarchies will be supported.

Information: It is all of the data and the derived information needed.

This descriptive term "FASMI" was suggested by Nigel Pendse. OLAP cube (also referred to as hypercube or multi-dimensional cube) forms the core of any OLAP system. Data in an OLAP cube is modeled in multiple dimensions. Dimensions are the perspective with respect to which organization would keep records. Each dimension may have a "dimension table" associated with it.

Facts are numerical quantities that are used to analyze relationship between the dimensions of an OLAP cube. A fact table contains the names of the facts (also called measures). An OLAP cube facilitates complex data mining queries to be answered quickly in comparison to a relational database. The use of aggregations (data summarized along dimensions) is the most important mechanism that supports the good performance of an OLAP system. The use of multiple hierarchies facilitates complex analytical and ad-hoc queries to be answered with a rapid response time. The most common OLAP applications include sales and marketing analysis, financial reporting, budgeting and forecasting.

9.8.3 Data Mining

Data mining has been defined as "the non-trivial extraction of implicit, previously unknown and potentially useful information from data." Data mining extracts useful information from large amount of data by the application of a computer based methodology. This is also known as knowledge discovery.

It can also be understood as the use of intelligent methods to discover meaningful patterns from large data sets. Data mining involves both knowledge discovery and pattern recognition.

Data mining, in fact, covers a broad spectrum of tasks. The data mining tasks include data characterization, mining association rules, data classification and evolution analysis.

9.8.3.1 Architecture of data mining system

A data mining system can be designed in any one of the following ways:

1. **No Coupling**
   In this architecture, a data mining system will not utilize any function of either a database or a data warehouse system. This architecture is poor as it fails to make use of the rich functionalities of the database and data warehouse system.
2. **Loose Coupling**
   In this design, the data mining system uses some of the facilities offered by a database or a data warehouse system, for e.g. the data mining system fetches data from the data stored in the data warehouse, performs data mining on the retrieved data and then stores the results in the database. This design is considered better than any coupling design.
3. **Semi-tight coupling**
   In semi-tight coupling a few essential data mining functions can be provided in the database/ data warehouse system. The intermediate data mining results can be stored in the database or data warehouse.
4. **Tight Coupling**
   Here, the data mining system is smoothly integrated into the database/data warehouse system. Tight coupling system efficiently implements data mining functions and has high system performance.

9.8.3.2 Data mining query language

Data mining Query Language (DMQL) is used to facilitate ad-hoc and interactive data mining in data mining systems. DMQL is based on certain data mining primitives. These are required for defining a data mining task and include the following:

1. Task relevant Data Specification: This involves specifying the portions of the database or the set of data that is relevant and in which the user is interested.
2. Kinds of knowledge to be mined: This determines data mining functionality that has to be performed on the data. Data mining functionalities include classification, association, and clustering or evolution analysis.
3. Interesting measures: This involve separating uninteresting patterns from knowledge. Interesting measures are used to evaluate the discovered patterns are support, confidence and simplicity.
4. Presentation and visualization of Data: It specifies the form in which the results of the query will be displayed to the user. Some forms in which data may be displayed are charts, graphs, cubes and decision trees.

LEARNING POINTS

1. A data warehouse is a repository of multiple heterogeneous sources of data. The data warehouse normally has three tiers. The tiers are as follows: Warehouse database server, OLAP server and client tier.
2. Enterprise data model starts by using the conventional relational data modeling techniques. Enterprise data model is typically used by the corporations that possess a corporate-wide data model. In other words, an enterprise warehouse collects all details about subjects spanning the whole organization.
3. Data Bus model is made up of a series of star schemas. The star schemas have gradually evolved over time.
4. A data mart contains a subset of corporate wide data that holds value only for a specific group of users.
5. In Process Neutral Model all the embedded business rules have been removed. The advantage of this data model approach is that as the business processes change there is little or no change required to the data model.
6. OLAP stands for "Online Analytical Processing". Data in an OLAP cube is modeled in multiple dimensions. Dimensions are the perspective with respect to which organization would keep records. Each dimension may have a "dimension table" associated with it.
7. Data mining has been defined as "the non-trivial extraction of implicit, previously unknown and potentially useful information from data."
8. The data mining tasks include data characterization, mining association rules, data classification and evolution analysis.
9. A data mining system can be designed in any one of the following ways: no coupling, loose coupling, semi-tight coupling and tight coupling.
10. Data Mining Query Language (DMQL) is used to facilitate ad-hoc and interactive data mining in data mining systems.

SUMMARY

MIS, DSS and EIS are the forerunners of the ERP systems. With the convergence of ERP, data warehousing and Internet, the forerunners of the ERP system have been phased out. An MIS processes data into useful information for various departments and levels of an organization. A decision support system supports the management to make quick and effective decisions by generating and evaluating decision alternatives. Various types of DSS include knowledge based DSS, group DSS, organizational DSS, distributed decision making systems (DDM) and active DSS. EIS is used to provide timely and critical information to the top executives.

According to Hammer and Champy, business process reengineering is defined as "the fundamental rethinking and radical redesign of business processes to achieve dramatic improvements in critical, contemporary measures of performance such as cost, quality, service and speed/" BPR and ERP go hand-in-hand. BPR improves the business processes which in turn are automated by ERP system.

Supply chain management refers to a wide variety of activities that firms and industries use to coordinate the key players involved in the procurement process. Planning systems, execution systems and performance measurement systems form the elements of supply chain management. Some of the key functions in SCM include customer asset management, integrated logistics, financial and accounting management, agile manufacturing etc. Kala Kota and Robin define CRM as "an integrated sales, marketing and service strategy." CRM supports tracking past purchases and payments made by customers. The main elements of a CRM system are operational CRM, analytical CRM and collaborative CRM.

The integration of e-commerce with ERP system enables the company to get a winning edge in the complex global environment. Integrating ERP with e-commerce requires careful planning on part of the vendor. A data warehouse is used to separate the operational data from historic data meant for performing business analysis. A data warehouse normally has three tiers: warehouse database server, OLAP server and client tier. OLAP, described by five keywords: Fast Analysis of Shared Multi-dimensional Information (FASMI), is used to support ad-hoc multi-dimensional queries. The most common OLAP applications include sales and marketing analysis, budgeting, forecasting and financial reporting.

Data mining has been defined as "the non-trivial extraction of implicit, previously unknown and potentially useful information from data." A data mining system can be designed in any one of the following ways: no coupling, loose coupling, semi-tight coupling and tight coupling. Data Mining Query Language (DMQL) is used to facilitate ad-hoc and interactive data mining in data mining systems.

POINTS TO REMEMBER

1. The use of ERP systems in an organization allows the automatic introduction of latest technologies such as Electronic Data Interchange (EDI), E-Commerce etc.
2. Management Information System (MIS) processes data into information which is sent to departments for appropriate decision making. A flawed MIS will cause operational risks. This will have an adverse effect on the business activities of the organization.
3. A decision support system is a computer based information system (CBIS) that supports the decision makers to take effective decisions quickly. There are different types of Decision Support System. They include: knowledge based DSS, Group DSS, Organizational DSS, Distributed decision making systems (DDM) and active DSS.
4. Geographic information system (GIS) is a special category of DSS. GIS uses data visualization technology to support decision making with digitized maps.
5. EIS is used to support the growing information needs of executives.
6. Business process reengineering (BPR) is defined as "the fundamental rethinking and radical redesign of business processes to achieve dramatic improvements in critical, contemporary measures of performance such as cost, quality, service and speed." This definition of BPR was given by Michael Hammer and Champy.
7. Depending upon the complexity of the business processes; some organizations may require only a partial, while others, a complete redesign of the business processes.
8. BPR and ERP go hand-in-hand. BPR improves the business processes and ERP automates those improved business processes to deliver better accuracy and higher efficiency.

9. Supply Chain Management (SCM) refers to a wide variety of activities that firms and industries use to coordinate the key players in their procurement process. In pull based approach to SCM the processes are initiated in response to an order from a customer. In push based model products are pushed to the customers in expectation of a customer order.
10. The key functions in supply chain management include the following: Customer asset management, Integrated Logistics, Financial and accounting management, Agile manufacturing.
11. According to Kala Kota and Robin, customer relationship management (CRM) is "an integrated sales, marketing and service strategy". A CRM system uses the CRM strategy that attempts to learn about the needs and preferences of customers in order to build healthier relations with the customers. The main elements of a CRM system are: Operational CRM, Analytical CRM and Collaborative CRM.
12. E-commerce is the exchange of information across electronic networks at any stage in the supply chain whether within an organization, between business and consumers, or between public and private sectors whether paid or unpaid.
13. Integrating the ERP system and e-commerce requires careful planning to be done by the vendor. Selecting vendors having a good experience in developing e-commerce wares is a good choice to make.
14. A data warehouse is a repository of multiple heterogeneous sources of data. The data warehouse normally has three tiers. The tiers are as follows: Warehouse database server, OLAP server and Client tier.
15. Enterprise data model starts by using the conventional relational data modeling techniques. Data Bus model is made up of a series of star schemas. The star schemas have gradually evolved over time. In Process Neutral Model all the embedded business rules have been removed. The advantage of this data model approach is that as the business processes change there is little or no change required to the data model.
16. OLAP stands for "Online Analytical Processing". Data in an OLAP cube is modeled in multiple dimensions. Dimensions are the perspective with respect to which organization would keep records. Each dimension may have a "dimension table" associated with it.
17. Data mining has been defined as "the non-trivial extraction of implicit, previously unknown and potentially useful information from data." The data mining tasks include data characterization, mining association rules, data classification and evolution analysis. A data mining system can be designed in any one of the following ways: no coupling, loose coupling, semi-tight coupling and tight coupling.
18. Data Mining Query Language (DMQL) is used to facilitate ad-hoc and interactive data mining in data mining systems.

REVIEW QUESTIONS

1. What is Management Information System?
2. Write short notes on the following:
   (a) Decision support systems
   (b) Executive information system

3. What do you understand by business process reengineering?
4. What is supply chain management? List some of the benefits of supply chain management.
5. Explain the push and pull approaches to SCM.
6. What are the elements of ECM?
7. Discuss the key functions in SCM.
8. Write a short note on supply chain application software.
9. What is CRM? Explain the elements of a CRM system.
10. What are the benefits of CRM?
11. How has web and e-commerce changed ERP structure? Explain giving examples.
12. What is a data warehouse? Why do you need a data warehouse?
13. What is data mining?
14. Explain OLAP and list some of the advantages offered by OLAP technology.
15. Explain the three-tier data warehouse models.
16. Explain the architecture of a data mining system.
17. Write a short note on Data Mining Query Language (DMQL).

OBJECTIVE QUESTIONS

SECTION A

TICK THE CORRECT ANSWER

1. The emergence of new __________ provides the business firms with many active tools to better conduct their business.
   (a) Technologies.
   (b) Products.
   (c) Systems.
   (d) None of above.
2. The growth of ______________ has resulted in the globalization of customer and supplier networks. This has eventually created a number of new opportunities and methods to do business.
   (a) Internet.
   (b) Web.
   (c) Both (a) and (b).
   (d) None of above.
3. Which systems can be used to integrate the firms across geographic boundaries?
   (a) Management Information System.
   (b) CRM systems.
   (c) Executive Information System.
   (d) ERP systems.
4. The use of ERP systems in an organization allows the automatic introduction of the latest technologies such as:
   (a) Electronic Data Interchange (EDI).

(b) E-Commerce.
(c) Both of above.
(d) None of above.

5. Some of the technologies that are being used along with ERP, in order to, overcome the limitations of a standalone ERP system and facilitate better decision making include:
   (a) Management information system, Decision support system, Executive information system
   (b) Data warehousing, data mining, on-line analytical processing.
   (c) Supply chain management and e-commerce.
   (d) All of above.
6. With the convergence of ERP, Data warehousing and Internet, the forerunners of the ERP system: __________ will be phased out.
   (a) MIS.
   (b) DSS.
   (c) Both (a) and (b).
   (d) None of above.
7. Management Information System (MIS) processes data into information which is sent to departments ______________.
   (a) For appropriate decision making.
   (b) For official use.
   (c) Only for manager's use.
   (d) None of above.
8. Which is true about MIS?
   (a) MIS is essential to manage an organization effectively.
   (b) MIS is mostly used at all levels of an organization.
   (c) It is used to support the day-to-day activities (such as financial accounting systems), as well as, the long-term strategic goals and objectives of the organization.
   (d) All of above.
   (e) None of above.
9. MIS is used to support:
   (a) Day-to-day activities (such as financial accounting systems).
   (b) Long-term strategic goals and objectives of the organization.
   (c) Both (a) and (b).
   (d) None of above
10. MIS emerged in _______ with the development of database management system (DBMS) to store and retrieve organized data.
   (a) 1960s.
   (b) 1970s.
   (c) 1980s.
   (d) 2000s.
11. ____________ extract useful management information from massive amounts of aggregated and summarized transaction data.
   (a) MIS.
   (b) DSS.

(c) EIS.
(d) Expert system.

12. Which system allows user-interactive queries to make routine (structured) decisions by implementing simple modeling and statistical techniques in the system?
    (a) MIS.
    (b) DSS.
    (c) EIS.
    (d) Expert system.
13. An effective MIS system helps in the following activities:
    (a) Enhancing communication among the employees.
    (b) Recording and aggregating information, generation of reports, delivering reports throughout the organization,
    (c) Reducing manual activities with use of automated procedures and supporting the goals of the organization.
    (d) All of above.
14. MIS system must provide:
    (a) Current information to users.
    (b) Correct errors promptly.
    (c) Provide complete useful information in summarized form.
    (d) Provide relevant information for effective decision making.
    (e) All of above.
15. A flawed MIS:
    (a) Will cause operational risks.
    (b) Adversely affect the business activities of the organization.
    (c) Both (a) and (b).
    (d) None of above.
16. Which is true about Decision Support System?
    (a) A decision support system is a computer based information system (CBIS) that supports the decision makers to take effective decisions quickly.
    (b) DSS solves managerial problems by generating and evaluating decision alternatives.
    (c) A decision support system must be able to perform the following activities: projection, deduction analysis, creation and comparison of decision alternatives, optimization and simulation.
    (d) All of above.
17. According to_______________, a decision support system must be able to perform the following activities: projection, deduction analysis, creation and comparison of decision alternatives, optimization and simulation.
    (a) Sprague and Carlson.
    (b) Peter Chuckland.
    (c) Herbert Schildt.
    (d) None of above.
18. Which is true about decision support system?
    (a) No longer a voluntary system for an organization.

(b) Has become a strategic tool in the hands of the management for the survival of an organization.
(c) Both (a) and (b).
(d) None of above.

19. Some DSS applications include:
(a) International business.
(b) Accounting.
(c) Auditing
(d) Marketing.
(e) All of above.

20. Which is not true about Geographic Information System?
(a) Geographic Information System (GIS) is a special category of DSS.
(b) GIS uses data visualization technology to support decision making with digitized maps.
(c) No longer a voluntary system for an organization.
(d) Both (a) and (b).

21. While ____________ provides managers with routine reports, __________ facilitates ad-hoc queries.
(a) DSS, MIS.
(b) MIS, DSS.
(c) EIS, MIS.
(d) None of above.

22. __________ primarily used to support structured problems but ________ is used to solve unstructured and semi-structured problems.
(a) MIS, DSS.
(b) DSS, MIS.
(c) EIS, MIS.
(d) None of above.

23. Types of Decision Support Systems include:
(a) Knowledge based decision support systems.
(b) Group DSS.
(c) Active Decision Support Systems.
(d) All of above.

24. Which systems are hybrid of DSS and expert systems (ES)?
(a) Knowledge based decision support.
(b) Group DSS.
(c) Active Decision Support Systems.
(d) None of above.

25. Which is true about KBDSS?
(a) KBDSS are used to solve a wide range of organizational problems.
(b) Knowledge acquisition serves as the major challenge in knowledge based systems.
(c) Both (a) and (b).
(d) None of above.

26. Which system is "an interactive computer based system which facilitates solution of unstructured problems by a set of decision makers working together as a group?

(a) MIS.

(b) Knowledge based decision support systems.

(c) Group DSS.

(d) None of above.

27. Which is true about Group DSS?

(a) Group DSS has special technological requirements of software, hardware, operational procedures and people.

(b) Special functional capabilities such as anonymous input of the user's ideas, listing ideas of the group members are included in Group DSS software.

(c) Both (a) and (b).

(d) None of above.

28. ________________ consists of several single user DSS, that work together in a distributed environment.

(a) Distributed decision making systems (DDM).

(b) Knowledge based decision support.

(c) Group DSS.

(d) Active Decision Support Systems.

29. ________________ make use of new tools and technologies to develop a new generation of active and intelligent DSS.

(a) Active Decision Support Systems.

(b) Distributed decision making systems (DDM).

(c) Group DSS.

(d) KBDSS.

30. Active DSS will be equipped with:

(a) Intelligent interfaces.

(b) Data mining tools.

(c) Both (a) and (b).

(d) None of above.

31. Which system is used to support the growing information needs of the executives?

(a) MIS.

(b) DSS.

(c) Executive information system (EIS).

(d) None of above.

32. Which system provides timely and critical information to the top executives for identifying malfunctioning of organizational activities, monitoring the situation and controlling it?

(a) EIS.

(b) MIS.

(c) DSS.

(d) Expert system.

33. EIS is used to:

(a) Provide strategic planning.

(b) Provide crisis management.

(c) Provide strategic control and monitoring of all the business operations.
(d) All of above.

34. Which is true about EIS?
(a) Has a menu-driven and user-friendly interface to provide easy and flexible access to corporate information.
(b) Provides timely and critical information to the top executives for identifying malfunctioning of organizational activities, monitoring the situation and controlling it.
(c) Both (a) and (b).
(d) None of about.

35. Who defined Business process reengineering (BPR) as "the functional rethinking and radical redesign of business processes to achieve dramatic improvements in critical, contemporary measures of performance such as cost, quality, service and speed"?
(a) Michael Hammer and Champy.
(b) Sprague and Carlson.
(c) Peter Chuckland.
(d) None of above.

36. Which is true about BPR?
(a) Provides a disciplined structured approach to organization that need to undergo a massive change for accomplishing the organization's goals and remain competitive.
(b) BPR uses Information Technology.
(c) In business process reengineering, the business processes are analyzed properly in order to identify the best way of performing jobs, the processes (jobs) are then changed accordingly.
(d) A failure of BPR in the organization will definitely lead to ERP implementation failure. BPR and ERP go hand-in-hand.
(e) All of above.

37. Depending upon the__________________; some organizations may require only a partial, while others, a complete redesign of the business processes.
(a) Complexity of the business processes.
(b) Nature of products.
(c) Organization's goals and objectives.
(d) Nature of employees.

38. The changes in the organization will affect:
(a) Company's business procedures.
(b) Organizational structure.
(c) Both (a) and (b).
(d) None of above.

39. Which is not true about BPR?
(a) BPR came earlier than the popularization of ERP happened.
(b) A failure of BPR in the organization will definitely lead to ERP implementation failure. BPR and ERP go hand-in-hand.
(c) BPR improves the business processes and ERP automates those improved business processes to deliver better accuracy and higher efficiency.

(d) Implementing BPR in an organization will ensure success to an ERP system implementation.
(e) None of above.

40. ERP serves as an ideal solution for reengineering the business processes, as ERP systems:
(a) Facilitate seamless information flow across departmental boundaries.
(b) Automates the business processes of the organization.
(c) Both (a) and (b).
(d) None of above.

41. What does BPR do?
(a) BPR improves the quality of products, services and operations.
(b) BPR increases the efficiency of the organization.
(c) BPR has continuously reduced the size of the workforce. As a consequence, the adoption of BPR approach has a challenging impact.
(d) All of above.

42. _________ refers to a wide variety of activities that firms and industries use to coordinate the key players in their procurement process.
(a) Supply Chain Management (SCM).
(b) ERP.
(c) CRM.
(d) None of above.

43. Which is true about supply chain?
(a) The concept of supply chain is usually supported by IT today.
(b) A supply chain that is being managed electronically with web-based software is referred to as an e-supply chain.
(c) A supply chain typically involves materials flows, information flows and financial flows.
(d) All of above.

44. _________ coordinates materials flows, information flows and financial flows among all the involved parties in the supply chain.
(a) ERP.
(b) CRM.
(c) Supply chain management (SCM).
(d) None of above.

45. The supply chain involves _________segments.
(a) Three.
(b) Five.
(c) Six.
(d) Four.

46. Which is true about SCM?
(a) SCM reduces the uncertainty and risks along the supply chain.
(b) SCM improves business processes by an effective coordination of information, material and financial flows among all parties involved in the supply chain.
(c) SCM helps provide better service to the customers.
(d) All of above.

47. Which is not true about SCM?
(a) SCM decreases the inventory level.
(b) SCM increases the cycle time.
(c) SCM reduces the uncertainty and risks along the supply chain.
(d) None of above.

48. A good supply chain management solution will improve:
(a) Critical business processes such as procurement-to-pay cycles.
(b) Order-to-cash cycles.
(c) Demand forecasting.
(d) All of above.

49. ____________ Tools monitor and optimize the entire supply chain to meet the specific needs of a company.
(a) Data mining tools.
(b) Advanced Planning and Scheduling (APS).
(c) Graphic.
(d) None of above.

50. In pull based approach to SCM:
(a) The processes are initiated in response to an order from a customer.
(b) Processes in pull based approach are also referred to as reactive processes because these processes react to the demands of the customers.
(c) Both (a) and (b).
(d) None of above.

51. In push based model:
(a) Products are pushed to the customers in expectation of a customer order.
(b) The push based processes are referred to as speculative processes since they respond to demand forecast rather than actual customer demand.
(c) Both (a) and (b).
(d) None of above.

52. There are ____________________ key processes in supply chain management.
(a) Three.
(b) Four.
(c) Five.
(d) Six.

53. The focus of the ______________ is to ensure the availability of the right product at the right time and at right place.
(a) Planning systems.
(b) Execution systems.
(c) Performance Measurement Systems.
(d) None of above.

54. Which is true about Execution systems?
(a) The system enables the efficient movements of products and services through the supply chain.
(b) Providing operational efficiency is the main focus of execution systems.
(c) Both (a) and (b).
(d) None of above.

55. What does Performance Measurement System do?
- **(a)** The system enables the efficient movements of products and services through the supply chain.
- **(b)** The system monitors and ensures the effectiveness of the supply chain.
- **(c)** The system ensures the availability of the right product at the right time and at right place.
- **(d)** None of above.

56. Use of web-based software agents and data warehousing allow the business operations:
- **(a)** To respond immediately to key business events.
- **(b)** To reduce the work force required.
- **(c)** Both (a) and (b).
- **(d)** None of above.

57. The key functions in supply chain management are:
- **(a)** Customer asset management.
- **(b)** Integrated Logistics.
- **(c)** Financial and accounting management.
- **(d)** Agile manufacturing.
- **(e)** All of above.

58. Customer asset management deals with:
- **(a)** Managing the flow of goods from suppliers.
- **(b)** Collecting and analyzing information about customer demand in order to have a better understanding of the customer needs.
- **(c)** Managing the financial flows with the suppliers as well as customers.
- **(d)** Managing the manufacturing process in such a way that the cost of production is low.

59. ____________ deals with managing the flow of goods from suppliers.
- **(a)** Customer asset management.
- **(b)** Integrated Logistics.
- **(c)** Financial and accounting management.
- **(d)** Agile manufacturing.

60. Financial and accounting management deals with managing the financial flows with:
- **(a)** Suppliers.
- **(b)** Customers.
- **(c)** Both (a) and (b).
- **(d)** None of above.

61. Which aspect of supply chain management deals with managing the manufacturing process in such a way that the cost of production is low?
- **(a)** Customer asset management.
- **(b)** Agile manufacturing.
- **(c)** Integrated Logistics.
- **(d)** None of above.

62. According to Kala Kota and Robin, ____________ is "an integrated sales, marketing and service strategy".
- **(a)** ERP.
- **(b)** Customer relationship management (CRM).

(c) SCM.
(d) None of above.

63. Customer relationship management (CRM) systems focus on the key elements of the organization, that is, __________.
(a) Customers.
(b) Relations.
(c) Marketing strategy.
(d) None of above.

64. Which is true about a CRM system?
(a) A CRM system uses the CRM strategy that attempts to learn about the needs and preferences of customers in order to build healthier relations with the customers.
(b) CRM systems support tracking past purchases and payments made by customers, updating the electronic customer profile, analyzing the behavior of customers and providing updated online-answers to the frequently asked questions (FAQs) about various products and services.
(c) CRM systems include all the tools, technologies and procedures related with sales, marketing and post-sale customer service.
(d) All of above.

65. Today, most of the companies are realizing the need to integrate CRM systems with __________ in order to achieve business improvements and better financial performance.
(a) ERP.
(b) SCM.
(c) Both (a) and (b).
(d) None of above.

66. __________ Systems include all the tools, technologies and procedures related with sales, marketing and post-sale customer service.
(a) SCM.
(b) ERP.
(c) CRM.
(d) None of above.

67. Which is true about CRM systems?
(a) CRM systems can be implemented by introducing CRM software within the company either in strategically selected areas or getting it fully installed.
(b) A CRM system implemented partially has limited functionality.
(c) The lack of standards in CRM activities often makes the implementation of a CRM system difficult.
(d) CRM systems should be designed in such a way that they address cross-functional business processes.
(e) All of above.

68. CRM vendors are now focusing on producing and delivering business process-based software solutions. These solutions are __________.
(a) More flexible.
(b) Highly configurable.

(c) Both (a) and (b).
(d) None of above.

69. ____________ is a new concept that attempts to overcome the limitations of the CRM systems.
(a) E-Commerce.
(b) Business process Management (BPM).
(c) ERP.
(d) Mobile agents.

70. The main elements of a CRM system are:
(a) Operational CRM.
(b) Analytical CRM.
(c) Collaborative CRM.
(d) All of above.

71. Which is true about Operational CRM?
(a) Operational CRM centres on all the activities of the business that are related to sales, marketing and customer service.
(b) Operational CRM deals with the collection and analysis of the data collected by the CRM system.
(c) Both (a) and (b).
(d) None of above.

72. ________ deals with the collection and analysis of the data collected by the CRM system.
(a) Operational CRM.
(b) Analytical CRM.
(c) Collaborative CRM.
(d) All of above.

73. Which is true about Analytical CRM?
(a) Different segments of customers and the relationship between them are identified, based on the results of the analysis.
(b) It provides support to decision making.
(c) Both (a) and (b).
(d) None of above.

74. Collaborative CRM facilitates the interaction with the customers by:
(a) Phone.
(b) Fax.
(c) Email.
(d) All of above.

75. Which of the statement is not true?
(a) Use of e-commerce together with ERP systems will enable companies to grow faster in the global environment.
(b) Both ERP and e-commerce are complimentary to each other.
(c) Both (a) and (b).
(d) None of above.

76. ____________ enables selling and purchasing of various products and services through web. Without ________ a company cannot fulfill the web orders accurately and speedily.

(a) E-Commerce, ERP.
(b) ERP, E-Commerce.
(c) E-Commerce, CRM.
(d) None of above.

77. Which of the statements is not true?
(a) The need of implementing ERP systems is growing in companies that desire to use E-commerce for doing business.
(b) ERP systems were initially meant only for employees within an organization.
(c) The customers want to get information that is free of all the ERP software jargon and easy to understand through the company's website.
(d) None of above.

78. In order to make the ERP systems available over the web, the company's IT department will have to build two new channels of access into the company's ERP systems. The access channels will be used to:
(a) Provide access to the customers for information such as order status and billing from the company's ERP system.
(b) Provide access to the suppliers and business partners so that useful and relevant information is made available more easily and efficiently from the ERP system of the company.
(c) Both (a) and (b).
(d) None of above.

79. Middleware and EAI software take information from the __________ system. The information captured is then converted into a format that the __________ applications can understand.
(a) E-Commerce, ERP.
(b) ERP, e-commerce.
(c) E-Commerce, CRM.
(d) None of above.

80. A data warehouse is a repository of __________ sources of data.
(a) Multiple.
(b) Heterogeneous.
(c) Single homogeneous.
(d) Multiple heterogeneous.

81. Which is true about data warehouse?
(a) Is primarily meant to separate operational data from the data stored for performing business analysis.
(b) The data stored in the data warehouse helps the managers in making quick and effective decisions.
(c) The data warehousing systems are now designed to support sophisticated online-analysis such as multidimensional analysis.
(d) All of above.

82. Data warehouses were initially used to generate ________ reports. They also had the capability to answer_________ queries.
(a) Useful, Predefined.

(b) Predefined, Useful.
(c) Useful, Ad-hoc.
(d) Complex, Ad-hoc.

83. Which is true about data warehouse?
(a) Data warehouse were initially used to generate useful reports.
(b) Later, the data warehouses began to be used to analyze the summarized data.
(c) Today, the data warehouses are used for strategic decision making.
(d) All of above.

84. ________ tools are used to discover knowledge from the vast pool of data stored in the data warehouse.
(a) Advanced mathematical.
(b) Data mining.
(c) Search tools.
(d) None of above.

85. Data warehouses applications include:
(a) Information processing.
(b) Analytical processing.
(c) Data mining.
(d) All of above.

86. The tiers of the data warehouse normally include:
(a) Warehouse database server.
(b) OLAP server.
(c) Client tier.
(d) All of above.

87. Warehouse database server is the ________ tier.
(a) Bottom.
(b) Top
(c) Middle.
(d) Client

88. __________ forms the middle tier of the data warehouse architecture.
(a) Warehouse database server.
(b) OLAP server.
(c) Client tier.
(d) EAI.

89. The topmost tier is the ________tier.
(a) Warehouse database server.
(b) OLAP server.
(c) Client.
(d) None of above.

90. The client tier contains:
(a) Query tools.
(b) Analysis and reporting tools.
(c) Data mining tools.
(d) All of above.

91. Which is true about data warehouse architecture?
(a) Defining the architecture for a data warehouse is a challenging task.
(b) A data warehouse architecture must meet challenges such as data integration, information reuse and business intelligence.
(c) The data warehouse model should achieve data integration, promote information reuse and provide rich business intelligence.
(d) All of above.

92. A data model defines:
(a) Objects that are of interest to the organization.
(b) The rules that describe those objects and govern them.
(c) Both (a) and (b).
(d) None of above.

93. The methodologies that are usually applied to design and implementation of a data warehouse are:
(a) Enterprise data model.
(b) Data Bus.
(c) Process Neutral Model.
(d) All of above.

94. ____________ starts by using the conventional relational data modeling techniques.
(a) Enterprise data model.
(b) Data Bus.
(c) Process Neutral Model.
(d) None of above.

95. Which is true about Enterprise data model?
(a) Describes the business in a conventional normalized database. A series of de-normalizations may then occur to improve performance.
(b) Enterprise data model is typically used by the corporations that possess a corporate wide data model.
(c) Both (a) and (b).
(d) None of above.

96. __________ is made up of a series of star schemas. The star schemas have gradually evolved over time.
(a) Enterprise data model.
(b) Data Bus model.
(c) Process Neutral Model.
(d) None of above.

97. Data models are views:
(a) Directly on the star schemas.
(b) Directly onto the aggregates of these star schemas.
(c) Either directly on the star schemas or onto the aggregates of the star schemas.
(d) None of above.

98. A __________ contains a subset of corporate wide data that holds value only for a specific group of users.
(a) Database.

(b) Data mart.
(c) Data warehouse.
(d) None of above.

99. Which of the statements is not true about Process Neutral Model?
(a) In Process Neutral Model data model all the embedded business rules have been removed.
(b) The advantage of Process Neutral Model data model approach is that as the business processes change there is little or no change required to the data model.
(c) The approach is generally used by organizations that are characterized by a rapidly changing corporate environment.
(d) The Process Neutral Model starts by using the conventional relational data modeling techniques.

100. Which is true about OLAP?
(a) OLAP stands for "Online Analytical Processing".
(b) An OLAP product is necessarily multi-dimensional.
(c) OLAP can be defined by five keywords: Fast Analysis of Shared Multi-dimensional Information (FASMI).
(d) OLAP cube (also referred to as hypercube or multi-dimensional cube) forms the core of any OLAP system.
(e) All of above.

101. The descriptive term "FASMI" for OLAP was suggested by:
(a) Nigel Pendse.
(b) Hammer and Champy.
(c) Robin.
(d) None of above.

102. Which of the statements is true?
(a) Data in an OLAP cube is modeled in multiple dimensions.
(b) Dimensions are the perspective with rcspect to which organization would keep records.
(c) Each dimension may have a "dimension table" associated with it.
(d) All of above.

103. Which of the statements is true?
(a) Facts are numerical quantities that are used to analyze relationship between the dimensions of an OLAP cube.
(b) A fact table contains the names of the facts (also called measures).
(c) Both (a) and (b).
(d) None of above.

104. Which of the statements is true?
(a) An OLAP cube facilitates complex data mining queries to be answered quickly in comparison to a relational database.
(b) The use of aggregations (data summarized along dimensions) is the most important mechanism that supports the good performance of an OLAP system.
(c) The use of multiple hierarchies facilitates complex analytical and ad-hoc queries to be answered with a rapid response time.
(d) All of above.

105. Common OLAP applications include:
(a) Sales and marketing analysis.
(b) Financial reporting.
(c) Budgeting and forecasting.
(d) All of above.

106. _______ has been defined as "the non-trivial extraction of implicit, previously unknown and potentially useful information from data."
(a) Data warehouse.
(b) OLAP.
(c) Data Mart.
(d) None of above.

107. Data mining involves:
(a) Knowledge discovery.
(b) Pattern recognition.
(c) Both (a) and (b).
(d) None of above.

108. The data mining tasks include:
(a) Data characterization.
(b) Mining association rules.
(c) Data classification.
(d) Evolution analysis.
(e) All of above.

109. Which is true about Data mining?
(a) Data mining extracts useful information from large amount of data by the application of a computer based methodology. This is also known as knowledge discovery.
(b) Data mining involves both knowledge discovery and pattern recognition. Data mining, in fact, covers a broad spectrum of tasks.
(c) The data mining tasks include data characterization, mining association rules, data classification and evolution analysis.
(d) All of above.

110. The ways in which data mining system can be designed are:
(a) No Coupling
(b) Loose Coupling
(c) Semi-tight coupling
(d) Tight Coupling
(e) All of above.

111. In _____________ architecture, a data mining system will not utilize any function of either a database or a data warehouse system. This architecture is poor as it fails to make use of the rich functionalities of the database and data warehouse system.
(a) No Coupling.
(b) Loose Coupling.
(c) Semi-tight coupling.
(d) Tight coupling.

112. Which is not true about Loose Coupling design?

- **(a)** The data mining system uses some of the facilities offered by a database or a data warehouse system.
- **(b)** This design is considered better than no coupling design.
- **(c)** The data mining system will not utilize any function of either a database or a data warehouse system.
- **(d)** None of above.

113. Which is true about semi-tight coupling?

- **(a)** In semi-tight coupling a few essential data mining functions can be provided in the database/ data warehouse system.
- **(b)** The intermediate data mining results can be stored in the database or data warehouse.
- **(c.)** The data mining system is smoothly integrated into the database/data warehouse system.
- **(d)** Both (a) and (b).
- **(e)** None of above.

114. In ___________, the data mining system is smoothly integrated into the database/data warehouse system.

- **(a)** No Coupling.
- **(b)** Loose Coupling.
- **(c)** Semi-tight coupling.
- **(d)** Tight Coupling

115. The advantage of tight coupling system includes:

- **(a)** It efficiently implements data mining functions.
- **(b)** It has high system performance.
- **(c)** Both (a) and (b).
- **(d)** None of above.

116. Which is true about Data Mining Query Language (DMQL)?

- **(a)** Data mining Query Language is used to facilitate ad-hoc and interactive data mining in data mining systems.
- **(b)** DMQL is based on certain data mining primitives that are required for defining a data mining task.
- **(c)** Both (a) and (b).
- **(d)** None of above.

SECTION B

STATE TRUE OR FALSE

1. The emergence of new technologies provides the business firms with many active tools to better conduct their business.
2. The growth of Internet and Web has resulted in the globalization of customer and supplier networks. This has eventually created a number of new opportunities and methods to do business.
3. The ERP systems cannot be used to integrate the firms across geographic boundaries.

4. The use of ERP systems in an organization allows the automatic introduction of the latest technologies such as Electronic Data Interchange (EDI), E-Commerce, etc.
5. Some of the technologies that are being used along with ERP, in order to overcome the limitations of a standalone ERP system and facilitate better decision making include management information system, decision support system, executive information system, data warehousing, data mining, on-line analytical processing, supply chain management and e-commerce.
6. With the convergence of ERP, Data warehousing and Internet, the forerunners of the ERP system—MIS and DSS will gain immense importance.
7. Management Information System (MIS) processes data into information which is sent to departments for appropriate decision making.
8. MIS is essential to manage an organization effectively. MIS is mostly used at all levels of an organization.
9. MIS is not used to support the day-to-day activities (such as financial accounting systems). It only meets the long-term strategic goals and objectives of the organization.
10. MIS emerged in 1980s with the development of database management system (DBMS) to store and retrieve organized data.
11. MIS extract useful management information from massive amounts of aggregated and summarized transaction data.
12. MIS allow user-interactive queries to make routine (structured) decisions by implementing simple modeling and statistical techniques in the system.
13. An effective MIS system helps in the following activities: enhancing communication among the employees, recording and aggregating information, generation of reports, delivering reports throughout the organization, reducing manual activities with use of automated procedures and supporting the goals of the organization.
14. MIS system must provide current information to users, correct errors promptly, information must be reliable, provide complete useful information in summarized form, provide relevant information for effective decision making.
15. A flawed MIS will cause operational risks and adversely affect the business activities of the organization.
16. A decision support system is a computer based information system (CBIS) that supports the decision makers to take effective decisions quickly.
17. MIS solves managerial problems by generating and evaluating decision alternatives.
18. According to Sprague and Carlson, a decision support system must be able to perform the following activities: projection, deduction analysis, creation and comparison of decision alternatives, optimization and simulation.
19. A decision support system is no longer a voluntary system for an organization but, in fact, has become a strategic tool in the hands of the management for the survival of an organization.
20. Some DSS applications include international business, accounting, auditing, marketing, finance etc.
21. Geographic information system (GIS) is a special category of DSS. GIS uses data visualization technology to support decision making with digitized maps.

22. While DSS provides managers with routine reports, MIS facilitates ad-hoc queries.

23.. DSS is primarily used to support structured problems but MIS is used to solve unstructured and semi-structured problems.

24. Types of Decision Support System include the following: Knowledge based decision support systems, group DSS, Distributed decision making systems (DDM) and Active Decision Support Systems.

25. Knowledge based decision support systems are hybrid of DSS and expert systems (ES).

26. KBDSS are used to solve a wide range of organizational problems. Knowledge acquisition serves as the major challenge in knowledge based systems.

27. According to DeSanctis and Gallupe, a group DSS is "an interactive computer based system which facilitates solution of unstructured problems by a set of decision makers working together as a group.

28. Group DSS has special technological requirements of software, hardware, operational procedures and people.

29. Special functional capabilities such as anonymous input of the user's ideas, listing ideas of the group members have not yet been included in Group DSS software.

30. Distributed decision making systems (DDM) consist of several multiple user DSS, that, work together in a centralized environment.

31. Active Decision Support Systems make use of new tools and technologies to develop a new generation of active and intelligent DSS.

32. Active DSS will be equipped with intelligent interfaces and data mining tools.

33. Executive information system (EIS) is used to support the growing information needs of the executives.

34. EIS provides timely and critical information to the top executives for identifying malfunctioning of organizational activities, monitoring the situation and controlling it.

35. EIS fails to provide strategic planning, crisis management and strategic control and monitoring of all the business operations.

36. An EIS has menu-driven, user-friendly interfaces to provide easy and flexible access to corporate information.

37. Business process reengineering (BPR) is defined as "the fundamental rethinking and radical redesign of business processes to achieve dramatic improvements in critical, contemporary measures of performance such as cost, quality, service and speed." This definition of BPR was given by Nigel Pendse.

38. BPR provides a disciplined structured approach to organizations that need to undergo a massive change for accomplishing the organization's goals and remain competitive.

39. BPR uses Information Technology. In fact, IT is a key factor that makes BPR work.

40. In business process reengineering, the business processes are analyzed properly in order to identify the best way of performing jobs, the processes (jobs) are then changed accordingly.

41. Depending upon the complexity of the business processes; some organizations may require only a partial, while others, a complete redesign of the business processes.

42. The changes while adopting Business process reengineering (BPR) will not only affect the company's business procedures but also its organizational structure.

43. ERP came earlier than the popularization of BPR happened.

44. A failure of BPR in the organization will definitely lead to ERP implementation failure. BPR and ERP go hand-in-hand.
45. ERP improves the business processes and BPR automates those improved business processes to deliver better accuracy and higher efficiency.
46. Implementing BPR in an organization will ensure success to an ERP system implementation.
47. As ERP systems facilitate seamless information flow across departmental boundaries and automates the business processes of the organization, ERP therefore, serves as an ideal solution for reengineering the business processes.
48. BPR improves the quality of products, services and operations.
49. BPR increases the efficiency of the organization.
50. BPR has continuously reduced the size of the workforce. As a consequence, the adoption of BPR approach has a challenging impact.
51. CRM refers to a wide variety of activities that firms and industries use to coordinate the key players in their procurement process.
52. The concept of supply chain is usually supported by IT today. A supply chain that is being managed electronically with web-based software is referred to as an e-supply chain.
53. A supply chain typically involves materials flows, information flows and financial flows.
54. Supply chain management coordinates materials flows, information flows and financial flows among all the involved parties in the supply chain.
55. The supply chain involves three segments. These are as follows: Downstream—the sourcing or procurement occurs from external suppliers; Upstream—the distribution or dispersal takes place; Internal—The packaging, assembly or manufacturing occurs.
56. SCM reduces the uncertainty and risks along the supply chain.
57. SCM improves business processes by an effective coordination of information, material and financial flows among all parties involved in the supply chain.
58. SCM helps provide better service to the customers.
59. SCM increases the inventory level and the cycle time.
60. A good supply chain management solution will improve critical business processes such as procurement-to-pay cycles, order-to-cash cycles and demand forecasting.
61. Advanced planning and scheduling (APS) tools monitor and optimize the entire supply chain to meet the specific needs of a company.
62. In pull based approach to SCM, products are pushed to the customers in expectation of a customer order.
63. Processes in pull based approach are also referred to as reactive processes because these processes react to the demands of the customers.
64. In push based model the processes are initiated in response to an order from a customer.
65. The push based processes are referred to as speculative processes since they respond to demand forecast rather than actual customer demand.
66. There are three key processes in supply chain management. These are as follows: Planning systems, Execution systems, Performance Measurement System.
67. The focus of the Execution systems is to ensure the availability of the right product at the right time and at right place.
68. The planning system enables the efficient movements of products and services through the supply chain. Providing operational efficiency is the main focus of planning systems.

69. Performance Measurement System monitors and ensures the effectiveness of the supply chain. Use of web-based software agents and data warehousing allow the business operations to respond immediately to key business events.

70. The key functions in supply chain management are as follows: Customer asset management, Integrated Logistics, Financial and accounting management, Agile manufacturing.

71. Integrated Logistics deals with collecting and analyzing information about customer demand in order to have a better understanding of the customer needs.

72. Customer asset management deals with managing the flow of goods from suppliers.

73. Financial and accounting management deals with managing the financial flows with the suppliers as well as customers.

74. Agile manufacturing aspect of supply chain management deals with managing the manufacturing process in such a way that the cost of production is low.

75. According to Kala Kota and Robin, Supply chain management (SCM) is "an integrated sales, marketing and service strategy".

76. Customer relationship management (CRM) systems focus on the key elements of the organization, that is, customers.

77. A CRM system uses the CRM strategy that attempts to learn about the needs and preferences of customers in order to build healthier relations with the customers.

78. CRM systems support tracking past purchases and payments made by customers, updating the electronic customer profile, analyzing the behaviour of customers and providing updated online-answers to the frequently asked questions (FAQs) about various products and services.

79. Today, most of the companies are realizing the need to integrate CRM systems with the other enterprise systems (ERP and SCM) in order to achieve business improvements and better financial performance.

80. CRM systems include all the tools, technologies and procedures related with sales, marketing and post-sale customer service.

81. CRM systems can be implemented by introducing CRM software within the company either in strategically selected areas or getting it fully installed.

82. A CRM system implemented partially has limited functionality.

83. The lack of standards in CRM activities often makes the implementation of a CRM system easy.

84. CRM systems should be designed in such a way that they address cross-functional business processes.

85. CRM vendors are now focusing on producing and delivering business process-based software solutions. These solutions are more flexible and highly configurable.

86. Business process Management (BPM) is a new concept that attempts to overcome the limitations of the SCM systems.

87. The main elements of a CRM system are: Operational CRM, Analytical CRM, and Collaborative CRM.

88. Operational CRM centres on all the activities of the business that are related to sales, marketing and customer service.

89. Analytical CRM deals with the collection and analysis of the data collected by the CRM system. Based on the results of the analysis different segments of customers and the relationship between them are identified.

90. Analytical CRM does not provide any support to decision making.
91. Collaborative CRM facilitates the interaction with the customers only by phone but not by fax or email.
92. "E-commerce is the exchange of information across electronic networks at any stage in the supply chain whether within an organization, between business and consumers, or between public and private sectors whether paid or un-paid".
93. Use of e-commerce together with ERP systems will enable companies to grow faster in the global environment.
94. ERP and e-commerce are not complimentary to each other.
95. E-commerce enables selling and purchasing of various products and services through web.
96. Without ERP, a company can fulfill the web orders accurately and speedily.
97. The need of implementing ERP systems is growing in companies that desire to use E-commerce for doing business.
98. ERP systems were initially meant only for employees within an organization.
99. In order to make the ERP systems available over the web, the company's IT department will have to build two new channels of access into the company's ERP systems.
100. One access channel will be used to provide access to the customers for information such as order status and billing from the company's ERP system.
101. The other channel will provide access to the suppliers and business partners so that useful and relevant information is made available more easily and efficiently from the ERP system of the company.
102. Integrating the ERP system and e-commerce requires careful planning to be done by the vendor. Selecting vendors having a good experience in developing e-commerce wares is a good choice to make.
103. ERP systems are complex and require a good deal of maintenance. The website will not be available to the public when the company shuts down the ERP system for maintenance work. This can be a costly affair.
104. In order to prevent huge losses, most e-commerce veterans build flexibility into the connecting links between e-commerce and ERP systems. This means that the e-commerce applications can keep running on the web during the ERP system shut down for upgrades and fixes.
105. Middleware and EAI software take information from the ERP system. The information captured is then converted into a format that the e-commerce applications can understand.
106. A data warehouse is a repository of multiple heterogeneous sources of data. A data warehouse is primarily meant to separate operational data from the data stored for performing business analysis.
107. The data stored in the data warehouse helps the managers in making quick and effective decisions.
108. The data warehousing systems are now designed to support sophisticated online-analysis such as multidimensional analysis.
109. Data warehouse were initially used to generate useful reports. They also had the capability to answer predefined queries.
110. Later, the data warehouses began to be used to analyze the summarized data. Today, the data warehouses are used for strategic decision making.

111. Data mining tools are used to discover knowledge from the vast pool of data stored in the data warehouse.
112. Data warehouses applications include information processing, analytical processing and data mining.
113. The data warehouse normally has five tiers.
114. Warehouse database server is the bottom tier. It almost consists of a relational database system.
115. Client forms the middle tier of the data warehouse architecture.
116. The client tier contains query tools, analysis, reporting tools and may also contain data mining tools.
117. The topmost tier is OLAP server the tier.
118. Defining the architecture for a data warehouse is a challenging task. A data warehouse architecture must meet challenges such as data integration, information reuse and business intelligence.
119. The data warehouse model should achieve data integration, promote information reuse and provide rich business intelligence.
120. A data model defines objects that are of interest to the organization and the rules that describe those objects and govern them.
121. The three methodologies that are usually applied to the design and implementation of a data warehouse are as follows: Enterprise data model, Data Bus, Process Neutral Model.
122. Enterprise data model starts by using the conventional relational data modeling techniques. The data model describes the business in a conventional normalized database. A series of de-normalizations may then occur to improve performance.
123. Enterprise data model is made up of a series of star schemas. The star schemas have gradually evolved over time.
124. Data Bus model is typically used by the corporations that possess a corporate wide data model.
125. A data mart contains a subset of corporate wide data that holds value only for a specific group of users.
126. In Process Neutral data model, all the embedded business rules have been removed.
127. The advantage of Process Neutral Model data model approach is that as the business processes change there is little or no change required to the data model.
128. The Process Neutral Model data model approach is generally used by organizations that are characterized by a rapidly changing corporate environment.
129. OLAP stands for "Online Analytical Processing". An OLAP product is necessarily multi-dimensional.
130. OLAP can be defined by five keywords: Fats Analysis of Shared Multi-dimensional Information (FASMI).
131. The descriptive term "FASMI" for OLAP was suggested by Nigel Pendse.
132. OLAP cube also referred to as hypercube or multi-dimensional cube) forms the core of any OLAP system.
133. Data in an OLAP cube is modeled in multiple dimensions.
134. Dimensions are the perspective with respect to which the organization would keep records.

135. A dimension in an OLAP cube may not have a "dimension table" associated with it.
136. Facts are numerical quantities that are used to analyze relationship between the dimensions of an OLAP cube.
137. A fact table contains the names of the facts (also called measures).
138. An OLAP cube facilitates complex data mining queries to be answered quickly in comparison to a relational database.
139. The use of aggregations (data summarized along dimensions) is the most important mechanism that supports the good performance of an OLAP system.
140. The use of multiple hierarchies facilitates complex analytical and ad-hoc queries to be answered with a rapid response time.
141. The most common OLAP applications include sales and marketing analysis, financial reporting, budgeting and forecasting.
142. Data mining has been defined as "the non-trivial extraction of implicit, previously unknown and potentially useful information from data."
143. Data mining extracts useful information from large amount of data by the application of a computer based methodology. This is also known as knowledge discovery.
144. Data mining does not involve knowledge discovery and pattern recognition.
145. The data mining tasks include data characterization, mining association rules, data classification and evolution analysis.
146. A data mining system can be designed in any one of the following ways: No Coupling, Loose Coupling, Semi-tight coupling and Tight Coupling.
147. In No Coupling architecture, a data mining system will not utilize any function of either a database or a data warehouse system. This architecture is poor as it fails to make use of the rich functionalities of the database and data warehouse system.
148. In Loose Coupling design, the data mining system uses some of the facilities offered by a database or a data warehouse system.
149. No coupling design is considered better than Loose Coupling design.
150. In semi-tight coupling, a few essential data mining functions can be provided in the database/data warehouse system. The intermediate data mining results can be stored in the database or data warehouse.
151. In Tight Coupling, the data mining system is smoothly integrated into the database/data warehouse system.
152. Tight coupling system efficiently implements data mining functions and has high system performance.
153. Data mining Query Language (DMQL) is used to facilitate ad-hoc and interactive data mining in data mining systems.
154. DMQL is based on certain data mining primitives. These are required for defining a data mining task.
155. Task relevant Data Specification involves specifying the portions of the database or the set of data that is relevant and in which the user is interested.

SECTION C

FILL IN THE BLANKS

1. The emergence of new technologies provides the business firms with many active tools to _______ conduct their business.
2. The growth of Internet and Web has resulted in the ___________ of customer and supplier networks. This has eventually created a number of new opportunities and methods to do business.
3. The ERP systems can be used to integrate the firms across ____________ boundaries.
4. The use of ERP systems in an organization allows the ___________ introduction of the latest technologies such as Electronic Data Interchange (EDI), E-Commerce, etc.
5. Some of the technologies that are being used along with__________, in order to, overcome the limitations of a standalone ERP system and facilitate _________decision making including management information system, decision support system, executive information system, data warehousing, data mining, on-line analytical processing, supply chain management and e-commerce.
6. With the convergence of ERP, Data warehousing and Internet, the forerunners of the ERP system—_______ and _________ will be phased out.
7. Management Information System (MIS) processes data into ____________ which is sent to departments for appropriate_________.
8. MIS is __________ to manage an organization effectively. MIS is mostly used at ________ levels of an organization.
9. MIS is used to support the day-to-day activities (such as financial accounting systems), as well as, the long-term __________ goals and objectives of the organization.
10. MIS emerged in ___________ with the development of database management system (DBMS) to store and retrieve organized data.
11. MIS extract useful management information from massive amounts of aggregated and summarized __________ data.
12. MIS allow user-interactive queries to make ___________ decisions by implementing simple modeling and statistical techniques in the system.
13. An effective ____________________ system helps in the following activities—enhancing communication among the employees, recording and aggregating information, generation of reports, delivering reports throughout the organization, reducing manual activities with use of automated procedures and supporting the goals of the organization.
14. MIS system must provide complete, useful, ________and _________information to users in ___________form for effective decision making and correct errors promptly.
15. A _________ MIS will cause operational risks and adversely affect the business activities of the organization.
16. A _________ system is a computer based information system (CBIS) that supports the decision makers to take effective decisions quickly.
17. DSS solves ________ problems by generating and evaluating decision ________.
18. According to ___________, a decision support system must be able to perform the following activities: projection, deduction analysis, creation and comparison of decision alternatives, optimization and simulation.

19. A decision support system is no longer a __________ system for an organization but, in fact, has become a strategic tool in the hands of the management for the survival of an organization.
20. Some __________ applications include international business, accounting, auditing, marketing, finance etc.
21. Geographic information system (GIS) is a special category of________. GIS uses data visualization technology to support decision making with __________.
22. While MIS provides managers with routine reports, DSS facilitates __________ queries.
23. MIS is primarily used to support __________ problems but DSS is used to solve ________ and semi-structured problems.
24. Types of Decision Support Systems include the following: Knowledge based decision support systems, __________, DDM and active DSS.
25. Knowledge based decision support systems are hybrid of ______ and __________.
26. __________ are used to solve a wide range of organizational problems. ________ serves as the major challenge in knowledge based systems.
27. According to DeSanctis and Gallupe, a __________ is "an interactive computer based system which facilitates solution of unstructured problems by a set of decision makers working together as a group.
28. Group DSS has special technological requirements of software, hardware, ________ and people.
29. Special functional capabilities such as anonymous input of the user's ideas, listing ideas of the group members are included in __________ software
30. Distributed decision making systems (DDM) consists of several single user DSS, that, work together in a __________ environment.
31. __________ Systems make use of new tools and technologies to develop a new generation of active and intelligent DSS.
32. Active DSS will be equipped with __________ interfaces and _________ tools.
33. ___________ is used to support the growing information needs of the executives.
34. EIS provides timely and critical information to the ____________ for identifying malfunctioning of organizational activities, monitoring the situation and controlling it.
35. EIS is used to provide strategic planning, ____________ and strategic control and monitoring of all the business operations.
36. An EIS has __________, user-friendly interfaces to provide easy and flexible access to corporate information.
37. ___________ is defined as "the fundamental rethinking and radical redesign of business processes to achieve dramatic improvements in critical, contemporary measures of performance such as cost, quality, service and speed." This definition was given by_______________.
38. BPR provides a disciplined _________ approach to organization that need to undergo a massive change for accomplishing the organization's goals and remain competitive.
39. BPR uses__________. In fact, IT is a key factor that makes BPR work.
40. In business process reengineering, the business processes are analyzed properly in order to identify the ________ way of performing __________, the processes (jobs) are then changed accordingly.

41. Depending upon the ________ of the business processes; some organizations may require only a partial, while others, a complete redesign of the business processes.
42. The changes will not only affect the company's __________ but also its organizational structure.
43. _______ came earlier than the popularization of ERP happened.
44. A failure of BPR in the organization will definitely lead to ERP implementation failure. BPR and ERP go _________.
45. BPR improves the business processes and __________ automates those improved business processes to deliver better accuracy and higher efficiency.
46. Implementing BPR in an organization will ensure success to an ________ implementation.
47. As ERP systems facilitate seamless information flow across departmental boundaries and _________ the business processes of the organization, ERP therefore, serves as an ideal solution for reengineering the ______________.
48. BPR improves the quality of products, services and__________.
49. BPR _________ the efficiency of the business processes in an organization.
50. BPR has continuously _________ the size of the workforce. As a consequence, the adoption of BPR approach has a challenging impact.
51. __________ refers to a wide variety of activities that firms and industries use to coordinate the key players in their procurement process.
52. The concept of supply chain is usually supported by _______ today.
53. A supply chain that is being managed __________ with web-based software is referred to as an ________ chain.
54. A supply chain typically involves___________, information flows and financial flows.
55. Supply chain management coordinates materials flows, information flows and financial flows among all the involved ________ in the supply chain.
56. The supply chain involves _______segments. These are as follows: Upstream—the sourcing or procurement occurs from external suppliers, ________—the distribution or dispersal takes place, _________—The packaging, assembly or manufacturing occurs.
57. SCM reduces the uncertainty and risks along the _______.
58. SCM improves business processes by an effective _________ of information, material and financial flows among all parties involved in the supply chain.
59. SCM helps provide better service to the __________.
60. A good supply chain management solution will improve _________ business processes such as procurement-to-pay cycles, order-to-cash cycles and demand forecasting.
61. ______________ tools monitor and optimizes the entire supply chain to meet the specific needs of a company.
62. In ________ approach to SCM, the processes are initiated in response to an order from a customer.
63. Processes in pull based approach are also referred to as ________ processes because these processes react to the demands of the customers.
64. In push based model, products are pushed to the customers in expectation of a __________.
65. The push based processes are referred to as ________ processes since they respond to demand forecast rather than actual customer demand.

66. There are three key processes in supply chain management. These are as follows: ___________, Execution systems, Performance Measurement System.

67. The focus of the ________ is to ensure the availability of the right product at the right time and at right place.

68. Execution system enables the efficient ________ of products and services through the supply chain. Providing ________ is the main focus of execution systems.

69. Performance Measurement System monitors and ensures the effectiveness of the ________. Use of __________ and data warehousing allow the business operations to respond immediately to key business events.

70. The key functions in supply chain management are: ____________, Integrated Logistics, Financial and accounting management, Agile manufacturing

71. Integrated Logistics deals with managing the flow of ________from suppliers.

72. Financial and accounting management deals with managing the ____________ flows with the suppliers as well as customers.

73. __________ aspect of supply chain management deals with managing the manufacturing process in such a way that the cost of production is________.

74. According to Kala Kota and Robin, customer relationship management (CRM) is "an __________ sales, marketing and service strategy".

75. _________ systems focus on the key elements of the organization, that is, customers.

76. A CRM system uses the ________ that attempts to learn about the needs and __________ of customers in order to build healthier relations with the customers.

77. CRM systems support tracking _______ purchases and payments made by customers, updating the electronic customer profile, analyzing the behaviour of customers and providing updated ___________ to the frequently asked questions (FAQS) about various products and services.

78. Today, most of the companies are realizing the need to integrate __________ with the other enterprise systems (ERP and SCM) in order to achieve business improvements and better financial performance.

79. _______ systems include all the tools, technologies and procedures related with sales, marketing and post-sales customer service.

80. CRM systems can be implemented by introducing CRM software within the company either in ___________ or getting it fully installed.

81. A CRM system implemented ________ has limited functionality.

82. The lack of ________ in CRM activities often makes the implementation of a CRM system difficult.

83. CRM systems should be designed in such a way that they address _______ business processes.

84. CRM vendors are now focusing on producing and delivering ________—based software solutions. These solutions are more flexible and highly ________.

85. ___________ is a new concept that attempts to overcome the limitations of the CRM systems.

86. The main elements of a CRM system are: __________, Analytical CRM, Collaborative CRM.

87. ________________ CRM centres on all the activities of the business that are related to sales, marketing and customer service.

88. Analytical CRM deals with the collection and ____________ of the data collected by the CRM system. Analytical CRM provides support to___________.

89. Collaborative CRM facilitates the interaction with the customers by ________, ________ or email.

90. "_________ is the exchange of information across electronic networks at any stage in the supply chain whether within an organization, between business and consumers, or between public and private sectors whether paid or un-paid".

91. Use of e-commerce together with ________ systems will enable companies to grow faster in the global environment.

92. Both ERP and e-commerce are _________ to each other.

93. E-Commerce enables selling and purchasing of various products and services through __________.

94. Without ___________, a company cannot fulfill the web orders accurately and speedily.

95. The need of implementing ERP systems is growing in companies that desire to use ________________ for doing business.

96. ERP systems were initially meant only for employees within an organization. But today's, __________ demand access to information such as order status, invoice reconciliation etc., that was only meant for employees in past.

97. Also, the customers want to get information that is free of all the __________ jargon and easy to understand through the company's website.

98. In order to make the ERP systems available over the web, the company's IT department will have to build _______ new channels of access into the company's ERP systems.

99. One access channel will be used to provide access to the ___________ for information such as order status and billing from the company's ERP system.

100. The other access channel will provide access to the ___________ and __________ so that useful and relevant information is made available more easily and efficiently from the ERP system of the company.

101. Integrating the ERP system and e-commerce requires careful planning to be done by the ________. Selecting vendors having a good experience in developing e-commerce wares is a ________ choice to make.

102. ERP systems are complex and require a good deal of _________. The website will not be available to the public when the company shuts down the ERP system for maintenance work. This can be a __________ affair.

103. In order to prevent huge losses, most e-commerce veterans build flexibility into the _________ between e-commerce and ERP systems. This means that the e-commerce applications can kept running on the web during the ERP system ___________ for upgrades and fixes.

104. Middleware and EAI software take information from the _______ system. The information captured is then converted into a format that the ___________ applications can understand.

105. A data warehouse is a repository of multiple __________ sources of data. A data warehouse is primarily meant to separate ___________ data from the data stored for performing business analysis.

106. The data stored in the __________ helps the managers in making quick and effective decisions.

107. The data warehousing systems are now designed to support sophisticated __________ such as multidimensional analysis.

108. Data warehouse were initially used to generate useful reports. They also had the capability to answer __________ queries.

109. Later, the data warehouses begin to be used to analyze the __________ data. Today, the data warehouses are used for __________ decision making.

110. Data mining tools are used to discover __________ from the vast pool of data stored in the data warehouse.

111. __________ applications include information processing, analytical processing and data mining.

112. The data warehouse normally has __________ tiers. The tiers are as follow: Warehouse database server, __________ and Client tier.

113. Warehouse database server is the __________ tier. It almost consists of a __________ system.

114. OLAP server forms the __________ tier of the data warehouse architecture.

115. The topmost tier is the __________ tier. The client tier contains query tools, analysis, reporting tools and may also contain __________ tools.

116. Defining the __________ for a data warehouse is a challenging task. A data warehouse architecture must meet challenges such as __________, information reuse and business intelligence.

117. The __________ model should achieve data integration, promote information reuse and provide rich business intelligence.

118. A data model defines objects that are of __________ to the organization and the __________ that describe those objects and govern them.

119. The three methodologies that are usually applied to the design and implementation of a data warehouse are: Enterprise data model, __________, Process Neutral Model.

120. Enterprise data model starts by using the conventional __________ modeling techniques. The data model describes the business in a conventional __________ database. A series of __________ may then occur to improve performance.

121. Enterprise data model is typically used by the corporations that possess a __________ data model.

122. Data Bus model is made up of a series of __________ schemas.

123. Data models are just views either directly on the star schemas or onto the __________ of these star schemas.

124. A data mart contains a subset of corporate wide data that holds value only for a __________ of users.

125. In Process Neutral Model, data model all the __________ business rules have been removed.

126. The advantage of Process Neutral Model data model approach is that as the business processes change there is __________ or __________ change required to the data model. The approach is generally used by organizations that are characterized by a __________ corporate environment.

127. OLAP stands for "Online Analytical Processing". An OLAP product is necessarily __________.
128. _______ can be defined by five keywords: Fast Analysis of Shared Multi-dimensional Information (FASMI). The descriptive term "FASMI" was suggested by ___________.
129. OLAP cube (also referred to as hypercube or multi-dimensional cube) forms the ________ of any OLAP system.
130. Data in an OLAP cube is modeled in __________ dimensions.
131. ___________ are the perspective with respect to which organization would keep records.
132. Each dimension may have a ___________ associated with it.
133. Facts are ________ that are used to analyze relationship between the dimensions of an OLAP cube.
134. A _________ contains the names of the facts (also called measures).
135. An OLAP cube facilitates complex data mining queries to be answered quickly in comparison to a ________ database.
136. The use of __________ is the most important mechanism that supports the good performance of an OLAP system.
137. The use of _______________ in an OLAP cube facilitates complex analytical and ad-hoc queries to be answered with a rapid response time.
138. The most common _______ applications include sales and marketing analysis, financial reporting, budgeting and forecasting.
139. ________ has been defined as "the non-trivial extraction of implicit, previously unknown and potentially useful information from data."
140. Data mining extracts useful information from large amount of data by the application of a computer based methodology. This is also known as______________.
141. Data mining involves both knowledge discovery and _________. Data mining, in fact, covers a broad spectrum of tasks.
142. The data mining tasks include___________, mining association rules, data classification and evolution analysis.
143. In __________ architecture, a data mining system will not utilize any function of either a database or a data warehouse system.
144. No Coupling architecture is poor as it fails to make use of the ___________ of the database and data warehouse system.
145. In __________ design, the data mining system uses some of the facilities offered by a database or a data warehouse system.
146. Loose Coupling design is considered _________ than no coupling design.
147. In _________ coupling a few essential data mining functions can be provided in the database/ data warehouse system. The intermediate data mining results can be stored in the database or data warehouse.
148. In Tight Coupling, the data mining system is smoothly _________ into the database/data warehouse system.
149. Tight coupling system efficiently implements data mining functions and has _________ system performance.
150. Data mining Query Language (DMQL) is used to facilitate _______ and _______ data mining in data mining systems.

151. DMQL is based on certain __________ primitives. These are required for ____________ a data mining task.

ANSWERS

SECTION A

(1) a **(2)** c **(3)** d **(4)** c **(5)** d **(6)** c **(7)** a **(8)** d **(9)** c **(10)** a
(11) a **(12)** a **(13)** d **(14)** e **(15)** c **(16)** d **(17)** a **(18)** c **(19)** e **(20)** c
(21) b **(22)** a **(23)** d **(24)** a **(25)** c **(26)** c **(27)** c **(28)** a **(29)** a **(30)** c
(31) c **(32)** a **(33)** d **(34)** c **(35)** a **(36)** e **(37)** a **(38)** c **(39)** e **(40)** c
(41) d **(42)** a **(43)** d **(44)** c **(45)** a **(46)** d **(47)** b **(48)** d **(49)** b **(50)** c
(51) c **(52)** a **(53)** a **(54)** c **(55)** b **(56)** a **(57)** e **(58)** b **(59)** b **(60)** c
(61) b **(62)** b **(63)** a **(64)** d **(65)** c **(66)** c **(67)** e **(68)** c **(69)** b **(70)** d
(71) a **(72)** b **(73)** c **(74)** d **(75)** d **(76)** a **(77)** d **(78)** c **(79)** b **(80)** d
(81) d **(82)** a **(83)** d **(84)** b **(85)** d **(86)** d **(87)** a **(88)** b **(89)** c **(90)** d
(91) d **(92)** c **(93)** d **(94)** a **(95)** c **(96)** b **(97)** c **(98)** b **(99)** d **(100)** e
(101) a **(102)** d **(103)** c **(104)** d **(105)** d **(106)** d **(107)** c **(108)** e **(109)** d **(110)** e
(111) a **(112)** c **(113)** d **(114)** d **(115)** c **(116)** c.

SECTION B

(1) True **(2)** True **(3)** False **(4)** True **(5)** True **(6)** False **(7)** True **(8)** True
(9) False **(10)** False **(11)** True **(12)** True **(13)** True **(14)** True **(15)** True **(16)** True
(17) False **(18)** True **(19)** True **(20)** True **(21)** True **(22)** False **(23)** False **(24)** True
(25) True **(26)** True **(27)** True **(28)** True **(29)** False **(30)** False **(31)** True **(32)** True
(33) True **(34)** True **(35)** False **(36)** True **(37)** False **(38)** True **(39)** True **(40)** True
(41) True **(42)** True **(43)** False **(44)** True **(45)** False **(46)** True **(47)** True **(48)** True
(49) True **(50)** True **(51)** False **(52)** True **(53)** True **(54)** True **(55)** False **(56)** True
(57) True **(58)** True **(59)** False **(60)** True **(61)** True **(62)** False **(63)** True **(64)** False
(65) True **(66)** True **(67)** False **(68)** False **(69)** True **(70)** True **(71)** False **(72)** False
(73) True **(74)** True **(75)** False **(76)** True **(77)** True **(78)** True **(79)** True **(80)** True
(81) True **(82)** True **(83)** False **(84)** True **(85)** True **(86)** False **(87)** True **(88)** True
(89) True **(90)** False **(91)** False **(92)** True **(93)** True **(94)** False **(95)** True **(96)** False
(97) True **(98)** True **(99)** True **(100)** True **(101)** True **(102)** True **(103)** True **(104)** True
(105) True **(106)** True **(107)** True **(108)** True **(109)** True **(110)** True **(111)** True **(112)** True
(113) False **(114)** True **(115)** False **(116)** True **(117)** False **(118)** True **(119)** True **(120)** True
(121) True **(122)** True **(123)** False **(124)** False **(125)** True **(126)** True **(127)** True **(128)** True
(129) True **(130)** True **(131)** True **(132)** True **(133)** True **(134)** True **(135)** False **(136)** True
(137) True **(138)** True **(139)** True **(140)** True **(141)** True **(142)** True **(143)** True **(144)** False
(145) True **(146)** True **(147)** True **(148)** True **(149)** False **(150)** True **(151)** True **(152)** True
(153) True **(154)** True **(155)** True.

SECTION C

(1) better **(2)** globalization **(3)** geographic **(4)** automatic **(5)** ERP, better **(6)** MIS, DSS **(7)** information, decision making **(8)** essential, all **(9)** strategic **(10)** 1960s **(11)** transaction **(12)** routine (structured) **(13)** MIS **(14)** reliable, relevant, summarized **(15)** flawed **(16)** decision support **(17)** managerial, alternatives **(18)** Sprague and Carlson **(19)** voluntary **(20)** DSS **(21)** DSS, digitized maps **(22)** ad-hoc **(23)** structured, unstructured **(24)** Group DSS **(25)** DSS, expert systems (ES) **(26)** KBDSS, Knowledge acquisition **(27)** group DSS **(28)** operational procedures **(29)** Group DSS **(30)** distributed **(31)** Active Decision Support **(32)** intelligent, data mining **(33)** Executive information system (EIS) **(34)** top executives **(35)** crisis management **(36)** menu-driven **(37)** Business process reengineering (BPR), Michael Hammer and Champy **(38)** structured **(39)** Information Technology **(40)** best, jobs **(41)** complexity **(42)** business procedures **(43)** BPR **(44)** hand-in-hand **(45)** ERP **(46)** ERP system **(47)** automates, business processes **(48)** operations **(49)** increases **(50)** reduced **(51)** Supply Chain Management (SCM) **(52)** IT **(53)** electronically, e-supply **(54)** materials flows **(55)** parties **(56)** three, Downstream, Internal **(57)** supply chain **(58)** coordination **(59)** customers **(60)** critical **(61)** Advanced planning and scheduling (APS) **(62)** pull based **(63)** reactive **(64)** customer order **(65)** speculative **(66)** Planning systems **(67)** Planning systems **(68)** movement, operational efficiency **(69)** supply chain, web-based software agents **(70)** Customer asset management **(71)** goods **(72)** financial **(73)** Agile manufacturing, low **(74)** integrated **(75)** Customer relationship management (CRM) **(76)** CRM strategy, preferences **(77)** past, online-answers **(78)** CRM systems **(79)** CRM **(80)** strategically selected areas **(81)** partially **(82)** standards **(83)** cross-functional **(84)** business process, configurable **(85)** Business process Management (BPM) **(86)** Operational CRM **(87)** Operational **(88)** analysis, decision making **(89)** phone, fax **(90)** E-commerce **(91)** ERP **(92)** complimentary **(93)** web **(94)** ERP **(95)** E-commerce **(96)** tech-savvy customers **(97)** ERP software **(98)** two **(99)** customers **(100)** suppliers, business partners **(101)** vendor, good **(102)** maintenance, costly **(103)** connecting links, shut down **(104)** ERP, e-commerce **(105)** heterogeneous, operational **(106)** data warehouse **(107)** online-analysis **(108)** predefined **(109)** summarized, strategic **(110)** knowledge **(111)** Data warehouses **(112)** three, OLAP server **(113)** bottom, relational database **(114)** middle **(115)** client, data mining **(116)** architecture, data integration **(117)** data warehouse **(118)** interest, rules **(119)** Data Bus **(120)** relational data, normalized, de-normalizations **(121)** corporate wide **(122)** star **(123)** aggregates **(124)** specific group **(125)** embedded **(126)** little, no, rapidly changing **(127)** multi-dimensional **(128)** OLAP, Nigel Pendse **(129)** core **(130)** multiple **(131)** Dimensions **(132)** dimension table **(133)** numerical quantities **(134)** fact table **(135)** relational **(136)** aggregations **(137)** multiple hierarchies **(138)** OLAP **(139)** Data mining **(140)** knowledge discovery **(141)** pattern recognition **(142)** data characterization **(143)** No Coupling **(144)** rich functionalities **(145)** Loose Coupling **(146)** better **(147)** semi-tight **(148)** integrated **(149)** high **(150)** ad-hoc, interactive **(151)** data mining, defining.

10
Chapter
ERP—A Manufacturing Perspective

HIGHLIGHTS

- **ERP — A MANUFACTURING PERSPECTIVE**
  - Various Manufacturing Modes
  - Manufacturing Strategy
  - Types of Manufacturing Information System

ERP has been used most widely by the manufacturing industries. As manufacturers realize the benefits of ERP systems such as improved efficiency, lowered cost, better customer service etc; implementation of ERP systems will gain more momentum. Today, manufacturers need to manage supply chains that are quite complex in nature. Extended ERP allows the manufacturers to effectively manage the complex supply chain by encompassing the suppliers and delivery channel partners into the enterprise-wide information system of the organization.

10.1 VARIOUS MANUFACTURING MODES

The manufacturing operations (modes) can be classified into the following types:

1. **Make-to-stock (MTS)**
   In make-to-stock, the manufacturer produces the product based on the demand forecast, the products are then stored in the inventory before he receives the customer's order. The products may also be sent to a distribution centre or a retail outlet from where a customer may purchase the product. Poor market analysis and demand-forecasting may result in heavy losses for the manufacturer. Make-to-stock also requires an efficient distribution planning feature.
2. **Make-to-Order (MTO)**
   In make-to-order operation, the manufacturer begins processing the raw material for the product only when he receives an order for that product from the customer.

3. **Assemble-to-order (ATO)**
   In this mode, the manufacturer manufactures the standardized option modules according to the demand forecast. But the assembling of a specific combination of modules is only done when he receives the order from a customer. Assemble-to-order, therefore, gets the advantage of both make-to-stock method as well as make-to-order operation.
4. **Engineer-to-order (ETO)**
   In this mode of operation, the manufacturer delivers customized orders to the customer. Since the product is being built according to the customer's choice, the cost of production is the highest in this manufacturing mode. It is also referred to as customer-driven manufacturing as customers solely determine what is built, how it is built and how it is delivered.
5. **Configure-to-order (CTO)**
   ETO manufacturers often feel a pressure to standardize at least some of the product lines in order to reduce delivery time and cost. CTO has emerged as a solution for the ETO manufacturers. In configure to order, the manufacturers meets the demands of the customers for personalized products by using a rules-based product configuration system.

LEARNING POINTS

1. As manufacturers realize the benefits of ERP systems such as improved efficiency, lowered cost, better customer service etc., implementation of ERP systems will gain more momentum.
2. Extended ERP allows the manufacturers to effectively manage the complex supply chain by encompassing the suppliers and delivery channel partners into the enterprise wide information system of the organization.
3. Manufacturing modes can be classified into following types: make to stock (MTS), make to order (MTO), assemble to order (ATO), engineer to order (ETO) and configure to order (CTO).
4. In make-to-stock, the manufacturer produces product based on demand forecast, the products are then stored in inventory before a customer order is received.
5. In make-to-order, the manufacturer begins processing the raw material for the product only when he receives an order for that product from customer.
6. In assemble-to-order, the manufacturer delivers customized orders to the customers.
7. In configure-to-order, the manufacturer meets demands of the customer for personalized products by using a rules-based product configuration system.

10.2 MANUFACTURING STRATEGY

To meet the increasing challenges of the global environment, manufacturing companies are trying different manufacturing strategies. Some of the strategies being used are just-in-time manufacturing, total quality control, customer-driven manufacturing etc.

10.2.1 Just-In-Time Manufacturing

Just-In-Time manufacturing refers to the production of the goods when needed, not too early and not too late. JIT manufacturing uses the pull based approach of Kanban. In Kanban system, the workstations placed along the production line only produce or deliver desired product components when they receive a card and an empty container (i.e., an order). This indicates that more components will be needed. When the workstations fill the entire container they stop. Thus components are pulled along the production lines as and when demand arrives. JIT eliminates storage of products anywhere in the production line.

JIT is a manufacturing strategy that makes use of a set of tools and techniques to bring about elimination of waste, total quality management and complete involvement of employees in the manufacturing process.

Some of the benefits of a JIT approach are as follows:

1. Increased Flexibility: Small batch sizes are used to achieve faster throughput.
2. Reduced Inventory: JIT minimizes the amount of inventory at all levels—raw materials, work-in-process and finished goods.
3. Simplicity of System: The number of cards in the system can be adjusted according to the changes in the product mix or volume.

LEARNING POINTS

1. Just-In-time manufacturing refers to the production of goods when needed, not too early and not too late.
2. Increased flexibility, reduced inventory and simplicity of systems are some are some of the benefits of JIT approach.

10.3 TYPES OF MANUFACTURING INFORMATION SYSTEM

Information systems are used broadly in all functional areas throughout an organization. The manufacturing information systems aim to automate the manufacturing process including all the stages of product life cycle, from computer aided designing to computer assisted production on the manufacturing plant floor.

The various types of information system used to facilitate speedy and quality production are described below:

1. **Materials Requirement Planning (MRP)**

   In 1970's many manufacturing firms realized that maintaining large volumes of inventory was uneconomical and unaffordable. This led to the development of materials requirement planning (MRP) systems.

   Materials requirement planning (MRP) system ensures that the right amount of required material is available to the manufacturer at the correct time. In other words, MRP systems are information systems facilitating automatic generation of purchase orders for stock that needs to be reordered. MRP system makes use of data from the master production schedule, bill of material (BOM) and inventory records (IR). A master production schedule (MPS) is a detailed production schedule for the finished product. MPS is supported by a BOM file that is used to describe the various components (along with their relationship) needed to produce the finished product. Inventory record contains information about stock-on-hand, stock-on-order etc.

2. **Closed-loop MRP**
   With the passage of time, MRP system was expanded to include capacity planning. New tools such as sales and operational planning were incorporated. The manufacturers could change production plans when necessary based on the feedback provided by the MRP system. The manufacturers now began to call these systems "closed-loop MRP".
3. **Manufacturing Resource Planning (MRP-II)**
   MRP-II systems include functions for production planning, business planning, sales and operations planning, order processing, and finance. In short, MRP-II systems provide information for all functional areas and support cross-functional communication. It supports financial planning by converting materials schedules into capital requirements.
4. **Enterprise Resource Planning (ERP)**
   ERP system is considered a natural extension of MRP-II. ERP systems help the manufacturers to translate demand forecast into a manufacturing plan of raw materials, gross capacity and production orders for the manufacturing plant floor. ERP systems integrate information system with both plant operations and the larger concerns of the whole enterprise.
5. **Manufacturing Execution Systems (MES)**
   These systems allow companies to track and monitor factory floor activities. MES facilitates maximum utilization of available resources, production monitoring via graphic display, electronic verification of each factory order for accuracy against accepted standards etc.
6. **Distribution Requirements Planning (DRP) systems**
   DRP systems integrate the physical distribution system with the production planning and scheduling system.
7. **Computer-aided Design (CAD) /Computer-aided-Manufacturing (CAM) Systems**
   Computer-aided-Design (CAD) systems are software packages that allow users to draw and modify product designs easily on a computer screen. CAD systems allow a designer to view a product from different perspectives and make appropriate modifications. The design characteristics of the products can be stored in the system. Apart from this, the CAD system also informs the designer whether or not the product specifications are being satisfied by the product design.

   Computer-aided-Manufacturing (CAM) systems automatically convert the CAD-engineered designs into software programs for automated production machines. CAD/CAM systems are being widely used in automotive companies. Though the use of CAD/CAM systems is spreading in other sectors too, yet the pace is slow.
8. **Product Data Management (PDM)**
   A product data management (PDM) system is used to maintain proper control of data. The master data (original copy) is stored in a secured manner. All the changes to the master data are made on the duplicate reference copies of the master data; the updated

copies are signed, dated and stored along with the master data (original copy). A single central vault system is used.

A PDM system groups similar types of component as a class. Classification is usually an essential characteristic of PDM system. PDM systems provide process management along with data management. Process management is concerned with the following activities:

(i) Work Management: It relates to the effects that are introduced on data when someone works on that data.

(ii) Workflow Management: It deals with managing the flow of data between people.

(iii) Work History management: It deals with recording the various stages the project has been through.

Some of the benefits of PDM systems are as follows:

(i) Data Integrity

Data integrity is safeguarded as the single central vault concept is used. The master document is stored in a central vault. Duplicate reference copies are made available to personnel to make changes. The changed versions are also stored.

(ii) Better Management of Engineering Change

PDM system supports the creation as well as storage of multiple revisions and versions of any design document. It provides the user a complete audit trail of changes made so far.

(iii) Improved Design Productivity

PDM system allows the identification, re-use and alteration of existing designs. This feature increases the productivity of the designers.

LEARNING POINTS

1. Materials requirement planning (MRP) system ensures that right amount of required material is available to the manufacturers at the correct time.
2. A master production schedule (MPS) is a detailed production schedule for the finished product.
3. MRP-II systems include functions for production planning, business planning, sales and operational planning, order processing and finance.
4. ERP is considered a natural extension of MRP-II.
5. DRP systems integrate physical distribution system with production planning and scheduling system.
6. Computer-aided-design (CAD) systems are software packages that allow users to draw and modify product designs easily on a computer screen.
7. A product data management system is used to maintain proper control of data.

SUMMARY

ERP has been used most widely by the manufacturing industries. Manufacturing operations are generally classified into the following types-make-to-stock, make-to-order, assemble-to-order, configure-to-order and engineer-to-order. Just-In-Time manufacturing refers to the production of goods when needed, not to early and not too late. It eliminates the storage of products anywhere in the production line.

Materials requirement planning (MRP) system is an information system facilitating automatic generation of purchase orders for stock that needs to be reordered. When capacity planning is included in the MRP system, it is referred to as closed loop MRP. MRP-II systems provide information for all functional areas of an organization. It also provides support to cross-functional communication. Manufacturing execution systems (MES) allow companies to track and monitor factory floor activities.

Distribution requirements planning (DRP) systems are used to integrate physical distribution system with production planning and scheduling system. Computer-aided-design ((CAD) system supports the designer to draw and modify product designs easily on the screen of computer. Viewing of the product designs from different perspectives is also possible. Computer-aided-manufacturing (CAM) systems automatically convert CAD-engineered designs into software programs for automated production machines. A product data management system is used to maintain a proper control of data in an organization.

POINTS TO REMEMBER

1. Manufacturing modes can be classified into following types: make-to-stock (MTS), make-to-order (MTO), available-to-order (ATO), engineer-to-order (ETO) and configure-to-order (CTO).
2. In make-to-stock, the manufacturer produces product based on demand forecast, the products are then stored in inventory till a customer order is received.
3. In make-to-order, the manufacturer begins processing the raw material for the product only when he receives an order for that product from the customer.
4. Just-In-Time manufacturing (JIT) refers to the production of goods when needed, not too early and not too late.
5. Materials requirement planning (MRP) system ensures that right amount of required material is available to the manufacturers at the correct time.
6. A master production schedule (MPS) is a detailed production schedule for the finished product.
7. MRP-II systems provide information for all functional areas and support cross-functional communication.
8. Computer-aided-design systems are software packages that allow users to draw and modify product designs easily on a computer screen.
9. Computer-aided manufacturing (CAM) systems automatically convert CAD engineered designs into software programs for automated production machines.
10. A product data management (PD) system is used to maintain proper control of data. PDM systems also provide process management along with data management.
11. PDM system supports the creation as well as storage of multiple revisions and versions of any design document.

REVIEW QUESTIONS

1. Write short notes on the following:
   (a) Make-to-stock
   (b) Make-to-order
   (c) Assemble-to-order
   (d) Engineer-to-order
   (e) Configure-to-order
2. Explain Kanban and Just-In-Time manufacturing.
3. What are the benefits of JIT manufacturing?
4. Explain materials requirement planning.
5. Discuss MRP-II.
6. What is closed loop MRP?
7. What are manufacturing modes?
8. What are Manufacturing Execution systems? Why are they used?
9. Explain Distribution Requirement Planning (DRP) systems.
10. What do you understand by CAD/CAM systems? Why are they used?
11. What is a PDM system? Give some of its benefits.

OBJECTIVE QUESTIONS

SECTION A

TICK THE CORRECT ANSWER

1. Which statement is true?
   (a) ERP has been used most widely by the manufacturing industries.
   (b) As manufacturers realize the benefits of ERP systems such as improved efficiency, lowered cost, better customer service etc; implementation of ERP systems will gain more momentum.
   (c) Today, manufacturers need to manage supply chains that are quite complex in nature.
   (d) All of above.
2. ___________allows the manufacturers to effectively manage the complex supply chain by encompassing the suppliers and delivery channel partners into the enterprise-wide information system of the organization.
   (a) Extended ERP.
   (b) SCM.
   (c) CRM.
   (d) None of above.
3. The manufacturing operations (modes) can be classified into:
   (a) Make-to-stock (MTS).
   (b) Make-to-Order (MTO).
   (c) Assemble-to-order (ATO).

(d) Engineer-to-order (ETO) and Configure-to-order (CTO).
(e) All of above.

4. In __________ production method, the manufacturer produces the product based on the demand forecast, the products are then stored in the inventory before he receives the customer's order.
(a) Make-to-stock (MTS).
(b) Make-to-Order (MTO).
(c) Assemble-to-order (ATO).
(d) None of above.

5. Which is true about make to stock production method?
(a) In make-to-stock production method, the manufacturer produces the product based on the demand forecast, the products are then stored in the inventory before he receives the customer's order.
(b) In make-to-stock production method, poor market analysis and demand-forecasting may result in heavy losses for the manufacturer.
(c) Make-to-stock requires an efficient distribution planning feature.
(d) All of above.
(e) None of above.

6. In __________ operation, the manufacturer begins processing the raw material for the product only when he receives an order for that product from the customer.
(a) Make-to-stock (MTS).
(b) Make-to-order (MTO).
(c) Assemble-to-order (ATO).
(d) Engineer-to-order (ETO).

7. In Assemble-to-order (ATO) mode:
(a) The manufacturer manufactures the standardized option modules according to the demand forecast.
(b) The assembling of a specific combination of modules is only done when he receives the order from a customer.
(c) Both (a) and (b).
(d) None of above.

8. Assemble–to-order gets the advantage of:
(a) Make-to-stock method.
(b) Make-to-order operation
(c) Both make-to-stock method as well as make-to-order operation.
(d) None of above.

9. Which is true about Engineers to Order (ETO) mode of operation?
(a) The manufacturer delivers customized orders to the customer.
(b) The cost of production is the highest in this manufacturing mode since the product is being built according to the customer's choice.
(c) Both (a) and (b).
(d) None of above.

10. ____________ mode of operation is also referred to as customer-driven manufacturing as customers solely determine what is built, how it is built and how it is delivered.

(a) Configure-to-order (CTO).
(b) Assemble-to-order (ATO).
(c) Engineer-to-order (ETO).
(d) None of above.

11. ETO manufacturers often feel a pressure to standardize at least some of the product lines in order to:
(a) Reduce cost.
(b) Reduce delivery time.
(c) Reduce delivery time and cost.
(d) None of above.

12. __________ has emerged as a solution for the ETO manufacturers.
(a) Assemble-to-order (ATO).
(b) Configure-to-order (CTO).
(c) Make-to-stock (MTS).
(d) None of above.

13. In ___________ production method, the manufacturers meet the demands of the customers for personalized products by using a rules-based product configuration system.
(a) Configure-to-order (CTO).
(b) Assemble-to-order (ATO).
(c) Make-to-stock (MTS).
(d) Make-to-order (MTO).
(e) None of above.

14. To meet the increasing challenges of the global environment manufacturing companies are trying different manufacturing strategies. Some of the strategies being used are:
(a) Just-in-time manufacturing.
(b) Total quality control.
(c) Customer-driven manufacturing.
(d) All of above.

15. Just-In-Time manufacturing refers to:
(a) The production of the goods early.
(b) The production of the goods not too late.
(c) The production of the goods when needed, not too early and not too late.
(d) None of above.

16. Which type of manufacturing uses the pull based approach of Kanban?
(a) Computer aided manufacturing.
(b) JIT.
(c) Both (a) and (b).
(d) None of above.

17. In Kanban system, the workstations placed along the production line only produce or deliver desired product components when they receive a card and an empty container (i.e.), an order). This indicates that ____________components will be needed.
(a) More.
(b) No more.

(c) Large sized.
(d) Small sized.

18. The number of cards in the system can be adjusted according to the changes in the:
(a) Product mix.
(b) Volume.
(c) Product mix. Or volume.
(d) None of above.

19. Which is true about JIT?
(a) JIT eliminates storage of products anywhere in the production line.
(b) JIT is a manufacturing strategy that makes use of a set of tools and techniques to bring about elimination of waste, total quality management and complete involvement of employees in the manufacturing process.
(c) JIT minimizes the amount of inventory at all levels-raw materials, work-in-process and finished goods.
(d) All of above.

20. The benefits of a JIT approach are:
(a) Increased Flexibility.
(b) Simplicity of System.
(c) Reduced Inventory.
(d) All of above.

21. The various types of information system used to facilitate speedy and quality production are:
(a) Materials Requirement Planning (MRP).
(b) Closed-loop MRP.
(c) Manufacturing Resource Planning (MRP-II).
(d) Enterprise Resource Planning (ERP).
(e) All of above.

22. In 1970's many manufacturing firms realized that maintaining large volumes of inventory was uneconomical and unaffordable. This led to the development of _______________.
(a) Materials requirement planning (MRP) systems.
(b) Closed-loop MRP.
(c) Manufacturing Resource Planning (MRP-II).
(d) Enterprise Resource Planning (ERP).

23. Which is true about Materials requirement planning (MRP) system?
(a) MRP system ensures that the right amount of required material is available to the manufacturer at the correct time.
(b) MRP system is an information system facilitating automatic generation of purchase orders for stock that needs to be reordered.
(c) An MRP system makes use of data from the master production schedule, bill of material (BOM) and inventory records (IR).
(d) All of above.

24. Which is true about master production schedule (MPS)?
(a) A master production schedule (MPS) is a detailed production schedule for the finished product.

(b) MPS is supported by a BOM file that is used to describe the various components (along with their relationship) needed to produce the finished product.
(c) Both (a) and (b).
(d) None of above.

25. Inventory record contains information about:
(a) Stock-on-hand.
(b) Stock-on-order.
(c) Both (a) and (b).
(d) None of above.

26. With the passage of time, MRP system was expanded to include___________.
(a) Capacity planning.
(b) Sales and operational planning.
(c) Both (a) and (b).
(d) None of above.

27. The manufacturers could change production plans when necessary based on the feedback provided by the MRP system. The manufacturers called these systems:
(a) Materials Requirement Planning (MRP).
(b) Manufacturing Resource Planning (MRP-II).
(c) Enterprise Resource Planning (ERP).
(d) Closed-loop MRP.

28. MRP-II systems include functions for:
(a) Production planning.
(b) Business planning.
(c) Sales and operations planning.
(d) Order processing and finance.
(e) All of above.

29. Which is true about MRP-II systems?
(a) MRP-II systems provide information for all functional areas and support cross-functional communication.
(b) MRP-II supports financial planning by converting materials schedules into capital requirements.
(c) Both (a) and (b).
(d) None of above.

30. ERP system is considered a natural extension of _________.
(a) Closed-loop MRP.
(b) MRP-II.
(c) Enterprise Resource Planning (ERP).
(d) None of above.

31. Which is true about ERP systems?
(a) ERP systems help the manufacturers to translate demand forecast into a manufacturing plan of raw materials, gross capacity and production orders for the manufacturing plant floor.
(b) ERP systems integrate information system with both plant operations and the larger concerns of the whole enterprise.

(c) Both (a) and (b).
(d) None of above.

32. Which systems allow companies to track and monitor factory floor activities?
(a) MRP.
(b) MRP-II.
(c) Manufacturing Execution system (MES).
(d) None of above.

33. MES facilitates:
(a) Maximum utilization of available resources.
(b) Production monitoring via graphic display.
(c) Electronic verification of each factory order for accuracy against accepted standards etc.
(d) All of above.

34. Which systems integrate the physical distribution system with the production planning and scheduling system?
(a) MRP.
(b) Manufacturing Execution system (MES).
(c) Distribution Requirements Planning (DRP).
(d) None of above.

35. Computer–aided-Design (CAD) systems are software packages that:
(a) Allow users to draw and modify product designs easily on a computer screen.
(b) Allow designer to view a product from different perspectives and make appropriate modifications. The design characteristics of the products can be stored in the system.
(c) The CAD system also informs the designer whether or not the product specifications are being satisfied by the product design.
(d) All of above.

36. Which is true about Computer-aided-Manufacturing (CAM) systems?
(a) Computer-aided-Manufacturing (CAM) systems automatically convert the CAD-engineered designs into software programs for automated production machines.
(b) CAD/CAM systems are being widely used in automotive companies.
(c) Both (a) and (b).
(d) None of above.

37. A product data management (PDM) system is used to:
(a) Maintain proper control of data.
(b) Groups similar types of components as a class.
(c) Provide process management along with data management.
(d) All of above.

38. Which statement is true?
(a) The master data (original copy) in a product data management (PDM) system is stored in a secured manner.
(b) All the changes to the master data are made on the duplicate reference copies of the master data.
(c) The updated copies are signed, dated and stored along with the master data (original copy) in a PDM system.
(d) All of above.

39. Process management is concerned with the activities:
 (a) Work Management.
 (b) Workflow Management.
 (c) Work History management.
 (d) All of above.

40. Work Management relates to:
 (a) The effects that are introduced on data when some one works on that data.
 (b) Deals with managing the flow of data between people.
 (c) Deals with recording the various stages the project has been through.
 (d) None of above.

41. ________________ deals with managing the flow of data between people.
 (a) Work Management.
 (b) Workflow Management.
 (c) Work History management.
 (d) All of above.

42. The benefits of PDM systems are:
 (a) Data Integrity.
 (b) Better Management of Engineering Change.
 (c) Improved Design Productivity.
 (d) All of above.

43. Which is true about a PDM system?
 (a) Data integrity is safeguarded in PDM systems as the single central vault concept is used.
 (b) PDM system supports the creation as well as storage of multiple revisions and versions of any design document.
 (c) PDM system provides the user a complete audit trail of changes made so far.
 (d) PDM system allows the identification, re-use and alteration of existing designs. This feature increases the productivity of the designers.
 (e) All of above.

SECTION B

STATE TRUE OR FALSE

1. ERP has been used most widely by the manufacturing industries.
2. As manufacturers realize the benefits of ERP systems such as improved efficiency, lowered cost, better customer service etc; implementation of ERP systems will gain more momentum.
3. Today, manufacturers need to manage supply chains that are quite complex in nature.
4. Extended ERP allows the manufacturers to effectively manage the complex supply chain by encompassing the suppliers and delivery channel partners into the enterprise wide information system of the organization.
5. The manufacturing operations (modes) can be classified into the following types: Make-to-stock (MTS), Make-to-Order (MTO), Assemble-to-order (ATO), Engineer-to-order (ETO) and Configure-to-order (CTO).

6. In make-to-stock production method, the manufacturer begins processing the raw material for the product only when he receives an order for that product from the customer.
7. Poor market analysis and demand-forecasting may result in heavy losses for the manufacturer.
8. In make-to-order operation, the manufacturer produces the product based on the demand forecast, the products are then stored in the inventory before he receives the customer's order.
9. In Assemble-to-order (ATO) mode, the manufacturer manufactures the standardized option modules according to the demand forecast. But the assembling of a specific combination of modules is only done when he receives the order from a customer.
10. Assemble-to-order gets the advantage of both make-to-stock method as well as make-to-order operation.
11. In Engineer-to-order (ETO) mode of operation, the manufacturer delivers customized orders to the customer. Since the product is being built according to the customer's choice, the cost of production is the highest in this manufacturing mode.
12. Assemble-to-order (ATO) mode of operation is also referred to as customer-driven manufacturing as customers solely determine what is built, how it is built and how it is delivered.
13. ETO manufacturers often feel a pressure to standardize at least some of the product lines in order to reduce delivery time and cost.
14. ATO has emerged as a solution for the ETO manufacturers.
15. In configure-to-order, the manufacturers meet the demands of the customers for personalized products by using a rules-based product configuration system.
16. To meet the increasing challenges of the global environment manufacturing companies are trying different manufacturing strategies.
17. Some of the strategies being used are just-in-time manufacturing, total quality control, customer-driven manufacturing etc.
18. Just-In-Time manufacturing refers to the production of the goods when needed, not too early and not too late.
19. JIT manufacturing does not use the pull based approach of Kanban.
20. In Kanban system, the workstations placed along the production line only produce or deliver desired product components when they receive a card and an empty container (i.e.), an order). This indicates that more components will be needed.
21. The number of cards in the system cannot be adjusted according to the changes in the product mix or volume.
22. When the workstations fill the entire container they stop. Thus components are pulled along the production lines as and when demand arrives.
23. JIT eliminates storage of products anywhere in the production line.
24. JIT is a manufacturing strategy that makes use of a set of tools and techniques to bring about elimination of waste, total quality management and complete involvement of employees in the manufacturing process.
25. Some of the benefits of a JIT approach are as follows: Increased Flexibility, Reduced Inventory and Simplicity of System.
26. Small batch sizes are used to achieve faster throughput.

27. JIT minimizes the amount of inventory at all levels—raw materials, work-in-process and finished goods.

28. Information systems are used broadly in all functional areas throughout the organization.

29. The manufacturing information system aims to automate the manufacturing process including all the stages of product life cycle, from computer aided designing to computer assisted production on the manufacturing plant floor.

30. The various types of information system used to facilitate speedy and quality production are: Materials Requirement Planning (MRP), closed-loop MRP, Manufacturing Resource Planning (MRP-II), Enterprise Resource Planning (ERP), Manufacturing Execution Systems (MES).

31. In 1970's many manufacturing firms realized that maintaining large volumes of inventory was uneconomical and unaffordable. This led to the development of Enterprise resource planning (ERP) systems.

32. Materials requirement planning (MRP) system ensures that the right amount of required material is available to the manufacturer at the correct time.

33. MRP system is an information system facilitating automatic generation of purchase orders for stock that needs to be reordered.

34. An MRP system makes use of data from the master production schedule, bill of material (BOM) and inventory records (IR).

35. A master production schedule (MPS) is a detailed production schedule for the finished product.

36. MPS is supported by a BOM file that is used to describe the various components (along with their relationship) needed to produce the finished product.

37. Inventory record only contains information about stock-on-hand.

38. With the passage of time, MRP system was expanded to include capacity planning. New tools such as sales and operational planning were incorporated.

39. The manufacturers could change production plans when necessary based on the feedback provided by the MRP system. The manufacturers now began to call these systems as ERP.

40. MRP-II systems include functions for production planning, business planning, sales and operations planning, order processing, and finance.

41. MRP-II systems fail to provide information for all functional areas and support cross-functional communication. It also does not support financial planning by converting materials schedules into capital requirements.

42. ERP system is considered a natural extension of MRP-II.

43. ERP systems help the manufacturers to translate demand forecast into a manufacturing plan of raw materials, gross capacity and production orders for the manufacturing plant floor.

44. ERP systems integrate information system with both plant operations and the larger concerns of the whole enterprise.

45. Distribution Requirements Planning (DRP) allow companies to track and monitor factory floor activities.

46. MES facilitates maximum utilization of available resources, production monitoring via graphic display, electronic verification of each factory order for accuracy against accepted standards etc.

47. Manufacturing Execution Systems (MES) integrate the physical distribution system with the production planning and scheduling system.
48. Computer-aided-Design (CAD) systems are software packages that allow users to draw and modify product designs easily on a computer screen.
49. CAD systems allow a designer to view a product form different perspectives and make appropriate modifications. The design characteristics of the products can be stored in the system.
50. The CAD system also informs the designer whether or not the product specifications are being satisfied by the product design.
51. Computer-aided-Manufacturing (CAM) systems automatically convert the CAD-engineered designs into software programs for automated production machines.
52. CAD/CAM systems are being widely used in automotive companies.
53. A product data management (PDM) system is used to maintain proper control of data.
54. The master data (original copy) in a product data management (PDM) system is stored in a secured manner. All the changes to the master data are made on the duplicate reference copies of the master data; the updated copies are signed, dated and stored along with the master data (original copy).
55. A PDM system groups similar types of component as a class.
56. Classification is usually not an essential characteristic of PDM system.
57. PDM systems provide process management along with data management.
58. Process management is concerned with Work Management, Workflow Management and Work History Management.
59. Workflow Management relates to the effects that are introduced on data when someone works on that data.
60. Work Management deals with managing the flow of data between people.
61. Work History management deals with recording the various stages the project has been through.
62. Some of the benefits of PDM systems are: Data Integrity, Better Management of Engineering Change and Improved Design Productivity.
63. Data integrity is safeguarded in PDM systems as the single central vault concept is used.
64. The master document is stored in a central vault. Duplicate reference copies are made available to personnel to make changes. The changed versions are also stored.
65. PDM system does not support the creation as well as storage of multiple revisions and versions of any design document. It fails to provide the user a complete audit trail of changes made so far.
66. PDM system allows the identification, re-use and alteration of existing designs. This feature increases the productivity of the designers.

SECTION C

FILL IN THE BLANKS

1. ERP has been used most widely by the ______________ industries.

2. As manufacturers realize the benefits of _________ such as improved efficiency, lowered cost, better customer service etc; implementation of ERP systems will gain more momentum.
3. Today, manufacturers need to manage supply chains that are quite _________ in nature.
4. Extended ERP allows the manufacturers to effectively manage the complex supply chain by encompassing the suppliers and delivery channel partners into ___________ of the organization.
5. The manufacturing operations (modes) can be classified into the types: ___________, Make-to-Order (MTO), Assemble-to-order (ATO), _____________ and Configure-to-order (CTO).
6. In __________ production method, the manufacturer produces the product based on the___________, the products are then stored in the inventory before he receives the customer's order. Make-to-stock also requires an efficient ___________ feature.
7. Poor market analysis and demand-forecasting may result in __________ for the manufacturer.
8. In make-to-order operation, the manufacturer begins processing the raw material for the product only when he receives an _________ for that product from the customer.
9. In Assemble-to-order (ATO) mode, the manufacturer manufactures the standardized option modules according to the demand forecast. But the __________ of a specific combination of modules is only done when he receives the order from a customer.
10. ___________ gets the advantage of both make-to-stock method as well as make-to-order operation.
11. In Configure-to-order (CTO) mode of operation, the manufacturer delivers _________ to the customer. Since the product is being built according to the customer's choice, the cost of production is the ___________ in this manufacturing mode.
12. Configure-to-order (CTO) mode of operation is also referred to as __________ as customers solely determine what is built, how it is built and how it is delivered.
13. ETO manufacturers often feel a pressure to __________ at least some of the product lines in order to reduce delivery time and cost.
14. _______ has emerged as a solution for the ETO manufacturers.
15. In configure to order, the manufacturers meet the demands of the customers for ___________ products by using a rules-based product configuration system.
16. To meet the increasing challenges of the global environment, manufacturing companies are trying different _________ strategies.
17. Some of the strategies being used are _____________, total quality control, customer-driven manufacturing etc.
18. Just-In-Time manufacturing refers to the production of the goods when needed, not too ________ and not too late.
19. JIT manufacturing uses the pull based approach of_________.
20. In Kanban system, the workstations placed along the production line only produce or deliver desired product components when they receive a ______ and an ___________. This indicates that _______ components will be needed.
21. The number of cards in the system can be adjusted according to the changes in the ____________ or volume.

22. When the workstations fill the entire container they stop. Thus components are pulled along the production lines as and when _________ arrives.

23. JIT eliminates storage of products ___________ in the production line.

24. JIT is a _____________ strategy that makes use of a set of tools and techniques to bring about elimination of waste, total quality management and complete involvement of employees in the manufacturing process.

25. Some of the benefits of a JIT approach are: Increased Flexibility, _______ and Simplicity of System.

26. _________ batch sizes are used to achieve faster throughput.

27. JIT minimizes the amount of ___________ at all levels-raw materials, _______________ and finished goods.

28. Information systems are used broadly in all ___________ areas throughout an organization.

29. The manufacturing information system aims to ____________ the manufacturing process including all the stages of product life cycle, from _________________ to computer assisted production on the manufacturing plant floor.

30. The various types of information system used to facilitate speedy and quality production are: Materials Requirement Planning (MRP), closed-loop MRP, Manufacturing Resource Planning (MRP-II), __________________, Manufacturing Execution Systems (MES).

31. In ____________ many manufacturing firms realized that maintaining large volumes of inventory was uneconomical and unaffordable. This led to the development of ___________ systems.

32. Materials requirement planning (MRP) system ensures that the ___________ amount of required material is available to the manufacturer at the________.

33. _________ system is an information system facilitating automatic generation of purchase orders for stock that needs to be reordered.

34. An MRP system makes use of data from the _____________, ___________ and inventory records (IR).

35. A master production schedule (MPS) is a detailed production schedule for the ______________ product.

36. MPS is supported by a _________ that is used to describe the various components needed to produce the finished product.

37. Inventory record contains information about______________, stock-on-order etc.

38. With the passage of time, MRP system was expanded to include_________. New tools such as sales and operational planning were incorporated.

39. The manufacturers could change production plans when necessary based on __________ provided by the MRP system. The manufacturers now began to call these systems “closed-loop MRP”.

40. ________ systems include functions for production planning, business planning, sales and operations planning, order processing, and finance.

41. MRP-II systems provide information for all functional areas and support cross-functional __________. It supports financial planning by converting materials schedules into ________.

42. _______ system is considered a natural extension of MRP-II.

43. ERP systems help the manufacturers to translate demand forecast into a ___________ of raw materials, gross capacity and production orders for the manufacturing plant floor.

44. ERP systems integrate __________ with both plant operations and the larger concerns of the whole enterprise.

45. Manufacturing Execution Systems (MES) allow companies to track and monitor __________ activities.

46. MES facilitates __________, production monitoring via graphic display, electronic verification of each factory order for accuracy against accepted standards etc.

47. __________ systems integrate the physical distribution system with the production planning and scheduling system.

48. Computer-aided Design (CAD) systems are software packages that allow users to draw and modify __________ easily on a computer screen.

49. CAD systems allow designer to view a product from __________ and make appropriate modifications. The design characteristics of the products can be stored in the system.

50. The CAD system also informs the designer whether or not the product specifications are being satisfied by the __________.

51. Computer-aided-Manufacturing (CAM) systems automatically convert the CAD-engineered designs into __________ for automated production machines.

52. CAD/CAM systems are being widely used in __________ companies.

53. A __________ system is used to maintain proper control of data.

54. The __________ in a product data management (PDM) system is stored in a secured manner. All the changes to the master data are made on the __________ of the master data; the updated copies are signed, dated and stored along with the master data (original copy).

55. A PDM system groups similar types of components as a __________.

56. __________ is usually an essential characteristic of PDM system.

57. PDM systems provide __________ along with data management.

58. Process management is concerned with activities: Work Management, __________ and Work History management.

59. Work Management relates to the effects that are introduced on __________ when someone works on that data.

60. Workflow Management deals with managing the __________ between people.

61. __________ deals with recording the various stages the project has been through.

62. Some of the benefits of PDM systems are: __________, Better management of Engineering Change and Improved Design Productivity.

63. Data integrity is safeguarded in PDM systems as the __________ concept is used.

64. The __________ document is stored in a central vault. Duplicate reference copies are made available to personnel to make __________. The changed versions are also stored.

65. PDM system supports the creation as well as storage of __________ revisions and versions of any design document. It provides the user a complete __________ of changes made so far.

66. PDM system allows the identification, re-use and __________ of existing designs. This feature increases the __________ of the designers.

ANSWERS

SECTION A

(1) d **(2)** a **(3)** e **(4)** a **(5)** d **(6)** b **(7)** c **(8)** c **(9)** c **(10)** a
(11) c **(12)** b **(13)** a **(14)** d **(15)** c **(16)** b **(17)** a **(18)** c **(19)** d **(20)** d
(21) e **(22)** a **(23)** d **(24)** c **(25)** c **(26)** c **(27)** d **(28)** e **(29)** c **(30)** b
(31) c **(32)** c **(33)** d **(34)** c **(35)** d **(36)** c **(37)** d **(38)** d **(39)** d **(40)** a
(41) b **(42)** d **(43)** e.

SECTION B

(1) True **(2)** True **(3)** True **(4)** True **(5)** True **(6)** False **(7)** True **(8)** False
(9) True **(10)** True **(11)** True **(12)** False **(13)** True **(14)** False **(15)** True **(16)** True
(17) True **(18)** True **(19)** False **(20)** True **(21)** False **(22)** True **(23)** True **(24)** True
(25) True **(26)** True **(27)** True **(28)** True **(29)** True **(30)** True **(31)** False **(32)** True
(33) True **(34)** True **(35)** True **(36)** True **(37)** False **(38)** True **(39)** False **(40)** True
(41) False **(42)** True **(43)** True **(44)** True **(45)** False **(46)** True **(47)** False **(48)** True
(49) True **(50)** True **(51)** True **(52)** True **(53)** True **(54)** True **(55)** True **(56)** False
(57) True **(58)** True **(59)** False **(60)** False **(61)** True **(62)** True **(63)** True **(64)** True
(65) False **(66)** True.

SECTION C

(1) manufacturing **(2)** ERP systems **(3)** complex **(4)** the enterprise-wide information system **(5)** Make-to-stock (MTS), Engineer-to-order (ETO) **(6)** make-to-stock, demand forecast, distribution planning **(7)** heavy losses **(8)** order **(9)** assembling **(10)** Assemble-to-order **(11)** customized orders, highest **(12)** customer-driven manufacturing **(13)** standardize **(14)** CTO **(15)** personalized **(16)** manufacturing **(17)** just-in-time manufacturing **(18)** early **(19)** Kanban **(20)** card, empty container, more **(21)** product mix **(22)** demand **(23)** anywhere **(24)** manufacturing **(25)** Reduced Inventory **(26)** Small **(27)** inventory, work-in-process **(28)** functional **(29)** automate, computer aided designing **(30)** Enterprise Resource Planning (ERP) **(31)** 1970's, materials requirement planning (MRP) **(32)** right, correct time **(33)** MRP **(34)** master production schedule, bill of material (BOM) **(35)** finished **(36)** BOM file **(37)** stock-on-hand **(38)** capacity planning **(39)** the feedback **(40)** MRP-II **(41)** communication, capital requirements **(42)** ERP **(43)** manufacturing plan **(44)** information system **(45)** factory floor **(46)** maximum utilization of available resources **(47)** Distribution Requirements Planning (DRP) **(48)** product designs **(49)** different perspectives **(50)** product design **(51)** software programs **(52)** automotive **(53)** product data management (PDM) **(54)** master data, duplicate reference copies **(55)** class **(56)** Classification **(57)** process management **(58)** Workflow Management **(59)** data **(60)** flow of data **(61)** Work History management **(62)** Data Integrity **(63)** single central vault **(64)** master, changes **(65)** multiple, audit trail **(66)** alteration, productivity.

11

Chapter

Learning and Emerging Issues

HIGHLIGHTS

- **LEARNING AND EMERGING ISSUES**
  - Emerging Issues
  - Learning Issues
  - Management Concern for ERP Success
  - Trends in ERP
  - Future of ERP

For most organizations, whether large scale or small and medium enterprises, ERP implementation opens the door for new opportunities. Opportunities abound, but only for those organizations who make efforts to learn the various issues associated with the ERP system and its implementation. In fact, several organizations are now realizing the need to understand and handle the big issues involved in ERP implementation.

11.1 EMERGING ISSUES

Some of the issues that need immediate attention are discussed below:

1. ERP security: ERP systems, today, integrate the organization's information system with trusted partners (extended ERP). As a result, new entry points to the information system from outside are introduced which jeopardizes the security of the information system. Worst still, most of the organizations do not configure their ERP system to maintain audit logs and avoid using internal controls.
2. ERP for SME's: ERP systems must be designed to provide the small or medium enterprises the business process capabilities they need and at an affordable price.
3. Cross ERP applications: Cross ERP products and applications are also referred to as XERP products and applications. XERP applications and products are dependent on

connectivity and web services. XERP emphasize the sharing of application programming interfaces (API's) to enable efficient working between products from different companies.

4. Service oriented architecture (SOA): The emergence of service oriented architecture (SOA) in ERP market has led to the development of a more flexible and extensible ERP system. SOA simplifies the interconnection of new system to legacy system thereby facilitating the usage of the existing (legacy) IT systems.

LEARNING POINTS

1. ERP systems, today, integrate the organization's information system with trusted partners (extended ERP). As a result, new entry points to the information system from outside are introduced which jeopardizes the security of the information system. Worst still, most of the organizations do not configure their ERP system to maintain audit logs and avoid using internal controls.
2. Cross ERP products and applications are also referred to as XERP products and applications. XERP applications and products are dependent on connectivity and web services. XERP emphasize the sharing of application programming interfaces (API's) to enable efficient working between products from different companies.
3. SOA simplifies the interconnection of new system to legacy system thereby facilitating the usage of the existing (legacy) IT systems.
4. The customization of ERP systems inhibits the development of standardized solutions for ERP security.

11.2 LEARNING ISSUES

Some of the lessons that must be learnt by any project team going for ERP implementation are as follows:

1. ERP implementation should be done on a solid foundation based on a clear definition of the organization's requirement, comprehensive project plan, best project team and management support.
2. Review the different ERP solutions available (considering best-of-breed versus integrated solutions) and select the option that best meet your requirements.
3. Decide carefully which approach to use—phased approach or big-bang approach. The approach you take may determine the fate of your ERP project.
4. Build an accurate picture of the projected costs of the ERP project. This is necessary so that the ERP project does not overshoot the expenses and be stopped in middle due to lack of finance.
5. Remember to limit the scope of the ERP project. "Scope creep" often leads to failure of ERP implementation.
6. Customization should be avoided unless they appear critical to the business needs. Customization often results in increased development costs, need for testing and difficulties in upgradations.

7. Hire consultants to conduct risk assessment and audit of the project.
8. Top management must commit to invest time and money in ERP upgrades.
9. Be careful while developing contract with the ERP vendor. The contract must allow for new functionality during the course of the ERP project.
10. An in-house implementation team will facilitate an easy transfer of knowledge about the ERP system and operations of the legacy systems.
11. The implementation team must include personnel from all the functional departments of the organization.
12. Project manager must create a "single team" atmosphere. A joint commitment to work together is a prerequisite for a successful ERP implementation.
13. Get the organization ready for change. Provide training to the employees so that the resistance is reduced to the lowest level.
14. Recruit and retain key personnel involved in ERP implementation.
15. Data conversion is a challenging task. It involves converting years of data stored in the legacy systems into the new format required for the new ERP system. One approach that may be used by an organization is to transfer the complete legacy data into a data warehouse and then start the new ERP system fresh.
16. Remember to maintain the morale of the team throughout the project duration.

11.2.1 Customization

Customization is the process of fitting the selected ERP software to the business requirements of a specific organization. Customization becomes a must whenever the processes used by the firm are significantly different from the processes represented in the selected ERP system. The only other alternative to customization is changing the business processes to suit the ERP software components. But this definitely is a costly choice often not acceptable to the organization.

Today complex customizations are the requirements of the business. As customization may affect every module of the ERP system, it must be avoided as far as possible. Customization adds to the integration costs of ERP implementation. It also suffers from the drawback that the next release of the ERP software would not support any customization done locally outside the core ERP software. Customization will need to be done all over again in the newer ERP version. Customization of the core ERP software will prove to be more damaging as the vendor will not be there to help you in the customization process.

By over-customizing the ERP software, the best practices in industry embedded in the software may get altered or completely lost, defeating the very purpose of implementing an ERP system. Firms must consider the following issues before they go for customizing the ERP software:

(a) Customization is costly and complex.
(b) Customization requires talented and skilled IT staff.
(c) Customization must be done correctly and adequately. All customization made in ERP software should undergo extensive testing. It must be remembered that any system is as secure as the weakest link.
(d) Customization is time-consuming.
(e) Customization if done moderately allows the customized functionality to be easily upgraded when the new version is released.

11.2.2 Data Migration

Data migration involves transferring of data from the legacy system to the new ERP system. Data migration is one of the most important activities. It determines the success of an ERP implementation in an organization. Before migrating old data to the new system the old data needs to be converted into new data. New data is data modified to a format acceptable to the new system.

According to KOOP and Rooimans, the old data needs to be converted into new data to be able to work with the data in the new system. As or when conversion is over, the new data needs to be loaded in the new system where its validity is checked. Data migration is costly. Data in most legacy systems is often dirty and most of it is only of little or no use.

LEARNING POINTS

1. ERP implementation should be done on a solid foundation based on a clear definition of the organization's requirement, comprehensive project plan, best project team and management support.
2. Decide carefully which approach to use—phased approach or big-bang approach. The approach you take may determine the fate of your ERP project.
3. Customization should be avoided unless it appears critical to the business needs.
4. Data migration involves transferring of data from the legacy system to the new ERP system. It is a costly but important activity.

11.3 MANAGEMENT CONCERN FOR ERP SUCCESS

The support of top management is critical in all the phases of the ERP life cycle. Strong commitment from top management would strongly mark the success of the ERP project. As the management is involved in a wide range of decisions that are vital to the success of the ERP implementation, top management support is considered a critical success factor for ERP implementation.

Support from management ensures that all the necessary resources will be made available at proper time. By communicating and sharing the ERP vision with the employees, the management can get the whole organization "ready for change". The management must expose the benefits of the ERP implementation to the employees by discussing the real-world case studies. This sincere attempt from the management's side will result in highly motivated employees willing to be a part of the change. Top management must also identify and analyze the sources of resistance within the organization and employ appropriate strategies to counter employee resistance.

A lack of commitment and support from the top level will be detrimental to the success of ERP project.

LEARNING POINTS

1. The support of top management is critical in all the phases of the ERP life cycle.
2. Top management must identify and analyze the sources of resistance within the organization and employ appropriate strategies to counter employee resistance.

11.4 TRENDS IN ERP

Change is the rule of nature. The field of ERP is constantly evolving. The introduction of new technologies is affecting the shape and nature of ERP. ERP developers are facing tremendous pressure from the companies to provide for upgradations that incorporate the new technologies.

Some of the latest trends in ERP are as follows:

1. New markets: ERP vendors are now focusing on small and medium businesses (SMB's) and home-based businesses. A number of initiatives are being taken to attract the mid-market sector.
2. Faster implementation: ERP vendors are now providing more effective tools and methodologies to achieve faster ERP implementation. As the ERP application becomes less complex to install and train, the implementation time needed for ERP gets reduced dramatically. Examples include ASAP from SAP and Fast Forward from Oracle.
3. Need-based applications: In the past, the firms had to purchase the whole ERP applications even if the company only intended to utilize the core function. This meant that most of the functions remained idle but had to be paid for. ERP vendors have now overcome this menace by offering need based ERP applications. With need based ERP applications, the firms get the liberty to purchase and install only the software program pertaining to the functionality required.
4. Increased focus on new business segments: The ERP vendors are now delivering specialized variants of their ERP applications to service vertical markets such as healthcare, finance and retail sector. Attempts are being made by each ERP vendor to make his ERP applications available to all sectors irrespective of the volume of transactions or the nature of business.
5. ERP vendors are integrating their ERP applications with OLAP tools, data mining web services, wireless etc.
6. ERP is being integrated with cutting-edge technologies such as sales force automation (SFA), customer relationship management (CRM) etc. New ERP systems are blurring the distinction between front-end and back-end systems by providing a unified solution driven by internet based commerce.
7. A web service is another big trend being witnessed. The use of web services and XML will enable any company to share its data with another company. Web services will enable an easy coordination of business processes across a number of cooperating firms.
8. Analytics is another trend in ERP. It is also referred to as business intelligence. Analysis codes embedded in the system are used to easily analyze large amounts of data created by ERP systems. Many ERP vendors presently rely on third-party systems for analytics.
9. Mid-tier vendors are beginning to offer workflow (automation of business process

such as alerting the manager when shipment is late) as a way to differentiate themselves.

10. Open Source technology: Open source ERP facilitates the user to download the software almost free of cost and install it. Even the source code is available free. It facilitates a large number of companies to go for ERP as they are no longer burdened with heavy ERP investments. The open-source technology saves the company from renewal and purchase of licences whenever an upgradation is made. Open source technology has its own drawbacks. It is unsuitable for many applications and may fail to meet the business needs of a particular company. As such the company's management must decide carefully whether or not to resort to open source ERP. Open source ERP may also result in lawsuit and incident claims.
11. Web-enabled ERP: Easy to use web interfaces are being made available in modern ERP systems. Organizations implementing web-enabled ERP can make their enterprise operations go online. Internet enabled ERP allows users to access ERP systems at anytime and from any place. It also enables separate ERP systems to share data with each other.
12. Wireless ERP: The advancement of wireless technology in ERP systems has facilitated the transfer of up-to-date information as and when required through the use of modern wireless communication devices such as mobile phones and laptops. The security needs are more profound in wireless ERP as compared to ERP.
13. Extended ERP: Extended ERP is a set of enterprise modeling tools that provide effective implementation of ERP. The concept of "extended ERP" was promoted by Baan Company. The idea is to design ERP in such a way that the customer is able to implement the ERP solution with minimum consultancy.
14. Portal modules facilitate the users to customize the browsers to receive the data that they use most.

LEARNING POINTS

1. ERP vendors are now focusing on small and medium businesses (SMB's) and home-based businesses.
2. ERP vendors are now offering need based ERP applications. With need based ERP applications, the firms get the liberty to purchase and install only the software program pertaining to the functionality required.
3. A web service is another big trend being witnessed. The use of web services and XML will enable any company to share its data with another company.
4. Open source ERP facilitates the user to download the software almost free of cost and install it. Even the source code is available free.
5. Open source ERP may result in lawsuit and incident claims.
6. The advancement of wireless technology in ERP systems has facilitated the transfer of up-to-date information as and when required through the use of modern wireless communication devices such as mobile phones and laptops.

11.5 FUTURE OF ERP

The automation of core business activities led to the rapid deployment of ERP systems in most organizations. Today, ERP systems are being integrated with new evolving technologies such as data mining, OLAP, web services, wireless etc. Many new ERP packages are now providing e-business applications. Some of the new e-business applications are sales force automation, e-procurement, supply chain management and analytics.

The use of portal modules in ERP system is gaining popularity. Portal modules facilitate the users to customize the browser to receive the data that they use the most. In order to keep pace with the rapid developments in e-business, the ERP systems have been extended to support e-procurement ands supply chain management. The new systems facilitate multiple enterprises to exchange data with each other. The trends and developments in ERP and evolving technologies are signaling a promising future for ERP ahead.

LEARNING POINTS

1. Some of the new e-business applications are sales force automation, e-procurement, supply chain management and analytics.
2. The use of portal modules in ERP system is gaining popularity. Portal modules facilitate the users to customize the browser to receive the data that they use the most.
3. In order to keep pace with the rapid developments in e-business, the ERP systems have been extended to support e-procurement ands supply chain management.
4. The new systems facilitate multiple enterprises to exchange data with each other.

11.6 EXTENDED ERP

Extended ERP is a set of enterprise modeling tools that provides effective implementation of ERP. The concept was promoted by Baan Company and is based on the premise that the customer must be able to implement ERP solutions with little or no need of consultancy.

Table 11.1 lists some of the characteristics of Extended ERP.

Table 11.1: Characteristics of Extended ERP

S No.	Characteristics of Extended ERP
1.	E-Commerce
2.	Intranet
3.	Decision support
4.	Cross enterprise integration
5.	Globalization

Table 11.2 lists the differences between ERP and ERP II.

Table 11.2: Differences between ERP and ERP II

S. No	ERP	ERP II
1.	It is not web enabled.	It is web enabled.
2.	It is characterized as monolithic and closed systems.	It is characterized as open systems.
3.	It looks after the needs of an enterprise: mainly concerned with optimizing the functioning of an enterprise.	It not only looks after the needs of enterprise but goes beyond by including suppliers, customers and other business partners and firms
4.	Does not include CRM and SCM.	Includes CRM and SCM.
5.	ERP preceded ERP II.	ERP II superseded ERP and its lesser known iterations—extended ERP and Enterprise application suite.
6.	Focuses mainly on manufacturing.	Crosses all business sectors and segments.

Figure 11.1 shows Extended ERP and Figure 11.2 illustrates the relationship between ERP and Extended ERP respectively.

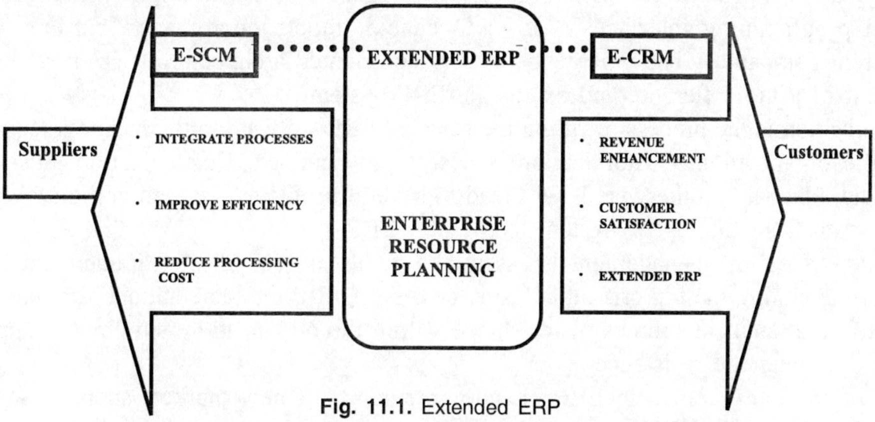

Fig. 11.1. Extended ERP

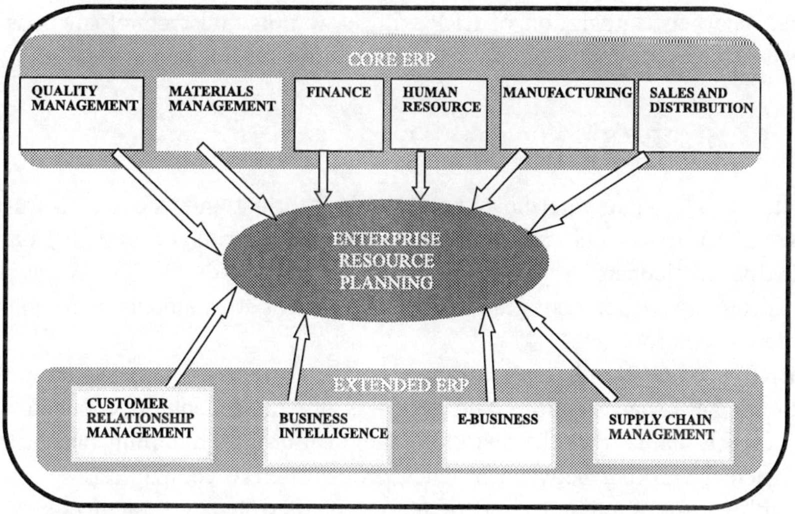

Fig. 11.2. Relationships between ERP and Extended ERP

LEARNING POINT

1. Extended ERP is a set of enterprise modeling tools that provide effective implementation of ERP.

SUMMARY

Some emerging issues that need to be immediately considered in the context of ERP include security-related issues, component-based ERP for SME's, cross-ERP applications, service oriented architecture etc. The security of an ERP system should be a prime concern of both the organization and the ERP vendor. Strict security measures should be developed and implemented to secure an ERP system. The ERP system of the organization must be configured to maintain audit logs and avoid using internal controls. The ERP vendors must provide only the specific functionality an SME needs at a price it can afford. Cross-ERP (XERP) products emphasize the sharing of application programming interfaces (API's) to enable smooth coordination between products from different companies. The emergence of service oriented architecture (SOA) has led to the development of a more flexible and extensible ERP system.

Customization is the process of fitting the selected ERP software to the business requirements of a specific organization. Customization is costly and complex. Customization must be done correctly and adequately otherwise it will lead to several problems. Data migration involves the transfer of data from the legacy system to the new ERP system.

The support of top management is essential for the success of ERP implementation. It is considered one among the top critical success factors for ERP implementation. Top management must identify and analyze sources of resistance within the organization and employ appropriate strategies to counter the resistance.

Some of the latest trends in ERP include emergence of new markets such as SME's and home-based business, fast ERP implementation, development of need based applications, increased focus on vertical markets, integration of ERP with new tools and technologies such as OLAP, data mining, sales force automation and customer relationship management.

POINTS TO REMEMBER

1. ERP systems today, integrate the organization's information system with trusted partners (extended ERP). As a result, new entry points to the information system from outside are introduced which jeopardizes the security of the information system. Worst still, most of the organizations do not configure their ERP system to maintain audit logs and avoid using internal controls.
2. Cross ERP products and applications are also referred to as XERP products and applications. XERP applications and products are dependent on connectivity and web services. XERP emphasizes the sharing of application programming interfaces (API's) to enable efficient working between products from different companies.
3. SOA simplifies the interconnection of new system to legacy system thereby facilitating the usage of the existing (legacy) IT systems.

4. The customization of ERP systems inhibits the development of standardized solutions for ERP security. Customization should be avoided unless it appears critical to the business needs.
5. ERP implementation should be done on a solid foundation based on a clear definition of the organization's requirement, comprehensive project plan, best project team and management support.
6. Data migration involves transferring of data from the legacy system to the new ERP system. It is a costly but important activity.
7. The support of top management is critical in all the phases of the ERP life cycle. Top management must identify and analyze the sources of resistance within the organization and employ appropriate strategies to counter employee resistance.
8. ERP systems are being integrated with new evolving technologies such as data mining, OLAP, web services, wireless etc.
9. Extended ERP is a set of enterprise modeling tools that provides effective implementation of ERP.
10. ERP vendors are now focusing on small and medium businesses (SMB's) and home-based businesses.
11. ERP vendors are now offering need based ERP applications. With need based ERP applications, the firms get the liberty to purchase and install only the software program pertaining to the functionality required.
12. A web service is another big trend being witnessed. The use of web services and XML will enable any company to share its data with another company.
13. Open source ERP facilitates the user to download the software almost free of cost and install it. Even the source code is available free. Open source ERP may result in lawsuit and incident claims.
14. The advancement of wireless technology in ERP systems has facilitated the transfer of up-to-date information as and when required through the use of modern wireless communication devices such as mobile phones and laptops.
15. Some of the new e-business applications are sales force automation, e-procurement, supply chain management and analytics.
16. In order to keep pace with the rapid developments in e-business, the ERP systems have been extended to support e-procurement and supply chain management. The new systems facilitate multiple enterprises to exchange data with each other.

REVIEW QUESTIONS

1. Discuss some of the emerging issues in ERP.
2. Discuss some of the learning issues in ERP.
3. Write a short note on service oriented architecture.
4. What is customization? Why do we need customization?
5. Discuss the advantages and disadvantages of customization.
6. What do you understand by data migration?
7. Write a short note on auditing of ERP systems.

8. Why is top management support considered vital for the success of the ERP project/
9. Write a short note on the latest trends of ERP.
10. List the major emerging trends in ERP in Indian context.
11. Discuss the future of ERP.
12. What is the role of top management in ERP implementaiton in any company?
13. What is extended ERP and how is it different from traditional ERP solution?

OBJECTIVE QUESTIONS

SECTION A

TICK THE CORRECT ANSWER

1. Some ERP issues that need immediate attention are:
   (a) ERP security.
   (b) ERP for SME's.
   (c) Cross ERP applications.
   (d) Service oriented architecture (SOA).
   (e) All of above.
2. Which statement is true about ERP?
   (a) ERP systems, today, integrate the organization's information system with trusted partners (extended ERP). As a result, new entry points to the information system from outside are introduced which jeopardizes the security of the information system.
   (b) Most organizations do not configure their ERP system to maintain audit logs and avoid using internal controls.
   (c) Both (a) and (b).
   (d) None of above.
3. Which is true about XERP?
   (a) Cross ERP products and applications are also referred to as XERP products and applications.
   (b) XERP emphasizes the sharing of application programming interfaces (API's) to enable efficient working between products from different companies.
   (c) Both (a) and (b).
   (d) None of above.
4. XERP applications and products are dependent on:
   (a) Connectivity
   (b) Web services
   (c) Connectivity and web services.
   (d) None of above.
5. Service oriented architecture (SOA) provides:
   (a) Support to the development of a more flexible and extensible ERP system.
   (b) Simplifies the interconnection of new system to legacy system thereby facilitating the usage of the existing (legacy) IT systems.

(c) Both (a) and (b).
(d) None of above.

6. ERP implementation should be done on a solid foundation based on:
(a) A clear definition of the organization's requirement.
(b) Comprehensive project plan.
(c) Best project team.
(d) Management support.
(e) All of above.

7. Review the different ERP solutions available (considering best-of-breed versus integrated solutions) and select the option that:
(a) Best meet your requirements.
(b) Provides vendor support.
(c) Requires less implementation time.
(d) Requires small fund.

8. ERP implementation success can be achieved by:
(a) Decide carefully which approach to use—phased approach or big-bang approach.
(b) Build an accurate picture of the projected costs of the ERP project. This is necessary so that the ERP project does not overshoot the expenses and be stopped in middle due to lack of finance.
(c) Remember to limit the scope of the ERP project. "Scope creep" often leads to failure of ERP implementation.
(d) All of above.

9. Which is true about customization?
(a) Customization should be avoided unless they appear critical to the business needs.
(b) Customization often results in increased development costs, need for testing and difficulties in upgradations.
(c) Both (a) and (b).
(d) None of above.

10. ERP can be implemented successfully by:
(a) Hiring consultants to conduct risk assessment and audit of the project.
(b) Top management must commit to invest time and money in ERP upgrades.
(c) Be careful while developing contract with the ERP vendor. The contract must allow for new functionality during the course of the ERP project.
(d) All of above.

11. Which is true about implementation team?
(a) An in-house implementation team will facilitate an easy transfer of knowledge about the ERP system and operations of the legacy systems.
(b) The implementation team must include personnel from all the functional departments of the organization.
(c) Both (a) and (b).
(d) None of above.

12. Which statement is not true?
(a) The project manager must create a "single team" atmosphere. A joint commitment to work together is a prerequisite for a successful ERP implementation.

(b) Get the organization ready for change. Provide training to the employees so that the resistance is reduced to the lowest level.
(c) Customization is easy and inexpensive.
(d) Recruit and retain key personnel involved in ERP implementation.

13. ______________ involves converting years of data stored in the legacy systems into the new format required for the new ERP system. One approach that may be used by an organization is to transfer the complete legacy data into a data warehouse and then start the new ERP system fresh.
(a) Data uploading.
(b) Data conversion.
(c) Data protection.
(d) Data hiding.

14. ____________ is the process of fitting the selected ERP software to the business requirements of a specific organization.
(a) Customization.
(b) BPR.
(c) ERP audit.
(d) None of above.

15. Customization becomes a must:
(a) Whenever the processes used by the firm are significantly different from the processes represented in the selected ERP system.
(b) Whenever top management changes.
(c) Both (a) and (b).
(d) None of above.

16. The only other alternative to customization is changing the ______________. But this definitely is a costly choice often not acceptable to the organization.
(a) ERP package.
(b) Business processes.
(c) ERP vendor.
(d) All of above.

17. Which is not true about customization?
(a) Today complex customizations are the requirements of the business.
(b) As customization may affect every module of the ERP system, it must be avoided as far as possible.
(c) Customization adds to the integration costs of ERP implementation.
(d) Customization suffers from the drawback that the next release of the ERP software would not support any customization done locally outside the core ERP software.
(e) None of above.

18. By over-customizing the ERP software, the best practices in industry embedded in the software:
(a) May get altered.
(b) May be completely lost.
(c) Both (a) and (b).
(d) None of above.

19. The issues that firms must consider before they go for customizing the ERP software are:
(a) Customization is costly and complex.
(b) Customization requires talented and skilled IT staff.
(c) Customization must be done correctly and adequately.
(d) Customization is time-consuming.
(e) All of above.

20. __________ involves transferring of data from the legacy system to the new ERP system.
(a) Data conversion.
(b) Data migration.
(c) Data hiding.
(d) None of above.

21. According to____________, the old data needs to be converted into new data to be able to work with the data in the new system.
(a) KOOP.
(b) Rooimans.
(c) Herbert Simon.
(d) KOOP and Rooimans.

22. Data in most legacy systems is often:
(a) Dirty.
(b) Most of it is only of little or no use.
(c) Both (a) and (b).
(d) None of above.

23. The support of top management is critical in ____________ of the ERP life cycle.
(a) Gap Analysis phase.
(b) Implementation phase.
(c) All the phases.
(d) None of above.

24. Which is true about top management support?
(a) Top management support is considered a critical success factor for ERP implementation.
(b) Support from top management ensures that all the necessary resources will be made available at proper time.
(c) By communicating and sharing the ERP vision with the employees, the management can get the whole organization "ready for change".
(d) Top management must also identify and analyze the sources of resistance within the organization and employ appropriate strategies to counter employee resistance.
(e) All of above.

25. Some of the latest trends in ERP are:
(a) Focusing on new markets—small and medium businesses (SMB's) and home-based businesses.
(b) ERP vendors are now providing more effective tools and methodologies to achieve faster ERP implementation.
(c) ERP vendors are now offering need based ERP applications.
(d) All of above.

26. Which statement is not true?

(a) As the ERP application becomes less complex to install and train, the implementation time needed for ERP gets reduced dramatically.

(b) In the past, the firms had to purchase the whole ERP applications even if the company only intended to utilize the core function. This meant that most of the functions remained idle but had to be paid for.

(c) With need based ERP applications, the firms get the liberty to purchase and install only the software program pertaining to the functionality required.

(d) The ERP vendors are now delivering specialized variants of their ERP applications to service vertical markets such as healthcare, finance and retail sector.

(e) None of above.

27. Attempts are being made by each ERP vendor to make his ERP applications available to all sectors irrespective of:

(a) The volume of transactions.

(b) The nature of business.

(c) Both (a) and (b).

(d) None of above.

28. ERP vendors are integrating their ERP applications with:

(a) OLAP tools.

(b) Data mining.

(c) Web services.

(d) Wireless technology.

(e) All of above.

29. ERP is being integrated with cutting-edge technologies such as:

(a) Sales force automation (SFA).

(b) Customer relationship management (CRM).

(c) Both (a) and b).

(d) None of above.

30. Which is true about a web service?

(a) A web service is another big trend being witnessed.

(b) The use of web services and XML will enable any company to share its data with another company.

(c) Web services will enable an easy coordination of business processes across a number of cooperating firms.

(d) All of above.

31. Which is true about Analytics?

(a) Analytics is a trend in ERP. It is referred to business intelligence.

(b) Analysis codes embedded in the system are used to easily analyze large amounts of data created by ERP systems.

(c) Many ERP vendors rely on third-party systems for analytics.

(d) All of above.

32. Which statement is not true?

(a) New ERP systems are blurring the distinction between front-end and back-end systems by providing a unified solution driven by internet based commerce.

(b) Mid-tier vendors are beginning to offer workflow (automation of business process such as alerting the manager when shipment is late) as a way to differentiate themselves.
(c) Organizations implementing web-enabled ERP cannot make their enterprise operations go online.
(d) Open source ERP facilitates the user to download the software almost free of cost and install it. Even the source code is available free.

33. Open source ERP facilitates:
(a) The user to download the software almost free of cost and install it.
(b) A large number of companies to go for ERP as they are no longer burdened with heavy ERP investments.
(c) Saves the company from renewal and purchase of licences whenever an upgradation is made.
(d) All of above.

34. Which is not true about Open source technology?
(a) Open source technology is unsuitable for many applications and may fail to meet the business needs of a particular company.
(b) Open source ERP may also result in lawsuit and incident claims.
(c) Both (a) and (b).
(d) None of above.

35. Which statement is false?
(a) Easy to use web interfaces are being made available in modern ERP systems.
(b) Internet enabled ERP allows users to access ERP systems at anytime and from any place.
(c) The advancement of wireless technology in ERP systems has facilitated the transfer of up-to-date information as and when required through the use of modern wireless communication devices such as mobile phones and laptops.
(d) The security needs are less profound in wireless ERP as compared to ERP.

36. Which is true about Extended ERP?
(a) Extended ERP is a set of enterprise modeling tools that provides effective implementation of ERP.
(b) The concept of "extended ERP" was promoted by Baan Company. The idea was to design ERP in such a way that the customer is able to implement the ERP solution with minimum consultancy.
(c) Both (a) and (b).
(d) None of above.

37. ______________ facilitate the users to customize the browsers to receive the data that they use most.
(a) ERP package.
(b) SCM.
(c) Portal modules.
(d) None of above.

38. Which is true about Portal modules?
(a) Portal modules facilitate the users to customize the browsers to receive the data that they use most.

(b) The use of portal modules in ERP system is gaining popularity.
(c) Both (a) and (b).
(d) None of above.

39. Which statement is not true?
(a) The automation of core business activities led to the rapid deployment of ERP systems in most organizations.
(b) Many new ERP packages are now providing e-business applications.
(c) In order to keep pace with the rapid developments in e-business, the ERP systems have been extended to support e-procurement ands supply chain management.
(d) None of above.

40. Some of the new e-business applications are:
(a) Sales force automation.
(b) E-procurement.
(c) Supply chain management.
(d) Analytics.
(e) All of above.

41. ______________ is a set of enterprise modeling tools that provides effective implementation of ERP.
(a) Extended ERP.
(b) Wireless ERP.
(c) XERP.
(d) None of above.

SECTION B

STATE TRUE OR FALSE

1. For most organizations, whether large scale or small and medium enterprises, ERP implementation opens the door for new opportunities.
2. Some of the issues that need immediate attention are: ERP security, ERP for SME's, Cross ERP applications and Service oriented architecture (SOA).
3. ERP systems, today, integrate the organization's information system with trusted partners (extended ERP). As a result, new entry points to the information system from outside are introduced which jeopardizes the security of the information system.
4. Most of the organizations do not configure their ERP system to maintain audit logs and avoid using internal controls.
5. ERP systems must be designed to provide the small or medium enterprises the business process capabilities they need and at an affordable price.
6. Cross ERP products and applications are referred to as XERP products and applications.
7. XERP applications and products are not dependent on connectivity and web services.
8. XERP emphasizes the sharing of application programming interfaces (API's) to enable efficient working between products from different companies.
9. The emergence of service oriented architecture (SOA) in ERP market has led to the development of a more flexible and extensible ERP system.

10. SOA simplifies the interconnection of new system to legacy system thereby facilitating the usage of the existing (legacy) IT systems.
11. ERP implementation should be done on a solid foundation based on a clear definition of the organization's requirement, comprehensive project plan, best project team and management support.
12. Review the different ERP solutions available (considering best-of-breed versus integrated solutions) and select the option that best meets your requirements.
13. Decide carefully which approach to use: phased approach or big-bang approach. The approach you take may determine the fate of your ERP project.
14. Build an accurate picture of the projected costs of the ERP project. This is necessary so that the ERP project does not overshoot the expenses and be stopped in middle due to lack of finance.
15. Remember to limit the scope of the ERP project. "Scope creep" often leads to failure of ERP implementation.
16. Customization should not be avoided as it often results in decreased development costs.
17. Hire consultants to conduct risk assessment and audit of the project.
18. Top management must commit to invest time and money in ERP upgrades.
19. Be careful while developing contract with the ERP vendor. The contract must allow for new functionality during the course of the ERP project.
20. An in-house implementation team will facilitate an easy transfer of knowledge about the ERP system and operations of the legacy systems.
21. The implementation team must include personnel from only the IT department of the organization.
22. Project manager must not create a "single team" atmosphere. A joint commitment to work together is not necessary for a successful ERP implementation.
23. Get the organization ready for change. Provide training to the employees so that the resistance is reduced to the lowest level.
24. Recruit and retain key personnel involved in ERP implementation.
25. Data conversion is a challenging task. It involves converting years of data stored in the legacy systems into the new format required for the new ERP system.
26. Remember to maintain the morale of the team throughout the project duration.
27. BPR is the process of fitting the selected ERP software to the business requirements of a specific organization.
28. Customization becomes a must whenever the processes used by the firm are significantly different from the processes represented in the selected ERP system.
29. The only other alternative to customization is changing the business processes to suit the ERP software components. But this definitely is a costly choice often not acceptable to the organization.
30. Today complex customizations are the requirements of the business.
31. As customization may affect every module of the ERP system, it must be avoided as far as possible.
32. Customization does not add to the integration costs of ERP implementation.
33. Customization will need to be done all over again in the newer ERP version.

34. Customization of the core ERP software will prove to be more damaging as the vendor will not be there to help you in the customization process.
35. By over-customizing the ERP software, the best practices in industry embedded in the software may get altered or completely lost, defeating the very purpose of implementing an ERP system
36. Customization is easy and cheap.
37. Customization requires talented and skilled IT staff.
38. Customization must be done correctly and adequately.
39. All customizations made in ERP software should undergo extensive testing.
40. Customization is not time-consuming.
41. Data migration involves transferring of data from the legacy system to the new ERP system.
42. Before migrating old data to the new system it is not necessary to convert the old data into new data.
43. According to Peter Chuckland, the old data needs to be converted into new data to be able to work with the data in the new system.
44. Data migration is costly.
45. Data in most legacy systems is often clean and most of it is of great use.
46. The support of top management is critical in only the gap analysis phase of the ERP life cycle
47. As management is involved in a wide range of decisions that are vital to the success of the ERP implementation, top management support is considered a critical success factor for ERP implementation.
48. Support from management does not ensure that all the necessary resources will be made available at proper time.
49. The management must not communicate and share the ERP vision with the employees.
50. The top management must reveal the benefits of the ERP implementation to the employees by discussing the real world case studies.
51. Top management must also identify and analyze the sources of resistance within the organization and employ appropriate strategies to counter employee resistance.
52. Lack of commitment and support from the top level will be detrimental to the success of ERP project.
53. The field of ERP is constantly evolving. The introduction of new technologies is affecting the shape and nature of ERP.
54. Some of the latest trends in ERP are: New markets, faster implementation, need-based applications and increased focus on new business segments.
55. ERP vendors are not focusing on small and medium businesses (SMB's) and home-based businesses.
56. A number of initiatives are being taken to attract the mid-market sector.
57. ERP vendors are now providing more effective tools and methodologies to achieve faster ERP implementation.
58. As the ERP application becomes less complex to install and train, the implementation time needed for ERP gets reduced dramatically.
59. In the past, the firms had to purchase the whole ERP applications even if the company only intended to utilize the core function. This meant that most of the functions remained idle but had to be paid for.

60. With need based ERP applications, the firms get the liberty to purchase and install only the software program pertaining to the functionality required.

61. ERP applications cannot be integrated with OLAP tools, data mining web services, wireless etc.

62. ERP is being integrated with cutting-edge technologies such as sales force automation (SFA), customer relationship management (CRM) etc.

63. New ERP systems are blurring the distinction between front-end and back-end systems by providing a unified solution driven by internet based commerce.

64. A web service is another big trend being witnessed. The use of web services and XML will enable any company to share its data with another company.

65. Web services will enable an easy coordination of business processes across a number of cooperating firms.

66. Analytics is referred to as business intelligence.

67. Analysis codes embedded in the system are used to easily analyze large amounts of data created by ERP systems.

68. Many ERP vendors rely on third-party systems for analytics.

69. Mid-tier vendors are beginning to offer workflow (automation of business process such as alerting the manager when shipment is late) as a way to differentiate themselves.

70. Open source ERP facilitates the user to download the software almost free of cost and install it. Even the source code is available free.

71. Open source ERP facilitates a large number of companies to go for ERP as they are no longer burdened with heavy ERP investments.

72. Open source technology is unsuitable for many applications and may fail to meet the business needs of a particular company. As such the company's management must decide carefully whether or not to resort to open source ERP.

73. Open source ERP may also result in lawsuit and incident claims.

74. Easy to use web interfaces are being made available in modern ERP systems.

75. Organizations implementing web-enabled ERP can make their enterprise operations go online.

76. Internet enabled ERP allows users to access ERP systems at anytime and from any place.

77. The advancement of wireless technology in ERP systems has facilitated the transfer of up-to-date information as and when required through the use of modern wireless communication devices such as mobile phones and laptops.

78. The security needs are less profound in wireless ERP as compared to ERP.

79. Extended ERP is a set of enterprise modeling tools that provide effective implementation of ERP.

80. The concept of "extended ERP" was promoted by SAP Company.

81. Portal module does not facilitate the users to customize the browsers to receive the data that they use most.

82. The automation of core business activities led to the rapid deployment of ERP systems in most organizations.

83. Many new ERP packages are now providing e-business applications.

84. Some of the new e-business applications are sales force automation, e-procurement, supply chain management and analytics.

85. In order to keep pace with the rapid developments in e-business, the ERP systems have been extended to support e-procurement ands supply chain management.

86. The new systems facilitate multiple enterprises to exchange data with each other.

SECTION C

FILL IN THE BLANKS

1. For most organizations, whether large scale or small and medium enterprises, ________ implementation opens the door for new opportunities.
2. Some of the issues that need immediate attention are: ERP security, ________ , cross ERP applications and Service oriented architecture (SOA).
3. ERP systems, today, integrate the organization's information system with ________. As a result, new entry points to the information system from outside are introduced which jeopardizes the ________of the information system.
4. Most of the organizations do not configure their ERP system to maintain ________ and avoid using internal controls.
5. ERP systems must be designed to provide the small or medium enterprises, the ________ capabilities they need and at an affordable price.
6. Cross ERP products and applications are also referred to as ________ products and applications.
7. XERP applications and products are dependent on connectivity and________.
8. XERP emphasize the sharing of ________ to enable efficient working between products from different companies.
9. The emergence of service oriented architecture (SOA) in ERP market has led to the development of a more ________ and extensible ERP system.
10. ________ simplifies the interconnection of new system to legacy system thereby facilitating the usage of the existing (legacy) IT systems.
11. ERP implementation should be done on a solid foundation based on a clear definition of the organization's requirement, ________, best project team and management support.
12. Review the different ERP solutions available and select the option that ________ meet your requirements.
13. Decide carefully which approach to use—________ approach or big-bang approach. The approach you take may determine the fate of your ERP project.
14. Build an accurate picture of the ________ costs of the ERP project. This is necessary so that the ERP project does not overshoot the expenses and be stopped in middle due to lack of finance.
15. Remember to ________ the scope of the ERP project. "Scope creep" often leads to failure of ERP implementation.
16. ________ should be avoided unless they appear critical to the business needs. Customization often results in increased development costs, need for ________ and difficulties in up gradations.
17. Hire ________ to conduct risk assessment and audit of the project.

18. ________ management must commit to invest time and money in ERP upgrades.
19. Be __________ while developing contract with the ERP vendor. The contract must allow for new ____________ during the course of the ERP project.
20. An in-house implementation team will facilitate an easy transfer of knowledge about the ERP system and operations of the ___________ systems.
21. The implementation team must include personnel from all the __________ departments of the organization.
22. Project manager must create a _______________ atmosphere. A joint commitment to work together is a __________ for a successful ERP implementation.
23. Get the organization ready for _________. Provide ___________ to the employees so that the resistance is reduced to the lowest level.
24. ________ and retain key personnel involved in ERP implementation.
25. ___________ involves converting years of data stored in the legacy systems into the new format required for the new ERP system.
26. Remember to maintain the __________ of the team throughout the project duration.
27. ___________ is the process of fitting the selected ERP software to the business requirements of a specific organization.
28. Customization becomes a must whenever the processes used by the firm are significantly ____________ from the processes represented in the selected ERP system.
29. The only other alternative to __________ is changing the business processes to suit the ERP software components. But this definitely is a _________ choice often not acceptable to the organization.
30. Today, complex customizations are the requirements of the___________.
31. As customization may affect _______ module of the ERP system, it must be avoided as far as possible.
32. Customization adds to the _______________ of ERP implementation.
33. Customization will need to be done all over again in the ___________ ERP version.
34. Customization of the core ERP software will prove to be more damaging as the ______________ will not be there to help you in the customization process.
35. By over-customizing the ERP software, the best practices in industry embedded in the software may get altered or ____________________, defeating the very purpose of implementing an ERP system.
36. Customization is costly and __________.
37. Customization requires talented and skilled _________ staff.
38. Customization must be done _________ and adequately.
39. All customizations made in ERP software should undergo extensive____________.
40. Customization is ___________.
41. Customization if done _____________ allows the customized functionality to be easily upgraded when the new version is released.
42. Data migration involves transferring of data from the __________ to the new ERP system.
43. Before migrating old data to the new system the old data needs to be converted into _________ data. New data is data modified to a format ___________ to the new system.
44. According to ____________, the old data needs to be converted into new data to be able to work with the data in the new system.

45. As or when conversion is over, the new data needs to be loaded in the new system where its __________ is checked.
46. Data migration is __________.
47. Data in most legacy systems is often __________ and most of it is only of little or no use.
48. The support of top management is critical in __________ the phases of the ERP life cycle
49. As management is involved in a wide range of decisions that are vital to the success of the ERP implementation, top management support is considered a __________ for ERP implementation.
50. Support from top management ensures that all the necessary __________ will be made available at proper time.
51. By communicating and sharing the ERP vision with the employees, the management can get the whole organization __________.
52. The management must reveal the benefits of the ERP implementation to the employees by discussing the __________case studies.
53. Top management must also identify and analyze the sources of __________ within the organization and employ __________ to counter employee resistance.
54. Lack of commitment and support from the __________ will be detrimental to the success of ERP project.
55. The field of ERP is __________ evolving. The introduction of new __________ is affecting the shape and nature of ERP.
56. Some of the latest trends in ERP are: New markets, faster implementation, __________ and increased focus on new business segments.
57. ERP vendors are now focusing on small and medium businesses (SMB's) and __________ businesses.
58. A number of initiatives are being taken to attract the __________ sector.
59. ERP vendors are now providing more effective tools and methodologies to achieve __________ ERP implementation.
60. As the ERP application becomes less complex to install and train, the __________ time needed for ERP gets reduced dramatically. Examples include __________ from SAP an __________ from Oracle.
61. In the past, the firms had to purchase the whole ERP application even if the company or intended to utilize the __________. This meant that most of the functi remained idle but had to be __________ for.
62. ERP vendors are now offering need based __________ applications.
63. The ERP vendors are delivering specialized variants of their ERP applications to s __________ markets such as healthcare, finance and retail sector.
64. Attempts are being made by each ERP vendor to make his ERP applications avai all sectors irrespective of the __________ of transactions or the nature of busines
65. ERP vendors are integrating their ERP applications with __________, data mir services, wireless etc.
66. ERP is being integrated with cutting-edge technologies such as sales force autor __________.
67. New ERP systems are blurring the distinction between front-end and back-end providing a unified solution driven by__________.

68. The use of ____________and XML will enable any company to share its data with another company.
69. Web services will enable an easy coordination of ______________ across a number of cooperating firms.
70. ________________ is referred to business intelligence.
71. Analysis codes embedded in the system are used to easily analyze ____________of data created by ERP systems.
72. Many ERP vendors are presently relying on __________ systems for analytics.
73. Mid-tier vendors are beginning to offer __________ as a way to differentiate themselves.
74. __________ facilitates the user to download the software almost free of cost and install it. Even the source code is available free.
75. Open source ERP facilitates a large number of companies to go for ERP as they are no longer burdened with heavy ERP______________.
76. Open source technology is unsuitable for many applications and may fail to meet the ____________ of a particular company. As such the company's management must decide carefully whether or not to resort to _________.
77. Open source ERP may result in ______________ and incident claims.
78. Easy to use __________ are being made available in modern ERP systems.
79. Organizations implementing web-enabled ERP can make their enterprise operations go _________.
80. ________________ allows users to access ERP systems at any time and from any place.
81. The advancement of wireless technology in ERP systems has facilitated the transfer of up-to-date information as and when required through the use of modern _____________ devices such as mobile phones and laptops.
82. The security needs are ________ profound in wireless ERP as compared to ERP.
83. _____________ is a set of enterprise modeling tools that provides effective implementation of ERP.
84. The concept of "extended ERP" was promoted by _________ company. The idea is to design ERP in such a way that the customer is able to implement the ERP solution with minimum __________.
85. _____________ facilitate the users to customize the browsers to receive the data that they use most.
86. The automation of core business activities led to the rapid deployment of __________ in most organizations.
87. Many new ERP packages are now providing __________ applications.
88. Some of the new e-business applications are _______________, e-procurement, supply chain management and analytics.
89. In order to keep pace with the rapid developments in e-business, the ERP systems have been extended to support _____________ and supply chain management.
90. The new systems facilitate multiple enterprises to exchange __________ with each other.

ANSWERS

SECTION A

(1) e	**(2)** c	**(3)** c	**(4)** c	**(5)** c	**(6)** e	**(7)** a	**(8)** d	**(9)** c	**(10)** d
(11) c	**(12)** c	**(13)** b	**(14)** a	**(15)** a	**(16)** b	**(17)** e	**(18)** c	**(19)** e	**(20)** b
(21) d	**(22)** c	**(23)** c	**(24)** e	**(25)** d	**(26)** e	**(27)** c	**(28)** e	**(29)** c	**(30)** d
(31) d	**(32)** c	**(33)** d	**(34)** d	**(35)** d	**(36)** c	**(37)** c	**(38)** c	**(39)** d	**(40)** e
(41) a.									

SECTION B

(1) True	**(2)** True	**(3)** True	**(4)** True	**(5)** True	**(6)** True	**(7)** False	**(8)** True
(9) True	**(10)** True	**(11)** True	**(12)** True	**(13)** True	**(14)** True	**(15)** True	**(16)** False
(17) True	**(18)** True	**(19)** True	**(20)** True	**(21)** False	**(22)** False	**(23)** True	**(24)** True
(25) True	**(26)** True	**(27)** False	**(28)** True	**(29)** True	**(30)** True	**(31)** True	**(32)** False
(33) True	**(34)** True	**(35)** True	**(36)** False	**(37)** True	**(38)** True	**(39)** True	**(40)** False
(41) True	**(42)** False	**(43)** False	**(44)** True	**(45)** False	**(46)** False	**(47)** True	**(48** False
(49) False	**(50)** True	**(51)** True	**(52)** True	**(53)** True	**(54)** True	**(55)** False	**(56)** True
(57) True	**(58)** True	**(59)** True	**(60)** True	**(61)** False	**(62)** True	**(63)** True	**(64)** True
(65) True	**(66)** True	**(67)** True	**(68)** True	**(69)** True	**(70)** True	**(71)** True	**(72)** True
(73) True	**(74)** True	**(75)** True	**(76)** True	**(77)** True	**(78)** False	**(79)** True	**(80)** False
(81) False	**(82)** True	**(83)** True	**(84)** True	**(85)** True	**(86)** True.		

SECTION C

(1) ERP **(2)** ERP for SME's **(3)** trusted partners, security **(4)** audit logs **(5)** business process **(6)** XERP **(7)** web services **(8)** application programming interfaces **(9)** flexible **(10)** SOA **(11)** comprehensive project plan **(12)** best **(13)** phased **(14)** projected **(15)** limit **(16)** Customization, testing **(17)** consultants **(18)** Top **(19)** careful, functionality **(20)** legacy **(21)** functional **(22)** single team, prerequisite **(23)** change, training **(24)** recruit **(25)** Data conversion **(26)** morale **(27)** Customization **(28)** different **(29)** customization, costly **(30)** business **(31)** every **(32)** integration costs **(33)** newer **(34)** vendor **(35)** completely lost **(36)** complex **(37)** IT **(38)** correctly **(39)** testing **(40)** time-consuming **(41)** moderately **(42)** legacy system **(43)** new, acceptable **(44)** KOOP and Rooimans **(45)** validity **(46)** costly **(47)** dirty **(48)** all **(49)** critical success factor **(50)** resources **(51)** ready for change **(52)** real world **(53)** resistance, appropriate strategies **(54)** top level **(55)** constantly, technologies **(56)** Need-based applications **(57)** home-based **(58)** mid-market **(59)** faster **(60)** implementation, ASAP, Fast Forward **(61)** core function, paid **(62)** ERP **(63)** vertical **(64)** volume **(65)** OLAP tools **(66)** customer relationship management **(67)** internet based commerce **(68)** web services **(69)** business processes **(70)** Analytics **(71)** large amounts **(72)** third-party **(73)** workflow **(74)** Open source ERP **(75)** investments **(76)** business needs, open source ERP **(77)** lawsuit **(78)** web interfaces **(79)** online **(80)** Internet enabled ERP **(81)** wireless communication **(82)** more **(83)** Extended ERP **(84)** Baan, consultancy **(85)** Portal modules **(86)** ERP systems **(87)** e-business **(88)** sales force automation **(89)** e-procurement **(90)** data.

References

1. Enterprise Resource Planning by Alexis Leon, TMH,
2. Enterprise Resource Planning by Brady, Thomson, 1980.
3. Enterprise Resource Planning: Concepts and Planning, Garg. Vinod Kr., PHI, 2nd edition 2003.
4. A framework for evaluating ERP acquisition within SMEs by Aurilio Ravarini, Marco Tagliavini, Federico Pigni and Donatella Sciuto.
5. Vinod Kumar et al., "ERP Systems Institutionalization: A Model for Organizational Effectiveness", ASAc 2002, conference, Winnipeg, Manitoba.
6. Holland, C.P., Light, B. and Gibson, N. (1999). "A Critical Success Factors Model for Enterprise Resource Planning Systems implementation", presented at 7th European conference on Information systems, Copenhagen.
7. Holland, C. and Light, B. (1999), "A Critical Success Factors Model for ERP Systems Implementation", IEEE Software, Vol. May/June, pp. 30-36.
8. Evaluating ERP Impacts through Soft Sytems Methodology by Adrien Presley, Division of Business and Accountancy, Truman State University, Kirskville, MO.
9. Checkland, P. (1981). Systems Thinking, Systems Practice, John Wiley & Sons, London.
10. Jose Esteves, Joan A. Pastor, "Towards the Unification of Critical Success Factors for ERP Implementations", Catalonia, Spain.
11. Davenport, T.H. (1998). "Putting the Enterprise into the Enterprise Systems", Harvard Business Review, Jul-Aug, pp. 121-131.
12. Markus, M. and Tanis, C. (2002). "The Enterprise Systems Experience- From Adoption to Success", In Framing the Domains of IT Research Glimpsing the Future through the Past, R.W. Zamud (Ed.), Pinnaflex Educational Resources, Cincinnati, OH.
13. David Allen, Thomas Kern, Mark Havenhand, (2002). "ERP Critical Success Factors: an exploration of the contextual factors in public sector institutions", In Proceedings of 35th Hawaii International Conference on System Sciences.
14. DeSanctis, G. and Gullupe. B. (1987), "A Foundation for the Study of Group Decision Support Systems", *Management Science* **33(5):** 589-609.
15. Kumar, K. and Van Hillegersberg, J. (2000), "ERP Experiences and Evolution", Communications of the ACM **43(4):** 23-26.
16. Esteves, J. and Pastor, J. (2001). Enterprise Resource Planning Systems Research: An Annotated Bibliography, *Communications of the Association for Information Systems* **7:** 1-52.
17. Manetti, J. (2001). "How Technology is Transforming Manufacturing", *Production and Inventory Management J.,* pp. 54-64.
18. Koppejan, S.A. "Factors Influencing the Purchase of an ERP System", Tilburg University, Netherlands.
19. Gencel, Orhan, (2003). "A study on the Enterprise Resource Planning Systems and Embedding them into the company Processes, M.S. thesis.
20. http://www.sba.oakland.edu/faculty/lauer/mis650/readings/ERP%20bib.pdf.
21. http://web.njit.edu/~jerry/OM/OM_ERP-Papers/ERP-framework.pdf.
22. http://grace.wharton.upenn.edu/~lhitt/erp.pdf.
23. http://www.umsl.edu/~sauterv/analysis/488-fo2-papers/erp1.htm.

24. http://www.igi-pub.com/articles/details.asp?ID=7251.
25. http://www.njit.edu/~jerry/OM/OM_ERP_Papers/ERP-10-Success.pdf.
26. Al-Mashari, M. and Zairi, M. (2000). Revisiting BPR: A Holitic Review of Practice and Development, *Business Process Management J.* **6:** 10-42.
27. Adam, F. and O'Doherty, O. (2000). Enterprise Resource Planning: Myth and Reality, Montpellier, France.
28. Al-Mashari, Abdullah Al-Mudimigh, M. Zairi, (2003). Enterprise Resource Planning: A taxonomy of critical success factors, *European J. Operational Research* **146:** 352-364.
29. Mabert, Vincert A. *et al.*, (2001a). Enterprise Resource Planning: Common Myths versus Evolving Reality, Business Horizons, May-June, 2001.
30. http:///www.erp-software-portal.com
31. http://www.wireless-erp-software.com.
32. Nagaraj Bhargava, (2007). ERP for SMEs-To buy or not to buy, August 2007 Management Next.
33. Milan ZDravkovic, Miroslav Trajanovic, Miodrag Manic, (2007). "SOA based approach to Enterprise Resource Planning Implementation in Small enterprises", Vol **5** No 1, 2007, Mechanical Engineering, pp. 97-104.
34. Satish Kumar, (2007). Life is easier with ERPII, August 2007, Management Next.
35. Ashley Davis, (2005). "ERP customization Imapcts on Strategic alignment and System Agility", In Proceedings of 2005 Southern Association of Information Systems Conference.
36. http://www.microsoft.com/dynamics/product/erp-primer.mspx.
37. Dr. Suresh Subramoniam, Nizar Hussain M, Dr. KrisnhnanKutty K.V., Dr. Gopal Krishnan Nair K., "ERP II: Next Generation ERP", Department of Business Administartion, Trivandrum.
38. Enterprise Systems from Supply chain to ERP to CRM, Systems Integration, 2003.
39. Milan Sterba, "The Managers view of Integration between CRM and ERP", Systems Integration, 2003.
40. http:///www.articles.techrepublic.com/5100-10878-11-1040167.htm.
41. Luis U. Bibiano, Enric Mayol, Joan A. Pastor, "Role and Imporatnce of Business Processes in the Implementation of CRM Systems".
42. S. Vijay Venkatesh,ERP for SMEs in SaaS Model, August 2007, Management Next
43. Ranganath Iyengar, ERP for SMEs- Keep it Lean, August 2007, Management Next.
44. Manage your way to ERP implementation success, Alice Hsu.
45. Critical Success Factors in ERP Implementation in Finland by Jiang Yingjie, Feb 2005, MSC thesis, Swedish School of Economics and Business Administration.
46. Higher education ERP: Lessons learned by Dave Swartz & Ken Orgill.
47. http://www.eccouncil.org/docs/ERP.pdf.
48. http://www.aberdeen.com/summary/report.benchmark/RA_ERP_MID_MARKET-3524.asp.
49. http:///www.nrf-arts.org/DW_MODEL_CHARTER%20_2.pdf.
50. www.ramco.com.

Index